THE ZONDERVAN 2027 PASTOR'S ANNUAL

For a *FREE* downloadable copy of the book, please visit www.Zondervan.com/p/zpa2027.

THE ZONDERVAN 2027 PASTOR'S ANNUAL

An Idea and Resource Book

T. T. Crabtree

ZONDERVAN REFLECTIVE

ZONDERVAN REFLECTIVE

The Zondervan 2027 Pastor's Annual

Published by Zondervan, 3950 Sparks Drive SE, Suite 101, Grand Rapids, MI 49546, USA. Zondervan is a registered trademark of The Zondervan Corporation, L.L.C., a wholly owned subsidiary of HarperCollins Christian Publishing, Inc.

Much of the contents of this book was previously published in *The Zondervan 2007 Pastor's Annual.*

Requests for information should be addressed to customercare@harpercollins.com.

Zondervan titles may be purchased in bulk for educational, business, fundraising, or sales promotional use. For information, please email SpecialMarkets@Zondervan.com.

ISBN 978-0-310-15610-9 (softcover)
ISBN 978-0-310-15611-6 (ebook)

HarperCollins Publishers, Macken House, 39/40 Mayor Street Upper, Dublin 1, D01 C9W8, Ireland (https://www.harpercollins.com)

Cover design: Angela Grit
Cover photo: © Helen Hotson / Shutterstock

Printed in the United States of America

26 27 28 29 30 LBC 5 4 3 2 1

CONTENTS

PREFACE

Of the many responsibilities of the average pastor, none is greater than that of preaching the Word of God every Sunday and, in many cases, every Wednesday. Each pastor should preach from his own experience with the Father God. Since we all need assistance in fulfilling our preaching ministry, however, this volume will be pleasing to God and beneficial to those who look to us for guidance, comfort, and help.

Letters from around the world encourage my heart that this volume is a valuable aid to some who are seeking to better preach the whole counsel of God to their congregations. I am grateful to the good people of Zondervan for their desire to provide assistance to pastors as they seek to be godly ministers of Jesus Christ.

Esteemed professors of preaching have been insisting over the years that pastors should seek the leadership of the Holy Spirit to plan a preaching program. Andrew Blackwood and J. Winston Pearce have published books with this emphasis. Vernon L. Stanfield has stated, "Planning will give purpose and direction to preaching.... Planning also helps the preacher with sermon preparation. . . . Planning removes much of the stress and strain of lack of preparation. For the pastor to plan his preaching will also help him to plan worship" (*On the Preparation and Delivery of Sermons*, ed. John A. Broadus [New York: Harper & Row, 1979], 257–60).

The production of a volume like this would be impossible without the valuable assistance of the contributors. On these pages you will find material from seventeen servants of our Lord who are ministering effectively in different places. Those who use the material are encouraged to amplify the principles for the specific needs of their congregations. Each sermon a pastor preaches should be borne out of a personal experience with God in seeking to meet those needs. If the manuscripts in this volume prove helpful, we will thank the Father and rejoice in each pastor's being a better undershepherd of the Great Shepherd who, in speaking to Peter, encouraged us to "feed my sheep."

Without reservation I dedicate this book to my beloved wife, Bennie Elizabeth, who is the helpmate God has provided for me.

—*T. T. Crabtree*

Contributing Authors

Tom S. Brandon	PM	December 5, 12, 19, 26
Mark Brister	PM	November 7, 14, 21, 28
Harold T. Bryson	AM	May 9, 16, 23, 30
		June 6, 13, 20, 27
	PM	January 6, 13, 20, 27
		February 3, 10, 17, 24
		March 3, 10, 17, 24, 31
		April 7, 14, 21, 28
Hiram Campbell	PM	April 4, 11, 18, 25
James E. Carter	AM	July 4, 11, 18, 25
		August 1, 8, 15, 22, 29
		September 5, 12, 19, 26
Bennie Cole Crabtree		Sentence Sermonettes
T. T. Crabtree		All messages other than those attributed to others
J. B. Fowler	PM	August 11, 18, 25
		September 1
Mike Fuhrman	PM	September 5, 12, 19, 26
Clyde Glazener	PM	October 3, 10, 17, 24
David L. Jenkins	AM	May 25
	PM	May 2, 9, 16, 23, 30
		June 6, 13, 20, 27
		August 1, 8, 15, 22
D. L. Lowrie	AM	October 10, 17, 24, 31
Jerold McBride	PM	August 4
		September 8, 15, 22, 29
		October 6, 13, 20, 27
Dale McConnell	AM	November 28
		December 5, 12, 29, 26
Alton E. McEachern	AM	March 7, 14, 28
		October 3, 31
	PM	December 2
Charles Sullivan	PM	July 4, 11, 18, 25
Bill Whittaker	PM	November 3, 10, 17, 24
		December 1, 8, 15, 22
Fred M. Wood	AM	April 1, 11, 18, 25
	PM	January 3, 10, 17, 24, 31
		February 7, 14, 21, 28
		March 7, 14, 21, 28
		May 5, 12, 19, 26

June 2, 9, 16, 23, 30
July 7, 14, 21, 28
Messages on the Lord's Supper
Messages for Children and Young People
Funeral Meditations
Weddings

SUGGESTED PREACHING PROGRAM FOR THE MONTH OF JANUARY

■ Sunday Mornings

Studying the joys and benefits of salvation yields new ways for us to appreciate our Lord. This new year starts with a series designed to accomplish just that. The theme of this set of sermons is "The Good News of Salvation for the New Year." Most of the sermons are derived from one of the great salvation passages, Titus 2:11–14.

■ Sunday Evenings

The Scriptures were written that we might receive encouragement to live in hope and righteousness. To read the Scriptures properly is to increase our faith in God's goodness as we face the pressures and pain of life (Rom. 15:4–6). "Messages of Hope from the Experiences of Abraham" is the suggested theme of this series.

■ Wednesday Evenings

Micah spoke hard truths to the people of Judah: their sins were going to be their destruction. Although Micah prophesied more than two thousand years ago, our lives today must be aligned to the truths he spoke. "Mighty Messages from a Minor Prophet" is the suggested theme for the series.

SUNDAY MORNING, JANUARY 3

Title: Three Great Words from God for the Coming Year
Text: "May the God of hope fill you with all joy and peace in believing, so that by the power of the Holy Spirit you may abound in hope" ***(Rom. 15:13 RSV).***
Scripture Reading: Romans 15:7–13
Hymns: "The Solid Rock," Mote
"O God, Our Help in Ages Past," Watts
"Lead On, O King Eternal," Shurtleff
Offertory Prayer: Father in heaven, we come to thank you for your blessings upon us during this past year. We come on this first Lord's Day of the new year to offer you the gratitude of our hearts and the praise of our lips. We desire that our offerings and our lives be used to advance your kingdom and to serve a needy world. Help us to be true followers of Jesus. In his name. Amen.

Introduction

Often we hear people speak disparagingly of making New Year's resolutions. They think these promises are worthless. This cynicism could indicate that they have no hope for the coming year being better than the last. It is certainly easy to give way to despair regarding oneself and others, the world and the church, the present and the future. In fact, Satan would have us do so.

But the words of our text challenge us to maintain an attitude about ourselves and our environs that is the exact opposite of pessimism and cynicism. How? It paints for us a picture of our God, who has high hopes for us and promises to fill us with hope and optimism as we face our present and our future.

I. The God of hope declares that we can abound in hope (Rom. 15:13 RSV).

The Bible speaks repeatedly of our God and his high hopes for us. Our Father is not in despair about our future; he wants us to face the future with hope. He makes his desires come to fruition by giving us all we need.

A. *Hope fills us with excitement and optimism.* Paul speaks the truth when he says that as Christians we are able to "rejoice in hope of the glory of God" (Rom. 5:2). He also speaks about rejoicing in hope (Rom. 12:12). Hope is one of the great characteristics that endures, along with faith and love, to the very end (1 Cor. 13:13).

B. *Hope produces patience and persistence.* Without hope, there is little chance of our developing the patience and persistence needed for living the Christian life.

C. *Hope helps us face our future.* Why should we have hope?
   1. Hope is a product of the promises of our Lord to us.
   2. Hope is a product of the presence of our Lord with us.
   3. Hope is a product of the power of our Lord, which works within us (Phil. 2:13).

II. The God of hope desires to fill us with joy.

It is significant that our text expresses the hope that God might fill us with "all joy." Joy is an elusive and misunderstood concept. First, it is mistaken for happiness. Happiness is linked to what *happens* to you and to those you love. Joy is something deeper. Second, joy and pleasure are often confused. Pleasure is the pause we experience between two pains.

Christian joy is not dependent on the circumstances of man. Joy is a thankfulness for who God is and for what he has given us through his Son's death.

A. *The Father God wishes to fill us with the joy of forgiveness.*

B. *The Father God wishes to fill us with the joy of eternal life.*

C. *The Father God wishes to fill us with the joy of belonging in his family.*

D. *The Father God wishes to fill us with the joy of knowing that we will go to heaven when this life is over.*

E. *The Father God wishes to fill us with the joy that comes as the result of serving others and helping others enter the life of faith.*

III. The God of hope fills us with his wonderful peace (Rom. 15:13).

People have always sought a trouble-free life. The heart longs for serenity. Humans, as sinners, experience inner tension, making serenity impossible. We are distracted by desires and ambitions that are contradictory. We are pulled apart as if we are in a civil war. The minds and hearts of people are battlegrounds on which they become split personalities like Dr. Jekyll and Mr. Hyde.

A. *God wants to bring order into the chaos of people's lives.* God wants to bring tranquility where there is turmoil. We live in a dangerous world. We need to be comforted by knowing that God will help us and will seek to bring good out of everything that life brings (Rom. 8:28).

B. *The Father God wants to give to us the gift of peace that comes through faith in Jesus Christ (Rom. 5:1).* The Holy Spirit of God, who dwells within us from the moment of our conversion, seeks continually to bring us into harmony with the will of God, making inner peace possible.

Our text affirms that it is through the power of the Holy Spirit that the life of hope, joy, and peace is made possible. This power of the Holy Spirit and these blessings from God come to us through believing in and trusting in the goodness and the graciousness of our God (Heb. 11:6).

Conclusion

Let us rejoice that God wants to give us hope and fill us with joy and peace. Our God will do this—in us, to us, for us, and through us—by the power of the Holy Spirit if we will respond to him with genuine faith.

In Romans Paul speaks of our God as the God of patience and encouragement (15:5); he is also the God of hope (15:13) and peace (15:33). As we face the new year, let us trust in and commit ourselves to him who gives the gifts of hope and joy and peace.

Sunday Evening, January 3

Title: Obey God and You Will Bless the World
Text: "So Abram went, as the Lord had told him" ***(Gen. 12:4 RSV).***
Scripture Reading: Genesis 12:1–8

Introduction

The flood is over. Humankind has started again with Noah's family. Sin, however, does not cease its ugly work! Once more the world is in trouble.

The sin of building the Tower of Babel causes the populated world to be scattered in various directions. Idolatry has become the order of the day. What will God do? He has promised that he will not destroy the world by water again. The first worldwide judgment did not change things: humans are still sinners and must be redeemed to live righteously.

God begins a new approach: he will choose a man and start a new race. Through this person's descendants, God will do two things. First, he will reveal his character as holy. This would be in contrast to the false gods who have no life and therefore no moral qualities to challenge humankind to proper conduct. Second, in the fullness of time, he will send a redeemer to bring salvation and forgiveness to all people regardless of who or where they are.

Where can God find such a person if all the world is contaminated by sin? He goes to Ur of the Chaldees and chooses a man named Abram whose father, Terah, is a moon-god worshiper (Josh. 24:2). An old Jewish tradition tells us that Terah ran a store where idols were sold. His son Abram did not like the idols and protested often to his father. One day when the boy was left in charge of the store, he took a stout stick and broke the idols into pieces. When his father came home and saw the ruins, he asked his son what had happened. The lad replied, "They all got in a fight and destroyed each other." The father insisted, "But they can't fight. They have no life." The boy replied, "Then why do you worship them?" This is the kind of man God needed to begin his redemptive program, and he called Abram to a new job and gave him a new name—Abraham.

I. Get into a new environment.

Though one's surroundings do not always determine his service, there are times when we need to get into a new location to start a new work.

A. *God had reserved the land of Canaan for the place he would put his new people.* He therefore relocated this man who would begin the new program. From secular history we know there was a general migration westward of a number of Semitic people about this time. The Hyksos, a group from the same ethnic background as Abram, went as far as Egypt, where they were successful in taking over the throne and holding it for several centuries. The call to Abram, however, was personal. Although he went with his father and other family members, he knew it was only a matter of time before he must go out on his own.

B. *God reveals himself to all people, but he selects certain ones at certain times for certain tasks.* He had chosen Abram but knew there must be a definite break with the old land. Too many memories remained there, and the temptation to yield to the customs of that environment might be too strong. Abram needed to move to a new area to serve God best. We, too, must leave the old behind.

II. Learn that life is for being a blessing.

A. *To do what Abram did required an awareness that God was with him.* How long he pondered the decision, we do not know, nor can we be certain of how his father, Terah, and the others fit into the scheme of things. Despite these questions, one thing is certain. Faith played a major role in the starting event and all that subsequently took place. The writer of Hebrews chose Abraham's faith as an illustration of his definition of this glorious trait that he calls "the substance of things hoped for, the evidence of things not seen" (11:1). Faith makes eternity as real as today. Why? Because it gives a reality to the new and limitless future where we will forget the sorrows and losses of our present world.

B. *As great as faith is, we need, however, to ask an important question about it.* In what are we to place our faith? The answer is simple: God's provision. What, though, did God offer Abram? This promise at first reading sounds fabulous, for God offered him so much; but look closer and see that the material things offered were not the most important. God offered Abram an opportunity to bless the world. The superficial reader emphasizes that God promised to make of Abram a great nation, to bless him, and to make his name great. The perceptive reader, however, sees something more. God said, "Thou shalt be a blessing" (Gen. 12:2). In fact, the literal Hebrew is imperative: "Be thou a blessing." Read a little further. The immature reader only notices, "I will bless them that bless thee, and curse him that curseth thee." The dedicated Christian emphasizes, "In thee shall all the families of the earth be blessed" (v. 3).

C. *Which is more important—to be blessed or to bless?* Unfortunately, too many of us become Christians for the wrong motivation or at least for the lesser one. Initially, we want to escape hell and go to heaven. Though this is a legitimate motive, it is not the highest one. We should come to Jesus because of who he is and the life of service he offers. Usually, however, we must grow in Christ before we make this the supreme motive of our lives. Abram did receive blessings, but most of all, God chose him as an instrument. Through him the world would be blessed. This is the meaning of life, for it is the one thing Jesus emphasized above everything else!

III. Serve where you are.

Although we emphasized at first the necessity of leaving home to gain a new identity, the time comes when we must settle down where we are and serve God in that place. We cannot be constantly moving every time things get tough.

A. *Abram served God where God put him.* At first God willed that Abram stay in Haran for a period of time. Perhaps it was to care for his father who may not have shared Abram's vision to go on to Canaan. For whatever reason, Abram waited patiently for a further word from the Lord. In the book of Acts, we learn that after Terah's death, Abram heard a new command from God. He then left Haran and went to Canaan. Notice that Abram "went forth to go into the land of Canaan; and into the land of Canaan they came" (Gen. 12:5). Nothing stopped Abram from doing God's will as he understood it.

B. *One thing that characterized Abram was that wherever he went, he built an altar and called on the name of the Lord (Gen. 12:8).* We need to worship where we are. The other side often looks better, but we must adjust to where God puts us.

Conclusion

Why did Abraham go down in history as such a great person? He had faith! Abraham's faith was proved by his faithfulness. God counted this faith as righteousness, and through his seed salvation has come to the world. We, too, can be a blessing if we obey.

WEDNESDAY EVENING, JANUARY 6

Title: A True Prophet for Our Times
Text: "The word of the LORD that came to Micah the Morasthite in the days of Jotham, Ahaz, and Hezekiah, kings of Judah, which he saw concerning Samaria and Jerusalem" ***(Mic. 1:1).***
Scripture Reading: Micah 1:1

Introduction

Harry Emerson Fosdick titled his autobiography *The Living of These Days.* He asserted that he was who he was because of specific experiences in his life coupled with his particular, inherent personality. Fosdick's life and ministry grew out of his social, political, and religious surroundings.

We can come to understand Micah in that way too. He lived in the eighth century BC. The superscription (Mic. 1:1) tells us something about his times. It follows the pattern of the other prophets' introductory verses: (1) "the word of the LORD that came to"; (2) "in the days of"; (3) "concerning."

Micah's message does not belong to only the days of Jotham, Ahaz, and Hezekiah. Micah is a prophet for our times. Our age needs to hear the words of a prophet of the Lord. Let us study Micah's superscription closely and see the qualities of a true prophet of the Lord.

I. A true prophet has a unique concept of God's Word.

Notice two expressions in Micah's superscription: "The word of the LORD which came to Micah" and "which he saw concerning Samaria and Jerusalem." These expressions describe the prophet's unique concept of God's Word.

A. *The true prophet speaks the word of the Lord.* The Hebrews had a high concept of God's spokesperson. They equated the words of the prophet with the Word of the Lord. Micah did not relate any of his experiences of faith, but he did indicate that God's hand was heavy on him when he spoke: "Thus saith the LORD." Micah's message originated from the Lord.

How does this apply to preachers today? When preachers remain true to the Bible, they speak the Word of the Lord.

B. *The true prophet has an inward perception through the influence of God's Spirit: "which he saw."* Micah's words were not his personal opinions. He disclosed what the Lord showed him.

No prophet arrives at inward perception without intimate fellowship with God. When a person lives close to the Lord, he or she begins to see what God wants.

II. A true prophet has great respect for the Lord.

Micah's great respect for God may be seen in the superscription and throughout the book as well.

A. *A true prophet respects the holy character of God.* Micah respected the majestic nature of God. He used the name Elohim to describe the power of God. He used the name Yahweh to describe the transcendental God.

No true prophet makes God a "buddy." Micah helps us to see the *otherness* of God. The proper responses to a holy God are reverence and awe.

B. *A true prophet respects the judgment of God.* Micah did not view God as a raging tyrant, but neither did he see him as an easy-going grandfather. He knew that God was a God of righteous judgment.

Being conscious of God's judgment gives one a profound respect for the Lord and his laws.

III. A true prophet has the ability to be himself as he is used by God.

The superscription has some pertinent facts about the personal life of the prophet. From the first verse we learn his name, his hometown, the times in which he lived, and his work.

A. *God works with all kinds of people.* Micah belonged to the illustrious group of eighth-century prophets. Each one of the prophets was different: Isaiah was a statesman, a city-dweller who prophesied to kings; Hosea learned his message from a domestic tragedy; Amos was a herdsman from the south who prophesied to Israel; Micah was a prophet from a small southern Judean village who prophesied to Jerusalem and Judah. God used each one of these unique prophets.

About all we know of Micah is his name and his hometown. His name means "Who is like Yahweh?" This obviously indicates his relationship to the Lord. Micah was from Moresheth, a small southern village in Judah near Gath.

God does not choose one kind of person to be his spokesperson. He works through all kinds of people.

B. *The prophet needs to learn about his or her true self.* Micah did not imitate the life and ministry of another prophet. He accepted his background and his personality and used them for the glory of the Lord.

No one can be an effective servant of the Lord while trying to be someone else. Find out who you are, then minister for the Lord out of your true being.

IV. A true prophet has an amazing relevancy to the times.

Two expressions in the superscription tell us about Micah's relevancy to his times. Look at these expressions: "in the days of Jotham, Ahaz, and Hezekiah"; and "which he saw concerning Samaria and Jerusalem." Micah spoke to the needs of his age.

A. *A true prophet relates to the times.* Micah's ministry took place during the reign of three of Judah's kings—Jotham, Ahaz, and Hezekiah. If we are to understand Micah's message, we need to know about the historical events during the reigns of these three kings. It was a time of international crisis. Israel had fallen in 722 BC to the Assyrians. During Micah's time the Assyrians under Sennacherib threatened Judah. Micah gave hope to the people during this crisis.

B. *A true prophet needs to commend or condemn a people's way of living.* Micah spoke "concerning Samaria and Jerusalem." These were the capitals of the northern and southern kingdoms. Micah spoke against all the evils he observed. And although he condemned sin, he encouraged the people. That is what a true prophet does.

Conclusion

Micah was a true prophet. He spoke to his day, and he still speaks to us today. His authenticity relays a message for us to be genuine before the Lord. His authenticity also demands that we listen to his message.

SUNDAY MORNING, JANUARY 10

Title: The Grace of God and Our Salvation

Text: "For the grace of God has appeared for the salvation of all men" ***(Titus 2:11 RSV).***

Scripture Reading: Titus 2:11–14

Hymns: "O Worship the King," Grant
"Great Redeemer, We Adore Thee," Harris
"Amazing Grace," Newton

Offertory Prayer: Thank you, Father God, for being the God of grace and mercy. Thank you for giving your Son Jesus Christ that we may receive the gift of eternal life. Help us, Father, to be generous, even as you have been generous, to give our all to advance your kingdom in the world. In Jesus' name we pray. Amen.

Introduction

Our newspapers are filled with bad news. As we listen to news reporters on television relating the tragic events happening around the world, we can easily become fatigued with the tragedy of what is taking place.

Our text contains some good news for this new year and for every year. It informs us that the grace of God has appeared in a remarkable form to make possible the salvation of all people. Paul had grown up in a world that believed only good Jewish people experienced salvation. The Great Commission was a new statement affirming that the grace of God had appeared for the salvation of all. Paul himself was included, though he was a persecutor of the church. You were included; I was included; and thus, we need to ask ourselves, "What is this great salvation that has been made possible by the grace of God?"

The apostle John affirmed, "For the law was given through Moses; grace and truth came through Jesus Christ" (John 1:17 RSV). The Jewish people considered the law as primarily being given to them. Both John and Paul proclaimed that the grace of God has come through Jesus Christ to all people.

The New Testament was written in Greek. The Greeks thought of grace as a favor conferred freely on a friend. In Hebrew thought God's grace is his unmerited favor freely conferred upon those who have made themselves his enemies. The grace of God is something much more than a favor conferred on a friend. It is God moving toward the undeserving sinner, offering freely the gifts that we so desperately need but do not deserve.

What, then, is this great salvation for all people that Paul is talking about?

I. Salvation by grace includes the new birth, or rebirth (John 3:3–7).

A. *There is no salvation apart from this spiritual birth of which Jesus speaks in his conversation with Nicodemus.*

B. *The appearance of Jesus has given humankind a chance.* Christ's work on the cross has made it possible for a sinful race to look to Jesus Christ by faith and receive this miraculous spiritual birth (John 3:14–16).

II. Salvation by grace includes spiritual rescue (Luke 19:10).

A. *The grace of God brought Jesus Christ into the world as a seeker of the lost.* We, by nature, do not seek God. The Holy Spirit seeks us by sending believers to communicate the good news of God's love to us.

B. *We have been rescued from our wanderings by the Good Shepherd, who searches for those who have strayed from God.*

III. Salvation by grace includes spiritual restoration.

A. *The apostle Peter says that we have experienced restoration to God because of the death of Jesus Christ on the cross for us (1 Peter 3:18).* He speaks of the substitutionary nature of the death of Jesus Christ on the cross for a guilty race. He affirms that it is by means of this that our Lord seeks to restore to the Creator God the sinful creature that was driven out of the garden because of sin.

B. *God the Father is eager to bring about the restoration of everyone who is willing to turn from sin to him through faith in Jesus Christ.*

IV. Salvation by grace includes spiritual renewal (Rom. 12:1–2).

A. *Salvation is more than just a ticket to heaven, and it is more than just being accepted by God on the basis of our faith. It involves a renewal of the mind.*

B. *Paul challenges believers to respond to God's mercy by presenting their total being to him.* He encourages them to refuse to be squeezed into the mold of a wicked, ungodly world and to experience renewal of mind that they might know and experience that the will of God is good, perfect, and right.

C. *God wants us to be like Christ in actions and attitude—indeed, in our very nature.*

V. Salvation by grace includes some revolutionary changes (2 Cor. 5:17).

A. *The conversion experience is described as a spiritual resurrection (Eph. 2:1, 5).*

B. *The grace of God that appeared in Jesus Christ for our salvation came to transform us.*

C. *The Father is eager to help each of us experience our full potential as his children.*

Conclusion

The good news is that the grace of God brings salvation for all people—including you. This salvation is experienced through the faith that makes Jesus Christ the Lord of your life. Today, if you have not already done so, let him become not only the Savior of your soul, but the transformer and enricher of your life.

Salvation is by grace: you cannot buy it, earn it, or steal it. You can receive it as a gift by faith when you open the door of your life to the Lord Jesus Christ.

SUNDAY EVENING, JANUARY 10

Title: Decision Determines Destiny

Text: "Let there be no strife between you and me, and between your herdsmen and my herdsmen; for we are kinsmen" ***(Gen. 13:8 RSV).***
Scripture Reading: Genesis 13:1–3

Introduction

Abram's experience in Egypt taught him a great lesson. When he returned he set up his camp at the original location between Bethel and Ai and once more built an altar. He seems to have been making an attempt to start over again and get back into full fellowship with God. Trouble came soon, however, and he was called to show his full commitment to God.

Life's adversities have a way of softening us and making us feel compassion for others. In times of distress we learn that God wants us to follow his will, and part of that is helping the weak. Too much prosperity can cause us to become selfish and unresponsive to the needs of those who are less fortunate and still striving for their "place in the sun."

Now Abram was ready to face a major crisis in his family relationship. He would do it against the background of his experience in Egypt.

I. The conflict.

Genesis 13:7 says, "And there was a strife between the herdmen of Abram's cattle and the herdmen of Lot's cattle." The preceding verse gives the background of the conflict: "And the land was not able to bear them, that they might dwell together: for their substance was great."

A. *In spite of Abram's sin in Egypt, God blessed Abram.* How great is God's grace!
B. *Often our prosperity is the very source of our troubles.* Many times children have been ruined because their parents have had too much. Some parents in our day would do well to give their children an example in unselfishness by giving a sacrificial amount to Christian causes.

II. The confrontation.

A. *Abram met the confrontation directly.* He was a person of peace and wanted things to go smoothly, especially since he and Lot were family. The solution was not only a fair one; it was more than fair. If anything, Abram was generous to a fault. He offered Lot his choice of the land. "Whatever you think is right" was his proposition to his nephew. Most people are astounded when a businessman settles a dispute by saying, "Pay me whatever you think you should, and we'll call the matter closed."
B. *Abram, however, was dealing with a person who did not have ethical integrity.* Lot interpreted meekness as weakness, as people in every generation do.

III. The choice.

A. *An outstanding educator once said, "It is by life's choices and not by life's chances that happiness comes to an individual."* Choices come to us every day, but sometimes a great one is thrust upon us that determines irrevocable events in our lives. Lot faced the major choice of deciding where he would live. Regardless of how we feel about Lot's choice, we must remember that the New Testament calls him a "righteous" man (2 Peter 2:7 RSV). He left his father's house and went with Abram, perhaps seeing something in this great patriarch that he wished to possess in his own life.

B. *The problem was, however, that Lot looked upon life with a spirit of worldliness and a desire to advance materially.* He represents those who believe that external advantages are the chief end of life, bringing true happiness. He failed to realize that when such values are considered the highest priority in a choice, the soul is easily corrupted.

C. *What should Lot have done?* If his finer feelings had not been blunted by selfishness, he would have deferred to Abram and insisted that the older man have the privilege of first choice. He, however, saw a chance to get rich quick and, since he was guided by no ethical principle, grabbed the opportunity without realizing the price he would pay in moral deterioration. Lot judged only by sight and sense: a person who operates from this set of priorities is always under the tyranny of appearances. Such an attitude always blurs the perceptions of moral beauty. No outward conditions, even though they seem fair and promising, will prove to be a paradise for one as long as he makes his own profit his highest goal in life. Selfishness will eat out the core of his happiness.

IV. The consummation.

A. *What happened as a result of Lot's choice?* The same thing that happens every time we make a decision: continuing consequences.

B. *The Bible tells us that Lot and Abram separated themselves.* Lot dwelled in the cities of the plain and "pitched his tent toward Sodom" (Gen. 13:11–12). Later, however, we read that Lot was dwelling in Sodom. In fact, he was sitting "in the gate of Sodom" (Gen. 19:1), which probably means he was "mayor" of the city.

During World War II on an island in the Pacific, the only tracks in the mud were those made by the trucks and jeeps. Before a person started down one of these, he saw a sign put up by the GIs that read, "Choose your ruts carefully. You'll be in them for the next ten miles." What a commentary on life's choices.

Conclusion

Abram and Lot represent two different approaches to life. Abram was the kind of man who, if his business interfered with his religion, gave up his business. Lot was the kind of man who, if his business interfered with his religion, gave up his religion. Which kind are you?

How far down the road of moral depravity can a wrong choice take us? Read the story of Sodom's destruction, but be sure to follow it all the way. The final "Ichabod" of Lot's life was when he brought children into the world by his own daughters. Moab and Ammon remained as perpetual enemies of God's people until they were completely destroyed. Decision determines destiny. We are what we choose.

WEDNESDAY EVENING, JANUARY 13

Title: One Person's Misfortune Is Another Person's Warning
Text: "What is the transgression of Jacob? is it not Samaria? and what are the high places of Judah? are they not Jerusalem?" ***(Mic. 1:5).***
Scripture Reading: Micah 1:2–9

Introduction

People learn from each other's actions. Many of our skills and behaviors come as a result of imitation. We learn both positive and negative things. While watching other people's actions, we can learn vocational or recreational skills. But also we can learn negative behavior by observing others. A well-known expression goes, "One person's misfortune is another person's warning." We could profit by observing the mistakes of others and avoiding the same.

Micah wanted Judah to learn from Samaria's mistake. In 722 BC the northern kingdom of Samaria fell to the Assyrians. Samaria's departure from the Lord evidently caused the fall. Micah saw that Judah moved in the same direction as Samaria. He called attention to Israel's mistake in hope that Judah would learn.

God's people could benefit from the mistakes of former generations, but some still continue to rebel against God. When will they learn? Let us learn some valuable lessons from Israel's mistake.

I. We can learn the awesome reality of God's judgment (Mic. 1:2–4).

A. *The reality of God's judgment is applicable to every person.* "Hear, all ye people; hearken, O earth, and all that therein is: and let the Lord God be witness against you, the Lord from his holy temple" (Mic. 1:2). Notice the universal terms Micah used—"all ye people," "O earth," "and all that therein is." Micah's message did not just apply to a small group of people in Judah; the Lord's judgment applies to every person on the earth.

B. *The reality of God's judgment on the world is analogous to the verdict of a judge in a courtroom.* "For behold, the Lord cometh forth out of his place, and will come down, and tread upon the high places of the earth" (v. 3). God's universal dominion entitles him to act as judge.

When God acts as judge, he takes powerful action. "And the

mountains shall be molten under him, and the valleys shall be cleft, as wax before the fire, and as the waters that are poured down a steep place" (v. 4). These images portray that the God who comes to judge his people has at his command all the powers of the universe.

II. We can learn the basic causes of God's judgment (Mic. 1:5).

A. *The cause of God's judgment is idolatry.* "For the transgression of Jacob is all this . . . What is the transgression of Jacob? is it not Samaria? what are the high places of Judah? are they not Jerusalem?" (v. 5). From the beginning of Israel as a nation, God demanded absolute obedience to him. He prohibited allegiance to idols. "Thou shalt have no other gods before me" (Ex. 20:3).

Even a casual reading of Samaria's history will disclose allegiance to idols. Israel kept some idols of Canaan. They also utilized some of the idols of their foreign neighbors. The Lord would tolerate no rivals; he responded in judgment.

Idolatry is not outdated. It does not belong to the superstition of ancient people. Anything that takes the place of God is an idol.

B. *The cause of God's judgment is sin.* "For the sins of the house of Israel" (v. 5). God's people had committed sins against the Lord. Micah did not name the specific sins; he simply accused both Israel and Judah of offending God. They deliberately rebelled against the Lord and failed to live up to his expectations. Failing to attain God's goal made the people liable to the prosecuting action of God.

God's judgment is not simply an outburst of rage. His judgment is a settled disposition against transgression and sins. When we rebel and choose to go our own way, we can expect judgment from the Lord.

III. We can learn the tragic effects of God's judgment (Mic. 1:6–7).

A. *God's judgment brings destruction.* Micah referred to the destruction of the impressive city of Samaria (1:6). This impressive city, noted for its beauty and military strength, became nothing more than a hill. The city wall toppled. Future generations used the site to plant vineyards.

Human beings must beware of what they call security. Feeling secure in wealth and military might can lead to destruction. Armies can be bested. Cities can be destroyed.

B. *God's judgment brings disappointment.* The Israelites gave allegiance to the idols, and the idols were destroyed by the Assyrians. They then had no place to turn. They were not only defenseless, but bitterly disappointed in their so-called gods.

IV. We can learn of God's great grief in his judgment (Mic. 1:8–9).

A. *God discloses his aching in judgment.* "Therefore I will wail and howl, I will go stripped and naked: I will make a wailing like the dragons

[NIV: 'jackals'], and mourning as the owls" (v. 8). God is portrayed by Micah as one distraught with grief. Vivid pictures such as jackals howling and owls crying in the night illustrate intense grief. Micah draws back the veil that allows us to see God's great grief over sin.

B. *God discloses his sadness in one person's failure to learn from another person's mistake.* "For her wound is incurable; for it is come unto Judah; he is come unto the gate of my people, even to Jerusalem" (v. 9). Not only was God hurt over Samaria's failure, but he was also sad because Judah failed to learn from their neighbor's mistake. Judgment was about to come to Jerusalem just as it came to Samaria.

Conclusion

God's people stand at a unique place in history. We possess the story of former generations. The lesson is obvious: we ought to learn from the errors of former generations.

Sunday Morning, January 17

Title: Three Motives for His Sacrifice

Text: "Jesus Christ, who gave himself for us to redeem us from all wickedness and to purify for himself a people that are his very own, eager to do what is good" ***(Titus 2:14 NIV).***

Scripture Reading: Titus 2:11–14

Hymns: "God, Our Father, We Adore Thee," Frazer
"There's a Wideness in God's Mercy," Faber
"At Calvary," Newell

Offertory Prayer: Heavenly Father, we accept the fact of your love for us even when we find ourselves in difficult circumstances. Thank you for demonstrating the greatness of your love through Jesus Christ and his sacrificial death for us. Grant to us a spirit of unselfish generosity toward those who are in need, even as you have been generous toward us in our need. Bless these tithes and offerings that they might express your love and grace to a needy world. In Jesus' name we pray. Amen.

Introduction

The motive that precedes action is supremely important. We all wonder about the motives that people have as they interact with us from day to day. They wonder about ours. The motive behind an action adds significance to that action.

It is encouraging to study the Word of God to discover the motives of our Father God. One can look through the New Testament and discover that our precious Lord had many motives that moved him in his ministry to bring salvation to a needy race. Our text focuses on three of these motives.

I. The proclamation of the good news.

As Paul spoke to Titus, he proclaimed the gospel in a sentence: "Jesus Christ gave himself for us."

A. *Jesus expected to die on the cross.* Death by crucifixion was not a last-minute emergency action on the part of Jesus Christ to bring about our salvation. A study of the prophetic Scriptures of the Old Testament indicate that somehow in the plan of God, the Messiah who was to be Prophet, Priest, and King, was also to be a suffering substitute for us (Isa. 53:4–9).

B. *Jesus chose to die for us.* Jesus was not a draftee who rebelled against his faith. Rather, he saw himself as a loving, obedient Son who chose to give his life (John 10:17–18).

C. *Jesus' death on the cross for us reveals to us the length to which his loyalty to the Father went.* Jesus' death for us shows the depth of the Father's love for us.

D. *The good news is that Jesus died for each of us.* By his death he bore the punishment that sinful people should have suffered. In doing so he opened the door to God for us. He permits us to enter the kingdom of God, where we are brothers and sisters to each other. Everyone is included in the offer.

II. The motives for his substitutionary sacrifice.

There were many motives moving our Lord to the cross, but our text speaks of three that we will consider today.

A. *Christ died for us that he might redeem us from all iniquity.* Isaiah was overwhelmed with a sense of his own wickedness and iniquity when the eye of his soul was opened and he saw the Lord (Isa. 6:1–6). These words may seem strange in this modern day when so many people lack a consciousness of sin.

Christ's atonement has many repercussions:

1. His death sets us free from all wrongdoing.
2. His death rescues us from our evil, self-destructive ways.
3. His death frees us from the wickedness that comes from living away from God.

To redeem someone is to purchase a person who occupies the role of a slave. It means to rescue someone from self-destructive attitudes, aims, and actions. Jesus liberates us from a lawless way of life that disregards the laws of God and pursues selfish disobedience.

B. *Christ Jesus gave himself that he might "purify for himself a people that are his very own."* Our Lord did not die on a cross to save us and then preserve us in a sinful state. He came that he might bring about wonderful changes within us. The conversion experience involves confession and forsaking the old way of life (Isa. 1:16–18).

Our Lord works to bring about this purification by making us aware of the imperfections in our lives. The apostle John encourages us to confess continually and forsake the ways that are contrary to the will of God (1 John 1:7).

1. A part of God's plan for bringing about our purification is the bestowal of the Holy Spirit at the moment of our conversion (Gal. 4:6–7; 5:16–17).
2. God has also given to us his Holy Word, by which it is possible for us to learn how to live a clean and holy life (Ps. 119:9).
3. The Father also uses chastisement to turn us from ways contrary to his holy nature and will for us (Heb. 12:4–11).

C. *Our Savior gave himself for us to produce a people zealous to do good.* Jesus did not die merely to rescue us from going to hell when we die; he did not give himself for us solely that we might go to heaven when we die. Rather, he gave himself for us that in us and through us he might bring a heavenly way of life to the here and now.

A part of Christ's motive for giving himself for us was to produce a special people to do what is right. He wanted to produce a people with real enthusiasm and ambition for doing good and noble deeds; he would have us set our hearts on living a life that is good.

Our Lord wants us to be characterized by enthusiasm for doing kind things for others.

1. God, our Father, is very good and wants us to do good.
2. Our Savior is described as one who went about doing good (Acts 10:38).
3. Paul wrote to the Ephesians, "We are his workmanship, created in Christ Jesus unto good works" (2:10).

One of Jesus' great motives for us was that we might be busy doing good deeds for the glory of God and for the welfare of others (Matt. 5:16).

Conclusion

Christ chose to die for me and for you. His motives behind the choice are clear. He desires to redeem, rescue, and deliver us from all that enslaves, harms, or disappoints. He also wants us to be pure and unstained in this wicked world. He yearns for us to be enthusiastic about doing good in the world today. Because of the grace that has appeared in Jesus Christ, let each of us decide to let him do his good work within us. Let us make that decision now and live the rest of our lives seeking to cooperate with the motives behind his death for us.

Sunday Evening, January 17

Title: Love Your Enemies—It Will Worry Them to Death

Text: "When Abram heard that his kinsmen had been taken captive, he led forth his trained men" ***(Gen. 14:14 RSV).***
Scripture Reading: Genesis 14:1–24

Introduction

The title of the message is a "tongue in cheek" way of saying that the best way to take revenge on somebody is to "kill him with kindness." Paul expressed it succinctly when he said, "Therefore if thine enemy hunger, feed him; if he thirst, give him drink: for in so doing thou shalt heap coals of fire on his head" (Rom. 12:20). A frustrated woman once complained to her pastor about her supposedly worthless husband who abused her constantly. The pastor asked her, "Have you ever tried heaping coals of fire on his head?" She replied, "No, but I once tried a bucket of hot water. It didn't do any good."

This passage depicts Abram risking all to rescue his nephew Lot, who had wronged him by taking the best lands. The lessons that spring from this story are best expressed in "negatives" as we see what we should avoid when tempted to seek revenge. Revenge is indeed tempting. It is also, however, "the sweetest morsel ever cooked in the oven of hell." Here is how to avoid tasting the bittersweetness.

I. Do not rebel against authority.

A. *Sometimes we must declare ourselves free from oppression, but we should be careful about the timing.* These five cities—Sodom, Gomorrah, Admah, Zeboiim, and Zoar—were ruled by the four kings of the East and, therefore, subject to taxation from them. The expression "Twelve years they served . . . and in the thirteenth year they rebelled" (Gen. 14:4) does not mean they formed an army and went forth to attack. Rather, they withheld the annual tribute. In the battles that followed, Lot was taken captive.

No one, of course, enjoys paying any form of taxes. We especially resent paying taxes if we feel the money is being spent unwisely. Taxation without representation is, of course, the most difficult to endure. These cities during Abram's day, no doubt, resented paying taxes to foreign powers, and so they rebelled. The point here is that they overestimated their strength. They were not able to defend themselves properly, and the taxers came to discipline the taxed.

Reformers who rebel need to be very careful and think through the matter properly. Is the issue big enough to put one's position, one's fortune, and sometimes even one's life on the line? This is precisely where the revolt might lead. If so, rebel, but be willing and prepared to pay the consequences if you fail!

B. *In this case, it wasn't the proper time to rebel.* War came with all the horrible results that accompany armed conflict. What a terrible thing war is! One of the terrible results of the fall of man in Eden is that the human race has wasted so much of its talents, resources, and energy in seeking to neutralize one another. Such a wretched loss of power is a folly that can only be corrected by the Spirit of Christ dwelling in our hearts. While we know that we shall never have permanent peace until Jesus comes, as Christians we need to work toward changing the lives of people through a transforming experience with the Savior. The lesson here is that we should be careful about going to war or conflicting in any way with a person or group of people unless we are certain we are right and also are confident the time is right for such action.

II. Do not hold a grudge.

A. *What did Abram do when he saw Lot taken prisoner?* He could have relaxed, smiled, and said, "Well, that impetuous young whippersnapper got what was coming to him. His greed caught up with him at last." Have you ever been tempted to have such an attitude? One man admitted that when another driver intimidated him on the highway, he became impatient with the driver's desire to pass. When the other driver dangerously passed on a hill, the man had to slow down considerably to prevent the other driver from a head-on collision with an approaching motorist. He admitted that, for a moment, he was tempted to speed up and leave the man exposed to the oncoming driver. He was saying to himself, "I ought to do it to teach him a lesson." This would, of course, have been criminally wrong, and he did not do it. Revenge, however, is part of all of us. We like to "play God" and take over his work. Paul, however, warned us, "Dearly beloved, avenge not yourselves . . . for it is written, Vengeance is mine; I will repay, saith the LORD" (Rom. 12:19).

B. *Now that we have seen what Abram did not do, let us see what he actually did.* The Bible tells us that he "armed his trained servants . . . and pursued them," not stopping until he had freed Lot and all those associated with him, including his goods. What a marvelous example of a godly attitude!

Beware of having an avenging spirit. Chaucer once wrote, "Vengeance is not cured by another vengeance, nor a wrong by another wrong; but each increaseth . . . the other." Bacon reminds us that "a man that studieth revenge keeps his own wounds green, which otherwise would heal and do well."

Why not take vengeance? Revenge is its own executioner. As John Milton said, "Revenge, at the first though sweet, bitter ere long, back on itself recoils."

III. Do not forget to be grateful.

A. *After the battle, Abram continued to show a marvelous spirit.* Two kings met him, and to each he acted graciously. Melchizedek, king of Salem, represented God, for he was the "priest of the most high God."

Abram gave him "tithes of all." The writer of Hebrews makes much of this noble example. There were no churches or religious organizations to which Abram might give, so he dedicated his "tithe" to God's representative, being confident he would use it properly.

B. *What do you do when you receive some unexpected bonus that overwhelms you?* One great Christian said, "I make a generous gift before my heart grows cold."

When the king of Sodom suggested that Abram keep all the material goods he had taken from the enemy (much of which belonged to the inhabitants of Sodom), Abram refused, saying, "I will not take from a thread even to a shoelatchet, . . . I will not take anything that is thine" (Gen. 14:23). Though Abram's motive, "lest thou shouldest say, I have made Abram rich" (v. 23), might be slightly suspect, his gratitude still shines forth. We should not fault Abram for his reason but should honor him for his unselfishness and gratitude. Samuel Johnson is incontestably correct when he says that gratitude is "a fruit of great cultivation; you do not find it among gross people."

Conclusion

Abram remembered these "do nots" and refused to be guilty of doing them. Sometimes it is as important to remember what not to do as it is to remember what we should do. Before God told Jeremiah he was to build and to plant, he warned him that he would be required to root out, pull down, destroy, and throw down. In other words, some negatives are necessary before the positives can be planted. The destruction of the devilish must come before the establishment of the Christlike.

Wednesday Evening, January 20

Title: Heartbroken over Sin

Text: "Declare ye it not in Gath, weep ye not at all: in the house of Aphrah roll thyself in the dust" ***(Mic. 1:10).***

Scripture Reading: Micah 1:10–16

Introduction

A pastor was contacted by law officials to deliver some bad news to parents who were members of his church: their son had committed armed robbery in another state. He went to break the news to them.

The pastor's apprehensions were high. He wondered how the parents would react. Would they be angry with their son? Would they be enraged over law enforcement? Or would they be angry with the pastor? With as much diplomacy as possible, he told them the shocking news. He was not prepared for their reaction: they were deeply grieved over their son's rebellious act.

Micah had to bring hard news to Judah about their sins. As he announced the sins of Judah, he also disclosed God's attitude toward sin. Some might think God's predominant attitude toward sin is anger, but by carefully studying Micah 1:10–16, we will learn that God was deeply grieved over Judah's sin. In verses 10–16 Micah skillfully describes God's attitude toward sin by using the meaning of the names of the towns in Judah.

God's people need to become heartbroken over sin. Let us study Micah and learn some reasons why. We shall choose some of Micah's wordplays on the cities.

I. Sin brings great sorrow.

A. *The exposure of our sin causes shame.* "Declare ye it not at Gath" (Mic. 1:10). Micah's dirge began with the same words as David's lament over the death of Saul (2 Sam. 1:20). The Philistines published the news of Saul's death to their cities. This grieved David greatly. Evidently Micah saw the approaching tragedy of defeat at the hands of the Assyrians. He hoped the seriousness of the Assyrian threat would not be told in Gath. In other words, Micah did not want Gath to glory in Judah's death. Judah's sin brought Micah great sorrow.

B. *The presence of sin prompts expression of grief.* "In the house of Aphrah, roll thyself in the dust" (Mic. 1:10). Aphrah means "house of dust." Rolling in the dust was a visual demonstration of great grief. Sin brings sorrow, and Micah called for people to express grief over sin.

II. Sin destroys beauty.

A. *Sin causes God's people not to live up to their name.* "Pass ye away, thou inhabitant of Saphir, having thy shame naked" (Mic. 1:11). Saphir means "beautiful." Micah predicted the doom of Saphir: it would not live up to its name.

B. *Sin destroys the beauty God intended.* Closely akin to not living up to God's name is the loss of beauty. God made Israel a beautiful nation, but Israel's rebellion destroyed all of it.

Micah predicted that when the enemy came, the residents would have to flee in shame. Sin always destroys the divine intention of the Lord.

III. Sin immobilizes initiative.

A. *Sin has a way of destroying human initiative.* "The inhabitant of Zaanan came not forth in the mourning of Bethezel; he shall receive of you his standing" (Mic. 1:11). The name Zaanan means to "go out." Evidently the inhabitants of Zaanan practiced hospitality. When travelers would near the city, people would go out and welcome them. Yet Micah said that rebellion had destroyed this initiative to go out.

B. *Sin has a way of immobilizing completely the desire for fulfillment.* Bethezel means "nearby town." Refugees from Jerusalem and other places fled to it. Yet when these refugees came to the city of Bethezel, they would discover that the inhabitants had lost their desire to welcome outsiders.

IV. Sin disappoints.

A. *Sin diminishes the hope of people.* "For the inhabitant of Maroth waited carefully for good: but evil came down from the LORD unto the gate of Jerusalem" (Mic. 1:12). Maroth means "bitterness." The people of "bitterness" longed for their town's name to change. They wanted hope, but the town remained bitter; hope never did come.

B. *Sin deceives the people.* "The houses of Achzib shall be a lie to the kings of Israel" (Mic. 1:14). Achzib means "lying, deceitful." In Jeremiah 15:18 the prophet spoke of deceitful or failing waters. The picture portrays a source of water that should have been trustworthy, but when a thirsty person went to get water, the waters failed.

To live a life in sin will always be a deceitful lifestyle. Sin seems to promise pleasure, but sin is deceitful; real pleasure never happens.

V. Sin enslaves.

A. *Sin brings even the mighty to destruction.* "O thou inhabitant of Lachish, bind the chariot to the swift beast: she is the beginning of the sin to the daughter of Zion: for the transgressions of Israel were found in thee" (Mic. 1:13). Lachish fell to the Assyrian ruler Sennacherib. A well-fortified city, it seemed indestructible, but Micah prophesied its fall.

B. *Sin will take you to another master.* "Therefore shalt thou give presents to Moresheth-gath" (Mic. 1:14). Micah used a pictorial image. Like a divorced person receiving a settlement, Moresheth-gath would receive farewell gifts, for she would then become the property of the Assyrians. Micah prophesied that this town would come under the rule of the Assyrians.

Conclusion

When Micah looked at the sins of Judah, he was heartbroken. He described an army advancing against Jerusalem from the direction of his own hometown. He used the meanings of the place names along the route to describe the tragic results sin brings.

Let us catch a glimpse of Micah's sorrow. Then let us try to take the heartbreak of the Lord over sin. Our response should be to see the seriousness of sin and repent.

SUNDAY MORNING, JANUARY 24

Title: The Negative Expression of True Religion

Text: "For the grace of God has appeared for the salvation of all men, training us to renounce irreligion and worldly passions" ***(Titus 2:11–12 RSV).***

Scripture Reading: Titus 2:11–14

Hymns: "Serve the Lord with Gladness," McKinney
"Our Best," Kirk
"Living for Jesus," Chisholm

Offertory Prayer: Gracious and loving Father, help us to recognize you as the giver of every good and perfect gift. We affirm that you are the giver of the power that we have to work and to accumulate wealth. We come today bringing tithes and offerings to indicate our love for you and our desire to be partners with you in bringing the good news of your love to a needy world. Bless these offerings to that end, we pray. In Jesus' name. Amen.

Introduction

Jesus came into a world where Judaism emphasized the negatives of the religious life more than the positives. Jesus made an impact on the world then as he does now by his emphasis on a positive response to God and a positive response to the needs of others.

While recognizing that the positive is of supreme importance, we should recognize that there is also a negative expression in genuine religion. Our text tells us, "The grace of God has appeared for the salvation of all men, training us to renounce irreligion and worldly passions." The New Testament in the Language of the People translates this verse, "For God's favor has appeared with its offer of salvation to all mankind, training us to give up godless ways and worldly cravings." With this word concerning the negative side of genuine religion, this translation continues this verse by saying that we are to "live serious, upright, and godly lives in this world while we are waiting for the realization of our blessed hope at the glorious appearing of our great God and Savior, Jesus Christ, who gave himself for us to ransom us from all iniquity and purify for himself a people to be his very own, zealous of good works."

It is highly possible that the greatest weakness in present-day preaching and in present-day Christianity is in the neglect to emphasize the biblical requirement of repentance. Repentance is basically and fundamentally a change of mind that affects the direction of a life. Repentance is far deeper than reformation. It is a transformation of the mind and attitude toward God, self, and others.

To be truly Christian, we must not only be positive about great spiritual values, we must be negative about ungodly values.

I. True religion calls for the repudiation of ungodliness.

A. *We need to ask God to help us become holier in all spheres of our lives.* This means repudiating—through repentance—ungodliness in our attitudes, ambitions, affections, and actions.

In our positive identity with the nature and character of our Father God, we must repudiate and renounce those things that are contradictory to his nature, character, and purpose.

B. *God is love, and this means that he repudiates hate.* We must not permit hate to occupy our minds and hearts.

C. *God is light and in him there is no darkness at all.* We must not tolerate attitudes and activities that are out of character with his perfect righteousness.

II. True religion calls for rejection of worldly cravings.

A. *One can become captivated by a desire for perishables.* Our Lord was not thinking about an offering plate when he counseled his disciples regarding true riches.

> Do not lay up for yourselves treasures on earth, where moth and rust consume and where thieves break in and steal, but lay up for yourselves treasures in heaven, where neither moth nor rust consumes and where thieves do not break in and steal. For where your treasure is, there will your heart be also. (Matt. 6:19–21 RSV)

Our Lord was concerned about his disciples putting their hearts into the eternal values of God's kingdom rather than living for the perishables of this earth.

B. *The apostle Paul gave similar advice to the church at Colosse.* He urged them to respond positively to God; to do this, he wrote, there had to be a negative response to the cravings and the appetites associated with this world system. In The New Testament in the Language of the People we read:

> So if you have been raised to life in fellowship with Christ, keep on seeking the things above, where Christ is seated at the right hand of God. Practice occupying your mind with the things above, not with the things on earth; for you have died, and your life is hidden in God through your fellowship with Christ . . . so once for all, put to death your lower, earthly nature, with respect to sexual immorality, impurity, passion, evil desire and greed, which is real idolatry. (Col. 3:1–3, 5)

Conclusion

The Father God wants to help us to repudiate all attitudes, ambitions, affections, and actions that are destructive to us and hurtful to others. We must be willing to say no to everything that is ungodly if we are to be true children of God and true followers of our Lord Jesus.

Sunday Evening, January 24

Title: Lord, Give Me Patience and Hurry Up!
Text: "Sarai said to Abram, 'Behold, now the Lord has prevented me from bearing children; go in to my maid; it may be that I shall obtain children by her'" ***(Gen. 16:2 RSV).***
Scripture Reading: Genesis 16:1–16

Introduction

The title of this message reflects the way most of us handle the matter of obtaining patience. Few people are willing for God to do things his way. One man admitted, "I do not have near as much trouble with God's will as I do with his timetable." Yet if we are out of step with the latter, we are weak in understanding the former. In the Scripture reading for this message, we see that Abram and Sarai had been waiting a long time for a son. This son was the one who would begin the fulfillment of God's promise made to them that their descendants would possess the land of Canaan. Because they were old, the delay of God to bless them with a child tested their faith.

I. Lack of faith is a common sin of God's people.

A. *All of us, regardless of how many blessings we have received, can recall times when we have tried to run ahead of God.* Can you not, however, look back now at something you wanted greatly and see that if God had given it to you when you first felt you needed it, the result would have been disadvantageous, perhaps even devastating?

> God knows when to send his blessings
> Just as well as when and how.
> Our time charts are merely guessings;
> The shallow shout, "I want it now."

B. *Though Abram and Sarai certainly failed to show patience, we should not judge them too harshly.* They were anxious to see God's plan unfold. Faith may be genuine and yet sometimes unsteady because of the severe trials to which it has been exposed. Abram had come a long way. He had choked on a lot of dust during his long journey across the desert from Ur to Haran and then on to Canaan. Would we not have been as vulnerable as he to falter and take matters into our own hands?

C. *The conflict between faith and reason is not merely a phenomenon of modern times but one as old as human nature itself.* The attempt to hasten God's work by plans devised from our own wisdom often seems so plausible that even the best of God's servants yield to the temptation and seek to take over for God the running of his universe or at least the part they feel they can handle.

II. However logical it might seem, lack of faith is wrong.

A. *All of us learn early in life to justify ourselves when we do wrong.* This process of rationalizing takes many forms. The established church in the Middle Ages reasoned like this: "If these people are not bright enough to come into our organization and escape hell, we will force them to, even if it takes bodily punishment to make them see the light." With Abram the twisted logic may have been, "God didn't make himself clear. Perhaps he meant for me to work it out in my own way. I wouldn't disobey him, but what's wrong with letting Sarai's handmaid be surrogate mother?"

B. *Of course, Abram was wrong!* God had not forgotten him. The tiniest dewdrop feels and obeys the same laws that control the movement of the sun and stars. The humblest wayside flower is formed and colored with the same patience as the most distinguished. No region of God's universe that we call nature, however obscure and minute, is given over to chaos and neglect. Likewise, in the world of spirit, no one lies under the neglect and abandonment of God. If the entire universe is in his hand, the details are also controlled by him. If he is behind and within the whole, he must be behind and within every part, because the whole consists of all the parts. Abram needed to learn these great truths, but even more, he needed to live in the light of that knowledge.

C. *Regardless of Sarai's suggestion to have Hagar act as surrogate, Abram stands as the guilty one.* One perceptive pastor shares this insight: "The source of Abraham's sin was in the old, evil nature that remains in us until we die. Sarai did not cause Abraham to sin; she just stirred his sinful nature until the sin in him surfaced. Even Satan cannot make us sin." Paul tells us: "But remember this—the wrong desires that come into your life aren't anything new and different. Many others have faced exactly the same problems before you. And no temptation is irresistible" (1 Cor. 10:13 TLB).

III. Our lack of faith can hurt others.

A. *Who is Hagar?* Most likely Hagar was one of the "maidservants" Pharaoh gave to Abram while he was in Egypt (Gen. 12:16). What a terrible price she paid in personal humiliation and harassment because Abram sired a child by her! Of course, Hagar was not without fault. None of us ever lives above error and sin. She, no doubt, must have become a threat and even an intimidation to Sarai, perhaps through a haughty attitude. Tradition, which seems reliable, tells us Hagar was of royal Egyptian blood, which, no doubt, aggravated the situation. The Hyksos were probably on the Egyptian throne at this time rather than the native Egyptians. Her sudden elevation from the state of slave to that of wife and mother changed her entire relationship to Abram. This brought severe complications to the household because, according to the Code of Hammurabi under which Abram and Sarai probably lived, a woman had a right to cast out her handmaid if she wished, even though she had borne a child by the master. In other words, Sarai was acting legally and Hagar suffered the most. It was not fair, but many things in life are not fair when sin moves in and takes over. Wrongdoing shows no logic in the people it affects adversely!

B. *The entire world has suffered greatly from this lack of faith Abram demonstrated.* The Israeli-Arab conflict today goes back to the birth of Ishmael. The descendants of Abraham from the line of Isaac would have been spared much misery if the patriarch had waited quietly for God's timing.

IV. God can overrule our lack of faith.

A. *Amazing grace, how sweet the sound!* God can and does bless us in spite of our sins. He did forgive Abram and Sarai, later sending Isaac.

B. *Look, however, at Hagar.* When she was driven away, God went with her. The angel of the Lord found the slave girl by a spring of water in the wilderness and sent her back to Sarai with a promise that he would watch over her. Hagar gave God a special name because of his compassion—El Roi—which means "a God who sees" (see Gen. 16:13).

Conclusion

So many lessons come to us from the story that we must be careful not to forget the first and most important one that underlies all others. Trust God and wait on him.

We may not always understand
Why we must wait so long,
But in his time, from his good hand
He always sends the song.

So if your faith is weak, still trust
Though hopeless it may seem.
He said he would and so he must;
Cling still in faith to him.

Leave all to God, pray, trust, and wait;
Our Lord does love and care.
The answer may come soon or late.
But God will answer prayer.

—*Frederick M. Wood*

Wednesday Evening, January 27

Title: On a Collision Course
Text: "Therefore thus saith the Lord; Behold, against this family do I devise an evil, from which ye shall not remove your necks; neither shall ye go haughtily: for this time is evil" ***(Mic. 2:3).***
Scripture Reading: Micah 2:1–5

Introduction

Frequently the media reports on near misses of airplanes. What causes near misses? The answer is simple. They are on a collision course, flying at the same altitude toward each other. Unless the course is corrected, a collision takes place.

Micah prophesied about a collision course. He spoke of God's will and God's way on one hand: he indicated that God would not change his way. He spoke, on the other hand, of human rebellion and transgression: if people continued to proceed on their course, there would be a collision. In striking contrast, Micah described God's way and the human way. Micah wanted to avoid a collision. He persuaded human beings to change course and align themselves with the Lord.

Look at today's society. Do you read the Bible and see God's way? Have you looked lately at the direction of human beings? If you have studied both courses, you will have to conclude that there is a collision coming. Let us carefully examine Micah's description of the collision course.

I. Look at the attitude and actions of the people (Mic. 2:1–2).

A. *Evil begins within the heart.* Micah addressed a particular group of people—the wealthy landowners. He identified the particular crime—the illegal appropriation of land.

Micah gave brilliant insight into the attitudes of the people. "Woe to them that devise iniquity, and work evil upon their beds! when the morning is light, they practise it because it is in the power of their hand" (v. 1). People lie awake at night devising schemes by which they may exploit others. Some of these people even use their influence to steal from the less fortunate.

Micah gives us insight into the nature and practice of sin, indicating that sin begins in the mind of a person. The expressions "devise iniquity" and "work evil" depict actions taking place in the mind of a person.

Sinful action begins in the mind. Jesus said that adultery begins with a lustful look (cf. Matt. 5:28). John said that murder begins with hate (1 John 3:15). Guarding our attitudes is important in controlling our actions.

B. *Evil planned in the heart results in evil actions.* "And they covet fields, and take them by violence; and houses, and take them away: so they oppress a man and his house, even a man and his heritage" (v. 2). What the people planned, they put in action. Rich people schemed and took away the heritage of the poor people. Notice the extremes to which people go with their greed. First, they devise legal schemes to secure land from the poor. If this does not work, they apply force. "Take" here means to snatch away by violence.

Greed has serious results. The sins of Micah's day prevail in our day. Many cases of shameless exploitation may be observed.

II. Look at the attitude and actions of the Lord (Mic. 2:3–5).

A. *The Lord plans and works against human plans.* While people had been devising evil, the Lord had been making plans against them. "Therefore thus saith the LORD; Behold, against this family do I devise an evil, from which ye shall not remove your necks; neither shall ye go haughtily: for this time is evil" (v. 3). God has the final word. The Lord had watched evil people bring calamity upon the defenseless. Now, according to Micah, the Lord will bring his own special calamity upon the designers of the wickedness. Just as their own victims were helpless, so will they be unable to extricate their necks from the Lord's yoke of calamity. They will swagger around haughtily, their heads high, but they will bend under God's yoke like laden beasts of burden.

B. *Micah went on to explain God's intervention against human exploitation.* He used an object lesson: "In that day shall one take up a parable against you, and lament with a doleful lamentation, and say, We be utterly spoiled: he hath changed the portion of my people: how hath he removed it from me! turning away he hath divided our fields" (v. 4). God would transfer land to others.

God's punishment matched the crime. The evil people took land from others. God then devised a plan to take the land from the exploiters.

Conclusion

The people in Micah's day traveled on a collision course. They refused to go God's way. They exploited others, taking the land of the poor. Micah predicted a collision when God would take the land from the exploiters.

Are you in the will of the Lord? If you are not in God's will, you are headed for a collision. Change to God's direction.

SUNDAY MORNING, JANUARY 31

Title: Living a Godly Life in an Ungodly World

Text: "... to live sober, upright, and godly lives in this world" ***(Titus 2:12 RSV).***
Scripture Reading: Titus 2:11–13
Hymns: "We Praise Thee, O God, Our Redeemer," Cory
"Let Others See Jesus in You," McKinney
"I'll Live for Him," Hudson
Offertory Prayer: Thank you, Father, for sending your Son from heaven to live on this earth to communicate your grace and love to us. Help us in this sinful and selfish world to imitate your character, becoming generous and helpful in all of our relationships. Bless these offerings as they are used to do your work. We pray in Jesus' name. Amen.

Introduction

Paul states his purpose for writing to Titus in the salutation of his letter: "to further the faith of God's elect and their knowledge of the truth which accords with godliness" (v. 1).

The Father God desires that his children become godly in their dispositions, beliefs, and behavior. To be ungodly in life is to be unlike God in nature, character, and disposition. To live a godly life, we must become, from the heart, imitative of the nature and character of our God.

How do we do that in an ungodly world? Some have given up trying. Others have accepted an oversimplified substitute for the clear teachings of God's Word. Here are some suggestions that can be helpful to a child of God who wants to live a godly life in this ungodly world.

I. If you would live a godly life in an ungodly world, you must recognize and respond to the grace of God.

We need to recognize and respond to the fact that our God is not a salesman. Our Father is the great lover who generously gives to those who come to him by faith. Life, with all of the talents and opportunities we have, is the gift of God, who is the giver of every good and perfect gift (James 1:17).

A. *Humans are workers.* They want to work their way to success, happiness, and even to heaven. Salvation, however, does not come through human works (Eph. 2:8–9).

B. *Humans are achievers.* Even so, apart from the grace of God, they cannot live godly lives in an ungodly world.

C. *Humans are consumers.* There are some who would like to purchase salvation and possess it like they do the gadgets that are available in the marketplace.

II. If you would live a godly life in an ungodly world, you must hunger to be holy more than you hunger to be happy.

A. *Our Father God is the Holy One of Israel.* The apostle Peter says, "As obedient children, do not be conformed to the passions of your former ignorance, but as he who called you is holy, be holy yourselves in all your conduct; since it is written, 'You shall be holy for I am holy'" (1 Peter 1:14–15 RSV).

B. *The holiness of God is a term that refers to the ethical and moral perfection of our God.* He is without sin; he is without flaw.

C. *Isaiah saw God in the temple as thrice-holy.* He heard the seraphim singing, "Holy, holy, holy is the LORD of hosts; the whole earth is full of his glory" (Isa. 6:3 RSV). This vision of the holy God overwhelmed the young prophet with his deficiency in moral and spiritual transparency, and there arose from his heart a confession of his uncleanness. Following his confession he experienced cleansing and heard the commission of God to become his prophet.

D. *As the essence of moral perfection, our God requires morality from those who worship him.* Our God is not an absentee landlord of the universe. He is the personal God who is available and accessible to all who will draw close to him for cleansing and forgiveness.

E. *To be holy, we must recognize that we belong to God and that we must act as those who belong to God.* That which is holy is that which belongs utterly and completely to God.

III. If you would live a godly life in an ungodly world, you need to respond to the generosity of God with generosity.

People have been plagued with insecurity ever since Adam and Eve were cast out of the garden of Eden. They have sought security in achievements and in the accumulation of material things. Our modern competitive economic system accentuates the acquisitive instinct humans have because of their lack of security in their relationship with God.

A. *Our God is not hungry in the sense that the human race is hungry.*

B. *Our God is not insecure as we are.*

C. *Our God is not acquisitive in the sense that he is seeking to accumulate an estate.*

D. *Our God is not materialistic.*

E. *Our God is not earthly minded.* He exists in eternity above and beyond planet Earth.

F. *If we would become generous, we need to understand and imitate this nature of our Father God.* We need to hunger and thirst to be like him at this point. We need to come to the place where we define our reason for being in terms of giving, sharing, caring, and helping.

G. *Think about the difference it will make in your life when you decide to define your reason for being in terms of being a giver.*

   1. Be a giver to your mate.
   2. Be a giver to your family.
   3. Be a giver in your vocation or profession.

If you would be like God, you must become a giver rather than a grabber.

Conclusion

Do you resemble your father or your mother the most? Is it possible that you resemble a grandparent even more than you resemble an earthly parent?

The more important question is this: Are people reminded of your Father God as they get acquainted with you? Do others see Jesus in you?

God aids his children in various ways to live godly lives in an ungodly world. He provides us with the strength and fellowship of a family of believers. He also speaks to us and teaches and corrects us through the reading of his Word. And he communicates with us through the Holy Spirit when we pray.

Sunday Evening, January 31

Title: Nothing Is Too Hard for God
Text: "Then Abraham fell on his face and laughed" ***(Gen. 17:17 RSV).***
Scripture Reading: Genesis 17:1–27

Introduction

The Bible does not give the details of the years when Ishmael grew up in the home of Abram and Sarai as the only child of the patriarch. We do not know how many times Sarai bit her lip and endured the slave girl and her son, secretly longing to cast them out again but perhaps fearing to do so lest she arouse the anger of both her husband and her God.

When Abram was ninety-nine years old, which means Sarai was eighty-nine, God reassured him that he would be a father of many nations. Surely he told his wife of the divine promise. Also, God instituted the rite of circumcision.

After having done this, God affirmed once more that Sarai (now Sarah) would have a child. This seemed so unlikely, even impossible, that Abram (now Abraham) laughed at the very idea. How could such a thing happen when both he and his wife were near the century mark in age? God insisted, however, that the covenant he would establish with Abraham's seed would be through the child Sarah would bear.

What about Abraham? He was a man of faith, but at times he failed to measure up to the quality of trust God desired. Notice some lessons from this story and the events that followed.

I. Abraham laughed.

A. *What type of laughter came from this man of God we are not told.* Surely it was not a mocking ridicule of the Lord's words, though it may have seemed that way.

B. *When we express disbelief, we show it in different ways.* The slow grin is often a sneer, as though we feel we possess a superior knowledge to the one at whom we smile. The nervous laugh is sometimes a cover-up for the fact that we really do not believe a person can or will do what he promises, but we hesitate to come out boldly and call him a falsifier. Of course, the rasping, mocking guffaw is the blatant denial of our confidence in the one speaking. This is, no doubt, the unkindest cut of all. Goethe once wrote, "Men show their character in nothing more clearly than in what they think laughable."*

II. Abraham pleaded for a substitute.

A. *Much pathos exists in Abraham's plaintive cry, "O that Ishmael might live before thee!" (Gen. 17:18).* This could be paraphrased, "Why not let Ishmael be my heir?" Before we condemn Abraham too much, let's examine our own lives.

B. *How many times have we tried to change God's will for our lives because fulfilling the ideal plan involved too much work or too much waiting or both?* What about the young man who feels a call to the foreign mission field but seeks to bargain with God by promising to support foreign missionaries with his money if God will only let him remain with family and friends? What about the young person who feels called into a full-time ministry but wishes to remain in the business world instead of going to school and preparing for a religious vocation? To bring it a little closer, what about the person who would rather remain secretary or some other officer in the Sunday school class than be dedicated enough to be a teacher? What about the man who would rather hire a "professional" Christian than go out himself on visitation night and give his personal witness to lost people? All of these are doing essentially what Abraham did when he cried for a substitute. They are seeking to change God's will because the task he has set before them is difficult, involving both faith and dedication.

III. God refused to compromise.

A. *Does God ever change?* This question has puzzled people and has resulted in some faulty answers. The truth is that God never changes in his essential nature. He is holy. That can never change, or else everything distinctive about God would disappear.

B. *Likewise, God is truth.* He cannot lie or be inconsistent with himself. Also, he is merciful, hating sin but loving the sinner. Such attributes never change, never vary. On the other hand, God does change his methods. The recurring phrase in the Old Testament "God repented"

---

* *5000 Inspiring Quotations: For Enlightenment, Support, Self-Growth & Self-Improvement,* Comp. Radharaman Agarwal (Upkar Prakashan, 2017), 199.

does not signify a moral action but rather a decision to alter his method because of man's response or lack of response to his commands and purposes.

C. *What about Ishmael?* Why did God insist that his covenant be with Abraham and Sarah's child? First, he had promised Sarah that she would have a child. God always keeps his promises. Second, God purposed to reveal through this covenant a higher type of life than the pagan people were practicing. His ideal was not only monotheism but also monogamy. True, God, because of the hardness of people's hearts, permitted divorce and seemingly did not condemn polygamy, but Jesus declared this was never God's ideal will. God felt it was right and proper to produce the heir through Sarah and Isaac, and he refused to compromise. Abraham had to accept this part of God's will as best and nonnegotiable.

D. *What did this mean for Abraham?* We do not discover all truth in a day. Even if we must wait for twenty years before we realize the fullness of God's plan for us, we should never be overcome by discouragement. Those who love God's will can "as little abstain from seeking it as the artist can abstain from admiring what is lovely."* Furthermore, we must hold open our hearts and minds, being assured that light is "sown for the upright and that all that is has lessons for the teachable."†

IV. Nothing is too hard for God.

A) *The one who made the world has the wisdom to sustain it.* He who breathed into us the breath of life can be trusted to guide us in the daily affairs of our earthly existence.

B) *We need to remember that God holds the solution to every situation facing us.*

Is there some problem in your life to solve,
Some passage seeming full of mystery?
God knows, who brings the hidden things to light.
He keeps the key.

Is there some door shut by the Father's hand
Which widely opened you had hoped 'twould be?
Trust God and wait, for when he shuts the door,
He keeps the key.

Is there some earnest prayer, unanswered yet
Or answered not as you had hoped 'twould be?

---

* Marcus Dods, *The Expositor's Bible: The Book of Genesis* (Double 9 Books, 2024), 106.
† Dods, *Expositor's Bible,* 106.

God will make clear his purpose by and by.
He keeps the key.

—*Anonymous*

C) *God will not leave us without his presence and guidance.* He will continue to hold out before us his intention for our lives. Sometimes this may irritate us because we want to settle for the easier way—the second or third best. He can and will, however, do what he purposes and promises because he is unlimited in resources and cares too much to let us have less than he wishes for us.

Conclusion

God does not reveal himself to us to satisfy our curiosity or even to grant our desire for knowledge merely for its own sake. Rather, he wishes to impart to us light and strength to do our duty. Through one of Israel's greatest prophets God said, "Call to me and I will answer you and tell you great and unsearchable things you do not know" (Jer. 33:3 NIV). Trust God and do right.

SUGGESTED PREACHING PROGRAM FOR THE MONTH OF FEBRUARY

■ Sunday Mornings

"The Good News of Salvation for the New Year" is the theme we will continue with through February 21 as we explore Titus 2:10–13. On the final Sunday morning of the month, begin the series "The Conquest of Spiritual Death by Spiritual Birth and Resurrection." Sin is a terrible reality. Only Jesus' death and resurrection can deliver us from it. Jesus was not only the Lamb who died, but he is the Lord who arose. This series will carry us through the Easter season.

■ Sunday Evenings

Continue the series "Messages of Hope from the Experiences of Abraham."

■ Wednesday Evenings

Continue with the theme "Mighty Messages from a Minor Prophet" based on the book of Micah.

WEDNESDAY EVENING, FEBRUARY 3

Title: What Constitutes Good Preaching?
Text: "Prophesy ye not, say they to them that prophesy: they shall not prophesy to them, that they shall not take shame" ***(Mic. 2:6).***
Scripture Reading: Micah 2:6–13

Introduction

A lot of preaching takes place each week. In America alone, five million sermons a year are preached. In large cities, in small towns, and in the country, people assemble to hear sermons. People also listen to sermons on radio, television, and online. In the twenty-first century there is no shortage of preaching in the land.

Perhaps we find this fact comforting. But before we take comfort, we need to ask what constitutes good preaching. Answers to that question would be diverse. Think of some criteria people have for preaching: short, long, conversational, loud, exegetical, topical, positive, negative, simple, profound, just to mention a few.

During Micah's ministry he was confronted by critics of his preaching. Listen to the objections to Micah's preaching, " 'Do not preach'—thus they preach—'one should not preach of such things; disgrace will not overtake us' "

(Mic. 2:6 RSV). Micah was asked to stop preaching about Judah's disgrace. He answered his critics with questions: "O thou that art named the house of Jacob, is the spirit of the LORD straightened? are these his doings? do not my words do good to him that walketh uprightly?" (v. 7). Micah contended that his preaching was authentic.

Today's preaching may be abundant, but it also needs to be authentic. Let us look closely into Micah's disclosures about good preaching. With his help we can make bad preaching good and good preaching better.

I. Authentic preaching causes opposition (Mic. 2:6).

A. *Micah's preaching produced opposition.* Read Micah 2:6 again. Micah insisted that one's relationship to God affected every area of life. Critics of Micah thought he should stick with religion and leave politics alone. Also, they thought he emphasized too much the judgment and wrath of God. The people wanted a preacher to emphasize solely the love of God.

Micah was not the only one to arouse opposition with preaching. Amaziah, priest of Bethel, sent word to Amos to leave town. "O thou seer, go, flee thee away into the land of Judah, and there eat bread, and prophesy there" (Amos 7:12).

B. *When God's way is presented, opposition comes.* Micah was neither the first nor the last preacher opposed. Many in today's world want a preacher to talk about a sentimental God who does not take sin seriously. They want a preacher to emphasize Sunday religion but not be concerned about social, economic, and political matters.

If preaching is to be authentic, opposition will come. When God's will and way are presented, an inevitable conflict occurs.

II. Authentic preaching declares God's Word (Mic. 2:7).

A. *Micah told his audience that the essence of true prophecy was the declaration of the Word of God.* Read Micah 2:7 again and notice the probing questions Micah asks his audience. The substance of false prophecy was the proclamation of the words of the prophet's masters. The real prophet of the Lord does not capitulate to the desires of people. The real prophet speaks God's Word, and God's Word is the only authentic word that does good to people.

B. *Declaring God's Word profits more than declaring what people want to hear.* The words of man may be false, but the Word of God is always true. The word of man may soothe for a while, but the Word of God will give long-lasting results.

III. Authentic preaching denounces evil (Mic. 2:8–10).

A. *Micah condemned the evils of society.* Micah exposed the wealthy land barons and their oppression of the weak (vv. 8–10). Micah blamed these wealthy barons for the forthcoming evil. These exploiters seemed to be for the people, but actually they were against the people. They attacked fellow citizens as enemies. They acted like conquerors and drove women from their homes.

B. *All preaching needs to include the bad news with the good news.* God's Word is not all good news; in the Bible there are many disclosures of bad news. Listen to some bad news: the whole world has sinned against God. People lie, cheat, and steal. People commit adultery and murder their fellow human beings. Whenever a true prophet observes the sins of society, the prophet needs to condemn the sins and announce the results.

IV. Authentic preaching differs drastically from false preaching (Mic. 2:11).

A. *Micah described the kind of preacher the people wanted.* The people wanted a preacher who walked about uttering lies and who would condone their vices.

B. *God's authentic prophet emphasizes truth.* Consequently, the true prophet has substance in his sermons. The authentic prophet has the ultimate welfare of the people in mind, not reputation for himself.

V. Authentic preaching offers hope (Mic. 2:12–13).

A. *Micah offered hope to a distressed people.* Even though Micah condemned the sins of society and predicted judgment, he still had hope. Following his announcement of expulsion of evildoers from the land, he predicted the return of a remnant (v. 12).

B. *While there is life, the authentic prophet offers hope.* Regardless of how far the people have gone in rebellion against God, the prophet holds out hope. The basis of hope is repentance and faith. God's real prophets may speak of sins and judgment, but they constantly share the good news of repentance and salvation.

Conclusion

What kind of preacher do you listen to? Listen to an authentic prophet of the Lord. Give your attention to one who speaks the Word of God rather than seeks popularity with the people.

SUNDAY MORNING, FEBRUARY 7

Title: Zealots for Good Works

Text: "Jesus Christ . . . gave himself for us, to redeem us from all iniquity and to purify for himself a people of his own who are zealous for good deeds" ***(Titus 2:13–14 RSV).***

Scripture Reading: Philippians 2:12–16
Hymns: "I Love Thy Kingdom, Lord," Dwight
"Make Me a Blessing," Wilson
"I'll Go Where You Want Me to Go," Brown
Offertory Prayer: Loving Father, we thank you for the zeal you have to save a needy race. Today we come offering our bodies as living sacrifices for your service. We also come offering back to you the time you have so graciously given to us. And we bring our tithes and offerings to support the work of your kingdom, not only in this community but to the ends of the earth. Accept these and bless them for that end. We pray in Jesus' name. Amen.

Introduction

Webster defines zeal as "eagerness in pursuing any course or object; ardent interest; fervor." And a zealot is "a person who shows zeal, especially excessive zeal; fanatic."

Jesus came to this world to do the works of God and to encourage others to engage in doing the things God wants them to do. He would have us serve him with eagerness and enthusiasm, not with apathy or indifference.

We see a lot of zeal around us. Many of us are zealous about a certain sport, hobby, or television show. To listen to some people talk, you would think that their reason for being is to travel and enjoy vacations. Others have a zealous greed for materialistic things. The god of gold often usurps the place that belongs to God. Still others are so intensely zealous for a cause that they commit acts of terrorism culminating in suicide and murder. But where are the zealots of love, helpfulness, and service?

Christ Jesus came into the world to choose, equip, and motivate a special people who would be eager to engage in doing things for the benefit of God and others.

I. A zealous eagerness for good works validates the genuineness of our faith in Christ.

A. *James has been called the book of practical religion.* It enumerates a number of tests by which it is impossible for us to validate the authenticity of our faith. This New Testament writer would have us seriously question the kind of faith that does not produce good works. He raises the question, "What does it profit, my brethren, if a man says he has faith but has not works? Can his faith save him?" (James 2:14 RSV). He then completes his thought. After illustrating the uselessness of a faith that does not evidence itself in good works, he affirms, "So faith by itself, if it has no works, is dead" (v. 17 RSV).

B. *In the Sermon on the Mount, our Lord speaks about the influence of the ideal citizen of the kingdom.* He exhorts us, "Let your light so shine before men, that they may see your good works and give glory to your Father who is in heaven" (Matt. 5:16 RSV).

II. A zealous eagerness for good works expresses the nature of our heavenly Father.

A. *God is good.* God is not a cold, impassive, unmoved, unconcerned deity in the distance somewhere. He is a doer of good and a giver of good to the sons and daughters of men. Jesus affirmed, "We must work the works of him who sent me, while it is day; night comes, when no one can work" (John 9:4 RSV).

B. *On another occasion, Jesus spoke about doing the works that the Father wanted him to do.* "But the testimony which I have is greater than that of John; for the works which the Father has granted me to accomplish, these very works which I am doing, bear me witness that the Father has sent me" (John 5:36 RSV).

When we give ourselves to the doing of good works, we give expression to the nature of our heavenly Father that came to us in the new birth experience.

III. A zealous eagerness for good works imitates the pattern of our Savior and Lord.

We read that "God anointed Jesus of Nazareth with the Holy Spirit and with power; . . . he went about doing good" (Acts 10:38 RSV). Jesus was a tireless worker in doing good to those with whom he came in contact. Here are some specific ways.

A. *Jesus was a healer of the sick.*
B. *Jesus was a teacher of the unlearned and needy.*
C. *Jesus was busy at the task of helping men to see, not only physically but spiritually.*
D. *Jesus worked to enable people to hear, not only with the ears but with the ears of their hearts.*
E. *Jesus worked with great zeal to point people to God.*
F. *Jesus continuously gave himself to the task of enriching and uplifting those who would permit him to enter into their lives.*

IV. A zealous eagerness for good works responds to the Holy Spirit.

A. *The Holy Spirit came into the world on the day of Pentecost to do a number of things that are of tremendous importance.* He came to help disciples become like Jesus Christ. The Holy Spirit is continually at work, helping Christians to be good and do good. He came to empower believers to be witnesses for Christ, to bring others to him, and to disciple them.

B. *The Holy Spirit empowers us and leads us to do good.* Many of us have grieved him by not following his signals and urgings to give ourselves to good works.

V. A zealous eagerness for good works exposes our very reason for being.

A. *In Ephesians 2 Paul climaxes his statement about salvation by grace.* He affirms, "We are his workmanship, created in Christ Jesus for good works, which God prepared beforehand, that we should walk in them" (Eph. 2:10 RSV). Some people never discover their reason for being; they merely drift through life. How different their lives would be if they sought out the divine purpose for their lives.

B. *Paul encouraged the Christians in Galatia.* He said, "So then as we have opportunity, let us do good to all men, and especially to those who are of the household of faith" (Gal. 6:10 RSV).

Conclusion

The greatest good that you can do for yourself is to give yourself to God through faith in Jesus Christ. The greatest good that you can do for another person is to help him or her come to know God through faith in Jesus Christ. Jesus sent his Holy Spirit that he might give you zeal and power for doing good works for his glory and for the benefit of others. God bless you as you respond to your highest reason for being.

SUNDAY EVENING, FEBRUARY 7

Title: Losing Our Influence Gradually
Text: "He seemed to his sons-in-law to be jesting" ***(Gen. 19:14 RSV).***
Scripture Reading: Genesis 19:12–14 (of Gen. 18:16–19:28)

Introduction

Although many lessons come to us from the story of Lot's choice and the results that followed, perhaps the chief one is that even a good man can so conduct himself that he loses the respect of his associates and his family. One of the saddest verses in the entire account of the various events says, "And Lot went out, and spake unto his sons in law, which married his daughters, and said, Up, get you out of this place; for the LORD will destroy this city. But he seemed as one that mocked unto his sons in law" (Gen. 19:14). Lot had made so many compromises that he had forfeited his ability to be taken seriously when he recommended a spiritual course of action for his family. What a terrible price to pay for indulgence in worldly things.

Lot's condition did not emerge suddenly. Much of it dated back to his early life and attitudes. Likewise, many factors enter into one's life to produce a character that comes across as false to our friends and acquaintances.

I. Concern for self.

A. *Go back to Lot's decision when Abraham gave him two alternatives.* Lot cared nothing that the older man may have lacked the energy and drive that he possessed. What he decided reminds us of the "rich fool" who said, "I will pull down my barns, and build greater; and there I will bestow all my fruits and my goods. And I will say to my soul, Soul, thou hast much goods laid up for many years; take thine ease, eat, drink, and be merry" (Luke 12:18–19). Count how many times the words "I" and "my" appear in the full story. He had no concern for anyone else but himself.

B. *The person who is wrapped up in self is clad in thin garments and will find out some day how inadequate the covering is to protect him from the chilling winds of adversity that come to all.* Self-love is a tragedy. Of course we need proper self-esteem to function, but we should never carry this so far that it becomes that which blinds us to the needs and burdens of others. Self-love has been called "the most inhibited sin in the canon" and the "mote in every man's eye." Benjamin Franklin wisely observed, "He that falls in love with himself will have no rival." Lot's first step downward was his concern for self.

II. Companionship with sinners.

Years ago a young lady from a Christian home went to college. She had been taught right and wrong and had always conducted herself as a Christian. During school days, however, she fell in with a group of not-so-dedicated people. Soon her life in Christ was questionable. Many people had doubts about her character. What caused this condition? A major reason was her companionship with the wrong kind of people. Happily this young woman later rededicated her life to the Lord.

A. *It is important to have as our personal friends those who live for Jesus.* When John Wesley enrolled at Christ's College in Oxford, he made a resolution. This young man, who later started an organization of Christian people who still have great influence for Christ, said, "I will have no friends except those who help me live a stronger Christian life."

B. *Look at Lot.* The New Testament speaks of him as "vexed with the filthy conversation of the wicked" (2 Peter 2:7). The significant thing is that Peter calls him "just," which means in New Testament language a "justified person," a saved man. Can a child of God lose his or her influence? Certainly! Peter did this when he denied the Lord. The fact that we have been saved by the blood of Christ does not mean that we never sin. Some strong Christians have had weak periods in their lives. Have you ever been embarrassed in the presence of a nonbeliever because you were at the wrong place for a Christian to be?

C. *How did Lot's downward trek begin?* He, first of all, "pitched his tent toward Sodom" (Gen. 13:12). Though we cannot be sure, this probably meant only that he moved in that direction. The final proposition of Abraham to the Lord in that classic negotiation process was that the city would be spared if ten righteous people could be found.

The contract was agreed upon, but ten righteous people could not be found and the city was destroyed. What had Lot been doing all these years? Had he not persuaded any of the people to accept God's way of life? His own family would have been eight of the number since he had two unmarried daughters and at least two married daughters and sons-in-law. Couldn't they be counted in the righteous crowd? If so, all Lot needed were two converts! His companionship with sinners had neutralized his witnessing for the Lord.

III. Compromise with sin.

Two recorded incidents reveal how low people can sink when they give free rein to personal ambition and lower their moral standards to accommodate the crowd.

A. *First, to protect his guests, Lot offered to give his single daughters to the mob for exploitation.* When evil men are dominated by their fleshly lusts, no type of reasoning can reach them. A polluted moral atmosphere is dangerous, and Lot had no business being in such an environment. Strong faith, on the other hand, teaches a person to do right even in the most perplexing and difficult situations. The results may be safely left with God, who knows how to "deliver the godly out of temptations" (2 Peter 2:9).

B. *After Sodom and Gomorrah were destroyed, another tragedy took place in Lot's life that further revealed how his compromise with sin had caused him to lose his influence.* Already his married daughters and sons-in-law had rejected him. Now his unmarried daughters got him drunk and engaged in incestuous relationships with him. Few sins are as disgusting as this one. The daughters had lost all respect for their father and even for themselves.

Conclusion

How strong is your influence with your family and friends? When we become concerned for self, fraternize with sinners, and compromise with sin, we lose our influence and our power in intercessory prayer. It is the "effectual, fervent prayer of a *righteous* man" that is powerful (James 5:16, author's italics). Lot loved worldly things too much, and because of this, he did not realize the spiritual blessings God had for him. We need to guard our lives constantly, maintaining uncompromising watchfulness against things that would destroy our influence.

Wednesday Evening, February 10

Title: Let Justice Prevail

Text: "And I said, Hear, I pray you, O heads of Jacob, and ye princes of the house of Israel; is it not for you to know judgment?" ***(Mic. 3:1).***

Scripture Reading: Micah 3:1–12

Introduction

There are two sides to the gospel: believing and behaving. What an important concept that is! It means that the relationship we have with God leads to proper relationships with others.

Micah did not neglect either side of the relationship. He spoke of walking humbly with the Lord, but he also spoke of practicing justice (Mic. 6:8). Micah's basis for doing justice came out of a relationship with the Lord.

In Micah's day injustice was rampant. Consequently, justice was a primary theme in Micah's preaching. He looked into the three areas of society that needed to check injustice and promote justice: the courts, the prophets, and the government.

Injustice was not a sin related solely to Micah's day. It prevails in every generation. Also, the three areas of society Micah addressed continually need to be the guardians of justice. Let us look into Micah's three areas and find relevancy for our day.

I. The judicial leaders (Mic. 3:1–4).

A. *The duty of leaders of the court was to know and to enforce the law.* Micah addressed the "heads of Jacob" and the "princes of the house of Israel" (v. 1) with a stunning question: "Is it not for you to know judgment?" The basic responsibility of these leaders was to be concerned with justice. They were responsible "to know justice" (v. 1).

B. *The tragedy of the judicial leaders was that they had forsaken justice.* The leaders of Micah's day demonstrated great greed. Listen to Micah's description of them: "Who hate the good, and love the evil; who pluck off their skin from off them, and their flesh from off their bones; who also eat the flesh of my people, and flay their skin from off them; and they break their bones, and chop them in pieces, as for the pot, and as flesh within the caldron" (vv. 2–3). The judicial leaders failed to protect the exploited. Instead, they became the exploiters. Micah compared their actions to a butcher slaughtering an animal.

C. *The judicial leaders should not turn to God for relief.* "Then shall they cry unto the Lord, but he will not hear them: he will even hide his face from them at that time, as they have behaved themselves ill in their doings" (v. 4). The exploiters failed to hear the cries of the citizens. The exploiters cried to the Lord but were told that God would hide his face from them in the time of their distress.

II. The religious leaders (Mic. 3:5–8).

A. *The prophets led people astray.* "Thus saith the Lord concerning the prophets that make my people err" (v. 5). Just as the people in Micah's time turned to the courts for justice, so too they turned to the prophets for guidance. The prophets should have given the people guidance, but they had become as corrupt as the courts.

B. *The prophets were motivated by selfishness.* "[They] bite with their teeth, and cry, Peace; . . . they even prepare war against God" (v. 5b). The people who paid these prophets a good honorarium would hear, "Peace, everything will be fine!" The poor people, however, could not meet the prophets' selfish desire for money, so the prophets gave them angry and abusive words. Tragically, the spiritual leaders sought for selfish fain. They were wicked people who worked in the garb of religion to get what they wanted.

C. *The false prophets would be punished for their evil.* Micah condemned the false prophets (vv. 7–8). He said that ultimately the false prophets would be disgraced before the people, for they had no answer, no vision, no word from the Lord. The people would turn from them in anger.

D. *One prophet testified to his credibility.* Micah knew himself to be a true prophet. "But truly I am full of power by the spirit of the Lord, and of judgment, and of might, to declare unto Jacob his transgression, and to Israel his sin" (v. 8).

   1. His message was consistent. It did not vary.
   2. His message came with the power of the Spirit.
   3. His message was true to the nature and character of God.

III. The political leaders (Mic. 3:9–12).

A. *The leaders considered themselves above the law.* They had lost their sense of fairness. "Hear this, I pray you, ye heads of the house of Jacob, and princes of the house of Israel, that abhor judgment, and pervert all equity" (v. 9). These leaders had become so distorted that they actually hated and rejected justice.

B. *The leaders became so engrossed in self-seeking that they abused people.* "They build up Zion with blood, and Jerusalem with iniquity" (v. 10). These leaders secured what they wanted by bribery and violence. Perhaps poor people had been exploited to pay for the building of government projects.

C. *The leaders presumed to serve as the ultimate answer for the people (v. 11).* People in ancient Israel looked in three basic directions for leadership—elders (heads), priests, and prophets. Micah said the people—and especially the leaders—did not look to the Lord for guidance.

D. *Corrupt leaders caused the collapse of a country.* "Therefore shall Zion for your sake be plowed as a field, and Jerusalem shall become heaps, and the mountain of the house as the high places of the forest" (v. 12). Those who proclaimed safety and ignored the injustices of society would see judgment come.

Conclusion

Micah's society was filled with corruption. Injustice prevailed in the courts, in religion, and in government. Micah called for justice to prevail.

Look at our society. Where are there injustices? The prison system? The courts themselves? The abortion clinics? These are just a few areas where justice does not prevail. We need to enter in and be willing to suffer so that wrongs can be made right.

SUNDAY MORNING, FEBRUARY 14

Title: Waiting for the Blessed Hope

Text: "Awaiting our blessed hope, the appearing of the glory of our great God and Savior Jesus Christ" ***(Titus 2:13 RSV).***

Scripture Reading: Titus 2:13

Hymns: "All Creatures of Our God and King," St. Francis of Assisi
"Crown Him with Many Crowns," Bridges
"Jesus Shall Reign Where'er the Sun," Watts

Offertory Prayer: Thank you, Father God, for being so extravagant in giving us gifts. We thank you for the gift of forgiveness. We thank you for the gift of eternal life. We thank you for the gift of your Holy Spirit. We thank you for the gift of letting us cooperate with you in your work of bringing salvation to a needy world. Bless our offerings today to that end, we pray. In Jesus' name. Amen.

Introduction

Have you heard someone make a statement concerning something and affirm it by saying, "It's as certain as death and taxes"? The second coming of Christ is even more certain than death or taxes. Carl F. Henry once said, "The second coming of Christ is the one event in the future that is more certain than physical death." This is true because those who are alive and remain when the Lord returns will not have to experience physical death (1 Thess. 4:15–17).

The first-century church eagerly awaited the return of the Lord Jesus Christ during their lifetime. As time passed, some began to doubt whether he would come back. The apostle Peter warned his fellow disciples against the danger of becoming discouraged because the Lord had not already returned. He made some great affirmations concerning the return of the Lord (2 Peter 3:8–10). Peter also challenged his readers to respond positively to the promise of Christ's final coming and to be ready for his return.

I. Christ first came after a long period of expectancy.

A. *The promise of his first coming is implied in his covenant with Abraham (Gen. 12:1–3).*

B. *Messianic promises were made through Moses.*

C. *Messianic promises were made through the prophets.*
D. *The psalmist looked forward with eagerness to the Messiah's coming.*
E. *John the Baptist came as Christ's forerunner to announce that the time had come for the Lord's ministry.*

In the fullness of time God did send his Son to be the Savior of the world.

II. Christ will come a final time.

Instead of referring to the *second* coming of the Lord, the New Testament emphasizes it as his *final* return. The prayer that comes almost at the end of the book of Revelation contains the attitude of early Christians toward this final return of the Lord. The inspired writer prays, "Come, Lord Jesus!" (Rev. 22:20 RSV). Some people dread the thought of being alive when the Lord returns; this is not the attitude we should have. Here are some of the events that will accompany his return.

A. *The resurrection of the saints will take place (1 Thess. 4:13–16).*
B. *Purification from sin will occur (1 John 3:1–3).* We shall be purified, for we shall see him as he is.
C. *Mortality will be replaced with immortality (1 Cor. 15:53–54).*
D. *Rewards will be presented (Rev. 22:12).* Eternal life is the gift of God. God chooses to reward his servants on the basis of their works. This will occur when our Lord returns.
E. *The reunion of God's people will occur: this will be heaven's homecoming.*
F. *Praises will be presented to our Savior (Rev. 22:3).* During our life of mortality we have sought to praise Christ. The activity of the saints is described as worshiping him and praising him.
G. *The fate of the unsaved will be sealed.* The final return of our Lord will be a tragic disaster for the unsaved who have rejected the Christ of mercy and love (2 Thess. 1:7–10). There is no evidence in Scripture to indicate that there will be another chance to receive Christ once he has made his final return to the earth.

III. Christ comes today and every day (Rev. 3:20).

Beloved professor Clyde T. Francisco taught that we should think in terms of the many comings of Christ rather than thinking solely of his first coming and his final coming. Christ conquered death and the grave, and he is alive and comes to us today and every day.

In the letters to the seven churches listed in Asia Minor, we discover something about the purposes of his coming day by day.

A. *Christ comes to commend us as we seek to do that which is good.*
B. *Christ comes to correct us with counsel that will help us.* He encourages us to trust and obey God. He encourages us to love and help people.

He encourages us to use things for God's glory and for people's good.

C. *Christ comes today to complain when we are not growing spiritually.* He complains when we are preoccupied with materialistic pursuits. He complains when we fail to worship the living God. He complains when we neglect the Holy Spirit. He complains when our major concern is for the comfort of our bodies rather than our souls' progress.

D. *Christ comes today and every day to cheer and to encourage.* He encourages us to go out in our personal world and live for the glory of God and for the good of others. He would use us to knock on the heart's door of a needy world to share the good news of God's love.

Conclusion

What is the great hope of your heart? Is your greatest desire to be popular? To be beautiful? To be handsome? To be a great achiever? To have a brilliant mind? Is your greatest hope to be successful in business? To live a long, fulfilling life? To be of service and help to others? The Bible suggests that your highest hope should be to live life with the values of eternity up front and to live so that you will be ready—fully and completely—if our Lord should make his final return today.

SUNDAY EVENING, FEBRUARY 14

Title: Some People Never Learn
Text: "Abraham said of Sarah his wife, 'She is my sister'" ***(Gen. 20:2 RSV).***
Scripture Reading: Genesis 20:1–18

Introduction

Why do some people repeat a sin again and again though they suffer every time they do it? For instance, the alcoholic knows what liquor does to him, but he cannot or will not abstain. Or, consider the woman who marries a wife beater and, upon securing legal freedom, marries the same type of man again. Clearly, a powerful habit is at work.

Wordsworth insists that habit "rules the unreflecting herd." None of us would believe that Abraham allowed falsehoods to become so much a part of his system that he became a pathological liar, but he certainly failed to learn from his experience in Egypt that misrepresenting the truth is not only wrong, it is dangerous.

I. One sin makes another easier.

A. *Many scholars feel Abraham made a mistake when he went to Egypt.* God had given him Canaan. Later he would will that Abraham's seed spend four hundred years in Egypt, but at that time Abraham's place was in Canaan. The famine threatened his lifestyle. Thus far he had probably lived with plenty, and this turn of events presented a problem with which he could not cope.

B. *How often we become anxious when the source of our food and clothing seems in doubt.* Jesus warned us not to worry about what we will eat or drink or wear. Life needs more than food. The body needs more than clothing. Did God send the famine to give Abraham a touch of hardship to make him stronger? Did Abraham then fail to be faithful in testing? We cannot be certain how God operates his universe. Nor is it wise to speculate too much. We can, however, profit from the lessons that emerge as we concentrate on the story. When we sin once, it is much easier to do it again. For instance, when a person crosses the line of sexual purity, the next time is easier; he or she yields much more quickly.

II. Sin destroys our creativity.

A. *When Abraham journeyed southward and sojourned in Gerar, he once more had the fear as when in Egypt.* He was certain the king would covet his wife and harm or perhaps kill him to take her. To a certain extent, Abraham was correct in diagnosing the situation, for Abimelech took Sarah when Abraham said she was his sister. But the point here is that Abraham not only did not learn that lying can produce dangerous consequences; he did not even have the originality to think of a new story (cf. Gen. 12:10–20). The old lie failed, but he reused it. Perhaps he rationalized that God had nothing to do with the evil sent upon Pharaoh, that it was all a coincidence.

B. *How prone we are, when the danger is over, to forget God's providential hand that delivers us.* Nothing clouds persons' minds and destroys both their initiative and creativity so much as a guilty conscience. Those who know God and understand their moral responsibility are never at their best when planning iniquity. We simply do not think clearly when we focus our minds on evil things.

III. Half-truths are lies.

A. *When confronted by Abimelech, Abraham resorted to a trick explanation.* He vaguely suggested that his statement was not entirely a lie. Technically speaking, if we accept the Jewish traditions and interpretations, Sarah was a kind of sister to Abraham. Haran, Abraham's brother, had a daughter named Milcah whom his brother Nahor married. He also had a daughter named Iscah whom Hebrew scholars and the Jewish historian Josephus say was Sarah, wife of Abraham (Gen. 11:30). Since granddaughters were often called daughters, Abraham gave a loose interpretation and considered Sarah as the "daughter" of Terah and therefore his sister. What a way to establish a case! When we want to prove a point, however, we, too, resort to any kind of reasoning to defend our contention.

B. *Lying, however disguised, is wrong.* A lie can be more than saying something false. It can be leaving a false impression by not telling all the facts; it can be telling the facts but either arranging or interpreting them in such a way as to convey a wrong conclusion. Those who serve God should "abstain from all appearance of evil" (1 Thess. 5:22) and "provide things honest in the sight of men" (Rom. 12:17).

IV. God still takes care of his own.

A. *In spite of our many shortcomings, God watches over us when he has a purpose for us, and we are earnestly seeking to fulfill it.* God watched over Abraham and delivered him from trouble. All of us are weak and therefore sinful, but great comfort comes to us when we remember this:

> There is an eye that never sleeps
> Beneath the wing of night.
> There is an ear that never shuts
> When sink the beams of light.
>
> There is an arm that never tires
> When human strength gives way.
> There is a love that never fails
> When earthly loves decay.
>
> —*James Cowden Wallace*

B. *Both in Egypt and in the land of Abimelech, God intervened and revealed to these rulers that their proposed course of action was wrong.* Let it be said to the credit of both men that they respected the moral code they lived by, whatever it was, and refused to take Abraham's wife.

C. *Have you ever had the experience of God's grace providing deliverance for you when you were about to do something that would have thwarted your ability to serve God's kingdom?* If so, thank him and ask him to help you not to repeat the mistake.

Conclusion

Though God directly intervened in Abraham's behalf, we should never be presumptuous. Jesus warned Satan in the temptation experience, "Thou shalt not tempt the Lord thy God" (Matt. 4:7). People can so condition themselves by repeated sins that they lose all control of their moral life. God is not obligated to rescue us from deliberate wrong choices. In the sacrificial system of the Israelites, as outlined in Leviticus, offerings could be made for all kinds of wrongdoing except one: if a person committed a deliberate wrongdoing, there was no sacrifice for it.

Mistakes should teach us lessons. Though error has been called the force that welds people together, it also must be said that truth is communicated to people only by deeds of truth.

WEDNESDAY EVENING, FEBRUARY 17

Title: Bright Hopes for Tomorrow
Text: "For all people will talk every one in the name of his god, and we will talk in the name of the LORD our God for ever and ever" ***(Mic. 4:5).***
Scripture Reading: Micah 4:1–8

Introduction

Perhaps one of the most famous social sermons ever delivered was Martin Luther King Jr.'s "I Have a Dream" sermon, in which he set forth many specific hopes he had for the black people of America.

Micah projected his dream for Judah in 4:1–8. Oddly enough, Micah had just announced Jerusalem's downfall and the destruction of the house of the Lord on Mount Zion (Mic. 3:12). He went from an announcement of catastrophe to a vision of victory and exaltation.

God's people need always to hold out hope. The days do not become so dark that hopes for tomorrow diminish. Let us learn from Micah's projections, his bright hopes for tomorrow. What did Micah want?

I. The universal worship of God (Mic. 4:1–2).

A. *The sovereign of the Lord would be made known (v. 1).* The prophet dreamed of a day when the house of the Lord would sit on a large mountain. The prophet was envisaging God's absolute sovereignty and perpetual presence in the world.

Not everyone worshiped the Lord in Micah's day; the people had all kinds of idols. The same is true today. How wonderful to conceive of a day when the people of the world would worship the true and living Lord!

B. *The people of the world would worship the Lord (v. 2).* The prophet spoke of a time when all the nations would come to Jerusalem, not to seek Israel, but to seek Israel's God.

II. The proper response to God's Word (Mic. 4:2).

A. *One proper response to God's Word is to learn it.* "He will teach us of his ways" (v. 2). The nations of the earth would come to the temple, not to offer sacrifices on its altar, but to learn about the law of the Lord.

People need to go to Bible study and worship services to learn the Word of God. Before one can obey the Bible, he or she needs first to learn its precepts.

B. *Another proper response to God's Word is to live it (v. 2).* The prophet longed for a day when the Word of God would be lived. It would be a day, not just when people read of love and forgiveness, but when they would put these traits into practice.

III. The harmony of personal relationships (Mic. 4:3).

A. *Interpersonal relationships will be based on a relationship with the Lord.* "He shall judge many people and rebuke strong nations afar off" (v. 3). Micah hoped for a day when people would relate to each other out of a common faith in the Lord, the only basis for harmonious human relationships.

B. *A common faith in the Lord leads to a peaceful world (v. 3).* The instruments of war would be replaced by implements of peace. The nations would practice war no more. The terror of violence and battle would be no threat.

What a bright hope for tomorrow! Micah caught a glimpse of the world as it should be. He allowed that vision to penetrate his efforts to change the world and to make it the world of his vision.

IV. The prevalence of vocation and security (Mic. 4:4).

A. *Harmonious relationships allow people to pursue their vocation.* "But they shall sit every man under his vine and under his fig tree" (v. 4). Rather than being involved in war, the people would have time for productive work, as God had originally intended.

B. *The Lord would cause people to dwell in security.* "And none shall make them afraid: for the mouth of the LORD of hosts hath spoken it" (v. 4). The prophet looked for a day when God would cause wars to cease. When wars ceased, people would not have to live in fear of enemies.

Micah conceived of no army as a match for the Lord. He described the Lord with the title "LORD of hosts." The reason God's people will dwell in security is because God has the capacity to subdue all their enemies.

V. The restoration of an influence (Mic. 4:5–8).

A. *God would gather his people again to accomplish his mission.* Micah promised the gathering of the scattered people of God. He depicted the nation as a flock whose members were lame and scattered. The future of the flock seemed hopeless, but the Lord himself would act to redeem his battered flock (vv. 5–6).

Listen to Micah's bright hopes for God's people. "I will make her that halted a remnant, and her that was cast far off a strong nation" (v. 7).

B. *God would use his people for his purpose.* God never intended just to make a nation. He intended for the nation to reflect God's character and to bring the nations to him. Micah saw a day when these purposes would be actualized (vv. 4–8). The Lord's chosen people would walk in the name of the Lord their God. People would see the Lord in their lives.

Conclusion

Do you have bright hopes for the future? No brightness can be gleaned from the world. Only a relationship with the Lord gives hope for tomorrow.

SUNDAY MORNING, FEBRUARY 21

Title: The Great Salvation God Offers
Text: "You shall call his name Jesus, for he will save his people from their sins" ***(Matt. 1:21 RSV).***
Scripture Reading: Titus 2:11–14
Hymns: "Holy, Holy, Holy," Heber
"Jesus Paid It All," Hall
"When We All Get to Heaven," Hewitt
Offertory Prayer: Heavenly Father, open our eyes to the greatness of your grace to us through Jesus Christ. Help us to see the extravagant generosity of your heart toward us. Thank you for giving us the gift of forgiveness. Thank you for giving us membership in your family. Thank you for giving us a commission to carry the good news of your love to the ends of the earth. Bless our tithes and offerings for the advancement of your kingdom. In Jesus' name. Amen.

Introduction

There are very few passages of Scripture that summarize the scope of God's great plan of salvation as this passage does. Paul speaks to Titus of the great salvation the grace of God makes available to all people.

Tragic, indeed, is our awareness of only fractions of God's great salvation for us through Jesus Christ. Some see Jesus only as a Savior of the soul. For them he is a spiritual funeral director whom they will need when death comes and they are ushered out into eternity.

The book of Titus emphasizes that our salvation has significance for the past, rich implications for the present, and glorious prospects for the future. We need to recognize and respond with gratitude to this great salvation that has appeared in the coming of Jesus Christ.

I. Salvation has significance for the past.

A. *Jesus Christ came into this world to save us from the guilt in our past.* Our Scripture passage declares that Jesus "gave himself for us to redeem us from all iniquity." That includes the transgressions of yesterday or last year. It is never too late to repent.

B. *It is good news to know that an innocent substitute has been provided by a merciful God to die in the stead of guilty sinners.* Paul wrote that "for our sake he made him to be sin who knew no sin, so that in him we might become the righteousness of God" (2 Cor. 5:21 RSV). Our past can be redeemed through the work of Christ. We should rejoice.

II. Salvation has implications for the present.

A. *The words of our Scripture passage for today affirm that salvation is a present, ongoing experience.* It is more than just a conversion experience that takes place in childhood without expressing itself in later life. Those who have only an emotional experience as a basis for their hope for heaven need to reexamine the teachings of the New Testament.

B. *The great salvation that the grace of God has made possible is one that continually trains us to "renounce irreligion and worldly passions, and to live sober, upright, and godly lives in this world" (Titus 2:12 RSV).*

C. *There is a negative side to the plan and purpose of God for us.* We must repudiate ungodly attitudes, activities, and ambitions. We must recognize that many of our desires are associated only with our earthly existence. Peter says that these earthly ambitions and desires war against the soul and prevent us from being what God wants us to be as his dear children (1 Peter 2:11–12). In Paul's letter to the church at Philippi, he urges his readers to work out, on a day-by-day basis, the salvation God worked into their lives at their conversion (Phil. 2:12–13 RSV). He affirms that God is at work within them to help them realize their potential as the sons and daughters of God. This is the gospel of God's activity within the heart of each believer.

D. *It is the will of our Father that we live productive, upright, godly lives.* We are to let the law of heaven control our minds and hearts in the present. Heaven is not just a place to which we go when this life is over. Heaven is a way of life we should adopt now.

III. Salvation has future consequences of great significance for each of us.

Titus 2:13 (RSV) says that we are "awaiting our blessed hope, the appearing of the glory of our great God and Savior, Jesus Christ."

A. *Salvation includes present membership in the family of God in which we rejoice in the love of the Father (1 John 3:1–2).* This passage also speaks of the future when, by the power of God, we will experience our full redemption, including the redemption of our body from its sinful state. "When he appears we shall be like him, for we shall see him as he is."

B. *Eliza Hewitt tried to express the joy that will be ours when we are in heaven.*

> Sing the wondrous love of Jesus,
> Sing his mercy and his grace:

In the mansion bright and blessed,
He'll prepare for us a place.

Onward to the prize before us!
Soon his beauty we'll behold;
Soon the pearly gates will open;
We shall tread the streets of gold!

When we all get to heaven,
What a day of rejoicing that will be!
When we all see Jesus,
We'll sing and shout the victory!

Conclusion

Salvation from the past, salvation in the present, salvation for the future—this is the salvation that God offers us through our faith in Jesus Christ and on the basis of his shed blood.

SUNDAY EVENING, FEBRUARY 21

Title: God Never Fails to Keep His Word
Text: "The LORD visited Sarah as he had said, and the LORD did to Sarah as he had promised" ***(Gen. 21:1 RSV).***
Scripture Reading: Genesis 21:1–34

Introduction

Habakkuk said, "The vision is yet for an appointed time, but at the end it shall speak, and not lie: though it tarry, wait for it; because it will surely come, it will not tarry" (Hab. 2:3). Although he was not speaking of Abraham and Sarah, his words have an application to their lives that also give us encouragement in our times of wavering faith. Many years of disappointment and longing had plagued the life of these two godly people. Since the time had long passed when they could expect offspring in the ordinary way, they were thrown entirely upon the strength of their faith. The substance of their hope was their confidence that God would do what he had promised. Many times they may have voiced the prayer uttered by a New Testament father concerning the healing of his child, "Lord, I believe, help thou my unbelief" (Mark 9:24).

Since both Abraham (Gen. 17:17) and Sarah (18:12), on separate occasions, laughed when told a child would be born to them, the baby was appropriately named Isaac, which means laughter. What joy must have come to them when they found their confidence in God, which had been tested by long and anxious waiting, was justified with the coming of their child. Let us look at the results in the lives of these two people and see some lessons from the events.

I. God often sends the greatest joy during the darkest hour.

A. *The pessimists we have with us always!* Take the year 1809, proclaimed by contemporary historians as the darkest time in the history of humankind. Napoleon was devastating Europe, and one writer predicted that future generations would call 1809 "the world's blackest year." Both freedom and social progress seemed doomed. Then look at the babies that were born that year: Abraham Lincoln; William Gladstone; Alfred, Lord Tennyson; Edgar Allen Poe; Oliver Wendell Holmes; Cyrus Hall McCormick; and Felix Mendelssohn. The year was not one of total destruction.

B. *Things had looked dark in the Abraham-Sarah household, but Isaac changed all that.* The mother's words have been called "the first cradle hymn." This is the first of its kind in recorded literature. The occasion's peculiarity justified Sarah's exuberance. Amazement and wonder were the order of the day. The miraculous nature of the event made it the occasion of extraordinary joy. In our own lives, the gifts of God's grace should cause us to say, "This is the LORD's doing, and it is marvelous in our eyes" (cf. Ps. 118:23 et al.).

C. *Abraham seems to have had the typical reaction of a serious-minded father.* He showed sober and thoughtful joy; the mother's, however, was an uncontrollable tide of emotion. Her feeling too great for many words, showed its humanly natural expression in laughter. Her words "All that hear will laugh with me" (Gen. 21:6) meant that she could not imagine anyone regarding her happiness with indifference. "Surely everybody is as excited about my baby as I am!"

D. *Sarah's greatest triumph, however, was that she had shown faith in a Creator who was able to perform his word.* Although we should never minimize correct doctrine in the life of a believer, we do not read of any detailed creedal statement to which she subscribed. Rather, she anchored her hope and trust in a personal God who would not fail her. Has this not been true of every great and effective child of God in all generations? Our faith exists not because we understand the revelation completely, but because we trust the Revealer implicitly.

II. Even the best faith falters.

A. *The Bible never fails to give an accurate appraisal of its characters.* Sarah was a great woman, but she was not without fault. In facing the issue of Ishmael, she failed miserably. Seeing Ishmael mocking on the day that Isaac was weaned, she realized she could not afford to compromise with the competition. We do not know exactly what Ishmael was doing that upset Sarah so much.

B. *We have mixed emotions about Sarah's attitude, but we can certainly identify with her.* We understand the resentment whether we agree with her entirely or not. We should note that the apostle Paul seems to side with Sarah in his allegory about the two covenants represented by the two children, even stating that "he that was born after the flesh persecuted him that was born after the Spirit" (Gal. 4:24–31). Paul insists that Sarah's command, "Cast out the bondwoman and her son," was an authoritative word from God. The point in this message is not the relationship of Ishmael to God's redemptive program but rather Sarah's humility in her lack of ability to cope with Ishmael's desire to have the same familial value as her son. Most of us would probably have reacted as she did, and thus we should be charitable in our evaluation of her action.

III. God's Word continues.

A. *The remaining material in chapter 20 shows that God had the entire world in mind, though he seemed to be working only with Abraham and his physical offspring through Sarah.* When Hagar and her child seemed doomed to painful starvation in the wilderness, God intervened and not only saved them, but promised the mother that her child would be the father of a great nation. Notice Hagar found a wife for Ishmael from her country of Egypt. Though God blessed Abraham in a significant way, he did not fail to show compassion to Ishmael.

B. *News of how God was blessing Abraham reached Abimelech, and he decided he should make peace with this man.* A great lesson comes to us at this point. When we conduct ourselves properly and receive God's approval and blessing, the nonreligious world respects us and seeks to be our ally. Notice that Abimelech seemed apprehensive about Abraham's success. He did not recognize all the factors involved and certainly did not understand that Abraham had received a special revelation, but he seemed to be aware that Abraham possessed some type of relationship that was paying off with material success. He reminded Abraham that on a previous occasion (probably when Abraham lied about Sarah and pretended she was his sister) he had shown kindness. Of course, astute businessman that he was, Abraham took advantage of the opportunity to remind Abimelech that his servant had violently taken a water well from him. Abimelech was quick to deny any knowledge of it. In the treaty that followed, Abraham insisted that Abimelech recognize that the well had been dug by Abraham and therefore belonged to him. When they agreed on the terms and planted a tree, Abraham called upon the name of his covenant God, not the deity employed by the larger world.

C. *God's redemptive program was now taking shape.* The heir had been born and the competition removed. The neighbors recognized the place of Abraham in the land, and the patriarch bore witness to his unique God who would some day send the world's Redeemer through the family of Abraham. Nothing can stop God's progress. Wise people find out where God is going and align themselves with him.

Conclusion

The God we serve never fails. He has no credibility gap. We can trust ourselves and all that we have to him. The skeptic who has become cynical never has the final word. God will not fail—nor will he even disappoint.

WEDNESDAY EVENING, FEBRUARY 24

Title: Helping People Get Through a Crisis
Text: "Now why dost thou cry out aloud? is there no king in thee? is thy counselor perished? for pangs have taken thee as a woman in travail" ***(Mic. 4:9).***
Scripture Reading: Micah 4:9–5:1

Introduction

Many churches today finance and staff a telephone counseling service. Trained counselors answer calls of people caught in crises and try to help them survive.

Micah was such a servant for the people of his day. They were in a crisis too. Old Testament scholars differ regarding the specific time of the crisis. Some say the material in Micah 4:9–5:1 referred to a time just before the Babylonian invasion of Jerusalem in 587 BC. Others say the material came during the reign of Zedekiah of Judah. Still others say that Micah 4:9–5:1 referred to the time when the Assyrians under Sennacherib surrounded the city and threatened its safety. Actually, the specific time does not matter because Micah's words could relate to people of any time.

Let us study Micah's therapeutic suggestions for times of crisis in 4:9–5:1. They can help us get through any type of crisis in our lives. Notice three "nows" (4:9, 11; 5:1). These represent Micah's three suggestions.

I. Keep your perspective during a time of crisis (Mic. 4:9–10).

A. *Recognize the reality of the crisis.* Micah wanted Judah to be aware of the seriousness of the problem. He spoke of the agonies of exile. The exile would mean the loss of king and counselor. It would mean pain like that of a woman in labor. It would mean being uprooted from Judah and transported to Babylon.

No one should fail to look at the reality of the crisis. Sometimes people pretend there is no real problem. At other times they do not see where their actions would lead to crisis. To keep perspective during a time of crisis, recognize its reality.

B. *Recognize the failure of the earthly kings and counselors.* For many years Judah depended on earthly rulers who had delivered them from enemies. Some of these kings had even made Judah a world power. But Micah predicted the failure of earthly rulers (v. 9).

Maybe we trust too much in earthly leaders. A crisis can teach us a valuable lesson: only the Lord is worthy of our trust.

C. *Recognize God as the ultimate Deliverer.* Micah again picked up the figure of a woman in childbirth. "Be in pain, and labour to bring forth, O daughter of Zion, like a woman in travail: for now shalt thou go forth out of the city, and thou shalt dwell in the field, and those shalt go even to Babylon; there shalt thou be delivered; there the LORD shall redeem thee from the hand of thine enemies" (v. 10). Micah urged the people to keep their perspective. God would ultimately deliver his people.

D. *God's people will go through great crises, yet there is hope.* God will bring them through. Even if death comes, God will give a better life. So keep your perspective during a crisis.

II. See God to be greater than the crisis (Mic. 4:11–13).

A. *Look at who you really are.* Judah considered herself to be strong. Micah spoke of the time when Judah's enemies would ridicule her. "Now also many nations are gathered against thee, that say, Let her be defiled, and let our eye look upon Zion" (v. 11). Other nations gathered to watch Jerusalem's agony and shame. The people of Jerusalem had been brought to their senses over the crisis.

Crises have a way of making us feel humble. They show us our inadequacies, putting us in the category of the created rather than the Creator. We easily see that we are not masters of our fate nor captains of our souls.

B. *God will not allow his plans to be stopped.* Look at how the nations gloated over the expected downfall of Jerusalem. "Arise and thresh, O daughter of Zion: for I will make thine horn iron, and I will make thy hoofs brass: and thou shalt beat in pieces many people: and I will consecrate their gain unto the LORD, and their substance unto the Lord of the whole earth" (v. 13). God would not stop until he declared his way to the nations. If Israel failed, he would turn to another.

C. *God can bring triumph out of great tragedy.* The crises of individuals or nations may not be comprehensive or ultimately detrimental. God can bring good out of bad. "But they know not the thoughts of the LORD, neither understand they his counsel: for he shall gather them as the sheaves into the floor" (v. 12). Those who came to thresh Judah would themselves be threshed by her.

Many times bad experiences happen to God's people and they

can see only the negative results. But God has the power to take the bad experiences and build character from them.

III. Seek the protection of God during a crisis (Mic. 5:1).

A. *The crises of life come with great severity.* Micah spoke in 5:1 of Jerusalem under the siege of an enemy. The leaders and the people suffered humiliation at the hands of the attackers. This could be a reference to the insults heaped on Hezekiah by Sennacherib's commander during the siege of Jerusalem in 701 BC.

Crises hand God's people great blows. They rob us of our energy, distort our thinking, and cause us great humiliation.

B. *People without God have a serious problem during a crisis.* Micah seemed to be talking about people boxed in by the crisis. Evidently the people of Judah had given themselves to idols. When the crisis came, their idols failed them. There is no greater time of panic than when one in whom you trust fails you in a moment of need.

Probably Psalm 46:1 was composed during Sennacherib's invasion of Jerusalem. Listen to the expression of faith in the Lord during a time of crisis. "God is our refuge and strength, a very present help in trouble" (Ps. 46:1).

Conclusion

Are you in a crisis? You can find help. The Lord helps his people. He may not take away the crisis, but he will give the strength and guidance you need.

Sunday Morning, February 28

Title: The Resurrection of Christ and Our Resurrection

Text: "Christ has been raised from the dead, the first fruits of those who have fallen asleep" ***(1 Cor. 15:20 RSV).***

Scripture Reading: 1 Corinthians 15:20–23, 35–45

Hymns: "Christ the Lord Is Risen Today," Wesley
"Majestic Sweetness Sits Enthroned," Stennett
"My Savior, First of All," Crosby
"O That Will Be Glory," Gabriel

Offertory Prayer: Loving Father, we are the recipients of your gracious and wonderful gifts. Thank you for loving us in Jesus Christ. Thank you for giving us assurance that our sins are forgiven and that we are accepted in Christ as members of your family. Thank you for the fellowship that we enjoy in and through the church. Thank you for the task that is ours of sharing the good news of a risen, living Lord with a needy world. Accept our gifts as tokens of our desire to be dedicated to the proclaiming of the good news of his death, resurrection, and living presence to the ends of the earth. In his saving name we pray. Amen.

Introduction

One of the great truths of Christianity is that death has been defeated, giving us hope for a life beyond this vale of tears in which we live. The word *resurrection* means a "state of standing up" or a "state of standing again." In the New Testament the word refers to the raising up of the body, the victory of the body from the cruel clutches of death. Our belief in resurrection is based solidly on the fact that Jesus Christ has conquered death and the grave.

I. The resurrection of Jesus Christ.

The New Testament writers based their belief in the resurrection of the saints firmly on the resurrection of Jesus Christ. They believed that the victory Jesus experienced over death is a victory that is to be experienced by those who believe in him and follow him as his disciples (1 Cor. 15:56–57; 1 Thess. 4:13–18).

A. *Jesus predicted his own resurrection (Matt. 12:39–40; John 2:19–22).*

B. *The resurrection of Christ.* The resurrection of Christ is the central fact of the New Testament. The Scriptures declare that Jesus' physical body did not decay in the grave. It was made alive again by the power of God. It was gloriously transformed so that it was no longer limited by time or space nor subject to change, decay, and death.

C. *The postresurrection appearances of the living Christ.* We have at least ten recorded instances in which the Christ who experienced crucifixion and death appeared to his disciples. Six of these are most significant for our consideration.

1. The appearance to Mary Magdalene in the garden (John 20:11–18).
2. The appearance on the road to Emmaus (Luke 24:13–32).
3. The appearance in the upper room (Luke 24:36–43).
4. The appearance one week later (John 20:26–31).
5. The appearance by the sea (John 21:4–19).
6. The appearance to Saul of Tarsus (Acts 9:1–22).

D. *The nature of Jesus' resurrected body.*

1. Jesus' body was tangible.
   a. The disciples saw Jesus.
   b. Jesus talked to the disciples.
   c. Mary clasped the feet of the resurrected Christ.
   d. Jesus ate the bread and honeycomb.
2. Jesus' body was transcendent.

   The resurrection of Jesus was not a restoration to the natural plane of life. His resurrected body was not subject to time, space, or material objects. As his precrucifixion body had been perfectly adapted to the needs of life in this world, so his resurrection body was adapted to the needs of the new plane of life.

II. The resurrection of believers (1 Cor. 15:20–22).

Christianity's belief in the certainty of a resurrection is based solidly on our belief that Jesus Christ conquered death and as such is the first fruits from among the dead.

A. *The resurrection of believers is based on the truth of the resurrection of Jesus Christ.* The gospel, stated in capsule form, relates to the truth taught in the Scriptures that Christ died for our sins, that he was buried in a tomb, and that he was raised from the dead on the third day. He was seen by many people, giving indisputable proof of his living presence (Acts 1:3).

That Christ has been raised from the dead is our proof that the kingdom of death has been invaded and the power of death has been defeated. The message of Christianity is that ultimately death will be completely destroyed.

B. *The resurrection of believers is based on our belief in the power of God (1 Cor. 15: 35–38).* In response to the question of "How are the dead raised?" Paul speaks concerning the power and wisdom of God.

1. The resurrection is possible because of God's power.
    a. God's power is demonstrated in the world of vegetation, where he is able to make from seeds planted in the ground a variety of plants and trees that are adapted to their habitats.
    b. In the realm of zoology, God the creator has given living creatures bodies adapted to their habitats. Although there are similarities between these living creatures, each is given a body suitable for its surroundings.
2. God's power is perfectly demonstrated in the creation of the heavenly bodies—the stars, the moon, the sun—for all are unique.

God's power makes it possible for him to do what he wishes regarding the resurrection of the saints.

C. *The resurrection of believers is possible because of the wisdom of God as well as his power.*

1. The body, planted in corruption, will be raised in incorruption.
2. The body is planted in dishonor because of sin, but it will be raised in honor, not subject to sin.
3. The body is planted in weakness, because it is subject to death, but it will be raised in power, not subject to death.
4. The body is planted as a natural body, but it will be raised as a spiritual body like unto the body of Jesus Christ.

The earthly body has been perfectly adapted to the needs of our physical plane of existence. The body in which we will exist in heaven will be perfectly adapted to the needs of that level of spiritual experience. Out of our relationship to Adam, we received a physical body subject to decay and death, but through our relationship with Jesus Christ, we will receive a spiritual body that is subject to neither decay nor death.

III. Responding positively to the prospect of resurrection.

If Jesus Christ be not risen, we are of all people most to be pitied (1 Cor. 15:12–19).

If Jesus Christ be not risen, we are whistling in the dark when we think about the possibility of survival beyond death.

If Jesus Christ be not risen, it is good-bye forever when we go to the cemetery that last time.

If Jesus Christ be not risen, there is absolutely no hope for a life beyond. The message of Christianity is that Jesus Christ is risen. Consequently, there are four great responses we should make.

A. *We should respond with gratitude (1 Cor. 15:57).*
B. *We would respond with comfort (1 Thess. 4:18).*
C. *We should respond with faithfulness and diligence in service with the conviction that what we do for God is not in vain (1 Cor. 15:58).*
D. *We should respond with joyful obedience to the living Lord as he commands us to carry the good news of his life, death, resurrection, and living presence to the ends of the earth (Matt. 28:18–20).*

Conclusion

Each one needs to respond to the resurrection of Christ by trusting him as Lord and Savior. Jesus Christ arose from the dead to give proof of the fact that his death on the cross was an adequate solution to your sin problem. He conquered death and the grave that he might be able to give you the gift of eternal life (Heb. 7:25). Today is the day in which you can do business with the living Christ. Let him become the Lord of your life now.

SUNDAY EVENING, FEBRUARY 28

Title: How Much Do You Love God?
Text: "Take your son, your only son Isaac, whom you love, and go to the land of Moriah, and offer him there as a burnt offering upon one of the mountains of which I shall tell you" ***(Gen. 22:2 RSV).***
Scripture Reading: Genesis 22:1–19

Introduction

No one except Jesus in Gethsemane ever faced such a testing as Abraham when God told him to take "your son, your only son Isaac . . . and offer him . . .

as a burnt offering" (Gen. 22:2 RSV). Likewise, no one else ever responded so quickly and completely to a command as this noble patriarch who "rose up early in the morning" to do the very thing God commanded him.

What was the purpose of this testing? God had selected Abraham as the recipient of the covenant. Abraham needed extraordinary faith since the entire redemptive covenant would be based on faith in God's promises. This man, who had been called to a high and singular destiny, was a person remarkable for intense feeling and fearless activity. He had obeyed the initial call with unwavering trust and hope in God. Gradually, Abraham had received further blessings, but he was at times forced to wait that he might learn to accept God at his word. This test of offering Isaac was used to refine his faith further and to make him more useful in God's purposes.

Underlying all of the story is a simple question. How much did Abraham love God? The pagan people offered their children to their gods. Did Abraham possess this kind of devotion? If so, let him prove it. God left him no loophole: "If you love me, do this thing I am asking." Each statement in the command grew with intensity. "Take your son. Take your only son. Take your son whom you love." One cannot conceive of a greater violence than that of killing one's own child. Add to that fact the reality that it was the son for whom Abraham had waited many years. All his hope for earthly immortality lay in this child. God called Abraham to give his best. God also wants our best.

I. The best of our love.

A. *The Old Testament laws instructed the people to love their neighbors as they loved themselves.* The motivation behind these laws was supposed to be a love for God. Jesus validated the importance of this when he compressed the code of morality into two commands: Love God. Love your neighbor. Furthermore, the first question he asked Peter after the resurrection was, "Simon, son of Jonas, lovest thou me?" (John 21:17).

B. *It is not what we know but rather how we love that determines our effectiveness in service to our Lord.* When we who are Christians think afresh of all our Savior has done for us at Calvary, we should, like Abraham, make any sacrifice necessary to show our Lord how much we love him.

II. The best of our labor.

A. *Abraham had labored many years building his herds: they were to be Isaac's, but if there was to be no Isaac, to whom would he leave them?* Abraham raised that question years earlier when he asked, "O Sovereign Lord, what can you give me since I remain childless and the one who will inherit my estate is Eliezer of Damascus? You have given me no children; so a servant in my household will be my heir" (Gen. 15:2–3 NIV). God wanted Abraham to face the fact that someone else might inherit the property that had come about because of his labors. The silver and the gold belong to God as do the cattle on a thousand hills.

B. *God wanted Abraham to recognize who truly owned his possessions.* Only then could Abraham's son truly be his covenant son. Consider this analogous example. A rancher in Texas took an evangelist to view his large ranch. He then made a request: "Preacher, I want you to pray a dedication prayer. Tell God that I'm giving all this to him, recognizing that he owns it. I'll be a good steward of the money I take in from it." When the preacher had finished the prayer, the rancher prayed, "Now, God I've given this to you. Will you do something for me? Give me back my boy. He is living a life of terrible sin. Will you give him back to me?" That night at a revival service, on the first stanza of the invitation hymn, the man's son came down the aisle and gave his heart to Jesus. God wants the fruit of our labor dedicated to him, and he must have it before he will deeply bless us.

> For we never can know, what the Lord will bestow
> Of the blessings for which we have prayed
> Till our body and soul, he doth fully control
> And our all on the altar is laid.
>
> —*Elisha Hoffman*

III. The best of our loyalty.

A. *Underlying the entire command was the matter of God establishing Abraham's loyalty.* Seneca called loyalty "the holiest good in the human heart." Jeremiah recalled that the heathen did not change their gods even though they were not gods. Then he chided Israel because they had left the God who is the fountain of living waters (Jer. 2:11–13). Shame on us Christians who show less loyalty to the one who has redeemed us from sin than the world does to the shallow things that cannot bring true profit and worth to life.

B. *Though we often make much of the fact that God intervened and prevented Isaac from being slain, we should remember that in his heart Abraham had already made the sacrifice.* In any action there is a time when we make the decision to do it. After that, we are emotionally incapable of changing unless some outside force stops us. This was true of Abraham. The author of Hebrews says that by faith Abraham "offered up Isaac: and he that had received the promises offered up his only begotten son, of whom it was said, That in Isaac shall thy seed be called" (Heb. 11:17–18). The writer explains that Abraham was convinced that God was able to raise him up, even from the dead. Perhaps no one other than Jesus Christ showed such loyalty to the Father's plan for his life.

C. *A parallel to Abraham's devotion is the martyrs in the first few centuries after Christ.* One of the greatest was Polycarp. Remember his famous words, "Eighty and five years I have served my Lord, and he has never failed me. Why should I fail him now?" At first the fire seemed to build a protective shield around him, but finally, as the executioners put on fresh fuel, he was consumed. One wonders, indeed, is almost convinced, that Polycarp remembered the words of his predecessor at the Ephesus church who wrote the letters to the seven churches from Patmos. To the church Polycarp served, John wrote, and perhaps the dying saint quoted it as the fire hovered round about him, "Be thou faithful until death and I will give thee a crown of life" (Rev. 2:10).

Conclusion

Three timeless truths may be gleaned from this account of the patriarch's faith. First, what one lays on the altar is never lost. Second, when we serve God faithfully, he will take care of our needs. Third, what we give to God, we get back with interest. The final truth was fulfilled remarkably in the life of Isaac. God not only gave him back to Abraham, but he multiplied him over and over through Jacob and his descendants.

Whatever our obvious rewards, we are called to a life of faith in and love for God. The greatest reward of these actions is intimacy with the Sovereign of the universe. With that, the obvious rewards pale and the bitter trials sweeten.

SUGGESTED PREACHING PROGRAM FOR THE MONTH OF
MARCH

■ Sunday Mornings

Continue the series "The Conquest of Spiritual Death by Spiritual Birth and Resurrection."

■ Sunday Evenings

Continue with the theme "Messages of Hope from the Experiences of Abraham."

■ Wednesday Evenings

Continue with the theme "Mighty Messages from a Minor Prophet" based on the book of Micah.

WEDNESDAY EVENING, MARCH 3

Title: God's Leader Is Always Better
Text: "But thou, Bethlehem Ephratah, though thou be little among the thousands of Judah, yet out of thee shall he come forth unto me that is to be ruler in Israel; whose goings forth have been from of old, from everlasting" ***(Mic. 5:2).***
Scripture Reading: Micah 5:2–9

Introduction

People constantly look for good leaders. They want good persons to lead in government. Corporations search for competent people to manage their business. Churches look for effective pastors and other leaders. Nevertheless, leaders sometimes fail. Such was the case in Israel and Judah.

Kings had risen and fallen in Israel and in Judah with regular monotony. Only a few kings in Israel had been godly leaders. Often the historian would remark about a king of Israel, "And he did evil in the sight of the LORD" (cf. 1 Kings 15:26 et al.). The kings of Judah were not much better than the kings of Israel. When Micah prophesied, Jerusalem was under attack, and the king was being insulted. Micah predicted that a new ruler would come in Judah, and he would be far better.

God's people need to look beyond present times and earthly rulers to a greater ruler, just as Micah did. Let us study carefully the characteristics of God's ruler.

I. God's leader would have impressive credentials (Mic. 5:2–3).

Micah gave some impressive credentials about the new leader. He compared the new leader with the days of David. Yet, according to Micah, this new leader would be Israel's Messiah and possess much more impressive credentials than David.

A. *The new ruler would originate from God (v. 2).* God used the unexpected to confound the strong. Bethlehem was the least likely place for God's ruler to originate, yet Micah predicted that God would take a ruler from Bethlehem. In the eyes of the people, Bethlehem held little prominence, but in the purpose of God, a new ruler would come from Bethlehem.

B. *The new ruler would radiate the character of God.* New vitality would spring out of the dead state of the Judean monarchy. God's ruler would be one "whose goings forth have been from of old, from everlasting" (v. 2). Micah and the nation longed for a ruler who would be a godly person like David (cf. v. 3).

Several words in Micah 5:2–3 disclose the unique character of the new ruler. The word *ruler* suggests more than an earthly king. Perhaps Micah reserved the title for one who would be a unique Messiah. The expression "goings forth" in verse 2 comes from one word that means "origin." It describes a child originating in the loins of his father. God's ruler would have impressive credentials, for he would come from the heavenly Father.

II. God's leader would have a shepherd's leadership style (Mic. 5:4).

Micah used the figure of a shepherd to describe the new leader's style of leading. In Micah's day people lived in a pastoral setting. They rejoiced to hear of a shepherd who would lead them.

A. *The leader would perform the role of a shepherd.* What did a shepherd in ancient Israel do for his flock? He gave guidance, offered protection, and provided for their needs.

God's new leader, the Messiah, would perform the role of a true shepherd. He would protect and defend, feed and nourish, and guide and direct his people. Israel's shepherd would do all three roles in an extraordinary way, for he would do them in "the strength of the Lord" and "in the majesty of the name of the Lord" (cf. v. 4).

B. *The people will trust the leadership of the shepherd.* "And they shall abide: for now shall he be great unto the ends of the earth" (v. 4). The new ruler's power would provide security and stability for Israel. This shepherd would be known and feared to the ends of the earth.

III. God's leader would have amazing power (Mic. 5:5–6).

A. *God's leader would be more powerful than all other leaders.* Micah spoke of the difficult times in the eighth century BC. Sennacherib laid siege to Jerusalem in 701 BC and boasted of his superior strength. According to Micah 5:5, Judah took measures to protect the nation from the invader. They raised up shepherds and princes to oppose Sennacherib. The numbers seven and eight could have been a Hebraic way of saying "a large group." But none of Judah's leaders could stop Sennacherib.

The new leader would be much more powerful than all of Judah's other leaders. God's leader is always better.

B. *God's leader would deliver his people from their enemies.* Micah confidently affirmed that God's new leader would conquer and impose dominion over Assyria (cf. v. 6).

Without a doubt, the Messiah continues to deliver his people from all of their enemies. No person or circumstances can ultimately defeat God's people.

IV. God's leader would have committed followers (Mic. 5:7–9).

Micah predicted that God's ruler would work with a special group of people called "the remnant." These were people who remained faithful to the Lord. Notice how God's leader used the remnant.

A. *God used faithful people as a silent influence.* Micah used the figure of dew to describe the silent influence of God's people. "The remnant of Jacob shall be in the midst of many people as dew from the LORD" (v. 7). The remnant of Israel served as a spiritual influence to others. God's people are called to live in the world and to exert their influence among the nations like dew from the Lord.

B. *God used faithful people as a militant army.* The second figure is the lion. "As a lion among the beasts of the forest" (v. 8), God's people would triumph over all adversaries.

Conclusion

Judah had many leaders. Some of these leaders were good leaders, but in most cases the kings and other leaders went in the way of idolatry. They forsook the Lord. Micah looked to the Lord for a better leader.

The ideal leader has come: Jesus is the long-awaited Messiah. We need to give ourselves gladly to his leadership.

SUNDAY MORNING, MARCH 7

Title: The Assurance of Our Resurrection

Text: "For as in Adam all die, so also in Christ shall all be made alive. But each in his own order: Christ the first fruits, then at his coming those who belong to Christ" ***(1 Cor. 15:22–23 RSV).***

Scripture Reading: 1 Corinthians 15:35–54

Hymns: "All Hail the Power of Jesus' Name," Perronet
"Christ the Lord Is Risen Today," Wesley
"He Lives," Ackley

Offertory Prayer: Holy Father, as we rejoice in the afterglow of Easter, we thank you for the assurance that you give us victory over sin, death, and the grave. We thank you for the glad consciousness of forgiven sin and the assurance of eternal life. Bless these tithes and offerings that we bring today that others might hear the good news of Jesus Christ. Amen.

Introduction

Death is such a mystery. What are we to make of it? Are we to conclude with Job that death is a screaming contradiction, that it is grossly unfair? Job said that if you cut down a tree and the spring rains come, it may sprout and grow, but if you cut down a man, he lies down and never rises again! What are we to make of this contradiction?

What can we know with certainty about life after death? How can we, indeed, know anything? Is all our faith in heaven simply a handful of pious guesses? Does it have some basis in reality, in historical fact? When we push back the curtains of this mystery and probe as deeply as we may, we will still not have all the answers, but we can catch a glimpse and learn that for those who are in Christ, glory awaits!

I. The natural fear of death.

First Corinthians 15 is the most informative and encouraging passage in all Scripture on the subject of death and resurrection. When I look death in the face with friends and family, I find comfort and help in this passage of God's Word.

A. *We have a natural fear of death and dying.* I have seen some concerned and even guilty about their anxiety concerning dying and death. I do not think we ought to feel guilty about it. I think we ought to accept it as part of our humanity.

If you have ever thought that fearing dying and death is a sign of weakness, then let me invite your attention to the Garden of Gethsemane. Or if you have ever doubted the sheer humanity of Jesus, you will not doubt it after reading of his agony in the garden.

B. *Look at Jesus, thirty-three years of age, facing the cross.* Who wants to die at thirty-three? Look at Jesus wrestling with death. What did he do? He prayed to the Father, not once, but repeatedly. He shrank back from death and the cross in Gethsemane. Isn't that a sign of his humanity? What would you or I do?

C. *We have a fear of dying because pain, suffering, and separation are unwelcome.* Paul calls death humankind's "last enemy" (1 Cor. 15:26 RSV). We are always uncomfortable about things with which we are unfamiliar.

If we died as Christians once, we would not be afraid to do it again, but because we have not, we may be anxious.

D. *Some have anxiety because they are not ready to meet the Creator.* This sense of being unprepared for death brings anxiety that should not be erased. It is natural and can lead one to the Savior.

The important thing then is that we get right with God, that we make our peace with him. By repentance, faith, and a faithful Christian life, we know that we have nothing ultimately to fear from death.

II. Victory over death by the resurrection of Christ.

Having affirmed the naturalness of our anxiety about dying and death, let me recall the great pronouncement of Paul in 1 Corinthians 15:20: "Now is Christ risen from the dead, and become the firstfruits of them that slept." We have no reason to hope that we will survive death apart from Christ and his resurrection. "Now is Christ risen . . . , the firstfruits of them that slept." This means that Jesus was the first to be raised from the dead but not the last. He was the firstfruits. Because of his death and his victory, we can believe that by faith in him we too will be raised to live with all those who have lived and died in Christ.

A. *A real body.* The resurrected Christ in his new body gives us our best glimpse of glory and our clearest hint of what our resurrected bodies are going to be like. What was Jesus' body like after the resurrection? It was a real body. He was not a ghost or a phantom or a figment of the imagination. The Scriptures record his appearances to as many as five hundred people. They touched him, ate with him, and talked with him, and they saw his wounds from the cross.

B. *A transcendent body.* Christ's resurrection body was real, but more than that, it was also transcendent. His resurrection body was not limited as his mortal body had been. His body had been transformed by the power of God. He was able to enter a room where the doors were locked and barred. He was able to be gone in the blink of an eye. His resurrection body was suited for that other realm, and thus we get a glimpse of what our resurrection bodies will be like.

C. *An imperishable body.* Paul gives us three key words to understanding what our resurrection bodies are going to be like. He said, first of all, that they are going to be imperishable (15:42). Our present perishable bodies will return to dust from which they came, and that process will begin the moment we breathe our final breath—suddenly. Our new bodies will be imperishable and immortal. They will live forever.

Paul is obviously not talking about the resuscitation of someone who had died "clinically." He is not talking about the raising of Lazarus, who was brought back from the grave, only one day to return. He is talking about resurrection. There is a tremendous difference. We need to believe that our bodies, like Christ's, will one day be changed, transformed into imperishable bodies.

D. *A glorious body.* Paul's second description is that our resurrection bodies will be glorious (15:43). Aren't you glad for that? Not many people are completely satisfied with their bodies or their appearance. We have inglorious bodies—ones subject to pain, aging, and decay. Our new, glorified, resurrected bodies are going to be glorious like Christ's. Our imperfect bodies will one day be replaced, transformed into perfect bodies, strong and beautiful.

E. *A spiritual body.* Paul's final word is that our new bodies will be spiritual ones (15:44)—not mortal, dying bodies, but spiritual ones, suited for that other realm. Think of the hope Paul's final word holds for us who are in Christ: one day we too are going to receive imperishable, glorious, spiritual bodies.

III. From destruction to departure.

Embedded in the middle of 1 Corinthians 15 is an ancient Christian hymn. Speaking of that new body, Paul sings: "It is sown in corruption; it is raised in incorruption: it is sown in dishonour; it is raised in glory: it is sown in weakness; it is raised in power: it is sown a natural body; it is raised a spiritual body" (vv. 42–44).

A. *Death wears two faces.* When one looks at death from the human point of view, it appears to be *destruction.* We are cut off, defeated. It seems grossly unfair that a child, a youth, a man, or a woman should be cut down. On its face death wears the appearance of destruction, defeat.

B. *But when you look at the same experience from the perspective of the Father, death is not destruction.* It is departure to be with the Lord. That is vastly different. From God's point of view, death is victory. There is a marvelous line in the Psalms: "Precious in the sight of the LORD is the death of his saints" (116:15). Can you imagine that? The death of God's children is precious to him because it means they are coming home to him.

In the last days of Paul's life, he dictated a letter to Timothy, his son in the ministry. As he came to the close of the letter, he gave an affirmation of his personal faith: "The time of my departure is at hand" (2 Tim. 4:6). Departure! He was about to be taken outside the city wall of Rome and decapitated. That looks like destruction to me. Paul saw it from God's point of view and called it departure. Isn't that wonderful? The word he used in the Greek is a rich word used of a soldier in the field striking his tent and heading for home. It is also the word that was used of a sailor loosing the moorings of his ship and sailing for home.

If you enjoy this world, friend, you haven't seen anything yet. The sweetest journey of all is the journey home.

Conclusion

Many years ago John Donne, a poet and pastor of St. Paul's Cathedral in London, wrote: "Death, be not proud. Thou, too, shall die." On Easter we celebrate Christ's resurrection. Today let us celebrate our own resurrection. How shall we be ready for it? By placing our faith and trust in Christ; by giving our life to him; by letting our work and daily tasks be dedicated to his glory and the service of others. Life everlasting is ours through faith in the Lord Jesus Christ.

Sunday Evening, March 7

Title: When We Try, God Helps

Text: "As for me, the Lord has led me in the way to the house of my master's kinsmen" ***(Gen. 24:27 RSV)***.

Scripture Reading: Genesis 24:1–67

Introduction

The heavenly Father, like a wise earthly parent, will help his children but will not complete a job for his children unless it is something they cannot do in their own strength and with their own abilities. The mission of Eliezer, servant of Abraham, to find a bride for Isaac clearly illustrates this truth.

Look at the setting. Sarah had been dead for three years. Abraham, though perhaps still mourning for Sarah, had to think about finding a wife for Isaac. He realized the divine redemptive program could not be perpetuated through his family unless Isaac had a child. Therefore, he must have a wife. God had promised that the seed of Abraham would come through Isaac not Ishmael. Notice the steps that not only provided a bride for the son but served as a channel for Eliezer to perform a task faithfully, serving as a noble example of duty well done.

I. Plain commission.

A. *Eliezer knew exactly what Abraham wanted.* Isaac needed a bride. (The custom of the parent finding a mate for his child was quite common.) The servant insisted on a clear definition of his duty. He asked, "Suppose I find a woman for him and she will not come here; do I take your son there?" Abraham spelled it out unmistakably: "No, do not take my son there. If the woman refuses to come here, you are free from your task" (Gen. 24:5, 8, author's paraphrase).

B. *How many times a plain understanding in advance of a job's requirements would have prevented problems.* Although job descriptions are not an infallible way of avoiding conflict, they have protected both employer and employee many times. When churches expand their number of staff members, such a policy is not only highly desirable but almost essential. Most important, however, is that we clearly understand the jobs God has given us. We need to consult his Word constantly to make sure we are fulfilling our job descriptions.

II. Prayerful counsel.

A. *A wise Christian of another generation said, "Until you have prayed about a situation, you can do nothing about it."* How true! Another said, "With reference to his kingdom's work, God operates only through prayer." Eliezer, of course, used all possible human means of help available to him. He took ten camels to carry provisions for the journey and presents for the bride.

B. *We cannot ignore the social customs and the culture of the day in which we live, but on the other hand, though faith and duty are one, the spiritual side is the more important.* The servant, when he came to the city, prayed and asked for a sign from God. In our day, as we learn from the teaching of Jesus, we do not feel that the highest means of determining God's will is to ask for a sign. One who constantly asks for a sign conveys the fact that he refuses to take responsibility for his choice. Such an attitude is unworthy of the Christian life, which should be led by the Holy Spirit.

Nevertheless, as Eliezer prayed, he asked for a sign. We should remember that the Old Testament is not the New Testament, and the full revelation of God's Son and the Holy Spirit had not yet been made. We who live in the light of the gospel should pray, of course, but we should be careful about asking for tangible signs. The New Testament teaches that the Holy Spirit will impress us.

III. Practical consideration.

A. *Notice that the sign for which Eliezer asked was not a neutral or mechanical one, but was related to practical matters.* He prayed, "Let it come to pass, that the damsel to whom I shall say, Let down thy pitcher, I pray thee, that I may drink; and she shall say, Drink, and I will give thy camels also: let the same be she that thou hast appointed for thy servant Isaac" (Gen. 24:14). Eliezer had a "method to his madness." He wanted someone who was kind and who was not afraid to work.

B. *Another practical consideration was related to the woman and her family.* Eliezer let them know he represented an outstanding man. He gave her a generous gift of a golden earring and two golden bracelets. Laban, her brother, was impressed. When he saw the gifts, he said to Eliezer, "Come in, thou blessed of the Lord" (Gen. 24:31).

Although food was set before him, Eliezer refused to eat until he had told of his errand. A practical man, indeed! He was not carried away with the emotional events in connection with his new friends. Although both the Old and New Testaments encourage compassion and motivation that come from affection, they avoid anything like a sick sentimentalism. The reality of life's duties is always insisted on along with impressive clarity of vision and firmness of aim. Though emotion is a part of any decision, it should never be an end in itself. When feeling evaporates without bearing fruit, it leads to the sure failure of moral vigor.

Conclusion

Once we have decided to do God's bidding, we should be insistent that it takes first place in all our life decisions. Eliezer was not even willing to wait a few days for Rebekah to enjoy a brief time with her parents. This story shows the determination of one who put forth his own best effort and was blessed. Only when we give our all do we have the right to ask for God's blessings. Eliezer did not stop until he performed his duty completely. Let us go and do likewise.

WEDNESDAY EVENING, MARCH 10

Title: What God Throws Away
Text: "I will pluck up thy groves out of the midst of thee: so will I destroy thy cities" ***(Mic. 5:14).***
Scripture Reading: Micah 5:10–15

Introduction

You have most likely cleaned a closet or a storage room at some point in your life. Wasn't it amazing how so many things accumulated over the years? In your desire to make the place neat, you had to decide what to throw away, and that probably was not easy.

Micah called for a house cleaning in Israel. He spoke of the Lord's purification of Israel in 5:10–15. He said God would look at Israel and determine what needed to be discarded. God's people needed to be purged of things that hindered their godliness. Notice the verbs in verses 10–15: "cut off," "destroy," "throw down," "pluck up." God wanted radical action.

The Christian life involves constant purging. Displeasing practices that pile up in the lives of Christians need to be discarded. The apostle Paul told the Colossian Christians to get rid of certain practices (cf. Col. 3:8).

As we study Micah 5:10–15 we will see things that need to be purified. What practices do we need to purge out of our lives?

I. God's people need to purge themselves of objects that destroy trust in the Lord (Mic. 5:10–11).

A. *Judah increased their military strength and fortified their cities in search of security.* During Micah's day the kings poured funds into developing troop strength, and they fortified their cities against invaders.

Sennacherib, king of Assyria, demonstrated the futility of earthly security. He surrounded the city, and Judah was helpless. Their large number of troops and chariots and their fortified walls were no match for Sennacherib's army. Micah condemned the things upon which Judah had built their hopes. Judah needed to trust in the Lord and in him alone.

B. *God is the only true source of strength and security.* The nation that builds its national security on military establishment and false faith will see it all collapse. People who build their lives on material things will see the erosion of these things.

II. God's people need to purge themselves of seeking guidance from someone other than God (Mic. 5:12).

A. *Judah sought guidance from soothsayers.* Evidently Judah had been influenced by their eastern neighbors to adopt witchcraft and soothsaying, methods of procuring information from supernatural sources. These persons practiced divination using omens derived from natural or manipulated signs.

Micah called for radical action. "I will cut off witchcrafts out of thine hand; and thou shalt have no more soothsayers" (v. 12). God made it clear that he did not want his people to be involved with witchcraft and sorcery (Ex. 22:18; Lev. 19:26).

B. *Oddly enough, Christians seek guidance for living from sources other than God.* Many believers seek guidance for the day by reading their horoscope in a daily newspaper. Some believers even go to fortune-tellers. God's people need to purge themselves of practices in which they seek guidance from sources other than God.

III. God's people need to purge themselves of idols that take the place of God (Mic. 5:13–15).

A. *Judah had adopted the practice of worshiping idols of wood or stone.* Their country was filled with idols (cf. Isa. 2:8). In Micah 5:13–14 the prophet used three terms to describe Judah's idols: "graven images," "standing images," and "groves." Three different words indicate that a variety of idol worship had found its way into Judah's religious practice.

Micah again called for radical action: "Thy graven images also will I cut off, and thy standing images out of the midst of thee; and thou shalt no more worship the work of thine hands" (v. 13).

B. *Idolatry is not outdated.* The temptation to worship the work of our own hands is as real today as it was in Micah's day. Consider our relentless pursuit of affluence, our assumed right of indulgence, or our constant desire to flee suffering of any kind. We are our own idols. We are our own gods.

Conclusion

God wants his people to be the best. For God's people to be spotless in character and effective in service, purification needs to take place. The Lord knows what needs to be thrown away. Listen to him and start discarding.

SUNDAY MORNING, MARCH 14

Title: How Can I Face Death?
Text: "O death, where is thy victory? O death, where is thy sting?" ***(1 Cor. 15:55 RSV).***
Scripture Reading: 1 Corinthians 15:47–56
Hymns: "Great Is Thy Faithfulness," Chisholm
"It Is Well with My Soul," Stafford
"What a Friend We Have in Jesus," Scriven
Offertory Prayer: Father God, we thank you for the bounty of your grace toward us. We thank you for material blessings. We thank you for blessings in the family. We thank you for your blessings upon the work of our heads and hearts and hands. Accept our tithes and offerings as indications of our love and of our desire to share your love with a needy world. In Jesus' name, we pray. Amen.

Introduction

The British Museum in London contains an exhibit of a human body that has been preserved in a remarkable way. It is not a mummy but is the body of a man dehydrated by the hot sands of Egypt in which he was buried. The body is in a crouching position, shaped like a human question mark. It seems to me that this is a parable of death. Death is an enigma though it is common to all. It is as much a part of our natural life as birth. Whether great or small, high or low, powerful or powerless, we all will die.

I. The Greek concept of death.

A. *The ancient Greeks examined the mystery of death and came up with an answer.* They decided that humans are by nature kin to the gods. Therefore, every person has a spark of divinity and is by nature immortal.

B. *The Greeks believed something else: a human lives in a body, the body is matter, and all matter is evil; but inside that evil body there lives a human soul and spirit that is good.* Therefore, the ancient Greeks saw humanity as a soul shut up in the cage of a body. They viewed death as liberation. The Greek view was that when a person died, his soul was emancipated from his body and returned to the deity from which it had come. The soul was then absorbed into that deity, like a drop of water returning to the ocean by evaporation.

C. *But the Greeks had no concept of resurrection.* They had no belief in a bodily resurrection; that would have been a contradiction in terms to them because they thought the body was evil. They had no concept of personal survival or personal identity beyond death.

II. The Hebrew concept of death.

A. *The Hebrews' understanding of death was very different from that of the Greeks.* The Hebrews believed in a place of existence after death that they called Sheol. The earth was the abode of humans and animals, and heaven was the abode of God and the angels. They had no concept of humans going to heaven where God was, but they knew that humans did not remain on earth. Therefore, they spoke and wrote of Sheol as the grave or the pit. It was the place of shadowy existence after death, a place where "shades" live. There was no personal identity there. They were nonpersons.

B. *The psalmist saw Sheol as a contradiction because the shades could not glorify God.* He wrote in Psalm 6:5 (RSV): "In death there is no remembrance of thee; in Sheol, who can give thee praise?"

The Greeks saw death as escape for the immortal soul. The Hebrews saw death as a shadowy existence in nothingness. Many modern Jews do not believe in life after death any more than their Old Testament predecessors did. They believe that there is no afterlife.

III. The New Testament concept of death.

A. *Immortality is the gift of God to those who believe.* "To all who received him, who believed in his name, he gave power to become children of God" (John 1:12 RSV). Jesus said that if we believe in him we have eternal life, beginning now.

The Christian view of death has been transformed. It has been revolutionized by the resurrection of Jesus Christ. We have an insight and understanding of death and life after death that is not characteristic of other groups.

B. *Christians, because of Jesus' resurrection and postresurrection appearances, are no longer left with blind guesses about life after death.* We have been given an authentic glimpse of glory. Therefore, we can have certainty of faith about things concerning death.

C. *Death wears two faces.* It is like the Roman god Janus, for whom the month of January is named. Janus had two faces facing opposite directions. Death is like that. Death from the human point of view looks like defeat and tragedy. But from God's point of view, death is victory and triumph. "Precious in the sight of the LORD is the death of his saints" (Ps. 116:15).

The apostle John got a glimpse of heaven and exhausted his vocabulary trying to describe its glory. Death wears two faces—destruction and departure.

D. *"Death is like blowing out a candle because the dawn has come."* This quote aptly describes the reality of death. Death can be terribly tragic, but death is not the worst phenomenon in this world. While the prospect of dying can be very bleak, there is no reason to have an ultimate fear of it. The resurrection of Jesus Christ means that death has died.

Lift up your hearts! Christ is risen from the dead, and every person who places faith and trust in him will rise and be clothed with immortality and live forever in the presence of the Lord.

> It will be worth it all when we see Jesus.
> Life's trials will seem small when we see Christ.
> One glimpse of his dear face,
> All sorrow will erase,
> So bravely run the race, till we see Christ.
>
> —*Esther Kerr Rusthoi*

Conclusion

Let me dare for just a moment to be intensely personal, to probe a bit, and perhaps plant a question in your mind that will set you thinking. The hope I have talked about belongs to every born-again believer. If today should be the day of your death, do you have the kind of faith relationship with God that would mean eternal life?

You can have this hope of glory. If you have never received Christ as your own Lord and Savior, I invite you to turn from sin and self right now and receive him as your personal Lord. If you will do that, God's Holy Spirit will work a miracle in your life.

Sunday Evening, March 14

Title: Live All the Days of Your Life

Text: "These are the days of the years of Abraham's life, a hundred and seventy-five years. Abraham breathed his last and died in a good old age, an old man and full of years, and was gathered to his people" ***(Gen. 25:7–8 RSV).***

Scripture Reading: Genesis 25:1–25

Introduction

A young lady invited a non-Christian to attend church. She was disappointed when the minister began to read the fifth chapter of Genesis as the Scripture lesson for the morning, preparatory to a sermon titled "Enoch Walked with God." As he droned on and on, the genealogical statistics became boring for her. She thought, "My friend will never feel his need for the Savior after this monotonous repetition." What she did not realize was that every paragraph ended with the same statement about each of the patriarchs:

"and he died." The young man did not pay attention to the number of years each lived, but he was greatly impressed, even disturbed, by the recurring statement that each one at last died. The man was later saved, having come under conviction through the reading of this Scripture.

All of us—from the greatest to the ungodliest—will some day face death. The New Testament says, "As it is appointed unto men once to die, but after this the judgment: so Christ was once offered to bear the sins of many; and unto them that look for him shall he appear the second time without sin unto salvation" (Heb. 9:27–28). Abraham lived a long time and did many things, mostly good, but some not so wise. The time finally came for him to face the fact that he would not live forever on the earth. Let us look at his years after Sarah died until the time he too passed away.

I. Provided for his posterity.

A. *Abraham, like many people, never thought about a cemetery plot until death came.* When Sarah died at the age of 127, he realized he must do something to show he intended for Canaan to be the possession of his descendants. Notwithstanding the fact that God had told him his seed must spend several centuries in a foreign land before they assumed full control of Canaan (Gen. 15:13–14), he purchased a burial place near what later became the city of Hebron. He did this to give a family identity to those who would come after him. Also, by this act, he showed his faith in God's promise to give this land to him and his descendants. Abraham paid for the land, thus assuring a clear title to it. In doing this he showed good business judgment.

B. *A second order of business lay on Abraham's agenda.* At the death of Sarah, Isaac was thirty-seven and still unmarried. How could he have grandchildren when he didn't have a daughter or daughter-in-law? Abraham took the initiative and sent his servant to find a wife for Isaac. To us such an action seems ludicrous, but in that day it was not without precedent and probably not infrequent. Nevertheless, this great man realized he must be sure his son married appropriately, so he sent Eliezer back to the land where his people lived.

II. Refused to stop living.

A. *As much as we love our earthly companion, we cannot quit because God takes our loved one first.* Abraham went on with his life after Sarah died, and he eventually married again. No evidence exists for the theory of some that Keturah was Abraham's concubine while Sarah was alive. The reference to Keturah's children by Abraham as "sons of a concubine" (1 Chron. 1:32) does not argue for this contention. The term probably refers to the fact that Sarah was considered by the genealogist as the primary wife and Keturah, though legally wedded to Abraham, as a subordinate in the family tree. Abraham strongly advocated monogamy, as is shown by his reluctance to have a child by Hagar until Sarah insisted on it. We find it difficult to believe this man would have had a mistress during Sarah's lifetime.

B. *Not only when we lose a companion or other loved one, but in all sorrows we must face life daily and refuse to quit when all our goals do not materialize.* It is dangerous to bargain with God by promising to do a certain thing if he will spare our loved one. If it is right to do a thing, it is right to do it whether we get our personal desires or not. Many good people have faced severe losses of various kinds and have continued to serve God, sometimes even more faithfully, because their tears have become telescopes by which they have seen God's will more clearly. Abraham had been promised that he would be the father of many nations. The marriage to Keturah made this possible.

III. Divided his estate while still living.

With wise foresight, Abraham made disposition of his property while still living. Another factor came from this decision: he kept alive the idea of family ties. Among all the ancient nations only the Romans and Jews seem to have strongly held on to the family concept. By giving Isaac the major portion of his property, Abraham said to future generations that this was his true family, the one God would use in the redemptive program. Through the centuries the Jews strengthened their moral constraints by remembering they were the descendants of their fathers Abraham, Isaac, and Jacob. The other groups did not feel such a closeness and therefore did not feel the necessity for being people of strong faith. One's heritage can be an important factor in motivating for high and holy living.

Of course, Abraham did not completely disenfranchise the other children. He provided for them, giving enough for each one's economic security. A person is wise today who can face the matter of his or her death with emotional maturity and make what he or she feels is a fair and just property settlement while still living.

IV. Died and was buried with dignity.

A. *The phrase "His sons Isaac and Ishmael buried him in the cave of Machpelah" (Gen. 25:9) is one we often overlook.* Much, however, is wrapped up in the statement. Both boys respected their father. Even Ishmael, who might have felt he received unfair treatment, stood with Isaac at the death of their illustrious father.

B. *An outstanding rabbi interprets the phrase "Abraham . . . died in a good old age . . . and full of years" (Gen. 25:8) to mean that he was "satisfied because he saw all the desires of his fulfilled and was pleased with all that he wished to see and do."* Another adds, "He was granted the privilege of seeing in his lifetime the reward stored up for him in the world to come." His long-awaited son Isaac was seventy-five years old, and his grandsons,

Jacob and Esau, were fifteen. If any character in the Old Testament saw his dreams come true, Abraham did. He even passed on before the clash between Jacob and Esau that resulted in the former leaving home for twenty years. He indeed "came to the end of a perfect day."

Conclusion

These eleven messages have traced Abraham from Ur to Machpelah. He was not without fault, but he was a genuinely dedicated man. He was "the friend of God" (James 2:23) and "father of the faithful" (cf. Gal. 3:7). Though three great religions trace their human origin to him, his greatest contribution was that Jesus Christ, the Son of the living God, came from his lineage. He did indeed leave us an example of faith.

WEDNESDAY EVENING, MARCH 17

Title: Going to Court with God
Text: "Hear ye, O mountains, the LORD's controversy, and ye strong foundations of the earth: for the LORD hath a controversy with his people, and he will plead with Israel" ***(Mic. 6:2).***
Scripture Reading: Micah 6:1–8

Introduction

Novelists and dramatists often use courtroom scenes as material for their stories. Prosecutors and defenders try their cases before jurors and a judge. Both call for witnesses. The audience gets caught up in the process. The tension builds until the verdict is passed and the sentence is given.

The prophets often used courtroom drama as well. Isaiah, Micah's eighth-century BC contemporary, used a courtroom scene in the first chapter of his book, "Come now, and let us reason together, saith the LORD: though your sins be as scarlet, they shall be as snow; though they be red like crimson, they shall be as wool" (Isa. 1:18). Look at the courtroom terms in our Scripture reading of Micah 6:1–8: "contend," "controversy," "plead." Micah structured his address according to a familiar covenant lawsuit pattern. God brought his people to trial for having broken their covenant with him.

Periodically, the Lord brings his people to court for rebelling against him. Let us follow the action of God's courtroom drama. We need to see if we are guilty before the Lord. If so, we have time to repent and mend our ways.

I. God summoned his people to go to court (Mic. 6:1–2).

A. *God invited people to plead their cases.* Micah, speaking on behalf of the Lord, issued a summons to the people of Israel: "Hear ye now what the LORD saith: Arise, contend thou before the mountains, and let the hills hear thy voice. Hear ye, O mountains, the Lord's controversy, and ye strong foundations of the earth" (vv. 1–2). Metaphorically, Micah used "mountains," "hills," and "strong foundations of the earth" to represent the whole world as witnesses.

B. *God gave his reason for calling the defendants and witnesses.* "For the LORD hath a controversy with his people, and he will plead with Israel" (v. 2). God had a charge to bring against Israel. They had promised to obey him, but they disobeyed. Whenever God's people disobey him, he summons them to bring the problem to him in repentance.

II. God reviewed his relationship with his people (Mic. 6:3–5).

A. *God summarized the good things he had done for Israel throughout their history.* Let us look at this review of blessings:
   1. When God's people were enslaved in Egypt, he gave them freedom. "For I brought thee up out of the land of Egypt, and redeemed thee out of the house of servants" (v. 4).
   2. When God's people needed leaders, God gave them gifted ones. "And I sent before thee Moses, Aaron, and Miriam" (v. 4).
   3. When the security of God's people was threatened, he rescued them. "O my people, remember now what Balak king of Moab consulted, and what Balaam the son of Beor answered him from Shittim unto Gilgal" (v. 5).

   God made explicitly clear his relationship with his people. Their failure could not be blamed on him. The fault is not with God, but rather with his rebellious people.

B. *God reminded his people of their rebellion.* "O my people, what have I done unto thee? and wherein have I wearied thee? testify against me" (v. 3). The historical recitations should have convinced Israel that God had done what was just. Israel had no right to rebel against the Lord.

Israel's first step in restoring their relationship with the Lord was to remember the great things God had done for them. The drama of the courtroom continued: witnesses had been summoned; a history of God's relationship with his people had been reviewed; and now God sought to help his people.

III. God sought to help his people get right with him (Mic. 6:6–8).

A. *God's people expressed a desire to get right with him.* Israel did not argue the charges. They did not dispute the evidence presented in the courtroom. Instead, the accused addressed a question to the court: "Wherewith shall I come before the LORD, and bow myself before the high God? shall I come before him with burnt offerings, with calves of a year old? will the Lord be pleased with thousands of rams, or with ten thousands of rivers of oil? shall I give my firstborn for my transgression, the fruit of my body for the sin of my soul?" (vv. 6–7).

The defendant desired to restore the relationship with God.

Would sacrifice in the temple restore the relationship? Would the Lord be pleased if Israel's firstborn son were offered as a sacrifice? The people were willing to do almost anything to restore the relationship.

B. *Micah told how a person can be right with the Lord.* "He hath shewed thee, O man, what is good; and what doth the LORD require of thee, but to do justly, and to love mercy, and to walk humbly with thy God?" (v. 8). Let us examine carefully each expression in God's requirements.
   1. To do justly. In Micah's context this expression means to set right the wrongs and to protect the helpless. It means to practice honesty and fairness in all transactions.
   2. To love mercy. The expression means to be faithful and kind to someone to whom one is bound in covenant relationship. It means loving someone sacrificially.
   3. To walk humbly with thy God. This expression describes the personal relationship a person has with the Lord. To walk humbly means to walk attentively with the Lord, yielding one's will to God's will.

Conclusion

God took his people to court. He presented the charges, and they could not be denied. The people deserved punishment, but the judge did not punish them immediately. He urged the people to get right with him.

SUNDAY MORNING, MARCH 21

Title: The Weeping King

Text: "As he approached Jerusalem and saw the city, he wept over it and said, 'If you, even you, had only known on this day what would bring you peace—but now it is hidden from your eyes'" ***(Luke 19:41–42 NIV).***

Scripture Reading: Luke 19:28–44

Hymns: "Crown Him with Many Crowns," Bridges
"Great Redeemer, We Adore Thee," Harris
"I Will Sing the Wondrous Story," Rowley

Offertory Prayer: Father, you have given us the power to attain wealth, and we rejoice in the fruit of our labors. Today we come bringing a portion of the income you have blessed us with, and we dedicate it to your service. Accept these gifts and use them for the advancement of your kingdom in this community and to the ends of the earth. Amen.

Introduction

One of the first references to Jesus Christ was the Magi's query, "Where is he that is born king of the Jews?" The last reference to Jesus was written on a crude sign over his head on the cross: "Jesus of Nazareth, the King of the Jews." And in between these references are many more that speak of Jesus' role as a king. In his temptation experience, Jesus was offered the kingdoms of this world on the Devil's terms, but he rejected kingship on that basis. In the Sermon on the Mount, Jesus described the nature of his kingdom and the characteristics of the citizens of his kingdom. Throughout his ministry, Jesus demonstrated kingly authority over the demonic, over disease, and over death. There were times when his disciples wanted to make him a king. They were thinking of him as a nationalistic and political king who would reestablish the sovereignty of the nation of Israel as a political force in the world. Jesus also rejected that kind of kingship.

In his triumphal entry into Jerusalem at the beginning of Passion Week, our Lord boldly and compassionately offered himself as the King of love and grace. The triumphal entry, which is recorded in all four of the Gospels (Matt. 21:1–11; Mark 11:1–11; Luke 19:29–44; John 12:12–19), was Jesus' bold declaration of his messiahship and his claim to be the Christ of God. He came into Jerusalem not to assert his sovereign rights to the throne of David's political kingdom, but to declare his kingship in the hearts of those who would trust and follow him. William Barclay has described this most beautifully and significantly:

> He came lowly and riding upon a donkey. We must be careful to see the real meaning of that. In western lands the donkey is a despised beast; but in eastern lands, the donkey could be a noble animal. Often a king came riding upon a donkey; but when he came upon a donkey, it was the sign that he came in peace. The horse was the mount of war! The donkey was the mount of peace. So when Jesus claimed to be king, He claimed to be the king of peace. He showed that He came, not to destroy, but to love; not to condemn, but to help; not in the might of arms, but in the strength of love. (*The Gospel of Matthew,* vol. 2 [Philadelphia: Westminster], 267)

Luke describes one experience in connection with the triumphal entry that is not recorded by the other apostles. "As [Jesus] approached Jerusalem and saw the city, he wept over it and said, 'If you, even you, had only known on this day what would bring you peace—but now it is hidden from your eyes'" (19:41–42 NIV). Here we see the King weeping over the city. The King was not weeping for himself. These were not tears of self-pity, remorse, or personal failure. They were the tears of a King suffering for his people.

I. The King was weeping because of his perfect knowledge.

Jesus' heart was filled with compassion for his people. He was experiencing the pain of a shallow acceptance that did not deceive him into believing that the people were willing to accept a King of love, grace, mercy, and righteousness.

He had a perfect knowledge of the situation in the past, present, and future; and this knowledge caused his heart to break with compassionate concern.

II. The King was weeping because of the blindness and deafness of the people.

Throughout his earthly ministry, Jesus restored sight to the blind and hearing to the deaf on many occasions. He did that to help the people see the need for really using their eyes for seeing and their ears for hearing. Jesus sought to minister to a group of people whose minds were filled with conceit and complacency. They had a feeling of spiritual superiority when they considered those around them. They were preoccupied with their own ways and goals and were unwilling to open up their minds to new truth about God as Jesus was trying to communicate it. They were spiritually and morally blind and deaf and would not permit themselves to see and hear. This caused the King to weep on their behalf.

III. The King was weeping because the city was passing up its opportunity forever.

Once opportunity comes to us, if it is not recognized and seized, we miss it and it is gone forever. Jesus knew that his people would never know what they were missing because of their unwillingness to believe and respond to him as the Messiah of love. He wept because they were passing up their unique opportunity.

IV. The King was weeping because the city was on a collision course with disaster.

Jesus could foresee that the nation was veering toward political disaster. He describes this in Matthew 24, in which he foretells the destruction of the temple and the calamity that would befall the city. His predictions became reality by AD 70, when the Roman general Titus captured and destroyed the city.

V. The tears of a weeping King give us insight into his character.

Jesus came to reveal God's nature and character to people. He came to reveal that God is not cold, distant, removed, and unconcerned. He came to reveal that God loves people and wants to save them from their self-destructiveness.

A. *Paul describes the compassion of this King who, though he existed in the form of God, did not hold on to the prerogatives of that position, but instead poured himself out into the form of a man so that he might come and rescue humans from sin (Phil. 2:5–8).*

B. *This God-appointed King submitted to the humiliation and pain of crucifixion so that he might reveal God's concern for his people (Matt. 27:32–44).* The tears of the King reveal the heartbreak of God.

VI. The tears of the weeping King reveal the divine helplessness.

A. *The King was omnipotent in creation.*

B. *The King is omnipotent in keeping the machinery of the universe in perfect coordination.*

C. *The King has no omnipotence in human hearts until he is invited to come in and take the place of authority.*

Conclusion

It is easy for us to be critical of those who rejected the claims of the King during his earthly ministry. Before we condemn them, however, we need to inquire as to whether we have rejected or ignored the claims of him who conquered death and the grave and who will someday come back as the King of Glory.

When we look at the world and see how few have even heard the good news of Christ, we must admit that we have either rejected or ignored the King's command to carry the good news to the ends of the earth.

As Jesus' disciples, we need to recognize that we have robbed ourselves of the promise of his companionship when we have neglected to recognize his authoritative command to evangelize the world (Matt. 28:19–20).

Jesus was born to be our King. We need to make him the Lord of our lives. We need to let him be the Lord of love in our homes. We need to let him be Lord in our vocations. We need to let him be Lord in our decision-making processes.

Jesus would have us do the will of God in the present even as it is done by the angels in heaven. Let us crown him King in our hearts today.

SUNDAY EVENING, MARCH 21

Title: Don't Take the Easy Way Out

Text: "Isaac dug again the wells of water which had been dug in the days of Abraham his father; for the Philistines had stopped them after the death of Abraham; and he gave them the names which his father had given them" ***(Gen. 26:18 RSV).***

Scripture Reading: Genesis 26:12–23

Introduction

How many parents with strong personalities have children who also have strong personalities? Though we do sometimes find vigor and dynamic transferred to the next generation, often the child will be mild compared with the parent. Isaac seems to have been that type of child. He may have fit the pattern of a young man in a modern novel who said, "Whatever I try to do, I couldn't ever be as successful as my father. He's already broken all the records and achieved enough greatness to last several generations. I somehow can't get motivated enough to even try." We might add, however, that sometimes the family zest is picked up in the grandchild who recaptures the drive of the first generation. In a sense, Jacob may fit that mold.

Look at Isaac and all the people like him. What is the temptation of their lives? Is it not to take the easy way out? To live on the previous generation's contribution? We do not have much recorded material about Isaac. Is this because he didn't do much? Perhaps. Or it may be that what he did was not very significant. To be sure, however, in our competitive and frenzied world, we sometimes admire, even almost envy, this type of person. He is not all bad; there is much to be said for his kind of life. The tragedy is, however, that taking the easy way out often means failing to do the things we could do for humanity both by contribution and by example. Let us try to draw several lessons from the life of this quiet young man.

I. His background.

A. *Beersheba, where Isaac was raised, was on one of two main routes to Egypt.* The last greenery before the start of desert land graced this area. One could look north and see the soft swelling hills of Judea. To the south were patches of fertile plain that gave way to barren, uninhabited land. In the immediate area was a place of shrubs with innumerable wildflowers, making the land adjacent to the desert a carpet of color for a number of weeks each year. Excellent pasture abounded, and grain crops could be raised on the lower slopes of the hills and in the valleys. Wells were easily dug because water was not too far beneath the ground. All in all, Isaac grew up in a comfortable environment.

B. *Add to this Isaac's position in the family.* He was the only child of his parents, born late in their lives. The word "spoiled" may be an oversimplification. When Ishmael continued to taunt Isaac, Sarah insisted that Abraham send the "bad boy" away. When Ishmael and his mother, Hagar, left, their absence left a clear field for the little lad. A strange lull may have followed their departure. No bickering, jeers, or persecution disturbed Isaac. He was the apple of his parents' eyes and probably enjoyed it. He stood in awe of his father and enjoyed the "smother love" of Sarah. Isaac had no need to develop a strong drive. He had all he could ask for.

II. A passive personality.

A. *Why did Isaac wait until he was forty years old to marry?* One could say that this was not that old considering the life expectancy of that day, but is that really an accurate appraisal? In any culture, especially the type in which Isaac grew up, he would have matured physically long before this time. Was he just not interested or was he too unmotivated to make a trip to Padan-aram himself? We do not know the facts, but he seems to have been content to let others make the decision for him. For a girl to let her father find a husband for her is one thing, but for a man to let a servant choose a bride for him seems almost irresponsible, regardless of the social customs of that day. Isaac took the easy way out.

B. *The biblical record does not tell us much about Isaac's life with Rebekah, but we can make some deductions from the meager amount of information we possess.* Rebekah seems to have dominated him completely. Look at the incident when Isaac was ready to give his blessing to his son. She schemed with her favorite son Jacob and deceived Isaac. How naïve could he be not to recognize the conspiracy! Again, Isaac took the easy way out!

III. Look at both sides.

A. *As said before, a low profile is not all bad.* Some people get much more done by maintaining a quiet stance. All of us must accomplish according to our personalities. "Train up a child in the way he should go" (Prov. 22:6) actually means teach and guide him according to his own personality. Work *with* the grain, not *against* it! Every parent who has had more than one child knows that no two are alike. Some children must be disciplined strongly; others cannot accept that kind of strictness. Some will respond to the slightest suggestion; others will not obey even if threatened with discipline. A parent must study each child.

B. *Likewise, every person must decide how to conduct his or her own life.* Some people cannot be strong, driving leaders. They must be followers. Some people are suited for the sales department, others for the research laboratory. This study of Isaac is not an effort to disparage him, for in the next message we will see a noble quality about him. Rather, the plea at this point is to be yourself but never be content to be less than you can be. Above all, develop your own personality. Profit from those you know by learning all the lessons you can from them. Final decisions, however, are up to you.

Conclusion

Although we should respect the religion of our fathers and mothers, we cannot build our lives on their faith. The time comes when we must launch our own *Mayflower* and set out on our own pilgrimage of faith. All of us are not pioneers like Columbus, but we all have a career to map out, and the glory of life is to do what God has planned for us.

Don't take the easy way out! Two men were dreaming. One said, "I wish I had five acres of watermelons." The other said, "If you did, would you give me one to eat?" The first one replied, "No. If you're too lazy to wish for your own melons, you can't have any of mine." Don't take the easy way out! Work for the night is coming!

Wednesday Evening, March 24

Title: The Essence of True Religion
Text: "He hath showed thee, O man, what is good; and what doth the Lord require of thee, but to do justly, and to love mercy, and to walk humbly with thy God?" *(Mic. 6:8).*
Scripture Reading: Micah 6:6–8

Introduction

Scores of different religions exist in the world today. Have you ever asked which religion is the true religion? People want to be right when it comes to religion.

Long ago Micah addressed the idea of true religion. He dealt directly with the universal question, What does a sinner do to restore his or her relation to God? Micah dealt with the issue by asking questions and then giving answers. His questions are found in Micah 6:7, and his answers are recorded in verse 8.

In our day the question of what is true religion is prominent. Once I heard someone put all the religions of the world into two categories. In the first category there are those religions that say human beings can do something to earn God's favor. In the second category is the religion that says God does something for human beings. The true religion is the final category. Let us study both categories carefully, using Micah as our source.

I. Some think we need to earn God's favor (Mic. 6:6–7).

A. *Look at the basic question about religion: "Wherewith shall I come before the Lord, and bow myself before the high God?" (v. 7).* The opening question "wherewith" indicates an intense desire of people to know how to be right with God.

B. *Every possible means may be tried in seeking to earn God's favor.* Micah mentions several ways human beings try to earn God's favor. "Shall I come before him with burnt offerings, with calves of a year old? Will the Lord be pleased with thousands of rams, or with ten thousands of rivers of oil? Shall I give my firstborn for my transgression, the fruit of my body for the sin of my soul?" (vv. 6–7). The possibilities are as follows:

1. Would God be pleased with sacrificed offerings? In some sacrifices all of the animal was consumed by fire on the altar.
2. Would God be pleased with year-old calves? Would tender, precious gifts please the Lord?
3. Would God be pleased with extravagant offerings? If so, one could offer thousands of rams and ten thousand rivers of oil.
4. Would God be pleased with human sacrifice? This would be the most costly sacrifice. The writer would have had in mind Abraham's willingness to offer Isaac as a sacrifice.

Micah does not list all the ways people seek to please God. Of course they try more ways than Micah mentioned. Yet after all human efforts are tried, the result is the same. No people can earn a right relationship with the Lord.

II. Others think we need to accept what God has done.

A. *Listen to the authoritative answer about real religion.* "He hath shewed thee, O man, what is good; and what doth the LORD require of thee?" (Mic. 6:8). The anxious uncertainty about what pleases the Lord is replaced by a calm certainty about what the Lord requires.

B. *God lists his requirements: "to do justly, and to love mercy, and to walk humbly with thy God" (Mic. 6:8).* Let us look carefully at God's requirements.

1. The first requirement of the Lord deals with community relationships. It is "to do justly." The Old Testament believer lived within a group of other faithful people. They were bound by a common covenant relationship to the Lord. To be committed to the Lord also involved commitment to the covenant community. The prophets used the word *justice* to characterize the covenant responsibility of social responsibility.
2. The second requirement of the Lord describes a single-hearted loyalty to the Lord. It is "to love mercy." The word "mercy" is *hesed*, and it is a word of partnership. It describes the faithfulness of God to humanity, but it also describes a person's faithfulness to God. The Lord often complained about Israel's fickle faith.
3. The third requirement of the Lord depicts a careful walk with the Lord. It is "to walk humbly with thy God." The word walk is *halak*, and it describes an intimate relationship with the Lord that results in a close communion with him.

Conclusion

Think about your religion. Is it the true one? If you have had to perform and give to gain God's approval, you have the wrong religion. Open your life to the Lord and accept his work on your behalf.

SUNDAY MORNING, MARCH 28

Title: Easter Joy

Text: "Jesus our Lord . . . was put to death for our trespasses and raised for our justification" ***(Rom. 4:24–25 RSV)***.

Scripture Reading: 1 Corinthians 15:20–23

Hymns: "Christ the Lord Is Risen Today," Wesley
"Jesus Shall Reign Where'er the Sun," Watts
"Wherever He Leads I'll Go," McKinney

Offertory Prayer: Father in heaven, open our eyes and help us to see on this Easter Sunday the richness of your gifts to us. Help us to respond to the gracious generosity of your heart. As we consider the empty tomb, help us to give not only our tithes and offerings, but help us to give ourselves to you totally, that we might be the means of proclaiming to the ends of the earth the death of Christ for our sins and his victory over death and the grave, that all might come to know him as Savior. In his name we pray. Amen.

Introduction

We don't celebrate Easter to the extent that we celebrate Christmas. That is really strange, because if there were no Easter, there would be no need to celebrate Christmas. If there were no resurrection, then Christ was born, lived, and died in vain. There would be no New Testament, no church, no Christianity, and no hope.

I. The resurrection means the assurance of forgiveness.

A. *We have been forgiven.* One writer has pointed out that the very first appearance of the risen Christ was to Peter. Christ appeared to Peter that he might forgive Peter for denying him three times. The resurrection means that the forgiveness of sin is a reality. Christ has atoned for our sins by his death on the cross. He paid our sin debt and opened up the way to the Father. We can be forgiven as surely as Simon Peter was forgiven.

B. *We can be grateful that forgiveness is not something we can experience only once.* Scripture says, "If we confess our sins, he is faithful and just to forgive us our sins, and to cleanse us from all unrighteousness"(1 John 1:9). To be forgiven once would be adequate if we only sinned once, but we need God's continued forgiveness.

Because we so graciously have been forgiven, we can learn to forgive others readily and happily. Indeed, Christ taught us in the Lord's Prayer and in the Sermon on the Mount that we will be forgiven as we forgive. An unforgiving spirit is a spiritual short circuit that does not let the power through. Someone has described forgiveness as a swinging door. If it gets stuck in one relationship, it will be stuck in other relationships.

Do you need to forgive someone on this Easter morning? Perhaps someone at work has wronged you. Maybe someone in your own household or in your church family has sinned against you. Let Easter swing wide the gate of forgiveness—not only of divine forgiveness, but of human forgiveness as well.

II. The resurrection also gives us bright hope.

A. *No one is beyond this hope.* John Masefield, the late poet laureate of Great Britain, wrote a fairly obscure poem titled "The Widow in the

By-Street" in which a young convicted criminal was to be hanged publicly. His mother was in the crowd of onlookers. The order was given, the trap door opened, and the rope came down and did its work. The mother muttered over and over about broken things "too broke to mend." Broken things, too broke to mend—that is the essence of despair. It is the realization that we have a past and we are living in the present, but we have no future.

B. *The disciples despaired like that.* Remember the two on the way to Emmaus? They said to the Stranger who walked with them, "We had hoped that he was the one to redeem Israel" (Luke 24:21 RSV). Oh, what high hopes they had! They had pinned their hopes on him. This one spoke with authority; this one performed miracles to demonstrate the inbreaking power of the kingdom of God. They really thought the Messiah had come in Jesus. "We had hoped," they said. They knew the past, they knew the present, but they had no future. Those early disciples saw the death of Christ as broken things "too broke to mend."

   Then Easter came, and suddenly they saw something they never suspected. That is what God can do with our despair.

C. *But even on this bright Easter morning, death is a screaming contradiction.* Death is the great mystery we all face. It is universal and inevitable. No one can be nonchalant for very long about death.

   German theologian Helmut Thielicke, out walking one spring day, turned aside to look at a lilac bush in full bloom. As he looked more closely, he discovered that the lilac bush was growing out of the body of a dead German soldier. Beauty and death side by side.

D. *Death is a contradiction.* Death is at times absurd. Death is absurd when a child dies before he ever has a chance to learn and live. Death is absurd when a patient lingers and lingers but is not really alive. Death is a dark mystery, and the brightest light we have to shed on it is Easter light.

Conclusion

While excavating some Roman ruins, archaeologists kept coming across the inscription "NFFNSNC." They finally determined that the initials reflected the pagan philosophy of the Romans: "I was not, I was, I am not, I do not care."

Is that the meaning of life or does Easter say it means something more? Easter gives us hope of life beyond the grave, of glory, of our own resurrection. Jesus is the firstfruit of the resurrection. Our resurrection will be the additional fruit. One day the trumpet of God will sound and the dead in Christ will be raised, clothed in immortality. They will receive new glorified bodies, like that of our Lord. Our new bodies will be suited for the spiritual realm.

Resurrection means forgiveness; hope, and victory over sin, evil, and death. Victory—that is what Easter is all about. The disciples' despair turned into glad discovery and joy. Good Friday turned into bright Easter morning with life and joy and a crown, not a cross; with laughter and victory, not pain.

One of the great themes of Christian theology is *Christus Victor,* "Christ is the victor!" You see, God does not save us *from* suffering and death; he saves us *through* suffering and death—his own. He gives us strength, courage, and grace.

Easter means that we have a future—a bright future in Christ. Therefore, lift up your hearts with faith, for your redemption draweth nigh! For now is Christ risen, the hope of glory!

Sunday Evening, March 28

Title: Back to Basics

Text: "He built an altar there and called upon the name of the Lord, and pitched his tent there. And there Isaac's servants dug a well" ***(Gen. 26:25 RSV).***

Scripture Reading: Genesis 26:23–25

Introduction

Perhaps you felt the evaluation of Isaac in last week's message was unfair. If so, let's look at the other side of the coin. One verse about this mild-mannered man shows us that he had a well-rounded life that made him a "whole personality," well-adjusted and integrated in all the essentials that make one a complete individual. The writer says of Isaac, "He built an altar there and called upon the name of the Lord, and pitched his tent there. And there Isaac's servants dug a well" (Gen. 26:25 RSV). Isn't it refreshing to see that Isaac reopened the wells his father had dug? A spiritual lesson emerges here. We, in our day, need to reaffirm some tremendous truths of the previous generations. In the educational field, it is called "getting back to basics." We need the same thing in our moral and spiritual lifestyles. Notice the threefold division of the verse about Isaac. Each part emphasizes a vital element of a genuinely dedicated and happy existence.

I. Religion—Isaac built an altar.

A. *In fact, the verse says more: he called upon the name of the Lord.* It is one thing to build a church building and another to have a true church in it. The church is the people, not the bricks and mortar. Isaac had both. He built an altar, and he also called upon the name of the Lord.

B. *No life is complete until it recognizes God not only as Creator, but as Redeemer and Lord of life.* Even the pagans recognized the need for some type of religion. The Israelites built many altars to their God on the sites of altars that had been used for sacrifices to Canaanite deities. They sought to purify the perverted concepts of Baal worship. Unfortunately, however, the opposite took place many times. The more secular type of worship triumphed over the spiritual approach. How hard it is to keep religion spiritual! We want to remake God into our image. The words of Jesus to the Samaritan woman remain as one of the most classic statements ever made, "God is a Spirit: and they that worship him must worship in spirit and in truth" (John 4:24).

C. *Civilization needs altars.* First, the Jewish, and then preeminently the Christian faith, has made the world a decent place in which to live. Remove monotheism—especially the Christian interpretation of it—from the world and chaos would soon set in resembling the days of Noah. James Russell Lowell heard someone criticizing religion and airing a cheap skepticism. He replied, "Show me ten square miles in any part of the world, outside of Christianity, where the life of man and the honour of woman are safe, and I can bring up my children decently, and I will emigrate there and give up my religion." Isaac recognized his need for the worship of God.

II. Home—Isaac pitched his tent there.

A. *The canvas that Isaac placed on a pole and used to cover himself and his possessions was frail and transitory, but it was home.*

We should never forget nor even minimize the value of home life. Is there a home inside your house?

J. G. Holland contends, "No genuine observer can decide otherwise than that the homes of a nation are the bulwarks of personal and national safety."

B. *The person who has only a tent or a house is the prey of passing time.* If that person has an altar within the home, however, that person has something that is superior to time. When the sacred ties and dear associates of a home are knit firm by prayer and faith, death has no power over it. The best and holiest of our homes go with us when we leave this world. In another sense, however, they remain in this world to bless the lives of those we have known and influenced.

C. *Today the expression "family altar" is more or less a figure of speech, but not too many years ago it was a reality in many homes.* Sir Henry Jones, in speaking of village families he had known in his youth, said, "Their homes were sacred with the daily prayers offered in them morning and evening, and sometimes at mid-day; and their knowledge of the Bible was marvelous." Such religious actions helped to develop standards, or integrity, in the lives of the family members. Right and wrong were clearly distinguished. If at times certain youths rebelled, after a period of reevaluation in the light of experience, they almost always returned to the faith of their fathers and mothers.

It is important that we remember that Christ wants to be a part of our home. Home is indeed what W. E. Channing called it—"the nursery of the infinite."

III. Work—Isaac's servants dug a well there.

A. *No amount of religious piety or domestic bliss can quite take the place of honest toil.* To overestimate the value of work ethic for our relationship to both God and others is impossible. The idle man gambles with his family's happiness and his children's character. Lack of industry is both the catalyst for and the symptom of that all-devouring selfishness against which no home can stand. A lazy person cannot serve God, for he or she has nothing with which to serve. An outstanding psychiatrist said that the most successful psyche is the one capable of love and work. He contends further that work is the most thorough and profound organizing principle in American life.

B. *Unless it is a dishonest or destructive profession, all work is honorable.* It is the way we "tend the world," the way people connect with each other, forming lasting and healthy relationships. Work is indeed "the most vigorous, vivid sign of life" in both individuals and civilizations. A well-balanced life is impossible without it.

Conclusion

Religion, home, work—a trilogy of virtues but even more. They form a group of essentials for building a happy and productive life. If we remain faithful in these three parts of life, we inherit true power and nobility. Notice the order: God comes first, and then the other two come from a right relationship with our Creator and Redeemer. Notice also the contrast between the altar and the tent. The first is built of solid and enduring stone while the second is of only slight intrinsic worth. When the first indwells the second, however, the temporary becomes permanent. A New Testament parallel reinforces this truth. If our relationship with God is vital and meaningful, when the earthly house of this tabernacle or tent is dissolved, we will receive from God a house not made with hands, eternal in the heavens.

WEDNESDAY EVENING, MARCH 31

Title: Death in the City

Text: "The LORD's voice crieth unto the city, and the man of wisdom shall see thy name: hear ye the rod, and who hath appointed it" ***(Mic. 6:9).***

Scripture Reading: Micah 6:9–16

Introduction

Over a decade ago French theologian Jacques Ellul wrote a book titled *The Meaning of the City*. The book gave theological insight to life in the large city. Several decades ago British writer Harvey Cox wrote a book called *The Secular City*. He wrote about people who lived as if God did not exist.

Micah had his own address to the city. It is preserved in Micah 6:9–16. More than likely, Micah observed life in the city of Jerusalem.

You will remember that Micah lived in a small village named Moresheth located about twenty miles southwest of Jerusalem. He observed how the farmers and herdsmen came to the city to sell their goods. Perhaps on a busy market day Micah delivered his timely address to the city of Jerusalem. He addressed the corruption and crime prevalent in the marketplace.

Go to any large city of the world, and you will see much the same crimes Micah saw. The cities of the world are full of cheating, violence, deception, and idolatry. Let us study Micah's address to the city with his charges of crimes and the consequences of these crimes. With Micah's words we can work to help our cities.

I. The charges against the city (Mic. 6:9–12).

A. *God judged the city.* Micah spoke the word of the Lord against the city. No city council or human court evaluated the city; the Lord himself judged it. "The LORD's voice crieth unto the city, and the man of wisdom shall see thy name: hear ye the rod, and who hath appointed it" (v. 9).

Micah acted as a herald of God. The charges were pronounced through the prophet, but they came from the Lord. Micah prefaced the delivery of the charges against the city with a call to the recipients to pay careful attention.

B. *God named the problems prevalent in the city.* Micah specified the charges (vv. 10–12); listen to them and note the relevancy to today's cities.

1. Merchants gained profit by evil means. "Are there yet the treasures of wickedness in the house of the wicked, and the scant measure that is abominable? Shall I count them pure with the wicked balances, and with the bag of deceitful weights?" (vv. 10–11). In the absence of standard weights and measures, the customer depended on the vendor's honesty.
2. People used violence. "For the rich men thereof are full of violence" (v. 12). Violence was a term for lawlessness. People lived against the laws of the land.
3. People used falsehood and deceit. "The inhabitants thereof have spoken lies, and their tongue is deceitful in their mouth" (v. 12).

There are many modern equivalents to the practices of Micah's day—false advertising, robbery, murder, rape, price-fixing, and improper labeling, to name a few.

II. The consequences of the crimes (Mic. 6:13–16).

A. *The consequences of sin are sure.* God had been a silent observer of the dishonesty, violence, and deceit of the rich. In his own time he moved to judge the crimes. The opening words of verse 13 are emphatic: "Therefore also will I." The people who have wronged others must answer to God. Sin against people is sin against their Creator.

B. *The consequences of sin are severe.* Micah proceeded to give some curses because of the people's sins.
   1. The curse of desolation. There will be food famines.
   2. The curse of dissatisfaction. "Thou shalt eat, but not be satisfied; and thy casting down shall be in the midst of thee; and thou shalt take hold, but shalt not deliver; and that which thou deliverest will I give up to the sword" (v. 14).
   3. The curse of disappointment. "Thou shalt sow, but thou shalt not reap; thou shalt tread the olives, but thou shalt not anoint thee with oil; and sweet wine, but shalt not drink wine" (v. 15). The enemy will overthrow Jerusalem, and Judah will not reap the crops.
   4. The curse of destruction. "For the statutes of Omri are kept, and all the works of the house of Ahab, and ye walk in their counsels; that I should make thee a desolation, and the inhabitants thereof an hissing: therefore ye shall bear the reproach of my people" (v. 16). Micah predicted invasion by an enemy. Judah had not learned the lesson from Israel. They left the Lord, and they perished. Judah was headed for the same fate.

Conclusion

Micah preached to the city. He observed the cheating, stealing, violence, lying, and deceit. He condemned the evil practices. If the city did not turn to the Lord, he said, Jerusalem would fall. But the people continued in their sinful ways; in 587 BC Jerusalem fell.

Will our cities ever learn? Death will come to the city if its people do not turn to the Lord.

SUGGESTED PREACHING PROGRAM FOR THE MONTH OF
APRIL

■ Sunday Mornings

On the first Sunday of the month, wrap up the series "The Conquest of Spiritual Death by Spiritual Birth and Resurrection." The suggested theme for the morning messages for the rest of the month and into the first Sunday in May is "Growing Quality Christians." The Father God is interested not only in our spiritual birth, but in our growing spiritual maturity. He has given to each believer the gift of the Holy Spirit that we might become quality Christians—mature children of God.

■ Sunday Evenings

Often the lives of others can stimulate us to deeper faith and good works. In light of that, a series of biographical messages is suggested. "Personalities from the Past That Speak to the Present" is the suggested theme for this look at four Old Testament characters.

■ Wednesday Evenings

Conclude the series of messages from the book of Micah using the theme "Mighty Messages from a Minor Prophet."

SUNDAY MORNING, APRIL 4

Title: Victory through Our Lord Jesus Christ
Text: "Thanks be to God, which giveth to us the victory through our Lord Jesus Christ" ***(1 Cor. 15:57).***
Scripture Reading: 1 Corinthians 15:51–58
Hymns: "Victory in Jesus," Bartlett
"There's a New Song in My Heart," Peterson
"There Is Power in the Blood," Jones
Offertory Prayer: Heavenly Father, we come to you through Jesus Christ our Lord. With appreciative hearts we thank you for what you have done and promise to do for us. Now out of gratitude for all our blessings, we bring our tithes and offerings into your storehouse for your kingdom's work. Bless them that they may lift burdens and advance your kingdom, through Christ our Lord. Amen.

Introduction

The apostle Paul gives expression to the gratitude of his heart for a unique victory that is assured to those who exercise a firm faith in Jesus Christ as

Lord and Savior. He is shouting with joy because of the confidence he has in the ultimate victory that will be ours through faith in Christ Jesus.

Paul has concluded his classic statement on the resurrection of Christ. He has expressed his confidence and conviction that those who trust Jesus Christ will likewise experience victory over death and the grave. His heart sings with joy and thanksgiving.

I. We can be thankful for victory over sin.

A. *Through Jesus Christ we have victory over the penalty of sin, which is death (Rom. 6:23).*

B. *Through Jesus Christ we can have victory over the power of sin (Phil. 2:13).*

C. *Through Jesus Christ we will one day have victory over the very presence of sin (Heb. 9:28).*

II. We can be thankful for victory over suffering (2 Cor. 12:7–10).

Sooner or later suffering becomes the lot of almost every person who lives. For some, suffering is a crushing blow that shatters them beyond repair.

How can one face suffering, disappointment, or defeat in a victorious manner?

Paul discovered that being a follower of Jesus Christ did not immunize one from hardship and suffering. There is no promise of exemption from suffering merely because one has faith and lives a life of faithfulness.

Paul discovered in the grace of God the strength and the wisdom to be victorious even in the midst of suffering. We can do likewise if we will keep our hearts open and let Jesus Christ have possession of our minds and spirits. Through Christ we can turn tragedy into triumph.

III. We can be thankful for victory over death.

Paul declared that the last enemy of humans is death (1 Cor. 15:26). Seemingly, death wins the victory over everyone. But our Lord came to demonstrate that life is more powerful than death. He came to taste death for every person (Heb. 2:9). He came to put death to death, destroying its power (Heb. 2:14). He came to deliver people from the fear of the power of death (Heb. 2:15).

Our Lord came to die for us that we might not have to die. He affirmed that his victory over death should be taken as a proof that we would also be rescued from death and that we would live as he lived.

First Corinthians 15 is the classic New Testament passage that affirms that through Jesus Christ we will experience victory over Satan, sin, death, and the grave. In view of this, it is understandable that this great chapter should close with an anthem of praise and with a challenge to faithfulness in working for the Lord Jesus Christ.

Conclusion

Victory is a beautiful word to those who are the victors. Through Jesus Christ we are assured of victory in the game of life in which everything is at stake.

Daily we should express our thanks to God for the joy and the assurance of this victory. To contemplate the full significance of the victory that is ours through Christ will fill our hearts with joy. Hearts that are filled with joy will find a way to communicate that joy to others. Our expressions of thanksgiving and joy will cause others to want to know our Savior.

The words of our text should be in our minds every day: "But thanks be to God, which giveth us the victory through our Lord Jesus Christ" (1 Cor. 15:57).

Sunday Evening, April 4

Title: Enoch: Initiated Before God

Text: "By faith Enoch was taken up so that he should not see death; and he was not found, because God had taken him. Now before he was taken he was attested as having pleased God" ***(Heb. 11:5 RSV)***.

Scripture Reading: Genesis 5:23–24

Introduction

One of the strangest occurrences in the Bible happened to a man named Enoch. Enoch's name means "initiated." He was chosen by God to give humanity a very special lesson on the value of holiness. God often works through individuals to reach other people. He gives different people varying ministries in accordance with differing circumstances. One may be called to serve as a layperson, another as a missionary, another as a pastor.

God may initiate a plan whereby he wants to show a whole society how Christians can be victorious even when they are ill, destitute, or under some great pressure. God chooses the person he desires for that ministry. Enoch was a man so selected by God. Let us look at several realities in the life of this man.

I. Enoch initiated by God.

A. *God's divine plan.* God's original plan called for man and woman to be placed in the garden of Eden to have a good life. God desired uninterrupted fellowship with them. He wanted to walk, talk, and exist with them in a total experience. Humankind was the crowning glory of God's creation. It was in humans alone that the "image of God" was placed.

B. *Human freedom of choice.* God could have made a robot and programmed it to obey his every desire, but its obedience would not have been motivated by love or respect. Therefore, God created humans with the ability to make our own decisions. We can choose to love God, or we can choose to reject God. The familiar story from Eden tells the world that humans chose to reject intimate fellowship with God in favor of experience with sin.

C. *God's circumstantial selection.* After only a few generations, humanity had degenerated to an appalling degree. The people were wicked. God wanted someone to have fellowship with, and he wanted the world to know that he still loved humans and longed for their companionship. Thus, he chose Enoch.

II. Enoch walked with God.

Enoch's relationship with God was distinct from that of others in his society. He had a perception of the character of God and was in contact with the "heart of God."

A. *God's holiness.* The primary characteristic of God is his divine holiness. In his holiness, God is totally separated from sin. He cannot abide sin. He is pure; he is light; he is love; he is honor and majesty. God's holiness sets him apart from his creation.

B. *God's desire for fellowship with humans.* God desires fellowship with us even though he is separated from a fallen humanity by his personal holiness. The initial purpose for man's creation was God's desire for fellowship with an intelligent, self-determined being. In the fall, this fellowship was thwarted.

C. *Enoch's attainment of holiness.* Enoch was chosen to reveal that total fellowship with God could be restored. Enoch made a personal decision to "walk with God." There was placed within his reach the power and the ability to experience an intimate, divine fellowship with God in all his holiness. In that Enoch could do it, so could others. But the question is how?

III. Enoch separated from man.

Enoch had a history of human failure and degradation to overcome. He had no example of victory among his contemporaries to follow. He was a pioneer in the truest sense.

A. *Humans are basically sinful.* Enoch had inherited a sinful nature from Adam. He was as prone to evil as his father, Jared, had been, and he lived in an environment that would encourage him to sin.

B. *Humans are destined to die.* Each generation had been placed under the condemnation of death. Enoch had gone through the grief of death time and again. He did not remain on earth long enough to see it, but his own father died under the curse of sin.

C. *Enoch was separated.* What was the secret to Enoch's experience with God? To walk in full fellowship with God, Enoch had to separate himself from the sins of humankind. He had to learn how to live apart from sin and close to God. He developed a hatred for sin and a love for God. This is the only way he could have walked with God and the only way we can walk with God today. "Come out from among them, and be ye separate," saith the Lord, "and touch not the unclean thing; and I will receive you" (2 Cor. 6:17). God chose Enoch to show humankind the end result of a person totally surrendered to him.

IV. Enoch translated by God.

God had a unique experience reserved for Enoch. Enoch had to meet certain conditions before he could receive this very special blessing. What was God's basic requirement for Enoch?

A. *Enoch was a man of faith (cf. Heb. 11:5).* God required Enoch to be a man of superior faith. It is impossible for any person to experience the divine presence of God apart from faith. Enoch's faith allowed him to communicate with God.

B. *Enoch was received by God.* God rejoiced over the faith of Enoch. The heavenly Father translated Enoch. He literally took Enoch bodily into the heavens. Enoch did not experience physical death. He did not feel the morbid results of sin in his life. His friends and family did not have to mourn over his death, but they must have had many questions when he was translated.

C. *Enoch received eternal life.* Enoch's presence with God was not a temporal experience; it was an eternal life shared by a man who dared to "walk with God."

Conclusion

The average Christian will never experience a relationship with God quite like Enoch's. As we surrender to God, our goal should not be to be translated as Enoch was. Rather, it should be to experience the awesome joy of fellowship with the holy God. A life of faith and dedication will open the way for complete, uninhibited joy with God.

WEDNESDAY EVENING, APRIL 7

Title: Confessions of a Frustrated Person

Text: "Woe is me! for I am as when they have gathered the summer fruits, as the grape gleanings of the vintage: there is no cluster to eat: my soul desired the firstripe fruit" ***(Mic. 7:1).***

Scripture Reading: Micah 7:1–7

Introduction

Many great, godly people have been candid about their deepest feelings. Jeremiah ventilated his feelings to Judah (cf. Jer. 11–20). The apostle Paul gave a spiritual autobiography in Romans 7. The fourth-century Christian preacher and theologian Augustine revealed himself in his monumental work titled *Confessions.* John Wesley shared himself in his *Journal.*

Micah was primarily a public prophet. He ministered and prophesied in the marketplace. On one rare occasion he shared his private feelings. He expressed his disappointment and distress over the moral condition of his nation by lamenting, "Woe is me!" (7:1).

Godly people have reason to be disappointed. When they see people rebelling against the Lord, they become frustrated. Let us examine closely the attitude of godly people toward rebellion against God.

I. Godly people experience great disappointment (Mic. 7:1–2).

A. *There is disappointment over the failure of God's people.* Micah likened himself to a hungry man going into a wheat field or a vineyard to glean after the reapers. The Hebrew law demanded farmers leave the remnants of their crops in the field for the poor to reap (cf. Deut. 24:19–22; Ruth 2:1–23).

The prophet went to the vineyard only to find that it had been stripped bare. No matter how diligently Micah searched, he could find no grapes or figs to eat (v. 1).

The application is obvious. God wanted Israel to be fruitful, but there was a sad lack of fruitfulness among his people. Any godly person should be disappointed when few godly works appear among a large population of people.

B. *There is a disappointment over the absence of godly people.* "The good man is perished out of the earth: and there is none upright among men" (v. 2). In the mind of Micah there seems to be only a few godly people left. Like Abraham before him (Gen. 18:23–33) and Jeremiah and Ezekiel after him (Jer. 5:1–5; Ezek. 22:30), Micah tried to find a righteous person. But the righteous seemed to be extinct.

II. Godly people experience justifiable anger (Mic. 7:2–4).

A. *Justifiable anger comes as a result of seeing extreme selfishness.* The prophet observed the self-centeredness of the people. "They all lie in wait for blood; they hunt every man his brother with a net" (v. 2). The godly had been replaced with murderers and robbers. Killing and robbing represent the ultimate in selfishness.

Murderers and robbers are not the only selfish people, however. Many people live their lives for themselves. Modern prophets should become justifiably angry over the malady of "me-ism."

B. *Justifiable anger also comes as a result of seeing masters of deceit.* Micah became angry when he observed shrewd people deceiving others. Rulers and judges, who should have maintained justice and order, had their hands out for bribes (v. 3).

The rulers used their knowledge and their position for evil

purposes: they sought bribes and exploited people. Any godly person would have to be angry at this deceit.

C. *Justifiable anger comes as a result of seeing the moral corruption of people.* Micah compared the ungodly people with briers and thorns (v. 4). Briers and thorns are figures that depict uselessness.

As the prophet looked on his society, he became angry. Godly people are indeed justified in becoming angry over futility, scarcity of godly people, and moral corruption.

III. Godly people experience deep depression (Mic. 7:5–6).

A. *There is a collapse of confidence.* Micah was depressed, for his relationships had disappointed him (v. 5). Micah felt that the closest people to him could not be trusted. Nothing causes greater negative feelings than to lose confidence in people.

B. *There is a cause for the collapse of confidence.* Micah expressed his lack of confidence and then proceeded to give the reasons for it (v. 6). The times were so evil that even the closest relationships could not be trusted. The prophet found himself deeply depressed because the closest relationships had deteriorated.

IV. Godly people experience confident trust (Mic. 7:7).

A. *Only one experience should dominate our lives.* The prophet ventilated his feelings—disappointment, anger, depression. He would not let any of these feelings dominate his life. Rather, he resolved to allow faith in the Lord to dominate. The text that began with "Woe is me!" ends with, "Therefore I will look unto the LORD" (v. 7).

B. *The experience of faith has grounds for certainty.* Look at the prophet's three affirmations:

1. I will look unto the Lord. The picture is of a watchman on the wall of a city waiting for the Lord to rescue.
2. I will wait for the God of my salvation. Here "wait" means to wait with certainty, not suspense.
3. My God will hear me. Micah knew other people might forsake him, but he was confident that the Lord would not ignore him.

Conclusion

To live a godly life will lead at times to frustration. The presence of evil and ungodly persons brings the mingling of moods. You cannot let negative moods dominate. Let faith in the Lord prevail.

SUNDAY MORNING, APRIL 11

Title: Understanding the Holy Spirit

Text: "But the Counselor, the Holy Spirit, whom the Father will send in my name, he will teach you all things, and bring to your remembrance all that I have said to you" ***(John 14:26 RSV)***.

Scripture Reading: John 14:15–18, 26

Hymns: "We Have Heard the Joyful Sound," Owens
"Saved, Saved!" Scholfield
"Amazing Grace," Newton

Offertory Prayer: Holy heavenly Father, we thank you for the opportunity to join with your children in your house for worship. We praise you for the bounty of gifts that comes from your hand. Help us to respond to world need with generous hearts and open hands. In Jesus' name we pray. Amen.

Introduction

Nothing is more satisfying than that climactic moment in a person's life when he or she discovers that God is love and that his love is expressed in his Son, Jesus Christ. The summit of all human experience is reached when, as a result of that discovery, one accepts Jesus Christ as his or her personal Savior and Lord.

It is at this point that a tragic mistake is often made. For many, the conversion experience is considered the completion of their relationship with God. The long struggle between enemy-human and pursuing-God is over. God has won; the human, the receiver of God's redeeming love, has "arrived." The battle is over.

But this is simply not true. It is a sad and disastrous delusion, for it means that such a person never sees the need to go beyond the conversion experience in his or her relationship with God. The result, then, is that the person soon regresses into the old habits and sins of his or her past life and the person's experience with Christ becomes an isolated event in the past.

What has happened? This person never established a pattern of spiritual growth. He or she was born as a babe into God's family but never began the growth process. Sadly, a major reason for these spiritual casualties in the church is that the church, which is so genuinely concerned about the rebirth of sinners, leaves them flailing in their cradles after they are born again as though helpless babies can take care of themselves.

There is an overwhelming need for consistent spiritual growth for the development of "quality Christians." The method by which God "grows" his people is the ministry of the Holy Spirit. The first of these five studies will be introductory, as we shall review the presence and ministry of the Holy Spirit from Old Testament times to the present.

I. The Holy Spirit in the Old Testament (Gen. 1:1–2).

A. *The opening words of Genesis fire the imagination.* They are full of mystery, awe, and power. In this first reference to the Holy Spirit in the Bible, we find the key to the understanding of all his works and ministry in the world. The picture Moses described is one of complete desolation.

B. *But God, in the person of his Spirit, saw potential and promise in that whirling, spinning mass of chaos and confusion.* He saw not only what it was but what it could become. Consequently, the Spirit of God *moved.* This is the Bible's first mention of action or motion. The Hebrew word translated "moved" is a word of incubation. It describes the mother hen who broods over her nest. Her body transmits life-giving warmth. So the Holy Spirit, like a great eagle, spread himself around this formless, empty world, encased in total darkness, and began to impart to that cold scene of death the warmth of life. In the midst of death, life stirred.

C. *After the universe was created the Holy Spirit did not retire.* Throughout the pages of the Old Testament we read of events in which he came upon men and women to continue to carry out God's plan and purpose. The Bible is a progressive revelation of God to man. Through the Spirit, God nurtured man as a mother nurtures a baby.

D. *Then humans were brought in God's school, with the Holy Spirit as the schoolmaster, to the threshold of the New Testament era.* It almost staggers the mind when we think of how much more the people of Malachi's day knew about God than Abraham knew. For whereas Abraham was nearly two thousand years away from the birth of Christ, the people of Malachi's day were scarcely four hundred years away from that signal event.

II. The Holy Spirit in the New Testament.

A. *With the coming of Christ we see a revelation of the Spirit of God that was never found in the Old Testament.* In Christ, where there was no trace of sin, the Holy Spirit was able to work in power and freedom. Jesus possessed the Spirit of God without measure. The total fullness of deity lived in the body of Jesus. He was God Almighty poured into a human form.

B. *Just before his death, Jesus promised the disciples that he would "send another Comforter" who would abide with them forever.* He told them that this Comforter had been with them, but that he would be in them. This came to pass on Pentecost. When the Holy Spirit came to indwell believers, his presence was permanent. The Holy Spirit did not come in as an overnight guest or as a weekend visitor, but to abide as the possessor, the owner of God's property.

C. *Three major things regarding the Holy Spirit happened on Pentecost.* First, he became the resident presence of God in the world until the end of the age. His abode became the bodies of believers, whom Paul called "temples" of the Holy Spirit (see 1 Cor. 3:16). Second, he initiated a new body called the church just as Jesus had promised. The Holy Spirit adds to this body as he draws people to Christ and they receive him as Savior. Third, at Pentecost the Holy Spirit empowered believers to witness, to share the reality of their faith with boldness and assurance.

III. The Holy Spirit today.

A. *The Holy Spirit has a ministry to unbelievers.* There is no way people can know they are lost and in need of a Savior apart from the Holy Spirit who opens their eyes to this fact. Scripture teaches that the lost person is "dead" in sin; the Holy Spirit awakens in the lost person the first recognition of God and awareness of personal sinfulness.

B. *The Holy Spirit has a ministry to believers.* He reveals God's will to them; he makes the Scriptures come alive and speak to their hearts. He works through their consciences to reveal truth and to encourage right decisions. The Holy Spirit is the constant companion, supporter, and guide of Christians.

The Holy Spirit also constantly reveals to believers more and more about God, his love, his purpose for the human race, and his purpose in believers' lives. He refines, teaches, encourages, and tenderly reworks.

Conclusion

What have we learned about the Holy Spirit? He is the divine mover. He is the agent in the Godhead who simultaneously moves a holy, all-powerful God toward sinful humans and sinful humans toward God. In the indescribable glory of this miracle, the Holy Spirit brings about the new birth. Just as he moved over the angry, chaotic waters of a spinning world of dead matter and brought forth life, so he moves over sinners who are "dead in trespasses and sins." Then he continues; he works with God's people to the end of the age.

SUNDAY EVENING, APRIL 11

Title: Lot: From Sodom to Salt

Text: "Lot dwelt among the cities of the valley and moved his tent as far as Sodom" ***(Gen. 13:12 RSV).***

Scripture Reading: 2 Peter 2:4–10

Introduction

The story of Lot is arresting. When his name is mentioned, we immediately think of his wife—the pillar of salt. This story could have been quite different. The writer of the epistle of Peter designates Lot as a righteous man. No Old Testament character had more unfulfilled potential than Lot. He allowed the opportunity of spiritual greatness to pass him by in small, near-insignificant doses. There are multitudes in the Christian churches of today that imitate Lot's life.

I. The potential of Lot.

All people are not born with equal opportunities. Some have more advantages than others by nature of their family's spiritual, economic, and/or social background. In many respects, Lot was born and reared with a silver spoon in his mouth as far as economic and spiritual opportunities were concerned.

A. *A nephew of Abraham.* Abraham is recognized as one of the greatest men in the Old Testament. God gave Abraham great promises and privileges. The close members of Abraham's family profited by the spiritual overflow. Lot was one of these so blessed. He held a unique position with Abraham; Abraham was without a male heir for a major portion of his life, and Lot was without parents during a substantial part of the time he was with Abraham. Consequently, Lot was drawn extremely close to Abraham in a near parent-child relationship.

B. *A companion of Abraham.* Abraham took Lot with him as he left his father's native land. Lot also shared with Abraham in his Egyptian experiences. Lot received many favors through his companionship with his uncle.

C. *The religion of Abraham.* Lot was a fellow believer in Jehovah God. His faith was centered in the God who made a covenant with Abraham.

D. *Numerous factors of life greatly favored Lot.* He had an excellent family background. He was a constant companion of a righteous man. He had a worship experience acceptable to God. He went to Bethel with Abraham. With all of these advantages, how did his life become so unproductive?

II. The fall of Lot.

We never like to recall the failures of others, but we can learn much by seeking to understand what happened in cases such as Lot's. We see stages of failure in the life of this man.

A. *Lot looked toward Sodom.* The city of Sodom was a place of blatant sinfulness. Righteous people avoided the place. Yet when Lot and Abraham had to separate their herds because of strife, the plains surrounding Sodom were very appealing to Lot. A fleshly desire aimed him in a downward direction.

B. *Lot camped toward Sodom.* Lot did not immediately invest his time and energy in the wicked city of Sodom. He camped nearby with his family and herds until he adjusted to the cultural shock of Sodom.

C. *Lot lived in Sodom.* Finally, Lot and his family were no longer content to camp near Sodom. They moved into the city and became part of that horrible society.

III. The agony of Lot.

Lot's mind and heart faced a constant bombardment from Sodom. So many Christians who try to identify with the world and with Christ at the same time know the realities of Lot's agony.

A. *A contrast with the environment.* According to 2 Peter, Lot maintained a semblance of righteousness while in Sodom. Imagine the horrible conflicts he continually faced between his remembrance of the righteous God at Bethel and the obvious despicable sins of the moral gutters of Sodom.
B. *A visit by the angels of God.* The angels of God visited Lot in Sodom in an attempt to escort him away. The horror of the sin of this city was magnified by the visits of these holy ones. God intervened in a miraculous manner to preserve his witness in Sodom.
C. *A destroyed witness.* Lot became convinced of the necessity to leave Sodom. His heart yearned for his family to go with him. Because of his life of compromise, his family members mocked his efforts to get them out of Sodom. His witness before the very ones he wanted to save was nonexistent. How terribly tragic was his flaccid faith.
D. *A devastated family.* In desperation Lot and part of his family fled Sodom just prior to its destruction by God. As they fled, Lot's wife looked back toward Sodom, contrary to a command by one of the angels, and God's judgment fell upon her. She was stricken and became a pillar of salt. Lot then fled to the safety prepared for him by God.

Conclusion

Lot maintained a personal righteousness recognized by the Holy Spirit, but the tragedy is that his power and influence as a godly witness failed at a critical point. Part of his family was destroyed in Sodom—and his wife died in disobedience as they fled. From this account we learn the importance of a consistent Christian witness.

WEDNESDAY EVENING, APRIL 14

Title: The Pilgrimage of Faith

Text: "I will bear the indignation of the LORD, because I have sinned against him, until he plead my cause, and execute judgment for me; he will bring me forth to the light, and I shall behold his righteousness" ***(Mic. 7:9).***

Scripture Reading: Micah 7:8–13

Introduction

John Bunyan wrote a classic when he penned *Pilgrim's Progress.* The work is sound allegorical literature; it also contains many helpful insights about the

Christian life. One of the contributions Bunyan made was to depict the Christian life as a journey, or pilgrimage. He pictured the pilgrimage with all kinds of experiences—trials, temptations, decisions, and many other happenings.

Every person who walks humbly with the Lord (Mic. 6:8) encounters various situations along the way. Micah 7:8–13 discloses some of the experiences in the pilgrimage. Not everything that happens to the godly is good. God's people encounter both good and bad during the pilgrimage of faith.

Let us not forget our historical setting. In the eighth century BC, Micah preached to Judah. Israel fell in 722 BC to the Assyrians while Micah ministered to Judah. The Assyrians threatened Jerusalem and Judah in 701 BC. Micah told of both the good and the bad of those who walked with the Lord. Look closely at Micah's description of the pilgrimage of faith. We can identify with every turn on the journey.

I. The pilgrimage of faith is an imperfect one.

A. *Micah admitted his sins as well as the sins of the people with such phrases as "when I fall" (7:8) and "I have sinned" (v. 9).* Micah would have been the last to say that either he or Judah walked perfectly. All of the people had stumbled along the road of the pilgrimage of faith.

B. *Faith in the Lord does not preclude stumbling.* Some of the most righteous people stumbled. Abraham, the prime example of faith, told the Egyptians that Sarah was his sister rather than his wife. David, described as a man after God's own heart, committed adultery with a woman and arranged for her husband's death. Simon Peter, a trusted member of the inner circle of Jesus' disciples, denied the Lord.

As Christians travel down the road of life, they sometimes fall, but their fall does not end their journey. Those believers need to confess their sins, accept God's forgiveness, and make more progress in their pilgrimage.

God's people are not perfect. They struggle with sin and temptation every day. At times they fall. Facing sin in the ecstasy of victory or the agony of defeat happens in every Christian life.

II. The pilgrimage of faith is a troublesome one.

A. *Micah mentioned the troubles of Judah.* The expression "when I sit in darkness" (7:8) could have referred to the Sennacherib crisis in 701 BC. For Judah those were dark days. Thousands of Assyrian soldiers surrounded the city. Fear filled Jerusalem. Defeat seemed inevitable. Judah's pilgrimage of faith involved some troublesome situations.

B. *Just because a person has faith does not mean he will lead a charmed life.* Some of the most righteous persons have experienced dark days of trouble. Job furnishes an example of a righteous person suffering. He was a good man, but he lost his children, his possessions, and his health.

The road of the Christian life has many bumps. All kinds of trials come to the believer's life. The only way to master trials is to trust in the Lord. Faith can help us cope with the adversities of life.

Having looked at two negative experiences—stumbling in sin and encountering trials—we will now turn to a positive encounter along the pilgrimage of faith.

III. The pilgrimage of faith is a trusting one.

A. *Micah recalled the times when Judah trusted the Lord.* There were times in Judah's history when there was no place to turn other than to the Lord. Listen to the expressions of trust: "He will bring me forth to the light"; "I shall behold his righteousness" (Mic. 7:9). Scholars cannot agree exactly when in Judah's history Micah 7:8–13 was written. Some think Micah referred to the Sennacherib crisis when the Assyrians surrounded the city. This situation seems to fit. When Sennacherib threatened Judah, there was only one place to turn: to the Lord.

B. *Life brings many situations where trust is the only logical response.* What does it mean to trust the Lord? It means to open your life to the Lord and to place complete confidence in him to help you through a particular situation.

IV. The pilgrimage of faith is a hopeful one.

A. *Micah spoke of Jerusalem's doom and its future hope.* Jerusalem's foes rejoiced over its fall and taunted its inhabitants. "Where is the LORD thy God?" (Mic. 7:10), they asked. Though for a moment Jerusalem had fallen, Micah predicted its restoration.

B. *The hope of God's people cannot be destroyed by circumstances.* God's people always have a better day. Even when death comes, believers have hope for victory. God has prepared a glorious eternity for his people.

Conclusion

Have you started the pilgrimage with God? Open your life to the Lord. That is the meaning of faith. With faith you can be faithful in anything that comes along the journey of life.

SUNDAY MORNING, APRIL 18

Title: Recognizing the Holy Spirit

Text: "The fruit of the Spirit is love, joy, peace, patience, kindness, goodness, faithfulness, gentleness, self-control; against such there is no law" *(Gal. 5:22–23 RSV).*

Scripture Reading: Galatians 5:16–26

Hymns: "Rejoice, Ye Pure in Heart," Plumptre

"I Will Sing of My Redeemer," Bliss
"Jesus, Keep Me Near the Cross," Crosby

Offertory Prayer: Dear Father in heaven, we come recognizing that every good and perfect gift comes from you. Help us to give good gifts to you and to those about us. Help us to be generous helpers to all who are in need. Help us to share the good news of your love with a needy world through the offerings we bring today. In Jesus' name. Amen.

Introduction

Satan is a master counterfeiter. He can take a genuine experience and reproduce a facsimile that, though it may look like the real thing, will bring about the opposite results. In no area does he enjoy doing this more than in regard to teachings concerning the Holy Spirit in the life of the Christian.

Satan counterfeits in the area of spiritual maturity. Sadly, many supposedly spiritual Christians are fake. Satan produces a counterfeit that has certain trappings of Christianity but no heart for the Lord. First, these imposters maintain a "holier than thou" air, an impression that they have reached a plateau of holiness that makes them superior to other Christians. Second, they feel capable of judging others' spiritual states. Third, they remember their good works, not only to compare their good deeds with those of fellow Christians, but also to remind God that they deserve special divine considerations and concessions in return.

The result is a tragic defamation of true Christianity. It repulses the unbeliever and stymies the new believer. Therefore, the importance of recognizing the Holy Spirit is vital. Why? Believers need to understand the working of the Holy Spirit in their own lives, and unbelievers who observe Christians may understand the truth about Christianity.

I. The Holy Spirit produces Christian character.

A. *What is Christian character?* The apostle Paul tells us plainly in Galatians 5:22–23 (the fruit of the Spirit). Compressed into these nine words is not only a portrait of the life Christ lived while he was on earth, but also a description of the kind of life God would have Christians live here and now. The question is, how do we cultivate these qualities in our lives?

B. *People have tried innumerable ways to cultivate the fruit of the Spirit in their lives.* Some have entered monasteries and taken vows of poverty, hoping to become more Christlike through techniques of self-denial. Others have tried to cultivate the Spirit's fruit by engaging in a feverish whirl of "religious activity." They have driven themselves to the point of exhaustion performing good works. Certainly there is nothing wrong with doing good; but people give the devil a foothold when they keep a record of their good works. Instead of producing the Christlike character qualities Paul describes, they cultivate pride, projecting themselves as supersaints before the world.

C. *If we do not work at bringing these qualities to pass in our lives, how do they grow?* Paul calls them the "fruit" of the Spirit. Fruit grows because of an inner compulsion. It develops in believers as they are willing to say, "Father, I surrender to your Holy Spirit working within me. I will not interfere with his work in my life. As you help me, I will be as clay in the potter's hands. Let this Christian character be produced *in* me, not *by* me!"

II. The Holy Spirit produces Christian service.

A. *Genuine Christian service is a direct result of the Holy Spirit working in and through believers.* Jesus told the multitudes one day, "He that believeth on me . . . out of his belly shall flow rivers of living water" (John 7:38). John explained that Jesus was speaking of the Holy Spirit who would come to indwell believers.

B. *We could never produce "living water" and certainly not "rivers."* We, at best, can be nothing more than channels, or instruments, for this divine outflow. Our Christian service, just as our salvation, has been designed within the eternal plan and purpose of God. Paul said, "We are his workmanship, created in Christ Jesus unto good works, which God hath before ordained that we should walk in them" (Eph. 2:10). According to this Scripture, God has already planned for a very special service he would have each of us perform. Who discovers the Christian service God would have them perform? Those who present their bodies as "a living sacrifice, holy, acceptable unto God" (Rom. 12:1).

C. *Christian service is never a chore when one has allowed the Holy Spirit to direct the path of service.* It would be a delightful experience for any church if every member were yielded to the Holy Spirit in the particular area of Christian service for which God planned. If that were the case, not only would the individual be doing exactly what God wanted, but the person would be doing it in the power of God's Spirit.

III. The Holy Spirit produces understanding.

A. *Jesus said to his disciples before his crucifixion.* "I have yet many things to say unto you, but ye cannot bear them now. Howbeit when he, the Spirit of truth, is come, he will guide you into all truth" (John 16:12–15). In other words, Jesus was saying that he was going to send the Holy Spirit, who would teach us and lead us beyond the range of mere human knowledge in regard to spiritual things.

B. *When does this ministry of the Holy Spirit begin in a believer's life?* It begins at the moment of spiritual rebirth. All of us have known new Christians who seemingly have grown by leaps and bounds in their faith. We have marveled at their development, at the wisdom and understanding they seem to have achieved so soon. That is no mystery! It is simply the Holy Spirit doing his work in them because they yielded to him.

C. *The process of learning in the Christian way continues until we see Christ face-to-face.* We must never become unteachable or inflexible and unwilling to receive new understanding from God's Word. God uses teachable Christians.

IV. The Holy Spirit produces identity.

A. *Paul said, "The Spirit himself testifies with our spirit that we are God's children" (Rom. 8:16 NIV).* Christians who are consciously aware of the Holy Spirit do not doubt their salvation, for one of the Spirit's ministries is to provide constant assurance that we are God's children.

B. *Do you know who you are—not just with your mind, but with your heart?* That is the difference between a dutiful Christian life and one filled with unbounded joy.

Conclusion

Have you recognized the presence and function of the Holy Spirit in your life? He produces Christian character, which is manifested in the fruit of the Spirit; he produces Christian service, leading us to perform the good works planned for us; he teaches us the meaning and application of the great truths of the Scriptures; and he makes it possible for us to know who we are—the people of God, the sheep of his pasture, the beloved of the heavenly Father.

SUNDAY EVENING, APRIL 18

Title: Aaron: Second Fiddle to Greatness

Text: "Then the anger of the LORD was kindled against Moses and he said, 'Is there not Aaron, your brother, the Levite? I know that he can speak well'" ***(Ex. 4:14 RSV).***

Scripture Reading: Exodus 4:14–16

Introduction

Everyone wants to be successful. It is very easy to have a good spirit when you are in first place. A type of humility may come rather freely when the laurels of victory are being worn, but real character is developed when a person is in second place or even lower.

Much is written and preached about Moses, the great leader of Israel, but the average Christian probably identifies more with Aaron who played a subordinate role to Moses. Let us see what we can learn from him.

I. Aaron—the natural healer.

In comparing the potentials of Aaron and Moses, one would probably select Aaron as the brother most likely to succeed. He had a number of natural qualities that gave him very distinct advantages over Moses.

A. *The meaning of the names.* Aaron was given a name meaning "rich," "fluent," or "enlightened." His name revealed a natural ability for leadership. Moses was given a name meaning "drawn out," "one who is born." His name was associated with an incident related to his birth rather than to his character.

B. *Aaron was the oldest son.* Since Aaron was three years older than Moses, it would be natural for him to be the leader. He would find additional favors with his father. The privilege of inheritance would be his rather than Moses'.

C. *Aaron was the fourth generation from Levi.* As the oldest son, Aaron would be expected to bear the family name and glory. He inherited the natural honor of the family tradition and religion. It is not a light matter that he had religious responsibilities passed down to him from the great Levi.

D. *Aaron had a full-family identification.* Aaron was identified entirely with his natural mother and father. There were no legal, national, or personal entanglements regarding his lineage. This was not so with Moses; Moses was identified as the son of Pharaoh's daughter. He was somewhat alienated from his natural family.

E. *Aaron was more talented than Moses.* Moses was placed in a high position of leadership early in his life because of his role as the son of Pharaoh's daughter. When Aaron and Moses are compared, however, Aaron immediately emerges as the more talented of the two. Aaron was chosen as the spokesman for Moses because of Moses' weakness in communication.

II. The call of Moses.

God did not choose the brother with the greatest talent. He chose the one he could best use. There were more problems to overcome through the selection of Moses rather than Aaron, but God made his choice.

A. *The burning bush.* Moses had fled Egypt after murdering someone. God revealed his will to Moses by speaking to him from a burning bush that was not consumed. Moses hesitantly yielded himself to God's service.

B. *The source of authority.* The faltering Moses exhibited all of his insecurities before the Lord. God proclaimed to Moses that he was not to depend on himself, but upon God: "God said unto Moses, I AM THAT I AM: and he said, Thus shalt thou say unto the children of Israel, I AM, hath sent me unto you" (Ex. 3:14).

C. *The appointment of an aid.* Moses refused to accept completely God's call to deliver Israel. He could only think of his personal shortcomings. God chose an individual of great personal talent to serve as Moses' aid. "The anger of the LORD was kindled against Moses, and he said, Is not Aaron the Levite thy brother? I know that he can speak well. And also, behold, he cometh forth to meet thee: and when he seeketh thee, he will be glad in his heart" (Ex. 4:14). Not only would Aaron be a good assistant to Moses, he would also have a good attitude.

III. The ministry of Aaron.

The first five books of the Old Testament center around the activities of Moses, but the ministry of Aaron cannot be neglected. Aaron had his good points and his weak points. When he was strong he was a great support to Moses. When he was weak (e.g., the golden calf episode) he brought out a godliness and strength in Moses that would not have been seen otherwise.

A. *Aaron the spokesman.* God had appointed Aaron to be the spokesman for Moses. It is probably correct to understand that in most places where it is stated that "Moses spake," Aaron was the actual mouthpiece used of God.

B. *Aaron the miracle worker.* Moses had Aaron cast down his rod before Pharaoh. As he did this it became a serpent. Aaron's rod became associated with awesome powers lent to Moses by God.

C. *Aaron the supportive minister.* In a battle between the children of Israel and the Amalekites, Moses was to serve as an inspiration to the warriors of Israel against the enemy (Ex. 17). Moses stood on the rock of Horeb. When he held his hands up over his head, Israel was victorious over Amalek. But as Moses grew tired, he lowered his arms, and Israel suffered defeat. Observing this, Aaron and Hur held up the weakened arms of Moses until Israel secured the battle in victory.

D. *Aaron the high priest.* God established a system through which Israel might approach God. It was the Levitical system of sacrifice and worship. He had Moses select Aaron to be the first high priest of the Levitical means of worship. Aaron carried this task out with great distinction before God.

Conclusion

Aaron had many faults in his ministry that led to great destruction. He created a golden calf for the Israelites to worship (Ex. 32); he rebelled against the leadership of Moses (Num. 12); and he joined Moses in sinning regarding the striking of the rock (Num. 20); but God used him in a great way despite his failures.

The lesson to be learned from the life of Aaron is that it is better to be "second fiddle to greatness" than to be "first in failure." Aaron realized this. His position required dedication to God, perseverance, faith, and humility.

Most of us are in second place or lower! Are we developing the character qualities necessary to serve God in this capacity?

Wednesday Evening, April 21

Title: Lord, Listen to Your Prophet Praying

Text: "Feed thy people with thy rod, the flock of thine heritage, which dwell solitarily in the wood, in the midst of Carmel: let them feed in Bashan and Gilead, as in the days of old" ***(Mic. 7:14).***

Scripture Reading: Micah 7:14–20

Introduction

Henry Ward Beecher once visited with Abraham Lincoln. After they exchanged pleasantries, President Lincoln called Beecher into a room away from people and requested prayer. Lincoln wanted Beecher to pray for him as a leader and for the people of his torn nation.

Still today there is a great need for people to engage in intercessory prayer. Micah interceded in prayer for Judah's deliverance from their enemies. He also asked God to guide Judah. Micah prayed for his nation.

Micah's prayer for Judah can help us learn to pray for other people. As we study Micah's prayer, we will see the times when petitions are needed.

I. Petitions are necessary for people's needs to be met (Mic. 7:14–15).

A. *Micah did not pray for the luxuries of Judah; he prayed for their necessities.*

1. Judah needed divine leadership. Micah prayed for that guidance: "Feed thy people with thy rod, the flock of thine heritage" (v. 14). Judah's history proved that they needed a leader.
2. Judah also needed to return to their former glory (vv. 14–15). Judah's former glory reflected the nature and character of God. Micah prayed for those days again.

B. *God's people need to pray for the necessities of life to be met.*

1. Jesus taught in his model prayer to petition for the necessities of life—food, the will of God, and deliverance from evil.
2. The biblical concept of prayer is to ask for necessities. God is interested in our essentials, not our luxuries.

II. Petitions are necessary for God's name to be honored (Mic. 7:16–17).

A. *Micah prayed for Judah to be restored to their former days.*

1. For Judah to be restored to their former days, their enemies had to be eliminated. Listen to Micah's prophecy about Judah's enemies: "The nations shall see and be confounded at their might: they shall lay their hand upon their mouth, their ears shall be deaf. They shall lick the dust like a serpent, they shall move out of their holes like worms of the earth" (vv. 16–17). The humiliation of Judah's enemies would mean the exultation of Judah.

2. For Judah to be restored to the glory of former days, she would have to reverence God. "They shall be afraid of the LORD our God, and shall fear because of thee" (v. 17). Strange as it may seem to us, Micah's concept of Judah's enemies meant that God would be considered the stronger of the gods. The name of the Lord would be held in great honor.

B. *God's people need to pray so that God's name will be honored.*

1. Jesus taught in his model prayer, "Hallowed be thy name" (Matt. 6:9). The Lord wanted people to recognize the power and the holiness of the sovereign God to whom they prayed.
2. One of the great opportunities of prayer is to adore and praise the Lord.

III. Petitions are necessary for sins to be forgiven (Mic. 7:18–20).

A. *Micah interceded to God for Judah's sins to be forgiven.*

1. Micah had a concept of the greatness of God. Remember that Micah's name meant "Who is like Yahweh?" Listen to how he speaks of the Lord. "Who is a God like unto thee . . ?" (v. 18).
2. Look closely at what Micah felt God would do for Judah (vv. 18–20): pardon iniquity, pass over transgression, not retain anger, delight in love, exercise compassion, put iniquities underfoot, and cast sins into the depths of the sea.

B. *God's people need to engage in petition for the forgiveness of sins.*

1. Jesus taught in his model prayer, "Forgive us our debts, as we forgive our debtors" (Matt. 6:12). Jesus disclosed the character of the heavenly Father as extremely gracious toward his erring children.
2. One of the necessary components of our prayer is to seek God's forgiveness for our sins.

Conclusion

Do you want to be more effective in your prayer life? If you do, listen to Micah, who prayed earnestly to the Lord. We can learn a lot from him.

SUNDAY MORNING, APRIL 25

Title: Cooperating with the Holy Spirit

Text: "Nevertheless I tell you the truth: it is to your advantage that I go away, for if I go not away, the Counselor will not come to you; but if I go, I will send him to you" ***(John 16:7 RSV).***

Scripture Reading: John 16:4–11

Hymns: "Holy, Holy, Holy," Heber
"Breathe on Me," Hatch
"Let Others See Jesus in You," McKinney

Offertory Prayer: Father in heaven, your Word teaches us that you give good gifts to your children. Thank you for the abundance of your grace and mercy to us. Help us to respond to others with an attitude of generosity that will reflect your generosity toward us. In Jesus' name we pray. Amen.

Introduction

One of the subtle insinuations about God that Satan has whispered throughout history is not that God does not exist, but that he is so great, so majestic, so powerful, and therefore so removed from lowly humans that there is no way he can be concerned with individual human beings. Satan's ultimate purpose in doing this is to convince us that we are the masters of our fate and the captains of our souls, that eventually we will be able to manipulate and control our destinies based on our own standards of right and wrong.

What this thinking does within an individual is to strike a death blow at the reality of the Holy Spirit—that member of the Godhead who deals personally and intimately with us. It is all right if one believes in a great, unapproachable creator or even in the historical Jesus who lived two thousand years ago, leaving the world some beautiful rules to live by. But the possibility that God would deal with individuals through the Holy Spirit is utterly preposterous to the natural person.

Why is this? Because Satan knows that when we cooperate with the Holy Spirit, there is established between us and God a relationship that is so glorious that it transcends all other relationships and experiences we may have. As we continue to focus on our theme, "Growing Quality Christians," we will examine what happens when a person cooperates with the Holy Spirit in his varied ministries in the world.

I. The ministry of the Holy Spirit to unbelievers.

A. *He convinces unbelievers of sin.* Jesus said, "And when he [the Holy Spirit] is come, he will reprove the world of sin . . . , because they believe not on me" (John 16:8–9). Note the singular word for "sin." The one sin in the life of the believer that most concerns God is unbelief. What does it mean to "believe on Jesus"? It means not only to agree intellectually with the Scripture that he lived, died, and rose again; it means to accept the "cure" he provided for humankind's sin in his death on the cross.

B. *He reveals to unbelievers what true righteousness is.* It is natural that independent, proud people believe that they can make themselves good by doing good deeds, by being lawful, by being kind to their neighbors, and so forth. But as good and commendable as these acts are, they are not good enough for God. The Scriptures declare, "All our righteousnesses are as filthy rags" (Isa. 64:6). God wants to give us the true righteousness of his Son. Paul calls it the "mind of Christ" (1 Cor. 2:16), the "Spirit of Christ" (Rom. 8:9), and "Christ in you, the hope of glory" (Col. 1:27).

C. *He declares to unbelievers the truth about judgment.* Jesus said, "The prince of this world is judged" (John 16:11). He meant that the forces of evil—personified in Satan—have been defeated because of Christ's death on the cross. It is not necessary for unbelievers to beg God for forgiveness, but rather to accept that God has already done it by sending his Son to die on the cross as full payment for people's sin debt. When individuals believe, they accept from God the receipt that declares the penalty for their sin of unbelief has been "paid in full." When people believe and receive Christ as Savior, they will never have to face judgment for the sin of unbelief; it is forever removed from God's attention.

II. The ministry of the Holy Spirit to believers.

A. *The Holy Spirit presides at a birth experience.* When one responds to the threefold ministry of the Holy Spirit to unbelievers, the experience of salvation takes place. Up to this point the Holy Spirit has been on the outside; but instantly upon the response of the unbeliever, he performs the miracle of the new birth. Then, because one has responded to the Holy Spirit in his initial ministry of convicting of sin and bringing to pass the new birth, three other ministries take place simultaneously upon conversion.

B. *The Holy Spirit baptizes.* Paul said, "For by one Spirit are we all baptized into one body, whether we be Jews or Gentiles, whether we be bond or free; and have been all made to drink into one Spirit" (1 Cor. 12:13). What is this "baptism of the Holy Spirit?" It is the act whereby, at the moment of one's conversion, the Holy Spirit places the believer into the body of Christ, the universal family of all believers in the Lord Jesus.

C. *The Holy Spirit seals.* "And grieve not the Holy Spirit of God, whereby ye are sealed unto the day of redemption" (Eph. 4:30). Here is more evidence of the way in which God protects his property. Not only does he "fuse" us into his family immediately upon our salvation, but he also "seals" us with his Spirit. That is, his presence within us is the divine mark of ownership. It is the heavenly brand stamped indelibly on every Christian. We are told that no cattle brand is so perfect that it cannot be altered, casting doubt on the rightful owner's claim. But not so with the brand God places on those who are his! Jesus said that the Good Shepherd knows his sheep and calls them by name. This seal God places upon us is to hold inviolably until the day of redemption when God comes to take unto himself those who are his "purchased possessions[s]" (Eph. 1:14).

D. *The Holy Spirit fills.* Again Paul said, "Be not drunk with wine . . . but be filled with the Spirit" (Eph. 5:18). This filling is not a one-time experience; it is continual. Literally, the word of Paul is, "Be *kept filled* with the Spirit." As we begin each day not knowing what awaits us with the unfolding of the hours, we should ask for a fresh filling of God's Spirit, a renewed awareness of his presence within us. We do not have to beg God for this. Jesus told his disciples that just as an earthly father in his imperfection is eager to "give good gifts" to his children, so the heavenly Father is eager to give the Holy Spirit to those who ask him.

Conclusion

When individuals cooperate with the Holy Spirit, they are brought to an awareness of their lostness, their sin, and God's provision for their salvation. They become members of the family of God as a result of the ministry of the Holy Spirit. They are baptized into God's family, sealed with God's mark of ownership, and filled with the Holy Spirit, who gives them power to resist temptation to sin and to live victorious Christian lives.

SUNDAY EVENING, APRIL 25

Title: Moses: The Burning Bush
Text: "And Moses said, 'I will turn aside and see this great sight, why the bush is not burnt'" ***(Ex. 3:3 RSV).***
Scripture Reading: Exodus 3:1–6

Introduction

When God has a big task to accomplish, he does not necessarily choose a great person. He simply takes a person who will become available to him for the task to be performed. In today's Scripture the task was to liberate God's people from Egypt and lead them to the Promised Land. Moses was the man God selected. Moses was not favored by his own people, and he did not have an abundance of talent, yet God wanted him, for he knew Moses could be used.

I. The man—his trials.

Moses had a rather dubious background when God selected him. Note the many obstacles God willingly overcame to select him as a choice servant for a particular task.

A. *Moses' heritage was tried.* Moses had been born of Hebrew parentage. He was adopted by Pharaoh's daughter when she found him floating in the river in a basket as his Hebrew mother's means of protecting him from the pharaoh's decree to kill all Hebrew male newborns. Thus, he was eventually raised in the household of the pharaoh. His natural and adopted heritages conflicted in social, economic, and spiritual qualities. His early life was scarred with conflicts.

B. *Moses' heart was tired.* Though Moses was an adopted Egyptian, his heart would never let him forsake his natural heritage as a Hebrew.

It was inevitable that these two worlds would find a major battlefield in his heart. He chose to favor his heart over his mind at a critical point of conflict.

C. *Moses' status was tried.* Moses interceded in an incident between an Egyptian and a Hebrew, killing the Egyptian. Overnight he became a fugitive from the justice system of Egypt and an alien from the hearts of the Hebrews. Moses had betrayed the Egyptians' trust and had broken the Hebrews' code of ethics. He then fled from an organized society. But God still wanted him!

II. The meaning—the burning bush.

God spoke to Moses in a wonderfully strange way. In an isolated stretch of desert, God communicated with Moses out of a fiery bush that was miraculously spared. Moses took note. Three significant messages were given to him from this bush.

A. *An awesome presence.* Moses was made aware of the angel of the Lord being present in the bush. God's call to a great task is always accompanied by a realization of his divine presence (cf. Paul's experience on the Damascus road). The present-day believer experiences this through the Holy Spirit.

B. *A staying power.* Moses' attention was drawn to the bush by the presence of the angel and the flaming fire, but he was amazed that the bush was not consumed by the fire. This abnormal phenomenon conveyed the message of God's miraculous power to preserve through all kinds of adversities. Also, his immutable nature of remaining unchanged may be reflected in this incident.

C. *A gracious power.* God's message to Moses revealed that he was a God of overwhelming grace. Though his justice had been experienced by those who disobeyed him, it could not overshadow his love for his chosen people. God's greatest message is always his love and grace.

III. The ministry of Moses—"Go."

God's revelation to Moses was not just to give him an awareness of his presence; God had a mission for Moses.

A. *The mission was surrounded by holiness.* God immediately made Moses aware that the ground on which he stood was "holy ground." This is a fact that is true in the life of every servant directly called of God. People do not select the ministry as a vocation. Rather, they are selected by God for the ministry.

B. *The mission was one of pathos (feeling).* God had felt the oppression of his downtrodden people. He knew of all of the injustices and felt the hurt of his people. This is always true of our holy God.

C. *The message was one of promise.* God's challenge was for Moses to lead the Hebrews out of Egyptian bondage into the land promised to their father Abraham. God's promises are as strong and as sure as his own character.

D. *The message was one of authority.* Moses anticipated great problems in this projected task. He could not do it because of his outlaw status within Egypt. God assured him that the ministry was God's—not Moses'! Therefore, it would be accomplished in his authority. Moses would say, "I Am hath sent me unto you."

Conclusion

God still calls for servants to lead sinners out of the life of bondage. The excuses of Moses are still utilized by those who are called. But by the authority of God, his present-day servants are able to go forth in victory.

Wednesday Evening, April 28

Title: Incomparable Forgiveness

Text: "Who is a God like unto thee, that pardoneth iniquity, and passeth by the transgression of the remnant of his heritage? he retaineth not his anger for ever, because he delighteth in mercy" ***(Mic. 7:18).***

Scripture Reading: Micah 7:18–20

Introduction

Think for a moment about gifts you have received. Probably many different kinds of gifts come to mind. You may have received clothes, sporting equipment, books, novelties, and various other items.

Now think for a moment about the great gifts of God. He has given us forests, sunny days, rain, wind, life itself—the list could be endless. Recently I began to think about some of God's gifts to me. One gift kept coming back to my mind—the gift of forgiveness. Even though I rebelled against the Lord, he forgave and restored me. Such a gift is incomparable.

I. God's forgiveness is incomparable because of the enormity of human guilt.

To see the greatness of God's forgiveness one needs to see how far human beings have gone away from the Lord. Seeing the depths of human depravity causes amazement over God's forgiveness. Look at the words that depict human guilt.

A. *People are guilty of iniquity.* The Hebrew word translated "iniquity" in Micah 7:18 means "to twist something that is straight and make it crooked." Human beings have taken the straightness of God's laws and twisted them.

B. *People are guilty of sins.* The Hebrew word for "sins" in Micah 7:19 means "to miss a target." God has an ideal intention for every life. No one has ever lived up to God's intention. Everyone sins or falls short.

C. *People are also guilty of transgression.* The Hebrew word for "transgression" used in Micah 7:18 means "to rebel deliberately." God has disclosed his way to human beings, and every person has chosen to rebel against God's way.

II. God's forgiveness is incomparable because of the greatness of his character.

To see the greatness of God's forgiveness, one needs to learn about his nature. Micah demonstrates an exalted concept of God throughout his prophecy. In Micah 7:18–20 we can see various traits of the character of Yahweh.

A. *The forgiving God has an incomparable character.* Micah asks, "Who is a God like unto thee . . ?" (7:18). The sole ground of forgiveness rests on the noble character of God. The pagans conceived of their gods as deities wanting revenge or judgment. The idols had to be placated. Our true and sovereign God wants to give mercy and love. There is no one like God.

B. *The forgiving God has great grace.* Nothing any human being can do will secure God's acceptance. The sole ground of forgiveness rests in the essence of God's character as one who forgives, forgets, and offers a new beginning.

C. *The forgiving God has great constancy.* God acts the way he always acted. He forgave Abraham and Jacob, and hundreds of years later he forgave Judah. Now hundreds of years after Judah, God has not changed his mind about wayward human beings; he continuously desires to forgive.

III. God's forgiveness is incomparable because of his solution to sin's guilt.

The greatness of God's forgiveness comes to light when we see the enormity of human guilt and the majesty of God's character. Yet take a look at God's solution to the sinner's guilt. From his action we get a glimpse of how seriously God takes sin.

A. *God pardons iniquity and passes over transgression.* Read Micah 7:18 again. The word "pardoneth" means "to lift up and to bear away." It conveys the picture of God taking away the guilt of our sins. The expression "passeth by" means that God ignores the reality of sin once it has been forgiven.

B. *God does not retain his anger, and he delights in steadfast love.* The verb translated "retaineth" means "to hold with your hands." This means that God does not continually hold our sins over us when he forgives us. For God to have steadfast love means that he keeps the commitment he made with his people.

C. *God treads our iniquities underfoot and casts our sins into the depths of the sea.* These expressions describe enemies to be subdued and banished from the earth. God works to get sin completely out of our lives.

Conclusion

Now think about a great gift. Isn't the greatest gift the gift of God's forgiveness? Rejoice and thank him for forgiving you.

Suggested Preaching Program for the Month of

May

■ Sunday Mornings

On the first Sunday of the month, complete the series "Growing Quality Christians." From Mother's Day through the end of June, use a series called "Strengthening the Family with Biblical Truths," which investigates various aspects of the family living in the light of the Holy Scriptures. The family is the fundamental institution in our society. The church can be no stronger than the families that constitute its membership.

■ Sunday Evenings

A series called "Job's Questions and Jesus' Answers" is suggested for Sunday evenings. The questions are taken from Job's depth of experience in his suffering.

■ Wednesday Evenings

The Psalms are often water to a thirsty soul because of their ingenuous approach to God. Glean the Psalms for your midweek messages in a series titled "Mining Spiritual Truths from the Psalms."

Sunday Morning, May 2

Title: Yielding to the Holy Spirit

Text: "Yield yourselves to God as men who have been brought from death to life, and your members to God as instruments of rightousness" ***(Rom. 6:13 RSV).***

Scripture Reading: Romans 6:14–18; 1 Thessalonians 5:19

Hymns: "We Praise Thee, O God," Mackay
"The Haven of Rest," Gilmour
"Holy Spirit, Faithful Guide," Wells

Offertory Prayer: Just as our Lord came to serve, to give, and to minister, we too have opportunities to serve, give, and minister. We thank you, heavenly Father, for the privilege of being used in rendering ministries of mercy and helpfulness to others. Accept our gifts and bless them to the end that they shall be expressions of your love to those in need. In Jesus' name. Amen.

Introduction

The key word to open the door to the understanding of God's very best for us is *yield.* To yield means "to give up, to surrender, to give place to."

What then is God's very best for us? It is simply the discovery of God's plan and purpose for our lives, beginning here and now and continuing throughout eternity. We do not arrive at this magnificent discovery as a result of the efforts of human ingenuity. Nor is there any magic formula we can apply nor any mystic experience that will instantly open up to us every detail of God's plan and purpose for our lives. Rather, God unfolds his will for us as we yield ourselves to his Holy Spirit within us.

Therefore, let us explore what is involved in this business of yielding to the Holy Spirit within us.

I. The proposition.

A. *What is involved in this proposition God makes to us?* "I beseech you therefore, brethren, by the mercies of God, that ye present your bodies a living sacrifice, holy, acceptable unto God, which is your reasonable service. And be not conformed to this world: but be ye transformed by the renewing of your mind, that ye may prove what is that good, and acceptable, and perfect will of God" (Rom. 12:1–2). "I beseech you," Paul says. It is not a command, but a pleading for believers to live the kind of lives that will mark them as children of God. This is not something we must do to be saved. Rather, it is something we should want to do because we are saved. It must be this way, for we truly yield ourselves only to a person or principle we love and have the deepest respect for. Yielding is not an act of the intellect exclusively; it is an expression of the heart, the soul, the very essence of a person's being.

B. *Paul indicates two areas that should be affected by this "yielding."* First, he calls for a dedication of the whole body as a living sacrifice to God. This is a dedication, not a consecration. Consecration is an act of God whereby he takes up that which has been dedicated to him and uses it according to his will. We dedicate ourselves to whatever God may choose for us. We do not presume to tell him what to do with our lives. That Paul singles out the body suggests that we are not compartmentalized into spiritual and physical insofar as our dedication to God is concerned. Thus, when we wholly dedicate ourselves to God, the Lord Jesus will be seen in everything we do. It will be obvious at home, in our social life, at work, at play, at school—wherever we are and in whatever we do.

C. *Second, Paul tells us how this dedication of our bodies is maintained.* "Be ye transformed by the renewing of your mind[s]." How are our minds renewed? It happens as Christ moves in and thinks through us. Charles Sheldon's classic, *In His Steps,* asserts this premise. A whole congregation of people determined not to do anything until they asked themselves, "What would Jesus do?" This, then, is what is involved in the proposition God had made to us in regard to yielding ourselves to his Spirit within us.

II. The pattern.

A. *In no uncertain terms, God sets down for us the "game rules."* One of the many evidences of perfection in the life of Jesus was his complete dedication to the will of his heavenly Father. Jesus' human body was the vehicle by which he carried out his Father's will while he was on earth. Likewise, the believer should view his body as the vehicle God has provided for him to carry out the will of his heavenly Father.

B. *But Jesus was the perfect Son of God.* There was no sin in him, no evil that would cause him to desire to respond to the unregenerate world around him. Our problem is that we are sinners by nature. It is "natural" for us to do that which is contrary to the will of God. So then, is it a hopeless case for us? Paul said, "Let this mind be in you which was also in Christ Jesus" (Phil. 2:5). The first word in this statement turns on the light for us: the little word "let" has compressed within it the whole Bible teaching concerning our responsibility toward letting Christ be seen in our daily lives. We cannot produce the Christian life in ourselves; we can only "let" it be done by the Holy Spirit. So the issue is not our dogged determination to do something ourselves; it is our willingness to let God do it through us by yielding to his Spirit within us.

C. *Because Jesus was dedicated to his Father's will, three things happened in his life.*

1. Jesus was willing to *go* where his Father chose. To do the will of his Father, Jesus came into this world on a mission of mercy. Are we willing to do the same?
2. Christ was willing to *be* whatever his Father chose him to be. He laid aside the glory he had with the Father in heaven to come to earth; he was willing to be rejected, humiliated, and crucified. That was the Father's will for him. How about us?
3. Jesus was willing to *do* whatever his Father chose for him to do. He became obedient unto death. Is our faith strong enough to yield to God's love in this way?

D. *Where does this leave us since we are not perfect like Jesus?* Again, Paul explains: "For God is at work in you, both to will and to work for his good pleasure" (Phil. 2:13 RSV). In other words, God tells us what he wants us to do; then by his Spirit within us, as we yield to that Spirit, he does it!

III. The purpose.

A. *Why are we to yield to the Holy Spirit?* What will such a yielding bring to pass in our lives? We will understand more fully, every day that we live, the will of God for our lives. First, God will lead us by his Spirit if we are willing to do what he chooses for us to do. Someone has said, "God will speak loudly enough for a willing soul to hear." It is one thing to conceive some great, vague will that God may have for our lives; it is quite another thing to say, "Lord, what would you have me to do *today*, in the midst of this humdrum, monotonous grind in which I live?"

B. *God's leading will always be according to the Scriptures.* It is never true with God that the end justifies the means. There is no such thing as sacrificing a minor principle to accomplish an ultimate goal.

C. *This divine leadership is provided by the Holy Spirit who indwells the Christian.* When we yield ourselves to God, we increasingly come to have "the mind of Christ." We start to think as God thinks. He is able not only to convince us of what is wrong, but also to give us a clear understanding of what is right.

Conclusion

Sometimes we get the idea that to sacrifice involves pain, and therefore the Christian who has sacrificed to yield himself or herself to do the will of God must be a sad-faced, morbid person. On the contrary, to sacrifice means simply to do another's will. There may be some pain along the way, to be sure; but the prevailing atmosphere will be that of joy, and the blessing of God in one's life will be that of peace.

SUNDAY EVENING, MAY 2

Title: A Man Named Job
Text: "In the land of Uz there lived a man whose name was Job. This man was blameless and upright; he feared God and shunned evil" ***(Job 1:1 NIV).***
Scripture Reading: Job 1:1–5

Introduction

What kind of mental picture do you get when someone mentions the name of Job? Most of us see a poor man, his body covered with painful boils, sitting dejectedly but stoically on a heap of ashes—a quivering mass of suffering humanity. To add to our pathetic depiction of Job, we see him as the plaything of a sadistic Satan. Perhaps most disconcerting is that his suffering was "permitted by God."

Bible scholars through the ages have made a multitude of conclusions about Job himself and about the purpose of the book in general. But to leave this book and this man Job in the ancient setting is to rob them of the value and purpose God intended. In fact, most of our Old Testament is without value to us until it is interpreted in the light of New Testament revelation.

This is true particularly of the book of Job. To study this book apart from the New Testament would be the most depressing and futile exercise we could undertake, for standing by itself, it remains the record of an answered agony. There is no answer to Job until we find it in Jesus.

In his sovereign wisdom, God allowed Satan to unleash on Job some inconceivably horrible "stress tests." The book of Job is a blow-by-blow account of how Job fared in this supernatural wind tunnel. There were fearful moments when he came frighteningly close to the brink of utter despair. But buried deep within Job was the spark of faith that God had placed there. If that spark had been snuffed out, and if Job had given up, then the rest of us might have reason to give up when life gets too painful. But in spite of his unanswered questions and agonizing frustrations, the spark of faith not only remained in Job; in the end, it was fanned into a blaze of faith and glory.

I. The man himself (Job 1:1–3).

A. *The author of this ancient book, which may be the oldest book in the Bible, tells us that Job lived "in the land of Uz."* We know practically nothing about Uz, except that it is mentioned in the book of Genesis. Some Bible scholars believe it was located northeast of Idumea, toward the Arabian desert. Job, the focus of the story, is described with two words: "blameless" and "upright." The word translated "blameless" means "whole, complete, innocent, and sincere." He had a simple faith in God. The literal translation of the Hebrew word translated "upright" means "straight, even, just, pleasing, and agreeable." One of the highest compliments that can be paid to anyone is that he is always "straight and just" in his dealings with others. Job was also well liked. He was the kind of citizen any community would covet.

B. *The author gives us the secret behind the uprightness and sincerity of Job.* He was one who "feared God," that is, he worshiped and reverenced God. He recognized God's majesty and power and also his approachability through prayer. Job also "shunned evil." This describes Job's morality, born out of his close relationship with God.

C. *The remarkable aspect about all of the suffering Job underwent is that God ratified it!* God described Job to Satan in the same terms the author uses to describe him in these opening verses. Furthermore, God had an amazing bottom line to all of this. He said, "There is none like him in the earth" (Job 1:8). So the one hero on stage for us—front and center—was a man of integrity who had a good relationship with God and who turned down evil and temptation whenever it presented itself.

II. Reviewing the story.

Our purpose is not to do a verse-by-verse study of the book, but rather to deal with the specific issues it raises and to see how the New Testament answers them.

A. *As we watch Job, we see him from three perspectives: physical, mental, and spiritual.* All three dimensions of his being are affected. By some mystic arrangement, the divine logic of which is too transcendent for us to comprehend, God allowed Satan to bring overwhelming calamities into Job's life. The reason for these calamities is not found in the book, in spite of the fact that Job's three friends were convinced that he harbored some deep, dark wrongdoing that precipitated these tragedies.

B. *We see Job stripped of everything humans depend on.* Suddenly Job was reduced from affluence to poverty—he lost all of his material possessions. Then his children died and his health broke. His wife could no longer bear to see him in agony. In deep depression over his pain, she said, "Job, why don't you curse God and die?" (Job 2:9, author's paraphrase). She would rather Job were dead than watch him suffer.

C. *So what do we see in this picture of Job?* We see emerging a fact of human life that has always caused overwhelming perplexity: tragic and terrible suffering that is not the result of the sin of the sufferer. We see it in the little child who suffers through no fault of her own. We see it in the agony and heartbreak of parents over the sins of a wayward child. We see it in death. We see it in the poverty and suffering of millions of people in the world. So the nagging, piercing question is there: "Why do good people suffer? Why do bad things happen to good people?"

D. *In the heavenly meeting between God and Satan that resulted in Job's suffering, the issue of why Job was a righteous man was posed by Satan.* Satan accused God of building a "hedge" around Job (Job 1:10) and blessing him on every side. God did not deny this, for he had protected Job, and he had blessed him with great material wealth.

So Satan said, "Stretch out your hand and strike everything he has, and he will surely curse you to your face" (Job 1:11 NIV). That was the devil's blasphemy against humanity—he was saying that people serve God for what they can get out of him. So God said, "Very well, then, everything he has is in your hands, but on the man himself do not lay a finger" (v. 12 NIV). Thus, Job became a battleground between God and Satan, between heaven and hell.

III. Making the application.

A. *Many people do not know the ultimate meaning of the heart-wrenching experiences they may be passing through today.* What is happening may well not be because of their own sin. Yet the story of Job suggests that there is a meaning and value in every experience God allows to come to us. Satan asserted that true followers of God serve the Lord strictly because of what they can get. Job showed dramatically that this was blasphemy. Do our lives refute Satan's theory?

B. *The book of Job as a whole presents a universe in which, whatever the problems, God reigns supreme.* There is no greater book in the Bible on the ultimate sovereignty of God than the book of Job. It may not explain all of the methods God uses, but it reveals him as present and acting. Satan, the archenemy of all, wanted to prove that people serve God only for what they can take from him. But the marvel of it all is that the devil could not touch a hair on the back of a single camel that belonged to Job until he had God's permission!

Conclusion

Over the next few Sunday nights, we will study Job's arguments, frustrations, and agonies. Then we will turn to the New Testament and see Jesus, who began without any wealth and without most of the material things other people depend on. Before we are through, we will discover that Jesus answered every question Job asked and supplied every need Job revealed.

In listening to the answers to Job's questions, perhaps we can find some answers to those better questions, those "whys," that we have flung toward heaven.

Wednesday Evening, May 5

Title: The Two Ways

Text: "For the Lord knoweth the way of the righteous: but the way of the ungodly shall perish" ***(Ps. 1:6).***

Scripture Reading: Psalm 1:1–6

Introduction

In the Psalms we find our deepest thoughts expressed. Reverence for God, excitement in knowing him, and terror when we feel cut off from his presence—all of these are set forth explicitly in these hymns of ancient Israel. The first, called "the threshold psalm," sets forth two ways of life and the destinies of those who choose them.

I. Happiness of the righteous person (Ps. 1:1–3).

The Hebrew word that begins this section can be best translated, "Oh, the happinesses of" and should be read as an exclamation.

A. *The psalmist gives three pictures that describe the righteous person.* The first verse tells what he does not do; the second, what he does do; and the third, what he is like.
B. *Verse 1 contains three things the righteous person does not do.* In it, we have three groups of three in descending order. First, walketh, standeth, sitteth. Second, ungodly, sinners, scorners. Third, counsel, way, seat. The Hebrew word rendered "ungodly" is a generic term for all wrongdoing. "Sinners" are those who miss the mark in life or fall short of

a standard. The "scornful" are those who openly scoff or mock at righteousness. The righteous person does not do these things.

C. *Verse 2 tells what the righteous person does.* The "law" to the Jew meant more than the Ten Commandments or even the entire Mosaic legislation. It was the complete ongoing revelation of God to his people. To us, God's will is brought first by the written Word, the Bible; second, by the Living Word, Jesus Christ; and third by the interpretation of the Bible and Jesus through the Holy Spirit. Thus, we would not be wrong if we spoke of the righteous person as meditating day and night on God's will for his life. John Wesley said, "To find God's will is man's greatest discovery, and to do God's will is his greatest achievement."

D. *Verse 3 tells us what he is like or what he becomes through righteous living.* The picture of a tree planted by water suggests both stability and fertility. His bearing fruit in season suggests his dependability, and the nonwithering leaf suggests constant fruit bearing. Because he has inner resources, he "causes to prosper" everything he starts. He is not a quitter. With God's help, he completes what he begins.

II. Picture of the unrighteous person (Ps. 1:4–5).

Everything the psalmist said about the righteous person is untrue of the wicked one. The Hebrew reads literally, "Not so, the wicked."

A. *The metaphor of chaff and wheat is so familiar that it does not need explaining.* The wicked person's deeds evaporate, for they have no lasting value in God's economy. The words "stand in the judgment" in this context probably mean the crises and testings of this life rather than in the New Testament sense of a judgment at the last day. The unrighteous person does not have the power to cope with the problems that arise in daily living.

B. *"Nor sinners in the congregation of the righteous" suggests that ungodly people are never comfortable with those who are godly in character and dedication.* They often feel threatened and intimidated even though righteous people do not want them to feel that way.

III. The fate of each (Ps. 1:6).

God divides people into only two classes: those who please him and those who refuse him.

A. *God "knows" the first group.* Of course, in the larger sense he knows everybody, but this word suggests intimate knowledge, experiential fellowship, and divine approval. This is the Hebrew word used so often in such passages as "Adam knew his wife; and she conceived, and bare Cain" (cf. Gen. 4:1 et al.).

B. *To "perish" means to go out into nothingness.* This is the true picture of a life without God. It is rootless, fruitless, and worthless.

Conclusion

This psalm emphasizes character and righteous living. Only when we are in Christ do we have the power to lead the kind of life the psalmist promises will bring happiness.

SUNDAY MORNING, MAY 9

Title: A Picture of Mother
Text: "Who can find a virtuous woman? for her price is far above rubies" ***(Prov. 31:10).***
Scripture Reading: Proverbs 31:10–31
Hymns: "Near to the Heart of God," McAfee
"I Need Thee Every Hour," Hawks
"O God, Who to a Loyal Home," Fosdick
Offertory Prayer: Our Father, we praise you for the emphasis of this day. Only you could have thought of the idea of mothers and fathers. We celebrate the gift of our mothers on this day. Just as you have given us the gift of parents, you also have given us material gifts. Accept our tithes as thanks for all you have given us. Help us to worship you as we give. In Jesus' name. Amen.

Introduction

Nineteenth-century artist James Abbot McNeill Whistler was most famous for the oil painting of his mother. Many art critics consider Whistler's painting of his mother to be one of the world's masterpieces.

An inspired writer from Israel gave a majestic word picture of a mother. It is recorded in Proverbs 31:10–31, and it ranks as a literary masterpiece. This portrait, like Whistler's, is old-fashioned in some respects, but although fashions and lifestyles change, the beautiful inner qualities of godly women will be admired generation after generation.

Let us study this picture in Proverbs. It will help us honor our mothers and will inspire them to imitate the biblical portrait.

I. Mothers should possess the quality of companionship.

Read through the writer's literary picture of a mother. The more you read, the more you see the idea of companionship showing up in the picture.

A. *The woman has camaraderie with her husband.* In the writer's day, wives shared in domestic responsibilities with their husbands. Men worked the fields and tended the flocks; women provided clothing and food. Teamwork in all areas of life was vital to marital stability.

B. *The woman has a companionship with her children.* There is more to motherhood than just giving birth to children. God made women to be friends to their children.

II. Mothers should possess the quality of nurture.

Read Proverbs 31:10–31 again. Do you see the idea of nurture emerging? *Mother* could be a synonym for *nurture.* To nurture means the mother attends to the needs of both her husband and children.

A. *Biological capability to reproduce does not make a woman a nurturing mother.* Motherhood is not basically a biological act or a physical relationship. Many women give birth to a child or to children but never become real mothers. Some regard children as a personal accomplishment or a biological accident. Others treat children as objects—toys to be played with, dolls to be dressed, tools for manipulating a spouse, or a means to gain benefits.

B. *Nurturing a child means accepting responsibility.* Motherhood means commitment. It means assuming responsibility to help develop the life of a child. It means getting involved with children—hurting, laughing, and crying with them, and experiencing good and bad times together.

Johnny, age four, appeared one day at the door of his father's study with a forlorn-looking chick that had apparently strayed from a neighborhood brood. The father said sternly, "John take that chicken right back to its mother."

"It has no mother," Johnny replied.

The father insisted, "Well, take it back to its father then."

But Johnny protested, "It has no father either. It has nothing but an old lamp."

An electrical lamp will serve the needs of a chick. It will hatch the egg and preserve the chick until it is old enough to face life, but that is about all. Mothers can give warm beds, nutritious meals, and adequate clothing but still fail to nurture.

III. Mothers should posses the quality of godliness.

Slowly read Proverbs 31:10–31 one more time. You will see that godliness should be a quality of a good mother. "Favour is deceitful, and beauty is vain: but a woman that feareth the Lord, she shall be praised" (v. 30).

A. *Many people speak of motherhood as a qualification for sainthood, but the fact is, many mothers are far from that.* In 2 Timothy 3:6–7 Paul speaks about women who were carried away by many kinds of false doctrines. In 1 Timothy 5:11–13 and Titus 2:2–5 Paul describes women who travel from house to house spending their time in gossip and slander. Probably many, if not most, of these women were mothers, but they were not good women.

One of the saddest words written about a mother was written concerning Ahaziah, king of Judah. "He too walked in the ways of the house of Ahab, for his mother encouraged him in doing wrong" (2 Chron. 22:3 NIV).

B. *Good mothers come as a result of a relationship with the Lord.* "But a woman that feareth the LORD, she shall be praised" (Prov. 31:30). The biblical writer used the word "LORD," the name used to describe a covenant relationship. The only way to become good is by a relationship with the Lord.

Godly mothers have had good influence. Augustine, the great fourth-century preacher and theologian, was influenced by his mother, Monica. He admitted that his mother's principles and actions affected him. She prayed fervently for Augustine's conversion.

Conclusion

Look again at the biblical portrait of a mother. She is not just a nice woman. Instead, she is a companion for her husband and children. A biblical mother gives her children more than life: she nurtures by deed and demonstration. A mother can fulfill her role only through the power of the Lord in her life.

Do you resemble the mother in the biblical picture?

SUNDAY EVENING, MAY 9

Title: Is There a Go-Between?

Text: "If only there were someone to arbitrate between us, to lay his hand upon us both, someone to remove God's rod from me, so that his terror would frighten me no more" ***(Job 9:33–34 NIV).***

Scripture Reading: Job 9:29–35; 1 Timothy 2:5

Introduction

Job was a man who had admitted God to his life. They had had a marvelous relationship. Job honored God, and God blessed Job in every imaginable way. Job had everything a man could hope for.

But now, with no prior warning and no apparent rhyme or reason, Job had been stripped of everything. The life of this dignified, affluent, self-assured, good man was reduced to little more than an animal existence.

All of Job's material possessions were gone, his children were all dead, and his body was covered with painful boils. His good wife, who was all in the world he had left, was begging him to "curse God, and die" (Job 2:9), for she could no longer stand to see her beloved husband in such agony.

An animal in such a predicament would simply run away to some hiding place where he could lick his wounds and try to restore himself to health. It would never occur to the animal that what had happened to him was unjust and unfair. All that would concern him is self-preservation. He would accuse no one, nor would he try to rationalize the situation.

But humans cannot do that. Because they are made in God's image, they ask questions and cry out for answers, justice, and mercy. They shout, "Foul! Unfair!" when they think what has happened to them is not right. In agony they search for answers.

So we come tonight to the first questions Job articulated.

I. The setting in which the questions arose.

A. *We learned last week that three of Job's friends had heard about his unbelievable dilemma and had come to visit him.* We commended them for that, realizing that it is often difficult to go to the side of someone who is in the midst of some overwhelming trouble that neither they nor we can understand.

Not only did these men *come,* but they *listened* to Job for seven days, resisting the temptation to give advice. Job poured out his soul to them, venting all of the bitter, accusing frustrations within him. But there came that time when they could resist no longer, and they began giving Job their advice. They were all eloquent philosophers, literate and articulate. They had thought through what they had to say to Job. Yet as humanly rational and sensible as their words sounded to them, they did nothing to help Job.

B. *Our text tonight appears during the first cycle of speeches, or conversations, between these three men and Job.* Here Job is in the process of answering Bildad, who had just spoken. Even though these men appeared to be pompous, self-righteous theologians, they were only reflecting the accepted theology of the day. But a remarkable thing happened. As they were reciting the popular concept of God and suffering, Job dared to question their theology. Why? Because he had never been in this situation before. There had never been a reason for him to reevaluate his beliefs about God and the way he dealt with people.

C. *We may have accepted some ideas about God that have been handed down to us through the years.* Suddenly one day we may be faced with a situation our traditional theology does not satisfy. Because we may have been taught never to question, we go on hurting, frustrated and disillusioned. The result is that we limp through life with a crippled faith.

II. The reaction of Job to Bildad's advice.

A. *The essence of Bildad's speech (Job 8) is that God must be just.* When bad things happen to us, it must be because we have sinned and offended God, and he is simply making us pay for our sins. Perhaps Bildad did not enjoy saying this to Job. It would have been much easier for him and his friends to have simply excused themselves with the proper condolences and left. But they were compassionate, and in spite of their wrong understanding of the situation, they were determined to try to help Job.

B. *Job's reply was that he knew God was just, but he did not understand his suffering.* Then he asked a legal question (9:2), the paraphrase of which would be, "How can a man argue his case with God in such a way as to justify himself?" Like a man in a maze, everywhere Job turned, he found a dead end. He felt trapped. At the climax of his bitter speech, he expressed his great cry for a "go-between" (vv. 33–35).

III. The cry for a go-between.

A. *We see demonstrated here the fact that there is a breakdown between humans and the God who made them.* There is an infinite sense of distance. But in the process of a person's coming to realize his or her spiritual need and incompleteness, there is that point at which he or she cries in despair, "I need God, but God is in heaven, and I, in my sin, in my weakness, am bound to this earth. I cannot reach God, and he cannot reach me. And there is no bridge between us!"

B. *Job's words echo through the corridors of time: "There is no go-between; thus, there is no hope!"* Yet there is an answer, and it rises out of the New Testament: "For there is one God and one mediator between God and men, the man Christ Jesus, who gave himself as a ransom for all men—the testimony given in its proper time" (1 Tim. 2:5–6 NIV). A "mediator" is a "middle man" standing between a person and God.

C. *And who is this mediator?* Paul named him: "the man Christ Jesus." And why is he so ideal in the performance of this task? Because he is God, he can touch God; because he was man, he can touch man! Because he is God, he understands the divine mind; because he was man, he understands the human situation.

D. *But that is not all.* We are told that this mediator "gave himself as a ransom." It is not merely that he is both divine and human, but also by him something has been done that makes the way of approach to God possible. What separates us from God? "Your iniquities have separated you from your God; your sins have hidden his face from you, so that he will not hear" (Isa. 59:2 NIV). The amazing thing is that this go-between was willing not only to represent us before almighty God (whom we never could have approached ourselves), but he paid the ransom with his life, which God's righteous and holy law demanded.

Conclusion

In Job's cry there was more than just an appeal for justice. Job was asking for a reconciliation with God. He was thirsting for love. Job was no prophet, but his cry to God for a go-between to "lay his hand" (Job 9:33 NIV) on both God and him, was an unconscious prediction of a coming Savior. Job had faith—and it was God-given, because it was a creative faith. In Job's darkest moment, the light of his faith shone forth in spite of his utter sense of hopelessness.

WEDNESDAY EVENING, MAY 12

Title: Serve the Lord with Gladness
Text: "Kiss the Son . . . Blessed are all they that put their trust in him" ***(Ps. 2:12).***
Scripture Reading: Psalm 2:1–12

Introduction

In the empires of the ancient world, when a new ruler took over, he was almost always faced with those who wanted to upset the new order to gain power for themselves. This psalm was written against the background of the death of a powerful king. The most natural king to fit the occasion was David, but such kings as Uzziah, Hezekiah, and Josiah could also qualify, since they kept the neighboring nations in subjection and collected revenues from them. Many aspects of this psalm also find ultimate fulfillment in Jesus Christ, the Messiah and our Savior. The song has four stanzas and was, no doubt, sung often by worshipers, perhaps especially at the installation of each new king. Four voices are heard, one in each stanza.

I. A word from the rebelling nations (Ps. 2:1–3).

A. *The poet begins with a question addressed to the rebels.* Why have they conspired to attempt that which is impossible?

B. *They cannot replace the one whom God has chosen, and they should have wisdom enough to realize their efforts are futile.* Their scheme to free themselves from this dominion is doomed.

II. A word from God himself (Ps. 2:4–6).

A. *The psalmist gave a graphic picture of the Almighty speaking sarcastically to the coalition formed against his chosen one.* He has utter contempt for them and lets them know how foolish they are to attempt to overthrow his plans.

B. *The word "wrath" in verse 4 comes from a Hebrew verb that means "to breathe through the nose," and thus "to snort."* The word rendered "displeasure" comes from a verb root with the idea of "hot."

C. *Terror, agitation, and dismay would take hold of those who tried to attack the king whom God had set on the throne.*

III. The word from the new king (Ps. 2:7–9).

A. *The king speaks, and we immediately recognize that the New Testament echoes his words and applies them to the Messiah, our Savior.* Just as God decided who would be king of ancient Israel, he chose the Messiah, his Son, to be the spiritual leader in his kingdom. Verse 8 includes more than the scope of Israel's king. The words picture the universal dominion of the Messiah's kingdom.

B. *The instruments of warfare pictured for the Old Testament king in extending Israel's dominion give way in the New Testament to instruments of peace—love, kindness, and tenderness.* As someone expressed it, these are the "little flowers that grow at the foot of the cross."

IV. An exhortation from the psalmist (Ps. 2:10–12).

A. *Since this work is of God, one is foolish to oppose it.* Let those who hear learn the lesson of this psalm. God will win the victory, and therefore the rebels should repent and commit their loyalty to this new king who symbolizes the eternal Messiah, the ultimate fulfillment of this poem. To reject God's way is suicide, but to surrender to him as Lord of life is peace.

B. *The phrase "Kiss the Son" has been translated "do homage in purity" and "lay hold of."* The idea is to acknowledge the Son as God's anointed. To kiss one's hand or foot was symbolic of recognizing the person's authority.

Conclusion

Nothing can permanently stop the progress of God's work in this world. The wise person will try to find out where God is going and go with him. Avoid aligning with those who plot against righteousness. Choose as friends those whose lives are in harmony with God's standards of holiness.

SUNDAY MORNING, MAY 16

Title: A Building Code for Homes

Text: "Therefore shall a man leave his father and his mother, and shall cleave unto his wife: and they shall be one flesh" ***(Gen. 2:24).***

Scripture Reading: Genesis 2:18–25

Hymns: "God Give Us Christian Homes," McKinney
"O Perfect Love," Gurney
"Faith Is the Victory," Yates

Offertory Prayer: Heavenly Father, we adore you for your character and your great works of nature and redemption. We give thanks for the gift of eternal life. Teach us to be responsible for the gifts you bestow. We give our tithes and offerings in worship of you. Teach us as a church to use these gifts for your missions. In Jesus' name. Amen.

Introduction

To build a house, numerous preparations have to be made. A person has to select a house plan, arrange for payments, purchase a plot of ground, secure a contractor, and then get a building permit. Yes, most cities and counties have building codes with which one has to comply. These building codes have regulations regarding location of the house, foundations, termite control, plumbing standards, wiring specifications, and numerous other matters. People cannot build their houses just any way they desire. They have to build according to standards.

To build a home, we need to follow God's building codes, which are found in the Bible. When God established the first home in the garden of Eden, he gave some building codes. Let us examine carefully God's instructions for building a home. To be sure, building a home matters more than building a house.

I. Build a home on a solid foundation.

Suppose you were going to build a house. You would want to put the house on the best soil possible. You ought to want to build a home on the best foundation.

A. *Some attempt to build a home on a faulty foundation.* Some people marry for the wrong reason. Some enter into marriage expecting an idyllic experience. If they are not happy with the results, they leave. Others marry out of infatuation: the girl gets overwhelmed by the physical looks of the boy, and the boy gets struck by the beauty of the girl. Others panic when they pass a certain age and marry out of a need for emotional security.

B. *The Bible has the only proper foundation for building a home.* "Therefore shall a man leave his father and his mother, and shall cleave unto his wife: and they shall be one flesh" (Gen. 2:24). To build a home two people need to give priority to their partner. The Bible says "to leave" and "to cleave." These words describe commitment as the biblical basis for marriage.

II. Build a home with the best materials.

City building codes have various requirements about the kind of material that goes into a house. Standards are specified for electrical systems, plumbing fixtures, and other building materials. But what kind of materials go into building a home? The answer is people.

A. *A born-again person with a desire to be holy is the best material.* Marrying an unbeliever does not comply with God's standards. Listen to the Bible: "Be ye not unequally yoked together with unbelievers: for what fellowship hath righteousness with unrighteousness? and what communion hath light with darkness?" (2 Cor. 6:14). Born-again believers make the best partners.

B. *A Spirit-filled person is God's requirement for the best material.* To be filled with the Holy Spirit means that we allow God's Spirit to control our lives. Submitting daily to the Spirit's control results in a transformed temperament and healthy interpersonal relationships.

III. Build a house with the best workmanship.

When you build a house, you try to find the best carpenter, brick layers, roofers, plumbers, cabinet makers, painters, and other skilled laborers. Likewise, to build a home, the best workmanship needs to be sought.

A. *Learn to adjust to the marriage relationship.* When two people get married, both have to work hard adjusting to decision making, gender roles, sex, relatives, money management, and other areas. To make a home beautiful, "overtime" work needs to be accepted.

B. *Learn to communicate with each other.* Marriages can be barely sustained, let alone improved and enriched, unless husband and wife get in touch with each other's thoughts, feelings, wishes, and intentions. Work hard in listening to your partner. Practice self-disclosure. Clarify meanings.

C. *Learn to fight fairly.* Conflicts come inevitably in marriage. To fight fairly, both partners need to keep in mind the nature of the conflict. They need to get anger out of the conflict, and they need to negotiate a settlement. Above all, both husband and wife need to practice Christian forgiveness.

IV. Build a home protected against storms and pests.

Houses need to be treated against termites while they are being built. These small creatures can destroy a house. Also, houses need to be built to withstand storms. Homes are threatened by the little things that grow and multiply and by the storms of adversity.

A. *Homes need protection from the little pests.* Little things can creep into a home and begin the destructive process. Couples need to watch for the "little foxes" that creep in to spoil a marriage.

B. *Homes need protection against the storms of life.* Storms came in the home of Adam and Eve: they lost their living quarters, and they saw one of their sons kill the other. All kinds of adversity come to homes today. Only when residents seek God's shelter can they find strength for the storms.

Conclusion

Jesus told of a man who built his house on the sand. The storms came. The house was washed away. Another man built his house on the rock. The storms came. The house stood. Will you yield to God's building code?

Sunday Evening, May 16

Title: If a Man Die . . . ?
Text: "If a man die, shall he live again? all the days of my appointed time will I wait, till my change come" ***(Job 14:14).***
Scripture Reading: Job 14:14; John 11:25

Introduction

In spite of all our incredible developments in science and technology, countless mysteries still plague us. In fact, nearly each new discovery uncovers yet more areas about which we are ignorant. So, in a very real way, we can identify with Job as he flings his seemingly unanswerable questions toward God. His questions are born out of his distress and calamity. Like pieces of red-hot iron, they are forged out of the fires of trouble.

As we see Job now, it is practically impossible to visualize the "Job that was"—the God-fearing affluent man who had been blessed by his Creator in lavish ways. For there sits before us now the most horrible spectacle, the most repugnant piece of humanity we can imagine.

Whereas this is true of Job materially, domestically, and socially, it is not really true of him spiritually. For even though he says some frightfully angry things to God and makes some chilling accusations, his trouble is forcing him to face life and ask some questions that had never been important to him before. In the midst of his anguish, there wells up within him a question born out of the mystery of life and death: "If a man dies, will he live again?"

I. The setting of this question.

A. *Having listened to Bildad and Zophar, his "comforting friends" who insisted he must have sinned greatly for God to punish him so severely, Job becomes furious, hurt, and frustrated.* His answer to them is one of the longest speeches he makes (Job 12–14). The essence of his lengthy reply is, "I am tired of listening to you! You aren't telling me anything! Therefore, I am going to address my remarks to God. I don't know if he can or will hear me—he is so majestic and powerful—but nonetheless, I am going to argue my case before him, and not before you!"

B. *Then there is a sudden outburst as Job pours his heart out to God (Job 12–14).* It is almost as though this outburst had been churning around in the depths of his soul all along. And suddenly, during some brief pause in his prayer, it explodes: "If a man die, shall he live again?" (14:14).

C. *Then Job continues to comment on this.* He says, in effect, that if he was sure that there is life after death, he could endure even all that he was experiencing. This is what he meant when he said, "All the days of my hard service I will wait for my renewal to come" (Job 14:14 NIV). Even here Job reflects the theology of his day. He sees himself as a soldier (in the hard service) who is destined for extreme suffering in war, a life that will be dismal and painful to its bitter end. Then he will "wait" in Sheol, that shadowy place of the dead, until God's anger with him is over, and he will be "released" to enjoy eternal bliss with his Creator. Even at best, there is not a great deal to look forward to in the life hereafter according to Job's understanding.

II. The question itself.

A. *It is really more of a "suggestion" from Job than a question. Even as he asks the question, a gleam of light shines through the gloom of his life.* Though the light is almost immediately extinguished by his despair, it nevertheless had appeared for a brief moment. There is no answer to that question from Bildad, Zophar, or Eliphaz, for they have adequate definitions for neither life nor death.

B. *In our translations of Job's question, we have added the word "again"—"If a man die, shall he live again?"* That is not what Job asked. He actually was asking whether or not one who dies physically still lives. The question has nothing to do with a possible return to this life; it is concerned with the continuity of life beyond what we call "death." His question could be paraphrased, "Is life something more than the present experience we are having? Could it be that what we call death is only a change? If a person dies, is he or she still living?"

III. The answer.

A. *Moving scores of generations through time, we come to the era of our Lord Jesus.* We are no longer in the dismal land of Uz, listening to this poor man Job. Instead, we are in the little village of Bethany, just outside Jerusalem. There are some amazing similarities to the scene where Job lived thousands of years before, however. For again, calamity has struck; deep grief is pervasive. It is a dark and stormy time for a family living in Bethany.

B. *Two sisters in Bethany are flinging questions at God much like those of Job.* Their brother, Lazarus, had been gravely ill. They had sent word to Jesus to come at once, for they were confident he could and would reverse this tragic situation and heal Lazarus. But Jesus purposely delayed his coming, and Lazarus died.

Now, when Jesus finally arrives, Martha meets him with a rebuke: "If you had been here, my brother would not have died" (John 11:21 NASB). Jesus says to her, "Your brother shall rise again" (v. 23 NASB). Almost in exasperation she replies, in effect, "Lord, I am a good Jew. I know my Torah. I also know there will be a resurrection at the last day, and my brother will rise. But that does not help my feelings now!"

Then Jesus answers her question—and the question of Job—in beautiful and powerful simplicity. He says, "I am the resurrection and the life. He who believes in me will live, even though he dies; and whoever lives and believes in me will never die. Do you believe this?" (John 11:25–26 NIV).

Now, what was Job's assessment of life? "Man that is born of a woman is of few days, and full of trouble. He cometh forth like a flower, and is cut down: he fleeth as a shadow, and continueth not" (Job 14:1–2). Later on he said, "For there is hope of a tree, if it be cut down, that it will sprout again, and that the tender branch thereof will not cease" (v. 7).

C. *Jesus simply expanded the definition of life.* He lifted it from the limiting confines of earthly existence. He said to Martha, "I am the resurrection and the life. He that believeth on me, though he die, yet shall he live." What was Jesus affirming? Not "resurrection," although he had taught and declared that. He was affirming life beyond what people look upon as death.

Conclusion

What then shall we say about life and death? Simply this: for the Christian, the "now" is ever leading to the "then." Every passing hour, every experience, however much we may misunderstand it, is linked with the life to come. And this places supreme value on all that is happening to us now, even though we cannot see the full meaning of these experiences.

WEDNESDAY EVENING, MAY 19

Title: Praise God for His Highest Creation
Text: "What is man that you are mindful of him, the son of man that you care for him?" ***(Ps. 8:4 NIV).***
Scripture Reading: Psalm 8:1–9

Introduction

The Hebrew songs praised God for many things: the sun by day (Ps. 19), the moon and stars by night (Ps. 8), the thunderstorm (Ps. 29), the harvest (Ps. 65), and the creation (Ps. 104). This psalm adds another note of glory to God. The writer uttered a doxology at both the beginning and the ending of his song for God's highest creation—who is made in the Creator's image and for fellowship with him.

I. Majesty of God (Ps. 8:1–2).

A. *Israel's God was more than a tribal or national deity.* He was the only God and, therefore, Lord of the entire universe. To the Hebrew mind, the name of a person stood for his complete personality and character. So when the psalmist praised God's name, he gave honor to him for all his attributes, such as holiness, truthfulness, and love. The "splendor . . . displayed . . . above the heavens" (NASB) suggests that God's glory is extolled by the angels above, thus mortal man, upon observing God's work, should certainly join in praising his majestic power.

B. *One of man's unique blessings is the God-given faculty of speech.* The Jewish Targum translates "Man became a living soul" (Gen. 2:7) as "Man became a speaking spirit." Humans are rational beings with power to verbally express their innermost thoughts. Reason cannot act without a word symbol. The first moment of rationality was also the beginning of some type of language. When we hear an infant's first prattle, we have proof of God's creative might. What is true of the physical infant is also true of the spiritual baby, the young Christian. Sometimes he or she can understand God's truth more easily and more quickly than one who has allowed the years to take away the wonder of God's marvelous salvation. The psalmist refused, at any level of life, to surrender his marvel at the Lord's greatness.

II. Humanity's physical insignificance (Ps. 8:3–4).

A. *When the psalmist first looked at the heavens and saw the stars, he was reminded of mankind's nothingness.* The obvious weakness of human nature is laid bare. With their impotence, frailty, and mortality, why are human beings an object of God's thoughts, let alone affections? Look at the stars—as a hymn by Joseph Addison says—"forever singing as they shine, 'the hand that made us, divine!'" What a contrast is mankind.

B. *The first Hebrew word denotes mankind in their weakness, while the second speaks of their earthly nature as formed out of the ground.* Compare creation's vastness with mankind's littleness, creation's power with humanity's feebleness, creation's duration with humankind's transience. One Old Testament writer said, "Generations come and generations go, but the earth remains forever" (Eccl. 1:4 NIV).

III. Mankind's spiritual worth (Ps. 8:5–8).

A. *Following his rhetorical question, the poet seemed to rethink the matter.* His pessimism could not remain the final word. After all, look where God has placed mankind! The King James Version says mankind is "a little lower than the angels," but the Hebrew says literally, "a little lower than Elohim," usually translated "God." Whether mankind is a little lower than just God or a little lower than the angels as well, it is still high in God's rating system.

B. *Mankind lost much in the Fall after sinning, but in Jesus Christ all that it lost can be regained—and more.* Thus God's highest creation, as the poet Thomas Moore wrote, is more than a "speck of life in time's great wilderness" or a "narrow isthmus 'twixt two boundless seas." Rather, human beings are those whom God loved enough to redeem from their sin by sending his only begotten Son to die on the cross. Praise God for mankind—when they remember who they are and to whom they belong!

Conclusion

The psalmist ended where he began—with a shout of praise (v. 9). This time, however, his words took on greater intensity. When we read the psalm seriously, we feel the final verse is an octave higher, after the intervening melody, than the first outburst of praise.

Sunday Morning, May 23

Title: What Do You Give a Child Who Has Nothing?

Text: "Train up a child in the way he should go: and when he is old, he will not depart from it" ***(Prov. 22:6).***

Scripture Reading: Deuteronomy 6:4–9; Proverbs 23:13

Hymns: "How Firm a Foundation," Rippon
"My Faith Has Found a Resting Place," Edmunds
"Be Thou My Vision," Byrne

Offertory Prayer: Our heavenly Father, we adore you. In this experience of worship we have sung your praises, heard your Word read, and sat in silence to hear you. We come to the part of our worship where we give to you. Help us to give with the right motive. Teach us to distribute what we receive in the offering for your kingdom's business. In Jesus' name. Amen.

Introduction

Two men were talking about what to give their children for Christmas. One commented that his son had a closet full of clothes, boxes full of toys, a storage room full of bicycles and scooters, and a go-cart in the garage. In his frustration of trying to think of a gift for his son, he asked, "What do you give a child who has everything?"

Think about this matter of parenting. Then turn the question around: "What do you give a child who has nothing?" Children come into the world with nothing. They come as pliable persons with enormous possibilities for good or for bad.

When God made a nation and called it Israel, he spoke frequently about the responsibilities of being a parent. Throughout the Scripture, God instructed Israel on what to give children. Our task this morning is to ask, "What do you give a child who has nothing?" and to answer the question from God's Word.

I. Parents need to give instructions to their children.

Think about the numerous instructions parents have to give a child. They give directions for talking, eating, hair combing, shoe tying, teeth brushing, bike riding, and a thousand other things. Parents need to give special consideration to this matter of instructing.

A. *Instructions constitute a necessary part of a child's life.* Children come into the world without instruction. They need parents to help them learn the many tasks needed in life. Training cannot be left to chance. The Bible teaches the necessity of a parent training a child.

B. *Instructions need to be given with a sense of urgency.* "Train up a child in the way he should go" (Prov. 22:6). Once T. DeWitt Talmadge preached a sermon titled "Things We Never Get Over." Among the things he mentioned was parental neglect. Training a child is one chance in a lifetime. A parent must have a sense of urgency in training a child, for a child becomes an adult all too quickly.

C. *Children need specific instructions.* The biblical writer said to train a child in the way he *should* go, not in the way he *wants to* go." The word "train" in Proverbs 22:6 can mean to imitate or to dedicate. Training a child means the parent has experienced the ways of the Lord and says, "This is the way; walk in it."

II. Parents need to give children the privilege of personhood.

Unfortunately, some parents depersonalize their children. Oftentimes they are objects to be adored. Sometimes parents seek to live their lives over again through their children. Many examples of depersonalizing a child could be cited. Let us see what is involved in treating a child as a person.

A. *Treating children as people means that parents seek to instill a good self-image in their children.* Dr. James Dobson stresses the necessity of parents creating a healthy self-image. He emphasizes that parents can so depreciate their children that the children will have negative feelings toward themselves. Dobson seeks to get parents to help their children have a realistic self-image.

B. *Treating children as people means that parents regard the autonomy of their children.* Children are not robots to be programmed or puppets to be manipulated. Parents must allow their children to be people. Parental tension comes at the point of commanding and granting freedom. Parents need to gradually allow their children to get away from their dominance and become persons with the right to choose.

Think for a moment about the father Jesus spoke about in Luke 15. The boy wanted freedom. The father granted the boy freedom, knowing the freedom could lead to good or evil. Yet the father was a good parent because he treated his son as a human being.

III. Parents need to discipline their children.

Though the subject is touchy, parents need to discipline their children. Listen to the wisdom of the writer of Proverbs: "Do not withhold discipline from a child; if you punish him with the rod, he will not die" (Prov. 23:13 NIV). Supervision and nurture are the positive sides of discipline. Punishment is the necessary negative side of discipline.

A. *Parents can misinterpret the real meaning of discipline.* Perhaps one of the most misunderstood aspects of parenting comes at the point of punishment or discipline. Let us think together of some abuses.

   Discipline is distorted when a parent responds out of anger to a child. Usually when this type of behavior happens, a parent has been inconvenienced. Also, discipline is distorted with tyrannical, strict punishment.

B. *Parents can use discipline in a beneficial manner.* Discipline helps train a child. It is an evidence of love. "He who spares the rod hates his son, but he who loves him is careful to discipline him" (Prov. 13:24 NIV).

IV. Parents need to give a godly example to their children.

Religion is not as much taught as it is caught. The best gift parents can give to their children is to live godly lives before them. Children imitate the parents either for good or for bad.

A. *Parents can provide a godly atmosphere for children.* The best thing a child can observe is a mother and father deeply committed and in love with each other. Children get a sense of security and peace from such an environment.

   Think about the influence of a child living in a home where prayers are offered, where the Bible is read, and where church is attended. Genuine expressions of God's love are powerful.

B. *Parents can live godly lives before their children.* The best way to explain what a Christian is, is to be one. What kind of example do you give to your children? I heard about a drunken father who returned home one cold winter evening. Snow covered the ground. The father staggered up the walk, went into the house, and went to bed. The next morning he looked out the window and saw his little son staggering in the snow. The father asked, "What are you doing, Son?" The boy replied, "I am trying to walk in your footsteps."

Conclusion

Parenting is one of life's great responsibilities. What do you give a child who has nothing? You give instruction, personhood, discipline, and a godly example.

Sunday Evening, May 23

Title: I Cannot Reach God
Text: "My intercessor is my friend as my eyes pour out tears to God; on behalf of a man he pleads with God as a man pleads for his friend" ***(Job 16:20–21 NIV).***
Scripture Reading: Job 16:18–21; Hebrews 9:24

Introduction

In the beginning of our studies from Job, we were complimentary toward the three friends who had come to see Job and to witness the tragedies that had come into his life. They had come, and they had listened; for seven days they sat in silence while Job vented the bitterness and hostility of his soul.

After that torturous week of listening to Job, these three men with their "prepackaged theology" felt they had to say something to Job. They may well have been just as perplexed as Job was, but they dared not risk turning loose their beliefs, which had been handed down to them and which, very obviously, they had never had reason to test in their own lives.

Countless Christians can recite many of the traditional beliefs and interpretations of their faith that have been handed down to them through the generations, but they have never put these beliefs to the test in their own lives. No doubt most of what they give intellectual assent to is true, but they have just never made those beliefs their own convictions. That is why many of us have real difficulty the first time we meet head-on with some baffling dilemma in our lives. This was the essence of Job's problem.

So traumatic was this discovery for Job that he cried out in anger, accusation, and even bitterness toward God. What I think we miss in all of this—what Job's friends did not hear—is that, in truth, Job's bitter words were not directed so much at the person of God as they were toward something Job did not understand. We come this evening to another of these rare insights that came like bits and pieces from Job's broken soul. In his stormy words and hot anger, these flashes of revelation give evidence that he had been in touch with God. His soul had absorbed some marvelous truths about God and his dealings with people. He just did not have them all sorted out yet; they were not in perspective.

I. The setting.

A. *In their tedious, almost pharisaical way, these three friends of Job had laboriously gone through their efforts to help Job deal with his problem.* Each had made a long speech, which really amounted to a negative condemnation of Job as a sinner who had brought all of this judgment from God upon himself. Job had answered each one of them in due course. After Job's rebuttal speeches, they were more frustrated than ever. All they knew to do was to start over again, so they began what we refer to in a study of Job as the second cycle of speeches. Actually they were saying the same things, just a bit more vigorously. Their points continued to be that it is only the wicked who suffer and that good people are rewarded with good things.

B. *These men were getting more emphatic with their words, and Job was following their pattern.* He was becoming increasingly impatient with their liturgy (see 16:1–5). Actually we are not really so far removed from the wrong attitudes and theology of Job's day. We still find it easy to condemn our brother when he is suffering, to see his faults, and to make our snap judgments. But according to the teachings of Jesus and Paul in the New Testament, those who know the Lord are to be loving and kind. Our assignment is not to pass judgment, but to search our own hearts and lives first. Our judgment is faulty because we do not have all the facts.

II. The great conviction.

A. *In the midst of Job's angry, sometimes sarcastic words of reply to Eliphaz, he suddenly says something that is almost totally out of context with what he had been saying against God (16:18–21).* It was an ancient belief that blood that is not covered up cries out for vengeance. According to this idea, Job is calling upon the earth not to absorb the blood of his suffering until he can be avenged or cleared of these false charges brought against him. And quite suddenly he says, "Even now my witness is in heaven; my advocate is on high" (Job 16:19 NIV).

B. *Only divine revelation could have caused Job to make such a statement.* Perhaps for the first time there was forming in Job's soul a conviction that God was not just a righteous God, always ready to pour out his wrath on people; he was a God of truth and ready to attest to that truth on behalf of his people. But as soon as Job had made the statement that somehow he believed he had a "sponsor" or a "bondsman" in heaven to plead his case, he declared that his problem was that he could not reach that witness, or else that one did not appear to be representing him.

III. The answer.

A. *"Christ did not enter a man-made sanctuary that was only a copy of the true one; he entered heaven itself, now to appear for us in God's presence" (Heb. 9:24 NIV).* The purpose of the book of Hebrews is to show that all of the Old Testament symbolism has passed away because it has all come to fulfillment in Jesus Christ. In this verse we learn that Christ does not dwell in a sanctuary made with human hands; he has entered into heaven itself, to appear in the presence of God for us.

B. *The writer of Hebrews speaks fully to Job's dilemma.* In effect, he says: "Job, you are so right as far as you have gone—for there is indeed one in heaven who has complete knowledge of us, and the records he keeps are true, with no trace of error or misunderstanding. But Job, what you do not understand is that this record-keeper, this advocate, who is God was also man! And now he stands in the presence of God, knowing us perfectly and understanding us completely! Don't despair, Job—you can reach God. For in his Son he has become your mediator, your perfect record-keeper, and you need not be concerned about the imperfect judgments of men."

Conclusion

A story is told of a great Oxford scholar and Bible student of England, Dr. Benjamin Jowett. One day at dinner a woman hoping to draw some clever response from him asked, "Dr. Jowett, we would like to know what is your opinion of God." His face became stern and serious, and he replied: "Madam, I should think it a great impertinence were I to express my opinion about God. The only constant anxiety of my life is to know what is God's opinion of me."

Job felt his need of that. He was conscious of his own innocence, but he could not prove it in the human courts. His friends had already tried him and found him guilty, but somewhere deep in his soul Job knew that there was one who would be perfect and totally impartial in his judgments. How wonderful it would have been had Job known the rest of the story—how that one day God's Son, Jesus, would come and so completely identify with us that he could be forever our advocate in heaven.

WEDNESDAY EVENING, MAY 26

Title: God's Guest

Text: "Lord, who shall abide in thy tabernacle? who shall dwell in thy holy hill?" ***(Ps. 15:1).***

Scripture Reading: Psalm 15:1–5

Introduction

The "character psalms" deal with the fundamentals of faith. The psalmist(s) put the ethical demands of religion into forms easily learned and easily repeated. Psalm 15 is such an example.

I. The question of the ages (Ps. 15:1).

A. *In a general sense, all religions seek the same thing.* They want to know what it takes to please God. A theology professor gave a definition of religion as follows: "Religion is a recognition of a power not ourselves and an effort to establish harmonious relations with it."

B. *The question is in two stages.* "Sojourn" means to dwell temporarily, and "tabernacle" means a temporary building. The idea would be "Who can spend the night?" In the second phrase, "dwell" and "holy hill" suggest permanence. The parallel questions inquire, What kind of person can find God's favor for a moment and then continue to please him?

II. The answer (Ps. 15:2–5).

A. *Verse 2 answers the question in general terms.* God allows no one to live in fellowship with him except a person of integrity, one who practices justice in his or her daily life and speaks the truth on every occasion. This means the person must have a wholehearted devotion to God and must deal honestly with others. The remainder of the section deals with the application of these general principles.

B. *The "law of the tongue" is that one should never use it to harm another.* The New Testament calls the tongue "a fire, a world of iniquity . . . that . . . defileth the whole body, and setteth on fire the course of nature; and it is set on fire of hell" (James 3:6). The same writer says that anyone who seems to be religious but "bridleth not his tongue, but deceiveth his own heart . . . this man's religion is vain" (1:26).

C. *Following closely upon the demand for a tender tongue, the psalmist insisted on treating one's neighbor properly.* Long before Jesus commanded his followers to love their neighbors, the Old Testament demanded justice and equity among those with whom one associated (v. 3). The opening phrase of verse 4 is, at first reading, difficult to understand. Closer scrutiny, however, leads the reader to see that the psalmist says one should be careful in evaluating people. Although God's followers must love everyone, they must be wise enough to spot a phony and avoid that person. At the same time, people who love the Lord and attempt to serve him must find their closest fellowship with kindred minds.

III. The promise (Ps. 15:5).

A. *The character psalms stress the stability of a life in harmony with the principles of God's righteous character.* Whereas the wicked are "like the chaff which the wind driveth away" (Ps. 1:4), the person who shows integrity has perpetuity even in this world.

B. *The New Testament picture is found in the words of Jesus, who said that one who hears his sayings and does them is like a "wise man who built his house on the rock" (Matt. 7:24 NIV).* What is his future? The rains may descend, floods may rise, winds may blow, but his house will not fall, because he has built on a rock.

Conclusion

Through the New Testament we understand even more clearly the life that is in the world beyond this one. We find this possible only through our

Savior's life, death, and resurrection. The Old Testament writer's message, however, has an integrity of its own and is profitable for our instruction. He emphasized that integrity of character, which was possible through the Lord's indwelling presence, meant a good life in this world. Righteousness is its own reward, and sin carries with it the seed of its own destruction. Only the person of faith can live in fellowship with God.

SUNDAY MORNING, MAY 30

Title: Long-Term Marriage
Text: "What therefore God hath joined together, let not man put asunder" ***(Mark 10:9).***
Scripture Reading: Mark 10:6–9; Ephesians 5:28–33
Hymns: "I Love Thee," Anonymous
"All Hail the Power of Jesus' Name," Perronet
"The Bond of Love," Skillings
Offertory Prayer: Our Father, we rejoice that you have chosen to be with us today. Our thoughts and our words are inadequate to offer you gratitude for your many blessings. We thank you for giving us time and energy. We thank you for our possessions. We offer our gifts as worship to you. We ask that these gifts may be used so others can know you. In Jesus' name. Amen.

Introduction

About half of all marriages end in divorce. Most of the time we talk about the half that fail. Let us consider for a few moments the half that last a lifetime.

How can two people make a life together and be close companions until "death do us part"? Let us search for the ingredients of a lifetime partnership.

I. Relationships deepen over a lifetime.

Marriage begins with a friendship. If the covenant lasts for a long time, that friendship deepens. So if you want to have a long-term marriage, marry a person with whom you have already developed a friendship.

A. *Relationships have various levels.* Think about how a relationship starts. It probably begins with "Hello, how are you?" or some other common greeting. Then the relationship grows to the point of sharing both separate and common interests. In sharing these interests, the relationship deepens. Many people marry at this point of relationship.

Unfortunately, many couples do not realize that relationships have potential for much deeper and more intimate involvement. The happiest marriages are made by people who choose to become open to their partners.

B. *Relationships in marriage need to go to the deepest level between human beings.* The deepest level of human relationships are caring, sharing, and intimacy. Couples need to become best friends. Becoming good friends and working together constitute a deep, lasting relationship.

God established sex as the ultimate in intimacy. Long-term marriages are likely to happen when couples commit themselves to making sex an expression of intimacy.

II. Covenants are kept for a lifetime.

A marriage ceremony is a miracle of words. "I take thee — — to be my wedded wife." "I take thee — — to be my wedded husband." At that moment the initial commitment of marriage begins.

A. *Many people live together—married or unmarried—without any real sense of commitment.* They live in the same house, eat at the same table, and even sleep in the same bed, but one or both parties are not committed to the other. There is no sense of belonging to each other.

In the past few decades we have seen the increase of men and women living together outside of marriage. Nevertheless, the general consensus is that living together without the commitment of marriage rarely works.

B. *Look at the meaning of commitment in marriage.* A commitment is a pledge to do something. One person tells another, "I promise," and the promise is kept, the obligation fulfilled. In marriage two people say, "I promise." The basis of their promises is the deep care marriage partners have for each other.

Christian commitment in marriage goes beyond mere feelings. It is a decision, consciously made. This decision has a maturing process. Long-term marriages are those in which the partners learn how to commit to each other.

III. Communication is active and open over a lifetime.

Marriage is two people being together. Not only are couples bound together by a covenant, but they have a lifetime to be together. In this lifetime of companionship, there is a desperate need to communicate with each other. Let us see how married partners communicate.

A. *Communication occurs with the exchange of words.* Of course communication involves the meeting of minds, but it also involves the exchange of words. Think how the words "I love you" say something to another person. Words can inflict hurt, cause feelings of inferiority, and stir anger. Yet words can also show appreciation, boost self-esteem, and stimulate sexual drives.

To communicate more effectively, couples need to analyze their verbal exchanges. Clarify to your mate the meaning of words. Watch how you say your words. Guard against direct or indirect insult. Time your words.

B. *Communication occurs with listening.* Communication involves a two-way process—sending and receiving. A problem occurs when one marriage partner wants only to be the broadcaster. Each partner needs to broadcast and receive. Listening is a key to knowing and understanding another person.

C. *Communication occurs with silence.* Theorists on communication say that 60 percent of messages come by body movement, gestures, and facial expressions. These theorists call this "body language." Such things as eye contact, the holding of a hand, a kiss, the movement of an eyebrow, a fidgety hand or leg, and other body movements tell other people volumes.

IV. Changes are accepted over a lifetime.

Marriage is a process. No couple ever remains stationary. As a couple lives together in holy marriage, their lifestyle may assume many different forms. For a marriage to last a lifetime, a couple needs to learn to grow together.

A. *Married couples go through various stages.* Generally people marry in their twenties. They are in a stage just beyond adolescence. They have exercised independence for only a few years. The early years of marriage are a time when critical vocational and family planning choices are made. These years are followed by many more years of raising a family. Then for many the midlife crisis comes when both physical and emotional changes take place. Many couples end their relationships during these years. When a couple survives middle age, retirement and the senior adult years come. Nothing is more beautiful than to see an older couple genuinely happy together in their golden years. They have made it!

B. *Relationships with children change.* Couples grow together in relation to their children. They have babies. They watch their babies grow up and go to school. They see their teenagers graduate. They attend their children's weddings. Later they welcome grandchildren. Through all these relationships couples have to learn to adjust to change.

V. God is active in relationships.

Marriages are not intended for two. God intends marriage for three. That is, God wants to be the other partner in the marriage covenant.

A. *To have a happy marriage one needs to marry a Christian.* Nothing helps a marriage relationship more than to have a born-again believer as a partner. Paul warned, "Be ye not unequally yoked together with unbelievers" (2 Cor. 6:14). Turn Paul's warning to a more positive picture. Seeing two oxen plowing together is beautiful. Also, seeing two believers yoked in marriage has great possibilities.

B. *To have a happy marriage one needs to be involved in godly activities.* Marriages can be enriched by praying together, attending worship together, and studying the Bible together.

Conclusion

Do you want your marriage to go the distance? Then heed these ideas: deepen your relationship, put commitment uppermost in mind, communicate with each other, grow together during life's changes, and keep God first.

SUNDAY EVENING, MAY 30

Title: Can I Know My Redeemer Lives?
Text: "I know that my Redeemer liveth, and that he shall stand at the latter day upon the earth" ***(Job 19:25).***
Scripture Reading: Job 19:25–27; Hebrews 7:25

Introduction

Physical suffering carries its own kind of pain that, indeed, can be excruciating. But when the human body can stand no more, nature provides a built-in release—the loss of consciousness. Mental torture can be even worse. It affects the mind and the emotions. It depresses, it distorts, it causes one to lose any concept of reality. It deteriorates, disintegrates, and tears down. Mental suffering attacks hope, which is a lifeline of human existence. It is the avowed enemy of faith, without which we cannot live—we only exist.

Therefore, when we visualize Job covered with boils from head to foot and dressed in rags, we know that he was suffering physically. But the more we read the words of Job to his three "friends," we realize that actually he was paying very little attention to his physical condition. The torture he was going through was mental and spiritual. It was tearing at his reason; it was blasting every lofty and reverent concept of life and God he had held dear.

Between the angry speeches in which Job vents the bitterness of his soul, there are interludes of fantastic revelations of divine truth—glimpses of what God is really like. So again tonight we will eavesdrop on Job and the conversations he is having with Bildad, Zophar, and Eliphaz. At chapter 19 we are in the second cycle of speeches, and Bildad has just finished his long harangue against Job.

I. The setting.

A. *Each time these men speak to Job, they become more hurtful and condemning.* No doubt they are retaliating somewhat for Job's angry words to them.

But as we have seen before, they were trying desperately to affirm their traditional concepts of suffering and of how God rewards good people with the good life and evil people with trouble. Chapter 18 contains Bildad's second speech, in which he rehearses the various sufferings Job was enduring. Like a broken record, Bildad again comes to the conclusion that Job's suffering must be related to some sin in his life.

B. *Just before God gave Job the next remarkable revelation, Job again sank into despair.* Job's emotions are like a yo-yo in these speeches. He goes to the very floor of the pit of despair, and then God comes. Job feels sure that his suffering is the result of God's wrath, but it is not. Behind all of Job's anxiety and suffering is God's marvelous love.

II. The revelation (Job 19:23–27).

A. *Job, who has been groveling in the mud and mire of utter distress, suddenly takes wings and soars to the highest pinnacle of faith.* He is like the fabled phoenix, the bird that apparently burned to ashes in the fire only to rise out of the flames in beauty and majestic splendor. Job, aware of the significance of a startling thought that has come into his mind and soul, has a sudden desire that what he is about to say be written down, to be preserved for all those coming after him. He wants the words engraved in stone with iron tools and then filled in with lead!

B. *Just before this, in his last speech to Eliphaz, Job declared that he had a witness in heaven, an advocate, who was keeping a true record of his life.* But here God takes Job a little further in his understanding. He gives this "witness in heaven" a name—he calls him Redeemer! The Hebrew word translated "redeemer" in the Old Testament is *goel,* and it comes from an ancient Hebrew custom. If a man sold himself into slavery, a kinsman was obligated to be his redeemer. In the story of Ruth, Naomi's closest relative was not able to redeem Naomi's land and marry Ruth. Since he could not do this, he transferred his responsibility to Boaz, who became Ruth's "redeemer." When a person was slain, a kinsman had a duty to secure vengeance against the murderer's family. Again, this person was the "redeemer." So, in another way, a redeemer in Old Testament times was one who defended the oppressed or who came to the aid of one in trouble.

C. *In the New Testament the meaning of the word* redeemer *has been gloriously expanded.* The closest substitute word would be "vindicator." But the redeemer's function was essentially one of *love,* while a vindicator's function was one of *law.* So what has happened to Job? There was no earthly redeemer living to defend him. His sons were dead, and all of his other relatives had apparently deserted him. Who, in Job's day, ever would have thought of this or dreamed that God could be called upon to act as redeemer for a human being?

D. *Job did not discover this for himself.* Rather, in the darkness and overwhelming sorrows in which Job was submerged, God beamed this glorious light, this marvelous revelation, into Job's soul. Job said, "I know that my Redeemer lives." He did not merely mean that he knew his Redeemer "existed." It is as though Job had said, "Even though I die, he lives!" He was saying, "I may die unjustified before men. But I know that I have a Redeemer in heaven who is not dead and who has not and will not forget me!" The climax to all of this comes when Job adds this final dimension to his new discovery: "Yet in my flesh I will see God; I myself will see him with my own eyes" (Job 19:26–27). For a fleeting moment, Job saw that there was more beyond this earthly life.

III. The answer (Heb. 7:25).

A. *The incarnation of Jesus—God coming to man in human flesh—was the glorious fulfillment of what Job had said.* Jesus' coming proved that what Job had said was literally true. This great God whom men, including Job, had always thought so unapproachable by sinful, imperfect humans, would one day come into this earthly life, stand on this "dust" with us, and argue our case.

B. *Sometimes we mistakenly say that when Jesus came to earth in human flesh he brought God closer to humans than he ever had been before.* That is not really true, for Jesus just made God visible to sinful humans. God had always loved them. For, from before the foundation of the world, God conceived this marvelous plan of salvation in which he would sacrifice his only begotten Son for our sins. But people would need a kinsman, an advocate, a *goel*, a redeemer with whom they could identify. Jesus became that Redeemer!

Conclusion

It is the wondrous teaching of our New Testament that we have not only a Redeemer who paid the price for our eternal salvation, but also one who stands near us at all times. If he seems to delay the revelation of his presence with us in our trouble, there is a reason within his sovereign will that ultimately serves our good.

SUGGESTED PREACHING PROGRAM FOR THE MONTH OF

JUNE

■ Sunday Mornings

Continue majoring on the needs of family living, using "Strengthening the Family from Bible Truths" as the theme.

■ Sunday Evenings

Continue the messages from the book of Job titled "Job's Questions and Jesus' Answers."

■ Wednesday Evenings

Continue with the series "Mining Spiritual Truths from the Psalms."

WEDNESDAY EVENING, JUNE 2

Title: Seeing God in His Work and His Word

Text: "The heavens declare the glory of God . . . The law of the LORD is perfect" ***(Ps. 19:1, 7).***

Scripture Reading: Psalm 19:1–14

Introduction

An outstanding philosopher once said that two things amazed him: "the starry sky above and the moral law within." This is exactly what Psalm 19 is all about—seeing God in his handiwork, especially in the marvels of the heavens, and seeing him in his law, the basic principles of morality taught in his Word.

I. God's wonderful world (Ps. 19:1–6).

A. *The writers of Scripture nowhere tried to prove the existence of God.* They took it for granted that only one who was morally deficient, the true meaning of "fool," would say in his heart, "there is no God" (Ps. 14:1). When the psalmist looked at the result of the Creator's activity, he saw an argument that the most skilled debater could not refute. A non-Christian philosopher once advised his students not to study astronomy because they could not make any practical use of it toward bettering the world. He was wrong! To see the vast expanse of the universe and the severe limitations of our own being will certainly lessen our selfish conceits; this, then, will be of practical benefit, especially for those who have to live with us.

B. *The cultivation of a sense of wonder when we contemplate the starry universe will fertilize the mind.* What can confirm our monotheistic faith more than to realize the unity and regularity of action in the heavenly bodies! No wonder the poet could say:

In reason's ear they all rejoice
And utter forth a glorious voice
Forever singing, as they shine,
The hand that made us is divine.

—*Joseph Addison*

C. *Modern translators eliminate the inserted "where" in verse 3, thereby showing the true meaning that the great creation stands as a "tabernacle for the sun."* And verses 5–6 compare that sun to a virile man, fresh from his wedding night, going out with boldness and confidence to make his mark in the world. Praise God for the wonderful world he has made!

II. God's wonderful word (Ps. 19:7–11).

A. *To most of us, the word of God is the Bible, but to the Jews it included all of God's revelation whether recorded or not.* The Torah was God's continued moral requirements. The psalmist stood amazed at the different ways God conveys his ethical demands. Whether we call them laws, testimonies, statutes, commandments, or judgments, they all present the fact that the universe is structured in righteousness, and those who cooperate with the Almighty by living in harmony with his plan will be blessed with an abundant life.

B. *The poet uses such words as "perfect," "sure," "right," "pure," "clean," "true," and "righteous" to describe God's revelation of himself and his law for us.* So wondrous is its effect on human beings that its messages have the answer for all our questions, govern all our ways, and meet all our needs. Truly God's Word is more to be desired than material gain, it is sweeter than any delicacy, it is to be completely trusted as a guide for our conscience, and it is a rewarder of those who follow it.

III. A fervent prayer (Ps. 19:12–14).

A. *Overwhelmed by the "starry sky above the moral law within," the psalmist cried out for help.* Realizing his finiteness and that he was "prone to wonder," he pleaded for guidance in the moral struggle.

B. *We who live on this side of Calvary have a higher revelation.* We know God in Jesus Christ and can find forgiveness in him. Transformed by his grace, we can live in the strength he gives and find an even more abundant life than the psalmist ever could have envisioned.

Conclusion

Psalm 19 is full of the glories of God. Yet we who know the final revelation of God in Jesus Christ see even more than this psalm teaches. He is indeed the true Word of God who became a man and lived among us. The written Word, the Bible, brings us to the living Word, our Savior. Both are vital; we must not minimize either. Neither can we fail to recognize God when we see his works in the created world. Above everything else, however, let us thank God that the one who spoke in times past unto the fathers by the prophets has spoken to us in these last days by his Son, whom he has appointed heir of all things (Heb. 1:2).

SUNDAY MORNING, JUNE 6

Title: Jesus Talks about Marriage
Text: "For this cause shall a man leave father and mother, and shall cleave to his wife: and they twain shall be one flesh" ***(Matt. 19:5)***.
Scripture Reading: Matthew 19:3–9
Hymns: "I Will Sing of My Redeemer," Bliss
"O God in Heaven, Whose Loving Plan," Martin
"Near to the Heart of God," McAfee
Offertory Prayer: Our Father, we celebrate the day. We give thanks as we think about the gifts we receive from you. We thank you for giving us eternal life. We rejoice in the spiritual gifts distributed so evidently among the members of your body. We long to worship you by giving. Help us as we give to you to learn the right spirit of giving. In Jesus' name. Amen.

Introduction

Because so many people get married in June, June has often been called the "wedding month." Before two young people get married, they should talk with various professional persons about certain aspects of married life. They may have premarital counseling sessions with their pastor to set priorities and discuss new family relationships. They may talk about family planning with a physician. And they may meet with a financial advisor to discuss budgeting, insurance, investments, and other money matters. But most important, a couple should find out what the Bible says about marriage.

I. Marriage is a unique relationship.

A. *Marriage is God's idea.* It did not originate from a law or a social trend or any other human invention. It started with God.

To begin the human race, God made one man and one woman. He united the man and the woman, intending for them to live together for companionship and to replenish the earth. God placed this sanction on marriage, calling it a good relationship. "Whoso findeth a wife findeth a good thing, and obtaineth favour of the LORD" (Prov. 18:22).

B. *Marriage is God's unique human relationship.* The language of Genesis 1–3 illustrates the natural unity of a husband and wife. The Hebrew words *ish* and *ishah* denote male and female. "So God created man in his own image, in the image of God created he him; male and female created he them" (Gen. 1:27).

II. Marriage is an intimate relationship.

A. *Marriage is a relationship designed for ultimate intimacy.* "What therefore God hath joined together, let no man put asunder" (Matt. 19:6 RSV). The expression "joined together" indicates the idea of being cemented or glued together.

B. *Marriage is a relationship designed to last a lifetime.* "They twain shall be one flesh" (Matt. 19:5). God intended the marriage relationship to last until death breaks the contract. No earthly contract is more intimate or has more lasting effects.

III. Marriage is an exclusive relationship.

A. *Getting married means to forsake a mother and father relationship.* "For this cause shall a man leave father and mother, and shall cleave to his wife: and they twain shall be one flesh" (Matt. 19:5). Jesus emphasized leaving and cleaving. Of course the Lord did not mean to disdain one's parents and have nothing else to do with them. The Lord emphasized that loyalty to one's married partner should have priority over one's parents.

    Some fail to forsake parents. They try to cleave emotionally and financially to their parents while trying to cleave to a married partner. A marriage is in serious trouble if a partner tries to cleave to both parents and partner simultaneously.

B. *Getting married means to forsake all other intimate partners.* Intimacy includes both emotional and sexual involvement. Sometimes a husband or a wife will turn to someone other than a spouse for intimacy and for sharing hurts, frustrations, dreams, and other matters. And unfortunately, some married partners do not forsake other sexual partners. But God commands, "Thou shalt not commit adultery" (Ex. 20:14).

IV. Marriage is a purposeful relationship.

A. *God intended man and woman to live together as companions.* "The Lord God said, It is not good that the man should be alone; I will make him an help meet for him" (Gen. 2:18). The expression "help meet for him" means someone to answer to all his needs.

    The Genesis writer described the purpose of marriage as a relationship. The husband answers to the needs of the wife. The wife answers to the needs of the husband. The needs of both include verbal exchange, emotional sharing, and sexual experience. No other relationship on earth can meet all of these needs except the marriage relationship.

B. *God intended man and woman to live together to propagate the human race.* After God united man and woman, he said, "Be fruitful, and multiply, and replenish the earth, and subdue it: and have dominion over the fish of the sea, and over the fowl of the air, and over every living thing that moveth upon the earth" (Gen. 1:28). Having children is a solemn responsibility of most couples. Rearing those children requires a team effort.

V. Marriage is an imperfect relationship.

A. *The marriage relationship at its best has strains.* Marriage at its best involves adjustments on the part of both partners. Marriage experts identify the primary areas of adjustment as gender roles, decision making, contrasting backgrounds, in-laws, values, social life, sex, money, and children.

Some marriages are better than others, but no marriage is perfect. Many couples have a sense of dissatisfaction because their marriages are not absolutely perfect. Couples need to identify problem areas and learn by God's help how to deal with the things that strain their relationship.

B. *The marriage relationship needs to experience constant forgiveness.* Inevitably one partner will hurt the feelings of the other. To keep the relationship healthy, the offender needs to learn to say, "I'm sorry, I was wrong. Please forgive me." The offended needs to learn to say, "You're forgiven."

Marriage involves a relationship of falling down and getting up, falling down and getting up. Of course some couples do not fall as regularly as others. Unfortunately, when some couples fall, they fail to get up and go on, and divorce severs the relationship.

Conclusion

Many people talk about getting married. They will hear advice from many persons: parents, counselors, friends, ministers, and others. Above everyone else, couples need to listen to what Jesus says about marriage: "For this cause shall a man leave father and mother, and shall cleave to his wife: and they twain shall be one flesh" (Matt. 19:5).

SUNDAY EVENING, JUNE 6

Title: If Only I Knew Where to Find Him
Text: "If only I knew where to find him; if only I could go to his dwelling!" ***(Job 23:3 NIV).***
Scripture Reading: Job 23:3–7; John 14:9

Introduction

No anguish can compare with that of a child who has become temporarily lost from his parents. We have seen the stark terror in the eyes of a child going frantically from one person to another, trying to find his parent. Perhaps it was in a crowded mall, on a busy carnival fairway, or down a long supermarket aisle. Why is being lost so traumatic?

Perhaps it is because we have been severed from a very important life-support system. There is security in knowing where we are and knowing that someone who cares deeply for us knows where we are. When this sense of security is threatened, one's world is shattered.

The most overwhelming sense of futility comes when a believer in God—one who has enjoyed an intimate closeness with the Lord—suddenly feels out of touch with God or that God has forgotten him or her. We know, because of what the Bible teaches, that this never happens as far as God is concerned. But Satan is shrewd and incredibly persuasive at this point. He can approach us at times of discouragement and trial, when we are caught in some great distress or trouble, and temporarily convince us that God is no longer close to us and no longer hears our prayers.

This is something of the experience Job had. According to God's own testimony, there had not been a human on earth who had a relationship as close and continuous with God as Job had. But now, from Job's standpoint, without rhyme or reason, all of that has been snatched away. God, Job feels, must be somewhere at the other end of his universe! Job has little or no concept of the omnipresence of God. Tonight we will visit Job again and hear another of the signs of exasperation coming from his soul.

I. The setting.

A. *We have already discovered that Job's three "friends" who have come to comfort him and express their concern for him are very organized in the way they are handling the situation.* They are disgustingly smug and snobbish in their remarks. Tonight we are in the third and final cycle of speeches. Eliphaz has just completed his third and last speech. It is considerably shorter than the other two, and he maintains the position he has held throughout—that Job's sufferings are the result of his sins (Job 22:1–30).

B. *There is little doubt that Eliphaz believes in salvation by works.* He says that when Job has returned to God, once more his prayers will be heard, his desires will be fulfilled, and he will be able to encourage others (Job 22:23–30). We would expect Job to react to Eliphaz as he had done following the other speeches—with bitterness and hostility, railing out in anger and disgust at him. But there seems to be a wistfulness about him we have not heard thus far.

II. The reply.

A. *Job begins with something of a prayer (23:2–9).* In so many words, Eliphaz had said to Job, "Get to know God, and all will be well!" Job replied, in effect: "That's just the problem! How am I going to do it? I thought I knew him. I know that I knew him! There is no way that I could have imagined or fantasized the relationship I had with God before all of this calamity came upon me. But now he's gone! North, south, east, and west I have searched for him."

B. *Then comes the prayer: "If only I knew where to find him; if only I could go to his dwelling!" (Job 23:3 NIV).* These were the words of a man who had strong convictions about God, regardless of the hot words of anger he had spoken previously. Nowhere is there any evidence that Job is becoming an agnostic, that he is doubting the existence of God. He decides that God is hiding himself, that he is not making himself accessible to his creatures. Perhaps there are times when we, in this enlightened New Testament era, come to something of this same conclusion. There are times in the midst of our troubles and heartaches and frustrations that we feel God is not watching and is not as concerned as we wish.

C. *Then Job goes on to reveal something else of his understanding of God.* He is convinced that if he can find God and get his attention, God will listen to him and reason with him about these unjust things that had come into his life. We see a double conviction of Job clearly here. He still believes in God's existence and in God's fairness; and he believes that God will be just concerning his case. His difficulty is that he cannot reach God; he cannot find him.

D. *With a plaintive, poetic beauty, Job describes his search for God (23:8–9).* A Puritan theologian commented on this in his quaint way: "Job, you have gone forward and backward, you have looked to the left and you have looked to the right. Why don't you try looking up?" But there is no doubt that even if Job had "looked up" at this time, he still would have said that he could not reach God. In one of the earlier speeches from these men, Zophar had said to Job, "Canst thou by searching find out God?" (11:7). So now, when Job's friend Eliphaz advises him to acquaint himself with God, Job restates the problem just as Zophar had expressed it earlier: "I have tried searching, but I cannot find him!"

III. The answer of Jesus.

A. *Many centuries have passed, and we find ourselves in an upper room in Jerusalem.* We join a group of men whose hearts, like Job's, have yearned for a relationship with God. In their midst is Jesus, a man, yes, but more than a man. Into that physical shell of humanity, God poured himself. Philip made a request of Jesus very much like Job's: "Lord, show us the Father and that will be enough for us" (John 14:8 NIV). These statements of Philip and Job reflect the basic cry of the human heart that has lost its consciousness of God through sin.

B. *Jesus answered Philip—and ultimately Job—with a clear and wonderful declaration (John 14:8–11).* A mere intellectual interest will never bring a person to discover God. Job and Philip were seeking God because they were convinced that he existed and that he was a just God. They were ready to receive a revelation of his glory. Revelation did come to Job ultimately—but not as fully, of course, as it came to Philip.

Conclusion

Of one thing we can be certain: we never search for God in vain. God is far more eager to find us than we are to find God. Have you "experienced" God—not just with your intellect, but with your soul? If you know that God exists only with your mind, your human reason, then your God is too small. For you have contained him in your mind. But if you know that he exists because you have experienced him, you have absorbed his glory in the little happenings of everyday life. You know him, and you know where to find him. He is always in the midst of his people.

WEDNESDAY EVENING, JUNE 9

Title: Value of Suffering
Text: "It is good for me that I have been afflicted; that I might learn thy statutes" ***(Ps. 119:71).***
Scripture Reading: Psalm 22:1–31

Introduction

The background of Psalm 22 is some event or series of events in David's life when he went through much opposition and physical abuse. While suffering on the cross, Jesus quoted part of the first verse. He may have quoted all of it but was so weak the crowd only heard the part recorded in Matthew's gospel. The journey the psalmist made from depression to victory gives us strength for our days of adversity.

I. Sufferings and plea for deliverance (Ps. 22:1–5).

A. *Every person has at some time, like David, felt that God has neglected to answer his prayers.* When such a time comes, God seems so far away that he cannot be reached even with repeated petitions.

B. *Yet one who has known God in days past knows God is sovereign in power and righteous in character.* The psalmist pleaded with God on the basis of his previous mercy to the nation. The fact that earlier generations trusted in God and were not disappointed made the psalmist confident and caused him to cry out for deliverance in his own crisis.

II. Innocent victim of scornful persecutors (Ps. 22:6–21).

A. *No Christian can read this portion of the psalm without being vividly confronted with the crucifixion of Jesus.* This song must have been one that was memorized and quoted by all careful students of the Hebrew Scriptures. These detailed statements used by New Testament writers to tell of Jesus' experience are amazing. We are startled to realize how God breathed words into David concerning his own suffering that would be reiterated and amplified in the life of the coming Messiah. Five times he penned words that were picked up by the Gospels in connection with the death of Jesus.

B. *The intensity of the suffering seems to transcend the limits endured by any ordinary human such as David.* Therefore, scholars see in him the ideal righteous sufferer, fulfilled in Jesus Christ, who died for our sins. Indeed, the most striking part of these verses is the sufferer's humility as he refused to cry out for vengeance on those who were causing him pain. No one but Jesus could have lived and died so nobly.

III. Anticipated victory of the sufferer (Ps. 22:22–31).

A. *Beginning with verse 22, the psalmist's entire outlook changed.* He considered his two outbursts of prayer (vv. 11, 19–21) completely answered, and he continued the psalm from that viewpoint. He looked forward with confidence, considering his deliverance an accomplished fact. First, he told of his intention to go to the place where believers gathered to worship that he might express in their presence his gratitude for God's mercy. Calling upon others to join him in praise, he also assured the people that he would fulfill the pledges he had made to God, which included the bringing of gifts to the sanctuary. What a beautiful parallel to our bringing our tithes and offerings for God's work to be accomplished.

B. *The psalmist then looked out beyond his small world to see the nations that did not know his God.* He was convinced that as a result of his sufferings and deliverance, they too would hear of God's great deliverance and turn to the Lord in love and service. Generations yet to be born would be told about this God who redeems. God's kingdom would know no end. It would bring the proud down in humility, and the family of God would worship in peace and plenty. All of this would take place because God's servant had suffered and called upon God in the midst of unbearable adversity. What a tribute to God and what a lesson to us who are called upon to suffer the arrows unjust people heap upon us. Whatever else we learn from life and the Lord in our suffering, we come to see that our suffering can be redemptive, and this is the most glorious truth of all.

Conclusion

This psalm is more than a foreshadowing of Christ's death. It is a picture of how all believers can approach suffering. We can use it as a lever to lift ourselves to a higher knowledge of God's nature and character. Suffering also can become a tool by which we who are believers can live redemptively, helping to heal the hurts of this battered world.

Sunday Morning, June 13

Title: Putting Sex in Its Place

Text: "Let the husband render unto the wife due benevolence: and likewise also the wife unto the husband" ***(1 Cor. 7:3).***

Scripture Reading: 1 Corinthians 7:1–7

Hymns: "Rejoice, Ye Pure in Heart," Messiter
"My Jesus, I Love Thee," Anonymous
"Love Is the Theme," Fisher

Offertory Prayer: Our Father, we reverence you. Holy is your name. Everything you have given us is good. Unfortunately, we have sometimes taken the good things and made them bad. We ask for your leadership in knowing how to use your gifts. Teach us to return a portion of our finances to your treasury so others can know you. Take these gifts and guide us in using them for your kingdom. In Jesus' name. Amen.

Introduction

The subject of sex is approached from many angles. Through the years the subject of sex has been repressed in many circles of conversation. Often children hear from parents, "You shouldn't talk about that." Oddly enough, many churches and many good, moral people think that the facts of sex should be kept secret.

Contrary to the opinion that sex should be a silent subject is the thought that sex should have free and open exposure. If we go to the movies, we can rarely see a film without a sex scene. Television soap operas, sitcoms, and dramas adopt fornication, adultery, and homosexuality as their themes. Newsstands contain magazines filled with explicit sex. Advertisers use sex to sell their products.

Perhaps no subject is more discussed and less understood than sex. People need to put sex in its place. But where is its place? Let us examine the subject from a biblical perspective.

I. Sex has various functions.

God thought of the idea of sex. All of God's creation has been described either as "good" or "very good." God designed sex for good purposes.

A. *God ordained sex to produce children.* In the opening chapters of Genesis, we have a magnificent commentary on the meaning of human sexuality. The biblical writer made a distinction between man and woman: "male and female created he them" (1:27). One of God's commands recorded in the creation account is "to replenish the earth" (v. 28). When a husband and wife have sex, there is the potential of producing children. God intended sex as a means of providing children, but this was not the only purpose for sexual activity of a husband and wife.

B. *God ordained sex to provide pleasure.* Intimacy in marriage was created for personal pleasure, not just for procreation. Read the Song of Solomon to learn what the Bible says of a husband and wife engaging in sex.

A wife can make her husband physically and emotionally fulfilled by the sex act. Likewise, the husband can make his wife extremely happy with the sex act. God did not intend for sex to be an experience to be endured, he intended it to be a tender time to be greatly enjoyed.

II. Sex has obvious failures.

Like every other gift of God, human beings have distorted the gift of sex. The human race has taken a perfectly beautiful act and corrupted it.

A. *Some sex failures happen outside the relationship of marriage.* "Now concerning the things hereof ye wrote unto me: It is good for a man not to touch a woman. Nevertheless, to avoid fornication, let every man have his own wife, and let every woman have her own husband" (1 Cor. 7:1–2). God prohibits any sexual activity outside the marriage relationship.

B. *Some sex failures happen within the relationship of marriage.* God intended sex to be mutually enjoyable. Various malpractices can come into a marriage to harm its function. When one of the partners wants sex for selfish purposes, there is a failure. Also, when sex is practical for only one of the married partners, there is a failure.

III. Sex has godly fulfillment.

We have examined the function and the failures of sex. To put sex in its right perspective, we need to see the great fulfillments of the sex experience.

A. *Sex gives a genuine happiness only in the marriage relationship.* Many psychologists testify of the great guilt that premarital and extramarital sex bring.

B. *Sex gives genuine happiness and fulfillment when it is an expression of love.* The sex act itself is a language. It is one partner saying to another, "I love you, and I desperately want to make you happy." It is a mutual endeavor. There is no greater expression for saying and showing, "I love you."

Conclusion

We can hear about sex in many places. We can read about sex in many books and magazines. But let us put sex in its place. Let us turn to the Bible—*the* Book—and see the functions, failures, and fulfillment of sex.

SUNDAY EVENING, JUNE 13

Title: Oh, That I Had Someone to Hear Me!
Text: "Oh, that I had someone to hear me! I sign now my defense—let the Almighty answer me; let my accuser put his indictment in writing" ***(Job 31:35 NIV).***
Scripture Reading: Job 31:35; Hebrews 7:22–24

Introduction

Have you ever said in utter exasperation, "Oh, if only there were someone I could talk with—someone who would really hear what I'm saying!" Perhaps the situation in which you found yourself at the moment was a suffocating and isolating one. It seemed that there was no one who really cared enough to listen, or if he or she did listen, could really "hear" what you were saying. No loneliness is quite so painful as that.

Our text for tonight is taken from the concluding words of Job's last speech to the three men who had, for some undetermined period of time, given their "advice" to him. They had reached their smug conclusions, had offered their "pat" answers, and had succeeded in wrenching from Job's soul almost every violent emotion he was capable of expressing. He had plumbed the depths of mental and spiritual depression.

As we learned in our past studies, in the midst of all of these negative reactions, God had given Job some amazing revelations of divine truth. Like a flash of lightning, they illuminated his soul and his understanding for a moment, but quickly the darkness of despair surrounded him again. Now the drama is about over. Job is mentally, physically, and spiritually exhausted. It seems to him that just about everything that could be said has been said. God, for no apparent reason to Job, has walked away from him—at least that is the conclusion Job has reached. Job has not lost his faith, nor has his belief in God's existence been shaken. It is God's attitude toward him, which Job, trapped and tortured as he is, cannot comprehend.

I. The setting.

A. *Job's last speech is a long one (Job 26–31).* We might call it "Job's summation." It is much like that of a defense lawyer presenting to the jury his last appeal on behalf of his defendant. Job surveys his past prosperity, rehearses his tragedy, and as he has done repeatedly, reaffirms his innocence.

B. *We should not be surprised or shocked at Job's harsh and sometimes violent words.* This is a common human experience in hours of overwhelming sorrow or trouble that seem to have neither reason nor explanation. Whether we express our feelings audibly or not, we are crying out, "God, why have you done this? Why have you let this terrible thing happen? This is not fair! There is no rhyme or reason in this!"

C. *While we are feeling these resentments and expressing these exasperations, our well-meaning friends, like Job's, may be saying, "But it is God's will, and we must not question it!"* Sometimes they will express the height of cruelty, saying, "Well, you can learn something from this. God chastens us, you know." The inference is, "You have sinned, and God is punishing you!"

II. Job's summation.

A. *It is interesting that the language Job uses is judicial—that is to say, the appeal he makes is based on the processes of a court of law.* He sees God as the "adversary" or "prosecutor," the one conducting the case against him, the defendant. In ancient courts of law, two things were always required. First, a charge was made by the prosecutor against the defendant. Second, a rebuttal of the charge brought against him was made by the defendant.

B. *Job's position is that his adversary, God, has never stated his case against him.* These three men have brought their charges against Job, but God has said nothing! Nonetheless, Job had prepared his rebuttal—even before the charge had been delivered. He says, "I sign now my defense—let the Almighty answer me; let my accuser put his indictment in writing" (Job 31:35 NIV). In spite of all that has happened, Job knows that the ultimate tribunal to which every person has a right to make an appeal is God.

C. *The current agony of Job's soul is simply that it seems to him that he is not getting a hearing in God's court.* Somewhere deep within, Job knows that the final judgment for man must be made by God, whose knowledge is perfect and whose decisions are absolutely just. Job's cry is the language of a man who believes in a moral universe over which God reigns and in which he governs. As we listen to Job's words, the question that comes to mind is whether we can have access to that ultimate court and stand before the perfect Judge.

III. The solution (Heb. 7:22–24).

A. *Through Jesus, the Son of God, we find the complete answer for Job.* "Yes, Job! It is possible to find the way to God and to have immediate access to him." The beauty of all this is that the one who can lead us to God is not just a majestic, far removed, unapproachable Creator-God, but one who became flesh for the express purpose of identifying with us and becoming involved in the human situation.

B. *The "unapproachableness" of God was a basic concept among the Hebrews.* It was demonstrated in the Holy of Holies, that sacred room in the temple symbolizing the presence of God. No one could approach him but the high priest, and that only in fear and trembling once a year on the Day of Atonement. When Jesus died on the cross, the heavy, separating veil was torn apart, and access to God was then provided for all people, not just for the high priest.

C. *Note what the author of Hebrews has said about Jesus' role as our "introducer" to God.* He says that "because Jesus lives forever, he has a permanent priesthood" (7:24 NIV). Because Jesus is living today, he is aware of our situation and sensitive to our cry. And not only that, his priesthood, his role as the Intercessor, is permanent! He will never cease to be available as our "go-between" before God.

Conclusion

Across the centuries the New Testament shouts to Job: "Yes, Job, there is someone who hears you! He has never stopped hearing you! And once you can release your troubled soul into his hands, you will know that he is there!"

It is a great experience for the human soul to stop listening to the opinions of neighbors and the arguments of philosophers and clever men, and to place its confidence in the clear and merciful judgments of God. When this happens, we find that Jesus is the mediator between God and humans. Furthermore, his blood brings another and even more blessed dimension of God's character—mercy is added to justice. For the repentant sinner, justice and mercy meet together, all because of what Jesus did for us on the cross. Do you need someone to hear you tonight?

Wednesday Evening, June 16

Title: God's World and Worshipers
Text: Who shall ascend into the hill of the Lord? or who shall stand in his holy place?" ***(Ps. 24:3).***
Scripture Reading: Psalm 24:1–10

Introduction

This great choral hymn, Psalm 24, was no doubt composed by David to be used when the ark of the covenant was moved from the house of Obed-Edom to the newly founded city of David on Mount Zion. The king, priests, people, elders, and other Israelites walked in solemn procession accompanied by music and song as they took the ark to its resting place on the holy mountain. The song reminds believers of all generations of how great God is and of what kind of character he demands in his worshipers.

I. The Creator of all (Ps. 24:1–2).

A. *What does God own?* Everything and everybody! Every square foot of ground and every building on it! Every business operation we carry out in this busy world! Because we often try to shut God into one corner of life, our spirits grow small and narrow. The inspired writer gave full credit for everything to his God.

B. *If we, like David, would remember God in all areas of life, how different our world would be!* What different people we would be! The poet's image of the earth as "founded upon the sea" is in harmony with the creation account in Genesis but contrary to the accounts of other ancient religions. Israel's God was "one God" as the Shema says, and all things belong to him.

II. Who can worship God? (Ps. 24:3–6).

A. *Anyone can fall down before God in fear and cry; whether this is true repentance or true worship is another issue.* The word *worship* is derived from "worth ship," denoting the worth or value of an object or person. Those who come in true worship recognize the moral qualities that exist in him and seek to reproduce these traits in their own lives. Worship is a form of fellowship with God, and only those with "clean hands and pure hearts" can understand the spiritual qualities necessary for personal communion with the one who is completely holy.

B. *The poet stressed both the inner and outer nature of character.* Purity of hands is expressed in righteous deeds. Purity of lips means proper speech. Purity of heart means controlled and guided desire. Those who worship will find that righteousness is its own reward, because the God they worship is one who can and will deliver them from harm. This, to the Jewish poet, was the highest concept of salvation. Verse 6 contains both the prayer and affirmation of the people that they were earnestly seeking to become a people of God.

III. A dialogue with the king (Ps. 24:7–10).

A. *This song was probably sung antiphonally as the people marched toward the site where the ark would be placed.* In verse 7 the people came to the Holy Place, symbolized in the song by a great citadel barred by a heavy door. When they cried for the door to be opened, a voice within called out to the worshipers to identify the great King they had with them, symbolized by the ark of the covenant.

B. *They represented him as the one who heads the forces of righteousness.* What a wonderful picture of our God! His glory is the reflection of his righteousness! We, too, can be righteous when we come in repentance and commitment to the one who revealed this righteousness in his own life and then paid our sin debt, rose for our justification, and lives to make intercession for us. What a privilege to worship him in spirit and in truth.

Conclusion

One of the greatest motivators for righteous living is to have a full view of God. The Jews conceived of their God as completely holy. For this reason, he demanded that those who worshiped him must reproduce in their own lives the traits that distinguished him from all others.

SUNDAY MORNING, JUNE 20

Title: The Ideal Father

Text: He arose, and came to his father. But when he was yet a great way off, his father saw him, and had compassion and ran, and fell on his neck, and kissed him" ***(Luke 15:20).***

Scripture Reading: Luke 15:11–32

Hymns: "Faith of Our Fathers," Faber
"God, Our Father, We Adore Thee," Frazer
"I'll Live for Him," Hudson

Offertory Prayer: Our Father, we celebrate the fact that you are our heavenly Father. We also give thanks for the gift of earthly fathers. Teach them on this day of their significance and their responsibilities. Many earthly fathers earn the daily bread for their families, so we pray for their continued health and strength. We dedicate these gifts to your kingdom. In Jesus' name. Amen.

Introduction

Most fathers face the perplexity of guiding the development of their children. They struggle between being an authoritative tyrant and a liberal benefactor.

What makes an ideal father? Fortunately, we can go to God's Word and learn a lot about being a father. Many of Jesus' parables draw on the dynamics of family situations. The matchless story of the loving father in today's Scripture reading deals with some of the situations earthly fathers face.

Jesus gave the parable of the loving father as a portrait of God. He wanted the scribes and Pharisees to see that the Lord loved everyone—including the prodigals. Nonetheless, from this father's relationship with his two sons, we get some amazing insights about an ideal father.

I. Ideal fathers grant freedom.

A. *Freedom is a difficult gift.* The father about whom Jesus spoke represented an ideal father in that he gave freedom to both of his sons. The younger boy requested his inheritance. The father knew that according to custom he could divide his estate between the two boys.

Yet by giving the boys their inheritance early, the father knew the boys could squander their possessions. He could have said, "I'll keep it for you," or "Let me invest the inheritance for you. I have the advantage of many years of experience." But he did not. Instead, the father divided the inheritance and gave freedom to both boys to do as they pleased.

B. *Freedom can be a disastrous gift.* The father in Jesus' story may have thought of the possibilities of the far country. What he feared would happen did happen. The boy took his freedom, went to the far country, and wasted his inheritance.

Evidences abound of children abusing freedom, but that is the risk of being a parent. A grandfather once said to his grandson, "God gives every person a rope. Each person can choose what to do with that rope. You can tie the rope on a bucket, put the bucket in a well, and get a drink of water. Or you can put the rope around your neck and hang yourself." What an accurate picture of freedom! Each father lives with the fear of abused freedom. He must have faith that God can intervene even in that.

II. Ideal fathers treat children kindly.

A. *Some children test the justice system of a father.* The younger son asked for his inheritance. After his father gave it to him, he went to the far country and wasted it. The prodigal son decided to return. He went back to the father, asking to be a hired servant. If the father had given the boy what he deserved, he would have made him a servant. Instead, the father gave him sonship.

A good father often treats a child not the way the child deserves to be treated, but rather with unmerited favor. The ideal father deals with all his children with grace, but he deals with the wayward child with mercy.

B. *Some children test the disposition of a father.* The father had an older son. When the older son came home one day, he found a celebration in progress. He learned from a servant about the return of his brother. The celebration made the boy jealous and angry. He would not join the celebration.

When the father came outside, he received the angry words of his older son. The father must have been sad and angry himself, yet he treated the sulking boy with extreme kindness.

Ideally, fathers should respond to children with a kind disposition: "Ye fathers, provoke not your children to wrath: but bring them up in the nurture and admonition of the Lord" (Eph. 6:4).

III. Ideal fathers provide an example.

A. *Children need to see the example of a good father.* Both boys in Jesus' story could see an example of a good father. They observed the father's love for each of them. The father showed no favoritism.

Some of the roles a good father plays are a masculine father figure, a friend who spends time, and a parent who teaches obedience with patience and firmness.

B. *Children need to see the example of a godly father.* A father's relationship of trust in the Lord provides an excellent model for children. The greatest gift a father can give a child is love for God and faith in Jesus Christ.

Conclusion

You can be a good father. Jesus' story of a father who had two sons provides good principles for fathering. Will you choose to be God's ideal father?

SUNDAY EVENING, JUNE 20

Title: I Am Unworthy

Text: "I am unworthy—how can I reply to you? I put my hand over my mouth, I spoke once, but I have no answer—twice, but I will say no more" ***(Job 40:4–5 NIV).***

Scripture Reading: Job 40:1–5; Matthew 16:26; John 3:16

Introduction

When God made man in the garden of Eden, he placed within him certain unique characteristics and qualities. God explains this difference between man and animals by telling us that he created man in his image, after his likeness (cf. Gen. 1:26).

One of these unique characteristics is the awareness of one's personal importance in creation. Psychologists have other names for it: self-esteem, self-worth, personhood, and so forth.

And this is good! This is what makes it possible for people to realize that they "have a place in the sun"; they have a unique personal dignity and importance imparted to them by their Creator. As they come to know God, one of the most exciting revelations of all is that they learn they are a part of God's master plan for eternity.

But as soon as each of us reaches what we call "the age of accountability," or "the moment of discretion," or the time in our lives when our consciences awaken to right and wrong, Satan attacks our self-esteem and sets about to play havoc with it. Sometimes he will try to exaggerate it, to cause us to have terribly inflated opinions of ourselves—to the point that we feel we are self-sufficient, that we do not need God. Then we strut like a proud peacock, disgusting to those who observe us and a grief to the heart of God.

Or if Satan fails here, he goes to the other extreme, seeking to destroy our self-esteem. Low self-esteem is one of the most damaging and devastating attitudes toward life that one can assume.

There is a point where these extremes meet. It is somewhat paradoxical: we have to be humbled to see the extent of our sinfulness against a loving God, yet we also have to acknowledge that God has indeed made us unique. We are special and we are fallen. This contrast works to increase our gratitude toward God.

I. The setting.

A. *The voices of Job's three friends are now silent.* They have said all that they knew to say. In fact, they have fallen to repeating themselves. Finally, Elihu, the last person who appears to give counsel to Job—but to no avail—is cut short by God himself. With a stroke of divine satire, God cuts Elihu short! Suddenly, in the midst of Elihu's performance, a fierce storm arises. Out of the storm God speaks to Job, and his words are a commentary on Elihu's speech! (Read Job 38:2–3.)

B. *Job had been begging for an opportunity to state his case before God.* Moreover, he wanted the privilege of having God speak to him. Finally, the moment had come. The first thing God did was remind Job that he was still who he said he was. "Brace yourself like a man; I will question you, and you shall answer me" (Job 38:3). God proclaims his immeasurable might in creation; he says that man cannot understand the ways of the Creator; and he declares that he alone is the ruler of the universe. Job has known that and admitted it all along. God confronts Job with recognizing the difference between God and man. He says, "Job, be a man—what I created you to be. Let me be God!"

C. *We have here the mystery and the miracle of faith.* As God brings Job face-to-face with the universe, he asks Job if he finds himself able to govern that universe. The point of God's argument with Job is to cause him to realize that since he can neither understand nor control the physical world around him, how can he understand God or enter into debate with him?

II. The remarkable revelation (Job 40:3).

A. *Job says in essence, "God, all at once, in the light of what you have said about yourself and your great power, I see how really insignificant I am and how utterly unworthy I am to be so important to you!"* Job's cry, "I am unworthy," is a great cry. He has seen God's greatness and his love and concern for people, and he is overcome with his unworthiness to be so considered by God.

B. *It is possible to grasp the greatness of the universe, the marvel of God's creation, without understanding it.* It is possible to be fully aware of the existence of God, even of something of the nature of God, without understanding all there is to know about him. But all of this realization of what God has created in the relationship between himself and man must produce in humankind a sense of unworthiness in the presence of a holy and righteous God.

C. *This is a crossroad for people.* Some go in one direction—the wrong direction—and come to see themselves as little demigods, little Caesars, who do not need God. But others, like Job, come to be so amazed and overcome at God's desire to have fellowship and a relationship with them, that all they can say is, "Lord, I am unworthy of this! There is no good thing in me!"

III. The consummation.

A. *What did Jesus do when he dealt with people?* First, he came to them just as he found them and spoke to them where they were. In the light and glory of his presence, they immediately saw their unworthiness. When God saw the sincerity of their hearts, he quickly lifted them to the point of realizing what they could become through his power and because of his saving grace.

B. *Two statements Jesus made bring together in marvelous revelation what God thinks about people.* In the first statement, "What shall a man give in exchange for his soul?" (Matt. 16:26), Jesus was using the terms of the marketplace, the world of trade. He made a man's soul of greater value than the whole world. Job had shouted, "I am unworthy!" (Job 40:3). But in God's sight, Job was greater than all of the world and its possessions.

C. *So then, when Jesus' question, "What shall a man give in exchange for his soul?" has brought us face-to-face with the value of our souls, we discover that we have no means of buying our souls back from the kingdom of darkness.* Then we hear Jesus say, "For God so loved the world, that he gave his only begotten Son . . ." (John 3:16). That is God's evaluation of the worth of a soul! To save us from hopelessly perishing, God gave his only begotten Son. We cannot understand this, but we can revel in its glory!

Conclusion

Frederick W. Faber expressed the wonder of God's love this way:

How Thou canst think so well of us,
And be the God Thou art,
Is darkness to my intellect
But sunshine to my heart.

G. Campbell Morgan, in thinking of God's inconceivable love for us, rephrased Faber's poem and wrote it this way:

And Thou dost think so well of us,
Because of what Thou art,
Thy love illumines my intellect,
And fills with fear my heart.

Indeed, God is mindful of us and visits us. When he visited us in the person of his Son, he came to reveal that each individual is worth more than all the world. We are so dear to him that he gave his only begotten Son for our salvation.

Wednesday Evening, June 23

Title: The Joy of Forgiveness
Text: "Blessed is he whose transgression is forgiven, whose sin is covered" ***(Ps. 32:1).***
Scripture Reading: Psalm 32:1–5

Introduction

As with Psalm 51, scholars virtually agree on the occasion of this Hebrew song. God heard the prayer of the penitent David and restored full fellowship to him. The forgiven man then composed this joyful testimony of the peace that comes when one finds forgiveness. Perhaps a year passed between Nathan's visit to David after he sinned with Bathsheba and the writing of his prayer for forgiveness (Ps. 51). Though no records exist to confirm it, most scholars believe a shorter time passed between that prayer for restoration and the writing of this beautiful psalm.

I. Happiness of the forgiven sinner (Ps. 32:1–2).

The Hebrew plural construct translated "blessed" in many versions is best rendered "Oh, the happinesses of" and expresses the many delights of the one who feels the burden of guilt lifted. Where David used three words for wrongdoing in Psalm 51, he used three figures of speech for God's way of dealing with such conduct in this psalm. They are "lifted up and carried away," "hidden from God's eye," "no longer charged against the sinner." The expressions used by Bible writers to express forgiveness are meaningful, containing great insights into how they felt about both sin and the removal of it.

II. Misery of unforgiven sin (Ps. 32:3–4).

As the poet looked back, he took a leaf out of his life's book and described his misery during the period of stubborn and willful silence. What did David do from the day he sinned until the time he was willing to pour out his soul to God in brokenhearted repentance? At first he probably refused to acknowledge his sin even to himself. Most likely, he continued to bluff and pose, playing the hypocrite and seeking daily to convince his neighbors that all was well. No confession came from his lips. Night after night, however, he could hear voices in his inner self accusing him of his vile deeds. No sleep came; remorse and dread burdened him.

III. Way to forgiveness (Ps. 32:5).

A. *How does forgiveness come?* Forgiveness comes only by complete confession to God and, when practical and wise, before the religious community. In this verse, David mentioned only that he confessed his transgressions to God. This neither confirms nor denies whether he said anything to others about his terrible deeds.

B. *The Old and New Testaments agree on the necessity for confession of sin.* The former says, "He that covereth his sins shall not prosper: but whoso confesseth and forsaketh them shall have mercy" (Prov. 28:13). The latter says, "If we confess our sins, he is faithful and just to forgive us our sins, and to cleanse us from all unrighteousness (1 John 1:9). If the condition is not met, the blessing cannot be received.

IV. Another word from the forgiven sinner (Ps. 32:6–11).

A. *The remainder of the psalm seems at first reading to be anticlimactic.* It is, however, the most important of all, for it contains practical advice to others who may be in a state of unconfessed sin.

B. *Do not be stubborn!* Follow the example of the one who wrote of his own experience: you will find relief when the sin is forgiven.

Conclusion

The sooner we repent and call out for mercy, the sooner joy and peace can come to our lives. No one can have perfect peace within or render effective service in God's kingdom as long as sin mars fellowship with God. Because God loves us, he is always ready to forgive, but we must take the initiative to repent and seek his favor.

SUNDAY MORNING, JUNE 27

Title: Bringing Up Mother and Father

Text: "Honour thy father and thy mother; that thy days may be long upon the land which the LORD thy God giveth thee" ***(Ex. 20:12).***

Scripture Reading: Ephesians 6:1–4

Hymns: "Crown Him with Many Crowns," Bridges
"The Solid Rock," Mote
"Take My Life, and Let It Be," Havergal

Offertory Prayer: Our Father, we celebrate your presence with us today. Thank you for putting us in this world. We adore you for the beauty and design of your creation. We also express gratitude for your work of redemption in Jesus Christ. We are amazed over your grace to us. Today we come to this part of our worship to express our gratitude in a tangible way. With this offering we thank you. In Jesus' name. Amen.

Introduction

We hear much about the responsibility of parents to children but little about the responsibility of children to parents. Our bookshelves contain volumes that have to do with rearing children, but have you ever seen a book dealing with the idea of children bringing up parents? Healthy relationships exist only when both sides fulfill their responsibilities.

The Bible speaks to both parents and children. Today let us look specifically at the obligations of children. Let us notice the implications of the command "Honour thy father and thy mother: that thy days may be long upon the land which the LORD thy God giveth thee" (Ex. 20:12).

I. This commandment implies respect.

A. *"Honour thy father and thy mother."* The Hebrew word translated "honor" means "to value" or "to treasure." The command means to treasure one's parents. Unfortunately, most children do not realize that their parents are a treasure they should cherish. Listen to these words: "Children now love luxury; they have bad manners, contempt for authority. Children are now tyrants, not the servants of their households. They contradict their parents, chatter before company, gobble up dainties at the table, tyrannize their teachers." Oddly enough these words were written by the ancient Greek philosopher Socrates.

B. *Look at the reasons for honoring parents.* Children should consider why they should respect their parents.

1. Children should respect their parents because of their parents' sacrifices. Mothers have experienced physical pain in giving birth. Both parents have worked hard to provide food, shelter, clothing, and luxuries for their children.
2. Children should respect their parents because of their parents' age and experiences. They have gained experience in the "school of hard knocks." Experience has the unusual ability to bring wisdom to parents.

II. This commandment implies responsibility.

A. *Children have the responsibility to love their parents.* Closely akin to the matter of reverence and respect is the idea of loving one's mother and father. Some children are ashamed of their parents. They are embarrassed over their parents' home, jobs, or physical appearances. The Lord wants children to have love for their parents. The best children are those who have an unconditional and unashamed love for their parents.

B. *Children have the responsibility to help their parents.* In ancient Israel household duties were the responsibility of all family members. Children helped run the household. In today's society we have reversed the roles. Now it seems that the parents work for the children. Mother, father, and children need to work together for the good of all.

C. *Children have the responsibility to obey their parents.* Part of growing up is to have parents to give rules and regulations. Complete freedom destroys children. When parents give rules and regulations, children need to obey.

III. This commandment implies a result.

A. *"That thy days may be long upon the land which the Lord thy God giveth thee."* This promise is sometimes misunderstood to speak about the longevity of individuals. But the expression "thy days" in the promise refers to the whole nation of Israel. For the children to respect their parents would result in long life for the nation.

B. *Failure to heed this promise has led to the downfall of many nations.* Edward A. Gibbon, in his book *Decline and Fall of the Roman Empire*, states several reasons for the fall of Rome, including the steady increase of sexual immorality and the dissolution of the Roman home.

One of the most tragic passages of Scripture comes from Judges 2:10: "And also all that generation were gathered unto their fathers: and there arose another generation after them, which knew not the Lord, nor yet the works which he had done for Israel." The survival of a nation depends greatly on the solidarity of the home.

Conclusion

The Bible tells children how to bring up their parents. Treat them with great respect. Regard them as precious treasures. Help them with household responsibilities. Love them.

What do you do if you are not obedient in any of these areas? Ask God and your parents for forgiveness. He will help you make a fresh start.

Sunday Evening, June 27

Title: My Ears Had Heard, but Now My Eyes Have Seen!

Text: "My ears had heard of you but now my eyes have seen you. Therefore I despise myself and repent in dust and ashes" ***(Job 42:5–6 NIV)***.

Scripture Reading: Job 42:5–6; Matthew 4:17

Introduction

Before we can have a positive relationship with God, we must first discover ourselves—learn who we really are—and then we will be in a position to begin to discover who God is. Job could write volumes about this. He had gone through some of the most devastating experiences that could possibly come to a human being. And in the process, God had peeled off a lot of veneers in

Job's life. Job was a good man—decent, moral, religious, and law abiding. He knew God, although not nearly as well as he thought he knew him. Somehow, throughout his past comfortable life, he had never had reason or occasion to find out who *he* really was—where he was strong and where he was weak.

In our study last Sunday night, we stood by while Job came to the stunning realization of *who he really was.* When he did, he cried out in complete sincerity before God. "I am unworthy" (Job 40:3). From that moment wonderful things began to happen. Job began to understand who *God* is. No, Job never fully and completely came to understand God. Neither his mind—nor ours—would ever be capable of that. But Job's discovery of himself moved him closer to God than he ever had been.

I. A secondhand knowledge of God (Job 42:1–4).

A. *A secondhand knowledge of God is better than no knowledge at all.* In fact, this is where we begin discovering God: someone else tells us what he or she knows about God, what he or she has experienced in regard to God's reality. Or perhaps we read what others say about him. We see around us the evidence of his handiwork in creation. During Job's experience, God paraded before him the majesty and awesomeness of his creation—the world and everything in it.

B. *Job could have gone either of two ways.* He could have sunk into despair, convinced that God is too far removed from man for there ever to be meaningful communication between the two. But because God was not through with Job, Job went the other way and saw that humans are unique within God's creation and that they are made in God's image and after his likeness. God did not explain the reason for Job's overwhelming troubles. In effect, God was saying to Job: "Some things come into a person's life that are beyond human understanding. But while these things are working themselves out, they are under divine control, and they are moving toward the fulfillment of my purposes in life!"

C. *When God made humans and gave them free will, God limited himself.* He gave people an incredibly long rope or, we might say, "a lot of space." Humans have been both the heartbreak and the ecstasy of God. They have vacillated from being the tools of Satan and the enemies of God to being friends of God, as was Abraham (Isa. 41:8), and people after God's own heart, as was David (1 Sam. 13:14).

II. Job's firsthand knowledge of God (Job 42:5–6).

A. *It is significant that Job had not been moved by all of the brilliant descriptions of God given by Bildad, Eliphaz, Zophar, and Elihu.* Job had heard all of that, but none of it had moved him—except to anger, hostility, and deeper frustration. But then God spoke. All the rhetoric of Job's friends was past. It was just "God and Job," and that was quite enough!

B. *After listening to God, Job came to two conclusions that had never truly broken in upon his consciousness before.* First, he said, "Lord, I know that you can do all things"; and second, "No plan of yours can be thwarted" (v. 2 NIV). Job came to the clear conviction that God was omnipotent, and that in the long run, no purpose of God could be frustrated. Whatever God willed or started would be carried out.

C. *Job said, "I despise myself."* The Hebrew word used here literally means "to disappear, to retract, to repudiate." Earlier Job had said, "I am unworthy" (40:3). But this statement goes far beyond that: "Lord, I retract all that I have said; I repudiate the position I had taken up. I cancel myself out completely."

D. *Then Job realized that, after all, he was a personality made by God.* So he continued, "I . . . repent in dust and ashes" (v. 6). The language of Job was that of complete submission to God, and in that submission we see the greatness of Job as we see it nowhere else in this book. Alfred, Lord Tennyson wrote:

> Our wills are ours, we know not how,
> Our wills are ours to make them thine.

People rise to the ultimate dignity, grandeur, and splendor of their own lives when they recognize their place and yield themselves in complete submission to God's will.

III. The knowledge of Jesus.

One of the key messages of Jesus' ministry was "Repent, for the kingdom of heaven is near" (Matt. 4:17 NIV).

A. *What was Jesus' fundamental point?* Simply that people must recognize God's authority and then submit to it! The way of entrance into the kingdom of heaven is that of repentance. Job repented when he recognized the power and love and mercy of God.

B. *God has many ways of breaking in upon the consciousness of the human soul.* We have seen how he did so with Job. He comes in other ways to other people, but the result is always the same. The person to whom God comes is brought face-to-face with God and has to say, "Lord, I am filled with sorrow! I am not worthy of you!" From the moment one says this from the depths of his or her heart and soul, God lifts that person from the dust to a place of fullness of life.

Conclusion

Once we repent and accept God's will, the "peace of God which transcends all understanding" (Phil. 4:7 NIV) will flood our lives.

Wednesday Evening, June 30

Title: Be Still, God Reigns
Text: "Be still, and know that I am God: I will be exalted among the heathen, I will be exalted in the earth" ***(Ps. 46:10).***
Scripture Reading: Psalm 46:1–11

Introduction

Most scholars believe this psalm was composed in the aftermath of God's delivering the Israelites from Sennacherib's army. This deliverance occurred after the siege of Jerusalem that ended when the angel of the Lord killed 185,000 Assyrian soldiers in one night. Martin Luther's famous hymn "A Mighty Fortress Is Our God" took its starting point from this mighty, moving Hebrew song that proclaims the sufficiency of God for the crises of life. This robust psalm, defiant of God's enemies, moves beyond the local situation that may have inspired it, to universal principles. Its great value, however, is the word it speaks to individuals to have faith in God's protecting hand and ample resources. It proclaims the ascendancy of God in three areas.

I. God has power over the forces of nature (Ps. 46:1–3).

Because communication technology is so advanced, news of earthquakes, hurricanes, floods, and other tragedies reach our ears instantly. We live in the face of grim reality, often seeing innocent people victimized by these terrible events.

A. *Yet God has ultimate control of these forces.* He limits them, allowing them to go so far and no farther. The important fact is that with God in our hearts, we can face even the possibility of world catastrophe with firm faith. Sometimes he spares his children, but sometimes they too must suffer or even die.

B. *God's children must not surrender their faith when they confront a tragedy they cannot understand or explain.* Every person will, at some time, have an experience in which all the elements seem to combine to overwhelm him. We must learn, with God's help, to endure with dogged persistency. Continued faith will produce courage. God controls this world and will never turn it over to evil or chance.

II. God has power over those who attack his strongholds (Ps. 46:4–7).

These verses refer to the city of Jerusalem, God's citadel, where his temple was. In it were the religious symbols that had served as a unifying force for the nation.

A. *Though they have their shortcomings, the institutions of religious faith are important.* They contain the depository of religious customs through the centuries. God protects his citadels. When some phase of institutional life needs to be destroyed, God is equal to the occasion. When, however, it needs only to be corrected and then protected, he is also equal to that task.

B. *God protects his Word, the Bible.* How else can one explain its existence when so many have sought to destroy it throughout the centuries? God's people need to trust him, continuing to believe in the integrity of his Word.

III. God has control over the whole warring world (Ps. 46:8–11).

What does a Christian do when he sees the nations of the world moving toward what seems to be an inevitable war that will bring universal destruction to the human race?

A. *The psalmist says, "He maketh wars to cease" (v. 9), and of course this is true.* Yet wars continue to arise. Christians must realize peace can come only when people have peace in their hearts, and this comes only through Jesus, the Prince of Peace. Thus, when we take the message of Jesus to the lost, we are doing the one thing that must have priority in all our service. We must, however, cooperate with all those who are seeking to promote peace, as long as we can do so without compromising our Christian convictions.

Finally, however, we must live with an attitude of trust, doing all that we can do but leaving the rest in God's hands. This is what the Lord meant when he said through the psalmist, "Be still, and know that I am God" (v. 10).

Conclusion

When the psalmist said, "Be still," he was, in a sense, speaking comfort to the harassed, but he had another audience in mind. His message was for the restless and turbulent world. His statement was more than mere assurance to God's people: he wanted to make it clear that God's glory would be manifested.

When the forces of evil have done everything they can to oppose God, he will stand victorious. Since this is true, his people can rejoice and be happy. If God be for us, who can be against us?

SUGGESTED PREACHING PROGRAM FOR THE MONTH OF

JULY

■ Sunday Mornings

The potency of a sermon is directly proportionate to the ways in which Jesus Christ meets the needs and answers the questions of the congregation. In light of this, a series titled "Questions People Most Ask Ministers" is suggested for Sunday mornings in July and August.

■ Sunday Evenings

Many of us are swayed by the shifts in our emotions; we have no control over them. More often than not these emotions harm us; despair, fear, and hate fill us with misery. Nevertheless, the Lord gives us great hope. The suggested series title to address these issues is "Salvation from Destructive Emotions."

■ Wednesday Evenings

Continue the series "Mining Spiritual Truths from the Psalms."

SUNDAY MORNING, JULY 4

Title: Why Are Prayers Not Answered?

Text: "Ask, and it shall be given you; seek, and ye shall find; knock, and it shall be opened unto you: for every one that asketh receiveth; and he that seeketh findeth; and to him that knocketh it shall be opened" ***(Matt. 7:7–8).***

Scripture Reading: Matthew 7:7–11

Hymns: "Teach Me to Pray," Reitz
"Tell It to Jesus," Lorenz
"Sweet Hour of Prayer," Walford

Offertory Prayer: Dear Lord, at this time when we celebrate our national independence, we confess our dependence on you. We are aware that all of our good gifts come from you. We praise you, our Father, for your gifts of love and grace. And now we return to you a portion of those gifts. From hearts overflowing with gratitude, we give this offering into your hands. We pray in Jesus' name and for his sake. Amen.

Introduction

Your mother was very ill, and you fervently prayed that God would heal her. She died. Was your prayer unanswered?

An opening came up in your company. All the pieces fit for you to get the job: you were prepared for it; you had paid your dues with the company; it was your time to receive the promotion. You prayed that God would allow you to have that job. But they passed over you and brought in someone from outside the company for the position. Was your prayer unanswered?

You lost a stone out of your ring. It was a ring that had both actual value and sentimental value to you. You prayed that God would help you find the stone, but you never did find it. Was your prayer unanswered?

Unanswered prayer is one of the biggest problems we face as Christians. We believe in prayer; we practice prayer; but it seems that many of our prayers are not answered.

"Why do some prayers go unanswered?" is one of the questions most frequently asked of ministers. Such questions will be the basis of our sermons for the next eight Sundays.

I. The problem: prayer with no answer.

A. *A limited view of prayer as petition.* We must recognize that we are thinking of only one kind of prayer—the prayer of petition—when we say that our prayers have not been answered.

Petition is only one form prayer takes. Our praying should also include prayers of adoration, confession, intercession, and submission.

B. *A limited expectation from prayer.* We decide beforehand how God must answer a particular prayer. If the prayer is not answered in exactly the manner we think it should be, then we may complain that God has not answered our prayer.

Such expectation overlooks the sovereignty of God. God is certainly not obligated to answer our prayers in the manner that we have determined beforehand.

Consider another way of viewing this point. The Bible contains many examples of prayers that are apparently unanswered.

Moses prayed that God would allow him to enter the Promised Land, but he died on top of Mount Nebo. The prophet Habakkuk began his book with the cry, "O LORD, how long shall I cry, and thou wilt not hear!" (Hab. 1:2). Paul prayed three times for the removal of the thorn in his flesh that was hindering his missionary labors, but for the rest of his life he was compelled to make the best of it (2 Cor. 12:9). Even the Savior himself in the Garden of Gethsemane prayed that the Father would remove his cup of suffering if it was his will (Luke 22:42). But he drank that cup to the bitter dregs.

How are we to understand these instances? Was God simply not listening? No, certainly not. Here again we have to examine our assumptions about what God *should* do. We pigeonhole God by expecting him to answer our prayers affirmatively. "Yes" is what we implicitly demand from God. We need to see that "no" is just as clear an answer as "yes." We need the faith to joyfully accept either answer.

II. The promise: prayer with assurance.

A. *Pray with persistence.* Jesus taught us to pray with assurance. When we pray with assurance, we can pray with persistence. We bring to God an undiscouraged life of prayer. Jesus expressed that persistence with three words:

1. Ask. When we ask of God, we see our need and are willing to make contact with God. We know that we have a need God can meet.
2. Seek. This indicates that there is some effort on our part along with the request to God. We can pray, "Give us this day our daily bread," but we must still work. We can pray, "Thy kingdom come," but we must still witness and preach. Someone has observed that there are three ways that persons can cooperate with God—by thinking, working, and praying. But each alone does not eliminate the others.
3. Knock. This would imply the persistence that we bring to prayer. But if we keep knocking on God's door in prayer, does this mean that we must badger God before he will answer us? No. But it does indicate that we must be serious in our prayer.

B. *Pray with patience.* Prayers can be answered in three ways: yes, no, and wait awhile. We may need to wait for things to be done on God's schedule. Charles Haddon Spurgeon likened waiting to a long sea voyage that would bring back great treasure from distant lands. "Coasters" were small boats that carried coal and ordinary things from port to port in the same country, hugging the coast while they traveled. But great treasures came from larger ships that sailed out of sight on the ocean. Some things are worth waiting for.

C. *Pray to a person.* Remember that our prayers are addressed to our heavenly Father. God is our Father, and he wants the very best for each one of us.

Conclusion

Are our prayers really unanswered? Toward the close of his life Adoniram Judson said that all his sincere and earnest prayers were answered. But Judson prayed to enter India and was compelled to go to Burma. He prayed for his wife's life, and he buried her and two children. He prayed for release from the king of Ava's prison and laid there for months, chained and miserable. He prayed for converts, and it was years before the first convert was made. Scores of Judson's petitions had gone without an affirmative answer. Nevertheless, he maintained that he had always been answered.

Paul had prayed for the removal of the thorn from his flesh, but he also testified that God's grace was sufficient for every need. And when Jesus prayed that the cup might pass, he had to drink it. He faced Pilate and the cross; we have salvation because of it.

Unanswered prayer? No, prayers answered beyond our imaginations.

SUNDAY EVENING, JULY 4

Title: Escape from Fear

Text: "When I saw him, I fell at his feet as dead. And he laid his right hand upon me, saying unto me, Fear not; I am the first and the last; I am he that liveth, and was dead; and, behold, I am alive for evermore, Amen; and have the keys of hell and of death" ***(Rev. 1:17–18).***

Scripture Reading: Revelation 1:9–18

Introduction

Delivering humanity from debilitating fear is both Jesus' mission and message. Certainly the problem of fear is a problem to be recognized in many lives. One of the most outstanding and surprising disclosures of stressful, nervous, modern civilization is that many people are in the clutches of fear.

Fear is a problem for all types of people: prestigious or alienated, rich or poor, educated or ignorant, old or young. All struggle with fear.

And people have all types of fears—fear of themselves; fear of others; fear of the past, present, or future; fear of sickness and death; fear of poverty. The list continues.

Some of our fears are normal. Normal fears can be an aid to our safety, comfort, knowledge, and health. A person void of fear is in a dangerous situation. However, many fears are abnormal; they undercut our efficiency, our happiness, and our mental and physical well-being. They paralyze us! They are enemies of the spirit and the flesh.

Throughout the Bible, God often tells people not to be afraid. Two words stand out in the Bible like mountain peaks: "Fear not!" With these words God comforted Abraham: "Fear not, Abram: I am thy shield, and thy exceeding great reward" (Gen. 15:1). With these same words he comforted Isaac at his lonely task of digging wells in the wilderness (26:24–26). With these same words he comforted Jacob when Joseph was lost in Egypt (46:3). And similarly he comforted the Israelites at the Red Sea: "Moses said unto the people, Fear ye not, stand still, and see the salvation of the LORD, which he will shew today" (Ex. 14:13).

The psalmist declared, "I will fear no evil: for thou art with me; thy rod and thy staff they comfort me" (Ps. 23:4). Isaiah gave this admonition from the Lord: "Fear thou not; for I am with thee: be not dismayed; for I am thy God: I will strengthen thee; yea, I will help thee; yea, I will uphold thee with the right hand of my righteousness" (Isa. 41:10). God wants us to walk and work without being overcome by fear.

Yet many Christians are tormented by fears. This should not be! We can—we must—break the fear habit before it destroys us. Application of the following positive techniques will help us to do this.

I. We must cultivate the habit of accepting change.

A. *We often love life's ruts.* We love familiar scenery; the dependable landmark; the security of job, family, and home. We often become afraid to change, and when change is forced upon us, we become fearful and confused.

B. *Recognize that life itself is the story of change.* Nothing in God's world is permanent. He made it that way. There is nothing we can do to alter that. Human existence is fluid. History is the record of the ebb and flow of the human tide. Nature itself tells the story of a restless universe.

C. *The fear habit is broken when we accept change as a normal, natural part of life.* Fear does not stop change; it only adds to its intensity. To live in constant fear of change is to betray our faith in God and in his world. It is imperative that we recognize:

1. Change has opportunity as well as danger.
2. Change has life as well as death.
3. Change makes living interesting and challenging.
4. Change often makes possible a better world.

D. *It is a mistake to try to re-create the past, freeze the present, or stave off the future.*

II. Cultivate the habit of adapting to the inevitable.

A. *Make the best of any situation.* This is not merely weak submission to the whims of fate. It is adjustment to the changes of life to use them for our very best.

B. *Walk by faith and not by sight.* The child of God must remember to do this. When we walk in this manner, we can be of good courage even in the face of death, the greatest change of all.

C. *Bible characters show us that we have power to make adjustments to the changes of life.* When God closes some doors, he opens others. This is seen in the lives of Joseph, Moses, Daniel, and Paul.

III. Cultivate the habit of being governed by facts.

A. *Many fears are not about existing situations.* They center around imaginary circumstances and events that we are afraid might happen.

When the Israelites were in search of the Promised Land, twelve spies went in to investigate it. They came back and reported to Moses that they found it to be a land of milk and honey. There was, however, one thing wrong: They reported that there were "giants in the land." At this report the people were fearful and wanted to turn back, but Joshua and Caleb thought otherwise. Far from being dismayed, they knew the "giants" were mere men. Thus they said, "The Lord is with us: fear them not" (Num. 14:9). We need to have the faith and common sense of Joshua and Caleb.

B. *Many fears are generated from prejudice.* We often feed our fears with preconceived ideas and generalities concerning others. God gave us our intelligence to use: he surely wants us to deal with things as they are.

IV. Cultivate the habit of complete trust in God.

A. *It is a truth presented in the Old Testament.* The Old Testament prophet presented trust in God as an antidote to fear. Isaiah declared, "Behold, God is my salvation; I will trust, and not be afraid" (Isa. 12:2). The psalms are full of expressions of trust in God as a remedy for fear. The psalmist said, "I sought the LORD, and he heard me, and delivered me from all my fears" (Ps. 34:4); and "The LORD is my light and my salvation; whom shall I fear?" (Ps. 27:1). Yet again, the psalmist declares, "What time I am afraid, I will trust in thee" (Ps. 56:3). The writer did not say that God delivered him from *some* fears or from *many* fears, but from *all* fears. When we cultivate the habit of complete trust in God, we can be free of our fears.

B. *The New Testament helps us cultivate the habit of complete trust in God.* Jesus frequently told his disciples that they need have no fear. Jesus wanted them to know that as God cares for the lilies, birds, and the grass, he would care for them (Matt. 6:25–30). Paul sounds the same note many times: "For ye have not received the spirit of bondage again to fear; but ye have received the Spirit of adoption, whereby we cry, Abba, Father" (Rom. 8:15). The author of Hebrews put it plainly, "The Lord is my helper, and I will not fear what man shall do unto me" (Heb. 13:6). In 1 John 4:18 we find these memorable words: "There is no fear in love; but perfect love casts out fear." How do we get perfect love? We ask God to fill us with his Holy Spirit.

Complete confidence in a great, good, gracious God gives direction and stability to life. We need to build the faith habit instead of the fear habit. The trust habit will keep us from being lonely by keeping us in touch with the Father above, and it will engender us with great power. Trust in God is sure protection for the hidden dangers that lie in wait for all of us.

Conclusion

People who find strength at all times by trusting the Lord are those who conquer fear. Their hearts are not fixed on trusting themselves, but on trusting God. Their hearts do not trust in circumstances and imaginary fantasies; their hearts trust in God. May God make us such men and women.

WEDNESDAY EVENING, JULY 7

Title: Prayer of a Penitent

Text: "Have mercy upon me, O God . . . Create in me a clean heart" ***(Ps. 51:1, 10).***
Scripture Reading: Psalm 51:1–19

Introduction

Psalm 51 tells of a man who has fallen into the snare of temptation. The trap has been sprung. He lies helpless, trembling in its grasp. With stern accuracy, a human soul's struggle for deliverance from an all-pervading malady is presented. So accurately does the writer describe the many-sided symptoms of spiritual sickness that one would think he was a contemporary man familiar with modern psychology. The truth is this poet was inspired by the almighty God before whom we all stand exposed in our sinful ways.

I. A plea for pardon (Ps. 51:1–6).

Scholars agree that the one crying for forgiveness is David after his adultery with Bathsheba.

A. *The first need we have as violators of the moral law is to know that God, the author of that law, has justified us from the guilt of our act.* David did not plead extenuating circumstances, but cried for mercy. His only hope to have the terrible deed erased from his record was that God would act from grace—free and unmerited love—which we find in Jesus Christ's atonement at Calvary.

B. *David gave three images of sin—rebellion, moral crookedness, and missing the mark.* His affair with Bathsheba and the following events included all three. His insistence that his sin was against God alone showed that in his intense desire for peace in his soul, he could think only of his relationship with his Creator. Of course, he had sinned against others—Bathsheba, Uriah, Joab, his family, the nation, himself—but they were not his immediate concern.

C. *David first needed to establish a right relationship with God.* We need to follow his pattern: reconciliation with God before any other relationships can be mended.

II. A prayer for purity (Ps. 51:7–12).

Pardon is not enough. Neither, in New Testament language, is justification enough. Jesus spoke of being "born again" (John 3:3), and Paul spoke of being "a new creature" in Christ (2 Cor. 5:17). Contrary to what some have said, there is no such thing as being justified but not regenerated.

A. *Unless both justification and regeneration have taken place in one's experience, neither has occurred.* However, as we read further, we see that David was not a "lost person" crying to be saved, but a child of God. In New Testament language we would say he was a "saved man," crying out for God to restore the joy of his salvation. This puts an entirely different light on the exposition! Can a member of God's redeemed family sink like that? David did, and he suffered terrible consequences! God restored the personal fellowship, but David still had to suffer for the things he set in motion when he took another man's life and wife. One of his sons raped one of his daughters; another son rebelled and sought to steal the kingdom from David, succeeding temporarily.

B. *What a terrible thing sin is, and how we need to guard ourselves against it, remembering that when we think we are strong, we may be in the greatest danger of stumbling.* David cried passionately for purity. The word translated "create" is the same Hebrew word used in Genesis where the writer says God "created" the heavens and earth. It means "to bring something out of nothing." This is what God does when he makes us clean. We have no ability to make ourselves clean from our impurities.

III. A promise to praise (Ps. 51:13–19).

Of course, the thoughts overlap in the three sections outlined. David continued to magnify the horror of his sin, calling it "bloodguiltiness" (v. 14), but the emphasis was on his promise to praise God before others and to instruct them so they would not follow his terrible example.

A. *Bringing others to a knowledge of God's forgiveness is still the highest form of service.* Soul winning, which was been called "the finest of the fine arts," stands first in fruit bearing. In fact, a tree bears fruit when it produces more of its kind. Reproducing believers is what being a Christian is all about!

B. *Let the redeemed not be satisfied until they have made certain they will not meet God empty-handed.* As the old hymn says, "Not one soul with which to greet him, must I empty-handed go?" That would, indeed, be a tragedy.

Conclusion

Repentance is more than being sorry for sin. It is realizing the full implication of sin's destructive power. Every part of one's personality is affected by wrongdoing. Also, the lives of others may be ruined. Repentance is feeling so strongly about sin that one adopts God's attitude toward it. Only then can forgiveness come and broken fellowship be restored between the sinner and God.

Sunday Morning, July 11

Title: What About Discouragement?

Text: "And he said, Go forth, and stand upon the mount before the Lord. And, behold, the Lord passed by, and a great and strong wind rent the mountains, and brake in pieces the rocks before the LORD; but the LORD was not in the wind: and after the wind an earthquake; but the LORD was not in the earthquake: and after the earthquake a fire; but the LORD was not in the fire: and after the fire a still small voice" ***(1 Kings 19:11–12)***.

Scripture Reading: 1 Kings 19:1–18

Hymns: "Faith Is the Victory," Yates

"O God, Our Help in Ages Past," Watts

"Lead On, O King Eternal," Shurtleff

Offertory Prayer: Dear Lord, we thank you this day for your grace. We praise you for your glory. We pray that you would receive these offerings as you have received us. We ask that you would use them for your work as we dedicate ourselves to you. In Jesus' name we pray. Amen.

Introduction

Have you ever felt discouraged? Have you felt so discouraged that you were ready to quit? Likely so. That kind of discouragement manifests itself in many ways.

Maybe you get discouraged over the repetitiveness of your work at home. Had you known there would be so many dishes to wash, clothes to clean, and beds to make on top of working a forty-hour week, you are not sure you would have married. There is surely not much romance or glamour in all that work. You get so discouraged you think of quitting. After all, you know others who have recently divorced.

Or you face discouragement in your job. Working hard, going beyond what is expected of you, you cannot see that you have received any recognition or reward for your work. You get so discouraged, you think seriously of resigning.

Maybe your discouragement has to do with your Christian life and morals. All of your life you have been taught that virtue has its own reward, that goodness will be rewarded. You have tried to live a good Christian life, but you cannot see that it has taken you very far. No one seems to appreciate it. You get discouraged and think that you may quit trying to live a Christian life and live any way that appeals to you.

Discouragement is a common feeling that prompts many people to ask, "What can I do when I am so discouraged I feel like giving up?"

Among contemporary Christians you are in good company when you ask that question. But also among biblical characters you are in good company when you feel discouraged. Take Elijah, the prophet of God, for instance.

In 1 Kings 18 Elijah confronted the prophets of Baal in a showdown on Mount Carmel concerning who was greatest, God or Baal. In an amazing show of power, God proved his reality and strength. Elijah had faced the prophets of Baal and had unmistakably destroyed them—both spiritually and physically. Then God sent a rain that broke the drought in the land.

Ahab, king of Israel, told his wife, Jezebel, who was largely responsible for the introduction of Baal worship into the land, what had happened. She threatened the life of Elijah. Elijah became discouraged and ran. He ran south to Beersheba where he left his servant. Then he went a day's journey farther into the wilderness, sat down under a juniper tree, and asked God to take his life.

But in that time of great discouragement, when the prophet wanted to give up, he was met by God, ministered to by God, and motivated by God. His experience can give us some help and assurance when we get discouraged.

I. The cause of discouragement: thinking about self, not about God.

The cause of Elijah's discouragement was that he was thinking about himself and not about God. Even after the great show of God's power on Mount Carmel, Elijah was concerned with Jezebel's threat. Notice some possible reasons for this way of thinking to show up in our lives.

A. *Physical exhaustion.* Elijah was physically exhausted after his encounter with the prophets of Baal and his race before the chariot of Ahab into Jezreel. Physical exhaustion is one cause of discouragement. We just do not have the strength to face life.

B. *Nervous reaction.* Stress causes a reaction in our nervous system. It has been said that such great military geniuses as Hannibal, Frederick the Great, and George Washington were never so hard to beat as the day after they had suffered a defeat. It is also true that we are never so vulnerable as the day after a victory. A victory or an achievement can cause such a powerful emotional reaction that we are more vulnerable than usual to moral defeat or temptation.

C. *Apparent failure.* Apparent failure brings on discouragement. Even though Elijah had won against the prophets of Baal, he had apparently failed against the queen. And that discouraged him.

D. *Loneliness.* In 1 Kings 19:10 and 14 Elijah emphasized that he felt totally alone in the service of God.

E. *Fear of the future.* Elijah did not know his future. After what he had done for God, he expected recognition and position; instead, he received a threat against his life.

II. The cure for discouragement: trusting in God, not in self.

There is a cure for the discouragement we face. Notice how his encounter with God helped to cure Elijah's discouragement.

A. *Deal with the physical causes.* God fed Elijah and gave him a restful sleep. He dealt with the physical causes of Elijah's discouragement. The physical causes must be taken seriously.

B. *Gain spiritual help.* Here are three ways to do that:

   1. A vision of God. Elijah went to Mount Horeb to find God. He found him in the "still small voice" (1 Kings 19:12). Elijah received

a new understanding of God. He had looked for him only in the evidences of power, but God came to him instead in a "gentle whisper" (NIV).

2. A call to service. 1 Kings 19:15–16 outlines the tasks that God assigned Elijah. Discouragement is overcome by doing something for God's honor. Activity helps to defeat discouragement.
3. A message of hope. 1 Kings 19:18 gives a message of hope. Elijah was not as alone as he thought he was: seven thousand other persons were faithful to God.

Conclusion

Elijah had God, he had a job, and he had seven thousand other faithful people. He had hope.

A. J. Cronin was an English medical doctor who became a novelist. He quit his practice, moved his family to a farm in Scotland, and spent a summer writing his first novel by hand on a lined exercise book. After receiving a draft from a secretarial firm that had done the typescript, he was so discouraged that he threw it out the back door on an ash heap. Then he went for a walk. He came upon Angus, the Scotsman who owned the farm, digging in a bog. Upon Angus's inquiry about the progress of the book, Cronin told him what he had done. The Scotsman said that he was sure the doctor knew best, but his father had dug that bog and had not made a pasture. But he knew that if he dug the bog long enough, some day there would be a pasture there.

With that word Cronin went back, dug out the manuscript, and dried the pages over a fire. Then he wrote a book that established him as an author and was translated into thirty languages.

In those times when you are so discouraged that you think of quitting, remember God.

SUNDAY EVENING, JULY 11

Title: Escape from Lonesome Valley

Text: "Two are better than one; because they have a good reward for their labour. For if they fall, the one will lift up his fellow: but woe to him that is alone when he falleth; for he hath not another to help him up. Again, if two lie together, then they have heat: but how can one be warm alone? And if one prevail against him, two shall withstand him; and a threefold cord is not quickly broken" ***(Eccl. 4:9–12).***

Scripture Reading: Ecclesiastes 4:9–12

Introduction

Loneliness is everywhere: from the heart of the socialite surrounded by the glitter of the world, to the heart of the mother surrounded by the demands of an active home; from the skilled surgeon's busy office full of waiting patients, to the modern rest home's quiet rooms full of elderly people waiting out their last days.

Someone has said, "Loneliness is the most devastating disease of our society." Sociologists call us "the lonely crowd."

Loneliness is the Christian servant's greatest enemy. Temptations that make little or no headway under normal conditions become almost irresistible in times of loneliness. Many a Christian in the midst of loneliness has given up the fight. Satan has struck some of his most devastating blows when Christians have been caught in utter loneliness.

In thinking about escaping from Lonesome Valley, it is imperative that we understand the difference between loneliness and solitude. In other words, it is one thing to be alone and another to be lonely. Many people who live alone are not lonely. In fact, the state of solitude where one is alone is many times helpful. But feeling alone can be a devastating experience. Many people who are almost always surrounded by a crowd are pathetically lonely. It is escape from this kind of loneliness that concerns us.

I. Factors contributing to loneliness.

A. *Self-pity.* Someone has said, "Loneliness is 90 percent self-pity." The next time you feel lonely, stop and see how much of it can be attributed to your feeling sorry for yourself. Self-pity causes loneliness, for it leads us to shut ourselves in and others out. Self-pity causes us to spin our own cocoons; thus, the sorrier we feel for ourselves, the lonelier we grow. We can expect loneliness as we surrender to self-pity.

B. *Self-sufficiency.* When we dethrone God and put self on the throne, we are headed toward loneliness. When we push God from the center of our lives and acquire attitudes of self-sufficiency, we are headed toward decay, defeat, and loneliness.

C. *Idleness.* We become dull and listless when we have nothing to do. A short while after Elijah prayed down fire at Mount Carmel and won a dazzling victory over pagan forces, he was found alone, praying to die. He was incredibly discouraged and lonely, saying, "I, even I only, am left" (1 Kings 19:10).

The Lord exposed Elijah's real problem by asking, "What doest thou here, Elijah?" (1 Kings 19:9). That was it—he was doing nothing! What famine and armies could not do to him, idleness did.

II. Factors to conquer loneliness.

There is a fourfold way to conquer loneliness.

A. *There is something to question.* We must ask ourselves, "Is my loneliness my own fault? Am I lonely because of self-pity or self-sufficiency or idleness? Am I lonely because I am wrapped up in myself?" If we are like that, we cannot help but be lonely. Loneliness cannot be overcome until we are willing to recognize the part that we play individually in being lonely and are willing to ask ourselves, "Is my loneliness my own fault?"

B. *There is something to remember.* Escape from Lonesome Valley is attained by building up a great reservoir of happy memories and thoughts. A mind full of pleasant memories, a heart that can count many blessings, and an eye that looks for beauty and good wherever it can be found will not brood long over being alone.

There is something else to remember. While every soul has its experiences of loneliness, God is at work holding every soul. In him we live, and move, and have our being. We can go as fast as we wish and as far as we will, but we will never out-distance God. The prophet Isaiah discovered this great truth when he heard God say, "Fear not: for I have redeemed thee, I have called thee by thy name; thou art mine. When thou passeth through the waters, I will be with thee; and through the rivers, they shall not overflow thee: when thou walkest through the fire, thou shall not be burned; neither shall the flame kindle upon thee" (Isa. 43:1–2).

C. *There is something to feel.* You must feel that you have been sent. Listen to the message from Christ's lips: "My meat is to do the will of him that sent me, and to finish his work" (John 4:34). "I can of mine own self do nothing: as I hear, I judge: and my judgment is just; because I seek not mine own will, but the will of the Father which hath sent me" (5:30). And best of all, "Then said Jesus to them again, Peace be unto you: as my Father hath sent me, even so send I you" (20:21).

What a glorious thought! The Father has sent you to that office, that business, that school, or that home for his glory! He sent you to that place of work to labor there that you might glorify him. Thus, you are never alone, for having sent you, he is with you. When you feel that you have been sent to glorify him, loneliness will flee.

D. *There is something to do.* When you find someone who is lonely and you tell that person that there is something to do, it often makes the person angry. I am not just talking about fishing, golfing, hunting, gardening, or some other hobby. The Scripture says, "He that loveth his life shall lose it" (John 12:25). "He that loseth his life for my sake shall find it" (Matt. 10:39). Loneliness is conquered when we find something to do for God and others.

Conclusion

There is an escape from Lonesome Valley. There is something to question: Is it my fault? There is something to remember: God is with me. There is something to feel: God has sent me! There is something to do: I must live for God and others.

Wednesday Evening, July 14

Title: A Doubter Goes to Church

Text: "When I thought to know this, it was too painful for me; until I went into the sanctuary of God; then I understood their end" ***(Ps. 73:16–17).***

Scripture Reading: Psalm 73:1–28

Introduction

What is your reaction when you see righteous people suffer and wicked people prosper? Do you become depressed? Do you lose faith? This is exactly what happened to the psalmist. The psalmist did not remain in despair, however; he saw God's goodness and power as the sole antidote to his sorrow.

The poem has an unusual structure: it begins with the conclusion. The psalmist then carefully examines the facts of the issue at hand and explains how the conclusion was reached.

I. The conclusion (Ps. 73:1).

A. *Many scholars translate "truly" as "I know now," indicating that the poet had done much investigating and weighing of the facts of the case.* He had decided that though he had doubted some beliefs he had been taught, they were true. What were these beliefs? Perhaps he was familiar with the psalm that says, "The Lord knoweth [approves] the way of the righteous: but the way of the ungodly shall perish" (Ps. 1:6). But that did not seem to correspond to the reality he saw. After questioning the belief, the poet then embraced once again his childhood teachings, accepting them as true. Often young people must do this before their faith can be their own. This is tragic, for they waste many precious years of service and training.

B. *Intellectual speculation, however, is different.* Sometimes we become stronger in faith when we investigate thoroughly that which we have been taught. When we do, we will find, as the poet did, that everything God says is true.

II. Why the psalmist was perplexed (Ps. 73:2–16).

A. *The poet was in great trouble.* Verse 2 says that he was about to go under, and the following verses give the reason. The wicked prospered, and he had become jealous of them. He observed that they did not suffer for their sins. Thus, they become conceited, strutting through life as though they owned the earth. Not only did they live selfishly, exploiting others frequently, but they mocked God's teaching openly, defying him publicly. To make matters worse, the people were deceived by them and urged their children to make them their role models.

B. *What could the psalmist do?* Was he foolish for serving God? What had it brought him? If he tried to complain, no one would believe him, and he might even offend some who were not strong in the faith, thinking he was doubting the reality of God. What do you do when you see people prospering whom you know are phony, pretending to be religious? If you condemn them, you could hurt the cause of Christ, so you bite your lip and keep quiet. This was hard for the poet to do.

III. What the psalmist learned and how he learned it (Ps. 73:17–28).

A. *Verse 17 is the transition verse of this poem: the poet decided to take his problem to God.* What finer way to do it than to go to God's sanctuary, a place separated and dedicated to God for public worship?

B. *While there, he received his answer.* God has his hand on everything in the world, including the wicked. They will be punished when God decides the time is right.

C. *When the poet understood this and accepted it, his attitude changed.* No longer was he depressed or rebellious. He was a new person! He realized the only certainty we can have is that of personal fellowship with God. This must suffice for our problems. Leave all to God. Pray, trust, and wait. God will make things right in his time, when he knows it is best.

Conclusion

Most people have trouble not so much with God's will as with his timetable. They are like the person who prayed, "Lord, give me patience and hurry up!" This spiritual autobiography says to the reader, "Take your doubts to the Lord just as you have taken your guilt. The one who bore your sins on the cross can show you the way to solving your personal problems of everyday living!"

SUNDAY MORNING, JULY 18

Title: How Do I Pass My Religious Beliefs to My Children?

Text: "Ruth said, Intreat me not to leave thee, or to return from following after thee: for wither thou goest, I will go; and where thou lodgest, I will lodge: thy people shall be my people, and thy God my God: Where thou diest, will I die, and there will I be buried: the LORD do so to me, and more also, if ought but death part thee and me" ***(Ruth 1:16–17)***.

Scripture Reading: Ruth 1:1–18

Hymns: "Come, All Christians, Be Committed," Lloyd
"O Love That Wilt Not Let Me Go," Matheson
"Take the Name of Jesus with You," Baxter

Offertory Prayer: Dear Lord, we thank you for your grace and majesty. We praise you for your involvement in our lives. We are conscious of the missionary obligation that we have to spread the gospel of the Lord Jesus Christ to the ends of the earth. We ask, then, that you use this offering for that purpose. In Jesus' name we pray. Amen.

Introduction

A family sent their son to a large, prestigious university. There he met an engaging teacher and adopted his skepticism toward religious beliefs. The staunch Christian family was disappointed at this budding agnosticism.

A Jewish family was shocked when their daughter came home to say that she had been so impressed with the truth of the music she had sung with the school glee club in the Christmas program that she was accepting Christ as her Savior and becoming a Christian.

A family had been mainline Protestant for generations. But the only son, the one in whom hope had been placed for carrying on all of the family traditions in both religion and business, announced that he had joined the Unification Church; he had become a Moonie. The family was distraught.

In the pluralism of the American religious scene, it is not unusual for a child to forsake his or her family's religious tradition to accept another faith or another expression of the Christian faith. The result is often difficult for families to handle.

One of the questions most often asked ministers is "How can I best pass on my religious beliefs to my children?" Our religious beliefs are very important to us. We would like for them to be as meaningful to our children as they are to us.

A biblical answer to this question is found in the experience of Ruth and Naomi. The decision of Ruth not to leave Naomi is often used in wedding ceremonies. Ruth 1:16–17 is a familiar passage that expresses a loyalty, devotion, and faithfulness that would honor any marriage.

The original meaning, however, was not for marriage, but rather for religion. Ruth's commitment to go with her mother-in-law meant that she would leave her home, her family, and her religion.

Naomi and her husband, Elimelech, had emigrated from Judah to Moab in a time of drought. There their two sons had married Moabite women who worshiped the god Chemosh. (People of a particular country usually worshiped the god who was considered powerful over that area. The Jewish people believed that there was only one God and that he was universal. Christians join in that belief.) Naomi's husband and sons died. After a time she decided to go back home to Judah, and Ruth went with her.

Because of Naomi, Ruth went to Judah, believed in God, and became one of the ancestors of Jesus. Her choice came about because Naomi was able to pass her religious beliefs on to her daughter-in-law. Why was Naomi able to pass her religious beliefs on to Ruth? It seems that Ruth chose Naomi's God because she had already chosen Naomi.

The personal element is the most important factor in passing on your religious beliefs to your children. If they perceive that faith is real, valid, and vital to you, they will be more likely to accept and follow that faith.

I. When religion is passed on to children, there is an active contagion.

A. *Where does faith begin?* For most people, faith does not begin with an argument, but with a desire. They are able to see something in Christians that they know is lacking in their lives, and they want it. The adage that the Christian faith is more caught than taught holds true.

Richard Swain, in *What and Where Is God?* testified that his first glimpse of God came in his mother's face. As a child, one day at church he leaned against her as she bowed to pray. When the prayer began, her face was tense and strained. As the prayer went on, her face relaxed and softened into a kindly glow. This experience impressed him as a boy; it stayed with him as a man.

B. *How is faith expressed?* Naomi had lived her faith so well in Moab that it made it easy for other people to believe in her God. Faith must be expressed for religion to have an attractive contagion.

II. When religion is passed on to children, compassion is manifested.

A. *Compassion is caring about a person.* It is a big part of the Christian witness. We often speak of compassion abstractly, but real compassion is shown in care for individuals. Ruth knew that Naomi was compassionate toward her personally.

B. *Compassion is expressed in consistent behavior.* Compassionate persons do not just talk about Christian faith; they live it. Compassion is not abstract in its expression; it is concrete. During World War II a Japanese girl released from a camp on the West Coast went to Chicago to find work. But before she got a job, she was stricken with appendicitis and was hospitalized. She was sick, a stranger, a Japanese during a time of war with Japan, unemployed, and facing a dark future. Some young people from a church in Chicago heard about her and went to the hospital offering to help in any way they could. Though brought up a Buddhist, that young lady decided that if Christianity made people act like that, she wanted to be a Christian.

III. When religion is passed on to children, there is absolute choice.

A. *A choice must be absolute.* Ruth stood by the Jordan River and made an absolute choice. There was no turning back.

B. *A choice may bring some surprises.* The big surprise in this story is the marriage of Ruth to Boaz and her place in the lineage of Jesus Christ. One choice brings other decisions in its wake. When you choose for Christ, you may be surprised where that choice will ultimately lead you.

C. *A choice may be influenced in unexpected ways.* When Naomi left for Judah, she had no way of knowing the extent of her influence over Ruth or of its ultimate outcome. In apparently incidental ways, witness can be given and can bring results for Christ.

Conclusion

Naomi was able to pass her religious beliefs on to her daughter-in-law Ruth. Your religious beliefs can be passed on to your children, too, when they are marked by the consistency and contagion exemplified in Naomi's faith.

SUNDAY EVENING, JULY 18

Title: Escape from the Blues
Text: "O wretched man that I am! who shall deliver me from the body of this death?" ***(Rom. 7:24).***
Scripture Reading: Romans 7:24

Introduction

Life for the Christian is not a bed of roses. Christ promised the abundant life to those who followed him, but the abundant life is not a life free of tension and conflict. Fear, worry, doubt, and boredom often attack us. In addition to these things, the Christian has to deal with despondency too! Like everyone else, there are times when Christians get horribly blue and discouraged. The apostle Paul was no exception. Read his letters closely, and on more than one occasion you will meet a discouraged man.

A good illustration of this is found in our text. Paul was miserable. Many times we have a problem understanding Paul, but all of us can identify with him in this hour of despondency. At one time or another we have all cried, "O wretched man that I am!"

Why did Paul feel discouraged? Why do you feel discouraged? What causes you to have the blues?

I. Why do we have the blues?

A. *People often have the blues because they think they are not significant.* Feeling that you do not count can be devastating. The third greatest cause of death among young adults ages fifteen to twenty-four is suicide. One of the leading causes of teen suicide is teens feeling that they have no significance to anyone.

Many senior citizens feel that few people are aware they exist and that even fewer care. It is indeed difficult for them to keep from the blues when they feel like a "nobody."

B. *People often have the blues because they lack confidence.* Abundant life eludes many people because they are plagued all their lives by self-doubt. They are shy and backward.

People who lack self-confidence constantly pour negativism into difficult situations. Many say, "Oh, isn't this awful! Isn't this terrible! I can't do anything about this! I am licked before I start! The odds are against me! The difficulties are just too many!" Such negativism is guaranteed to produce despair.

The Bible regards confidence as very important. Hebrews 10:35 says, "Cast not away therefore your confidence, which hath great recompense of reward." Self-confidence is destroyed in many people because they think with their emotions instead of their minds.

No one can live effectively in this world without self-confidence. A Christian should never be lacking in self-confidence. Why? A Christian's life is based on something unshakable, something enduring, something completely secure—namely, Almighty God, the Father of our Lord Jesus Christ, and our Savior himself. When we live by our emotions, we encounter a typhoon that destroys our confidence. The desire of God is that we turn such typhoons into tailwinds that carry us to the glorious destination that he wants each of us to reach. If we fail to do so, it will result in destruction of our own self-confidence and in our reaping the blues.

II. How can we escape the blues?

A. *Recognize that you are not overlooked by God.* He made you just the way you are, and he loves you! One little boy said, "I am me, and that's good! Because God don't make no junk!" His grammar may have been all wrong, but his outlook on life was right.

Jesus was driven by the hostility of the loveless world outside the city wall of Jerusalem and hanged on a cross. The sight of him dying was a message for everyone who passed by. To those who saw him there, it was God's way of saying, "I love you." Yes, God loves you and God loves me. When we recognize that God does love us and has not overlooked us, we cannot help but drive away the blues.

B. *Recognize that you must cultivate the lifestyle of being a holy person.* Our quest to become holier people is not always a simple one. Many times we are thwarted by our own sinful desires; they powerfully keep us from the Lord.

This was the problem that made Paul despondent. He knew that he was a child of God; he felt like a somebody. But he found it extremely hard to do the right thing. There was a civil war going on within his soul. "When I want to do right," he said, "I don't! And when I try not to do wrong, I do it anyway" (Rom. 7:15, author's paraphrase). No wonder Paul said, "O wretched man that I am!"

If you want to know what kind of lifestyle will help you to escape the blues, read Matthew 5. It has within it a blueprint for escaping the blues. Pointers on what you have to do to be happy and to escape the blues continue throughout the chapter. If anyone makes you travel a mile, go two miles. If anyone takes your coat, give him your cloak also. Not only should you not commit adultery, you should also keep your thoughts pure and surrendered to the Holy Spirit. And it says you are not only to love your friends, but also to love your enemies and "pray for them which despitefully use you" (v. 44). This great sermon rises to a climax when it says, "Be . . . perfect, even as your father which is in heaven is perfect" (v. 48).

You say, "That is unattainable. That's too hard!" Our Lord Jesus Christ is telling us that Christianity is not a soft religion. If you rise to the high challenge of life, you will experience happiness you cannot get any other way. Your life will be great, and you will escape depression.

C. *Realize that the Lord has given you all that you need to stand up against anything.* In 2 Corinthians 5:17 we read, "If any man be in Christ, he is a new creature; old things are passed away; . . . all things are become new." That is to say, if a person will take Jesus Christ and set him deeply in the center of his or her life, that person will be a new creature in Christ. No one needs to remain as he or she is. Have you ever been dissatisfied with yourself? Even sick of yourself? Who hasn't? But you can be changed. You can enter into a new world of real living. You can escape the blues when you realize that with Christ in the center of your life, you have within yourself what it takes to stand up against anything.

D. *Recognize that a spirit of enthusiasm makes the difference.* Enthusiasm for life is perhaps one of God's greatest gifts and one of the greatest tools for defeating the blues. If you want to escape the blues, do not let your enthusiasm be drained.

What is the outstanding characteristic of children? Enthusiasm! They think the world is terrific. Everything fascinates them. If they keep that spirit until the day they die, they will more than likely escape the blues. Truly one of the secrets of maintaining happiness is to never lose your enthusiasm.

Enthusiasm makes the difference in our attitudes toward other people, toward our jobs, and toward the world. It makes a difference in whether our lives are blue or delightful.

Conclusion

To escape the blues and experience a beautiful life in Jesus Christ, you must realize that God has not overlooked you. You must recognize the importance of having a holy lifestyle. You must realize that Christ is within you, and with him you can stand. Your enthusiasm for that can make the difference.

Wednesday Evening, July 21

Title: Revive Us Again
Text: "Wilt thou not revive us again: that thy people may rejoice in thee?" ***(Ps. 85:6).***
Scripture Reading: Psalm 85:1–13

Introduction

Ask any pastor the greatest need of the church, and you will likely receive the answer, "Revival!" Sometimes that means only new converts and new church members; at other times, however, it means that the present members become revitalized and renew their dedication. This psalm is about a land that needed revival and a psalmist who poured out his heart for God to grant it. The most probable time of writing is during the time of Nehemiah when the Jews had returned from Babylon, rebuilt the temple and the walls, but had then dropped back into a state of apathy and low morals.

I. Remembering previous revivals (Ps. 85:1–3).

A. *The review of happier times is a profitable and illuminating use of history.* Though someone has said that "a sorrower's crown of sorrow is remembering happier things," this is not the entire truth. The Bible continually reminds us of past mercies for terrible sins. One of Israel's greatest prophets challenged his people with the memory of better days: "I remember thee, the kindness of thy youth, the love of thine espousals, when thou wentest after me in the wilderness, in a land that was not sown" (Jer. 2:2). No conversion story is more inspiring than one that reminds us of what we once were. When our fires are burning low, we can take heart as we remember redeeming love.

B. *The motive of "return" is one of the strongest in religious appeal because it reminds us that God never does things just once.* He is the God of the recurring opportunity. Each day gives us another chance to surrender to God's love. The psalmist looked at Israel's history and realized it was a great evidence of God's love: truly Israel was a product of God's grace.

II. Praying for present plight (Ps. 85:4–7).

A. *Moved by conditions in the land, the psalmist focused inward and pleaded with God to act in the present to dispense anew the loving-kindness of former days.* "Restore" in verse 4 (RSV) can mean, as in most other places, "turn."

B. *If so, the writer could be praying for God to lead the people to repent and forsake their wickedness.* This is, of course, the only way sinful people can be restored to fellowship with God. The emphasis is not on God removing his wrath, but on the people changing their attitude and being willing to turn to him so he can bless them and make them rejoice.

III. Anticipating future blessings (Ps. 85:8–13).

A. *How glorious it is to see someone so convinced of the efficacy of prayer that God is thanked in advance.* The psalmist knew nothing of the dreary pessimism that comes so often in this modern world. He knew God would bring revival.

B. *When revival came, the restored community would reflect God's attributes because it owed its existence to him.* God demands righteousness but gives peace as he overlooks the weaknesses and sin of people when they show a genuine sorrow for their shortcoming and an earnest desire to serve him. Every revival of love for God brings joy to the land. The psalmist saw his glorious future and rejoiced as he sang about it.

Conclusion

Do you want revival in your church? Look to the times when you have been close to God. Ask yourself what factors were present, and then ask God to reproduce them in your situation.

SUNDAY MORNING, JULY 25

Title: How Do I Recharge My Spiritual Batteries?

Text: "Truly God is good to Israel, even to such as are of a clean heart. But as for me, my feet were almost gone; my steps had well nigh slipped. For I was envious at the foolish, when I saw the prosperity of the wicked. . . . Until I went into the sanctuary of God then understood I their end" ***(Ps. 73:1–3, 17).***

Scripture Reading: Psalm 73

Hymns: "Come, Thou, Almighty King," Anonymous
"My Jesus, I Love Thee," Anonymous
"It Is Well with My Soul," Spafford

Offertory Prayer: Dear God, this day we thank you for the outpourings of your blessings upon us. We are grateful for life, for the abundance of sunshine, for your love that shines on our lives as brilliantly as the sunshine, and for the opportunities to express our love to you through giving of our gifts. Bless the gifts as you bless the giver. We pray in Jesus' name and for his sake. Amen.

Introduction

Did you ever have battery problems with an automobile? Maybe you had a car that you had trouble starting in the morning. Each morning you would grind and grind on the starter until you gave up. Then you would get some jumper cables and jump-start the car. It would run all right during the day as you built up power in the battery, but then the next morning it would not start again. The whole process had to be repeated.

There are times when you recharge a battery. The battery is still good. The cells in the battery are not dead; it just does not have sufficient power to operate. That battery needs recharging to carry out its function.

Spiritually we get that way too. There are times when it seems that our spiritual power just runs down. If someone can give us a boost as with booster cables, or a shove as in shoving a car to get it started, we can function all right. But it seems to us that our power diminishes.

One of the questions that people ask ministers most frequently is, "How can I recharge my spiritual batteries?" Most likely it is a question you have asked. It is a problem that faced the psalmist as expressed in Psalm 73: "My feet were almost gone; my steps had well nigh slipped" (v. 2).

The specific problem that had rendered the psalmist powerless was the apparent prosperity of the wicked. He just could not seem to understand how the unrighteous people fared so well while his life was fraught with so much difficulty. As a result, his spiritual batteries were very low. They needed recharging.

I. You can recharge your spiritual batteries by acknowledging that you need them recharged.

A. *An honest admission (vv. 1–2).* We are immediately struck with the honesty of the psalmist, who expressed his own spiritual staleness. We must acknowledge to God and to ourselves our own spiritual weakness and our need for spiritual recharging. Lloyd John Ogilvie, in his book *Falling into Greatness,* tells of an unsophisticated frontier preacher who once pointed to the casket during a funeral service and said that he wanted the people to know that the corpse had been a member of that church for thirty years. Perhaps the same could be said for some of us. We need to acknowledge our spiritual state both to God and to ourselves.

B. *An accurate appraisal (vv. 3–14).* Notice the appraisal that the psalmist gave of the wicked people around him. He was judging simply on appearances. On the outside all he could see were wealth, comfort, and the approval of the community. At that point he was not able to make an accurate appraisal and see things from either their perspective or from God's. In the acknowledgment of our need we should see things as they really are, not simply as they seem to be.

II. You can recharge your spiritual batteries by taking a spiritual inventory.

A. *Confession (vv. 15–16).* Start your spiritual inventory with a confession to God concerning the things that bother you. The psalmist indicated that he could not handle his spiritual problems. They had become wearisome to him. What do you need to confess to God?

B. *Cleansing (vv. 21–22).* With confession and repentance comes a cleansing from God. God gives the one who confesses understanding, perspective, and strength.

C. *Commitment (vv. 23–26).* When the heart has been cleansed and the life renewed, a commitment to God and his work follows. That commitment brings a sense of fellowship with God and an awareness of the strength that God gives.

III. You can recharge your spiritual batteries by being a part of a fellowship of Christians.

A. *The reality of that fellowship (v. 17).* Notice that it was only when the psalmist went into the sanctuary of God, the place of worship, that he began to get his perspective on life and to recharge his spiritual batteries. For us that would be a church. In the church, the fellowship of believers, we can begin to see the truth more clearly.

B. *The function of that fellowship (vv. 18–20).*

1. To give perspective.
2. To share strength.
3. To give support through fellowship, openness, and prayer.
4. To worship God.

C. *The faith of that fellowship.* In the worship of God and the expression of faith, we are able to find strength and renewed spiritual life.

IV. You can recharge your spiritual batteries by expressing your faith through witness and ministry.

A. *The problem comes when faith goes too far inward (v. 27).* The psalmist had turned his thoughts inward. He had become, perhaps, too introspective.

B. *A solution comes through turning faith outward (v. 28).* When faith is expressed through witness and ministry, it helps to give us spiritual strength.

Do something for someone else. Share your faith. George W. Truett told the story of a college boy who came home for the Christmas holiday and told his mother that he was no longer sure of his Christian faith. His mother asked him if he would carry a meal to an old man she had been helping. She explained that the man was not a Christian and suggested to her son that he read to him from the Bible while there. When the boy asked what he should read, his mother suggested the Gospel of John. The boy came back home with a radiant face and renewed faith. In sharing his faith, in doing something for someone else, faith had become real to him.

Conclusion

There are times when you may feel that you are run down spiritually. Ask God to help you recharge your spiritual batteries.

Sunday Evening, July 25

Title: Escape from Boredom's Path
Text: "I am come that they might have life, and that they might have it more abundantly" ***(John 10:10).***
Scripture Reading: John 10:10

Introduction

Jesus said, "A man's life consisteth not in the abundance of things which he possesseth" (Luke 12:15). Yet men and women today feverishly are seeking satisfaction in power, profit, and pleasure. As the poet Cowper has said, these people will be disappointed in their search, for they are seeking in the wrong places for happiness—"letting down buckets into empty wells, and growing old with drawing nothing." Thus they have come to walk only on boredom's path.

Lord Byron was a genius with position and wealth in his possession. All of these advantages could not bring him lasting satisfaction and inward peace. On his thirty-third birthday, he was standing in the center of boredom's path, and he wrote:

> Through life's dull road so dim and dirty,
> I have dragged to three and thirty.
> What have these years left me?
> Nothing, except thirty-three.

Scores of people can be classified as being both bored and boring. Seeing no real meaning in life, they scowl and accuse. Having their own pattern of thoughts, they choose never to widen the circumference of their outlook. To such people, every ship seems romantic except the one on which they sail. Boredom's path is indeed crowded.

I. How does one enter boredom's path?

A. *By being content with mediocrity.* Willingness to be mediocre leads to boredom's path. The scope and magnitude of this mediocrity is seen in many facets of our society. Public education is not as strong as it should be. Industry is satisfied to manufacture cheap products. Employees do substandard work and waste company time. Even the church must come in for a scathing indictment at this point: programs are often poorly planned, music is often ineffectively rendered, and sermons are often more noise than content.

B. *Purposelessness brings one to boredom's path.* For many, life is not going anywhere. It seems to be only a series of circles, an endless round of routine. People who have no sense of mission, or who have undertaken so many diverse endeavors that their lives are fragmented, need to organize their lives so that they can say with Paul, "One thing I do!" (Phil. 3:13).

C. *Idleness brings one to boredom's path.* An old saying goes, "An idle mind is the devil's workshop." True enough. Extended idleness is also a breeding ground for boredom. People who do not work, have not worked, and are not planning to work are bored half to death. In the last days of the Roman Empire the people demanded not only bread but also a circus. Why? They wanted something to care for their stomachs and to minister to their boredom. Idleness often brings one to boredom's path.

D. *A wrong attitude toward life leads to boredom's path.* You will find yourself in the middle of boredom's path if you have a wrong attitude toward life. A spirit of selfishness that says, "I'm going to do my own thing!" leads to boredom's path.

II. What does it cost to stay on boredom's path?

A. *It costs the loss of reverence.* Boredom makes us irreverent toward all life. We pass by some of life's most sacred things without a glance, with no reaction whatever. Life becomes perfunctory.

B. *It costs the loss of enthusiasm.* Enthusiasm is a word that has for its root meaning, "God in us." It means to be possessed by God. When one is caught in the midst of boredom, the childish wonder and awe of life disappear, and the dullness of life takes control.

C. *It costs the loss of superior work.* A bored person will produce inferior work. Employees bored with their jobs can hardly be expected to produce an acceptable product. A housewife who is bored usually finds her house in disarray, and she wonders why.

D. *It costs the loss of contentment and happiness.* Boredom slows down the clock and lengthens the days. The day never ends for someone caught on boredom's path.

III. Boredom's path leads to many dead ends.

Various unbiblical answers abound.

A. *There is the answer of despair.* Despair says, "Life will always be boring, empty. There is no escape. Just curse God and die. End it all!" This is the decision that thousands choose every year.

B. *Stoicism says boredom of life can be escaped by sealing your heart to all feeling.* Put it away. Deaden your emotions. Refuse ever to give in to tears.

Turn away from the thought that life is empty. Harden your heart until it does not bother you.

C. *There is the answer of denial.* A young girl who found life in her hometown empty and boring said to a group of her young friends, "Go with me to Florida, and there we will have the fragrance of orange blossoms. Every night we will have the lilt of the dance, and we will sleep in the daytime and forget it all." Many people have chosen denial as a means to overcome boredom. They have merely tried to tell themselves over and over again, "Life isn't empty. It's not boring. Forget it." Such a procedure does not alter the facts as they exist.

IV. The only escape from boredom's path.

We can escape boredom if we know Jesus Christ as Savior and have a growing experience with him. If there is no growth, boredom is certain to come.

A. *Growth in Christ leads to abundant life.* Jesus said, "I am come that they might have life, and that they might have it more abundantly" (John 10:10). "Abundantly" is a rich adverb. It is overflowing compensation for effort. The only escape from boredom's path is growth in Christ, for only Christ can make life more abundant.

B. *Growth in Christ will engender a song in the soul.* Growth in Christ will drive away the discord of life and leave new harmony in its place. Remember the state of Paul and Silas who were thrown into a Philippian jail. The despondency and gloom of the hour was driven away because of their growth in Christ. There was a song in their souls.

C. *Growth in Christ will produce a radiance on the face.* One of the great compliments Jesus paid his followers was this: "You are the light of the world" (Matt. 5:14 NIV). We are to be shining lights in a world of darkness. We ought to have an inner glow resulting from our relationship to the source of light, Christ. Just as the moon has no light of its own and reflects the light of the sun, so Christians are to reflect the light of Christ. Escape from boredom's path is found whenever we grow in Christ; it will produce radiance on the face.

D. *Growth in Christ will produce a joyful religion.* Growth in Christ will make one's heart merry and one's mind active. The promise in Psalm 1 is this: "[The godly man] shall be like a tree, planted by the rivers of water, that bringeth forth his fruit in season; his leaf also shall not wither; and whatsoever he doeth shall prosper" (v. 3). Escape from boredom's path is found whenever we grow in Christ, for it will produce a joyful religion.

Conclusion

A woman remarked in disgust as she threw down a book, "I believe that is the dullest book I have ever read." A few years later the same woman met the author of that dull book. Eventually she found herself in love with the author, and they were married. Under those conditions, she reread the book. The second reading produced a different impression altogether. Why? Because love gives meaning to anything and anybody. Many think that life is empty and boring. They find themselves wandering on boredom's path. But life can become a magnificent obsession when you come to know and love the Author.

WEDNESDAY EVENING, JULY 28

Title: O Worship the Lord
Text: "I was glad when they said unto me, 'Let us go into the house of the Lord'" ***(Ps. 122:1).***
Scripture Reading: Psalm 122:1–9

Introduction

Anyone who wishes to serve God must learn to worship him. Ralph Waldo Emerson said, "What greater calamity can fall upon a nation than the loss of worship?" That worship, however, must be properly motivated. Thomas Fuller said, "They that worship God merely from fear would worship the devil too if he should appear." To worship God for what he has done for us is good, but the problem is that if we should feel he is not doing enough for us, we might quit worshiping him. The greatest motive for worshiping God is to worship him for himself—for who he is. The other motives will then fall into proper place. This psalm is about worship, written by a man who had been to God's house and, on returning home, had wonderful memories of the occasion.

I. The invitation to worship (Ps. 122:1).

A. *This verse is a flashback.* The author saw himself as a person, perhaps in a rural place, standing along the road when the pilgrims passed by on their way to Jerusalem where they were going to worship at one of the annual festivals. They called out for him to accompany them. Though he had not intended to go to that feast, their invitation moved him to join them. Looking back after the event, he was happy that he made the decision to go with them to God's house.

B. *Have you ever had this experience?* You were not sure if you wanted to go to church to worship on a Lord's Day. Someone, perhaps even at the last minute, came to see you or called and said, "Let's go to church today." You decided to go and later were happy that you went.

Reverse the scenario. Invite some people to church. Perhaps they will thank you for urging them to go to God's house. Many people go to church because someone invites them. Try it! You will be glad you did!

II. The worshiper at worship (Ps. 122:2–5).

A. *Verse 2 is translated, "Our feet shall stand within thy gates, O Jerusalem."* The poet was impressed anew at the city. Though he had been there before, each time was a fresh and exhilarating experience. The group stood spellbound by the city's magnificence and by memories of its ancient glories.

B. *The tense of "go" (v. 4) in the Hebrew means something that the people had done and continued to do.* The psalmist called this practice of the people a "testimony." How true of worship! When we go to God's house regularly, we are giving a silent witness to the world that we love God and want to be recognized as being on his side in issues that confront the world.

III. The result of worship (Ps. 122:6–9).

A. *The poet returned to the present with an exhortation to his peer group.* His recollection of the joyful worship caused him to bid others to have this same happy experience. The city of Jerusalem was dear to every Jew because it symbolized the place where God was present in a unique way. The ark of the covenant had been placed there. The temple was later built on the same spot. The glory of the Lord was in the Holy of Holies. No more sacred spot could be found in all the earth! When the poet prayed and urged others to pray for Jerusalem's peace, he was praying for God's cause to be advanced in the world.

B. *Christians do not worship exclusively in one spot, for Jesus revealed to his followers that God is everywhere and is to be worshiped in spirit and truth.* Local churches, however, are places where Christians go to experience God's presence in a unique way. Assembling together with other Christians regularly is necessary for the highest form of joy and the most effective service.

Private worship, in the form of quiet meditation, is good and necessary, but Christians also need the strength that comes from corporate worship. The more people worship, the more they will realize its value and begin to encourage others to join in this wholesome and profitable activity.

Conclusion

If the ancient Jew found joy in worshiping the God he knew, how much should those who have a higher revelation of him find ecstasy and great delight in the fervent worship of this God who has, in Jesus Christ, redeemed the world from sin! Public worship makes religion practical and prevents our devotional lives from becoming isolated piety and our personalities from becoming introverted, making our witness virtually worthless. Come, let us go with others to worship our God!

SUGGESTED PREACHING PROGRAM FOR THE MONTH OF AUGUST

■ Sunday Mornings

Continue the series "Questions People Most Ask Ministers."

■ Sunday Evenings

Someone has said that all people need three homes: the home of their birth, their church home, and their heavenly home at the end of this life. In the evening services we will discuss our church home with a series on "The Church Jesus Built."

■ Wednesday Evenings

People have always been concerned about life beyond the grave. The suggested title for a five-part series on this topic is "Looking Heavenward."

SUNDAY MORNING, AUGUST 1

Title: Where in the World Is God?

Text: "Why art thou cast down, O my soul? And why art thou disquieted in me? Hope thou in God: for I shall yet praise him for the help of his countenance" ***(Ps. 42:5).***

Scripture Reading: Psalm 42:1–11

Hymns: "Great Is Thy Faithfulness," Chisholm
"Abide with Me," Lyte
"O God, Our Help in Ages Past," Watts

Offertory Prayer: Dear Lord, we are reminded of your constant care for us: we know that our times are in your hands. We thank you for your continuous care. We acknowledge that all good gifts come from you. Today we give gifts to you, knowing that you have given us many gifts of grace, of love, and of life that we could never repay. Accept these gifts then, dear Lord, not as any attempt to repay you for your grace, but as expressions of our love and gratitude to you for that grace. We ask these favors in Jesus' name and for his sake. Amen.

Introduction

A call came to a pastor early in the morning from the church secretary. She called to say that there was a dire emergency in the community. When he arrived at the address given him, he found the residence surrounded with fire trucks and police cars.

The husband and father of the household had some mental and emotional problems. He had just been released from the hospital and gone back to his work on the night shift. After his wife had gone to work and his daughters to school, he had doused himself, his son, and the bed on which they were lying with gasoline and ignited it. The house burned, and they both died. Where was God when that happened?

At 2:00 p.m. that same day, the pastor conducted the funeral service for a fifty-one-year-old woman who had died quickly from cancer. She and her husband had no children. He had no brothers and sisters, and his parents were dead. He was totally alone in the world and had no church affiliation. Where was God in all of that?

Following the funeral service, on the way back to the church, the pastor stopped at the hospital to visit an executive in the denomination. During minor, elective surgery he had suffered an aneurysm in the brain. At that time there was question as to whether he would survive and, if he did, what the extent of the brain damage would be. Where was God then?

One of the questions pastors hear most is, "How can I believe in a loving, merciful God when I see what goes on in the world?" Another way of phrasing that question is, "Where in the world is God?"

We would have no problem if we did not believe in a loving, merciful God who acts with power in the world. But believing in that kind of God, we often are struck with questions when we see the evil and sorrow in the world.

Psalm 42 is a song of anguish. The reason for the psalmist's deep anguish is not known. From the first verse it appears that he was not in Jerusalem, perhaps not even in the land of Israel. He could have been in exile. In those times when we are in anguish and ask, "Where is God now?" this psalm will help to give us answers and assurance. Here are ways to help us determine where God is during our times of trouble.

I. Start with a memory of God (Ps. 42:1–4).

A. *A memory of the presence of God.* Verses 1–4 indicate a memory of better times. Some of those better times were in the presence of God. Because he could remember when he was in the presence of God, the psalmist longed for God as a deer chased in the hunt longs for a cool drink of water. Our memory of previous experiences with God helps us to know what we miss when we do not have the consciousness of God's presence with us.

B. *A memory of the worship of God.* Verse 4 shows that there was once a time when this psalmist went with the throngs to worship God. Those memories of past times of worship help to sustain in times of questioning and doubt brought on by the bad experiences of life.

II. Consider a moment with God (Ps. 42:5–8).

A. *A moment to meet God.* The psalmist felt anguish until that moment with God. Those who had opposed and perhaps even oppressed him were laughing at him, ridiculing him, and asking him about the presence of the God he trusted. And then he met that God. The psalmist then rhetorically asked why, when he had God, he was so downcast (v. 5).

B. *A moment to respond to God.* The response to God is expressed as "deep calleth unto deep." At the cataracts of the Jordan where that river of promise begins at Mount Hermon, the psalmist had a moment with God and responded to him.

C. *A moment when God responds to us.* But God responds to us too. He gives us songs to sing even in the nighttime of our souls.

III. Where in the world is God? Observe the message from God (Ps. 42:9–11).

A. *It is a message of hope.* Psalm 43 ends with the same refrain as found in Psalm 42:5 and 11. Some feel that it was originally another stanza of Psalm 42. But notice that it is more positive than Psalm 42. It is as though the message that gave hope to the psalmist came from God "Hope thou in God" is the instruction in verse 11.

B. *It is a message of help.* A personal relationship with God assures us of his help. We can refer to God as "my God."

Conclusion

In times of anguish and sorrow, we often wonder where God is. Then we meet God in personal experience and know that God is with us to give help and hope.

SUNDAY EVENING, AUGUST 1

Title: Laying the Foundation

Text: "Thou art Peter, and upon this rock I will build my church; and the gates of hell shall not prevail against it" ***(Matt. 16:18).***

Scripture Reading: Matthew 16:13–18

Introduction

Christians in the universal family of God hold differing views of the church. The most profoundly simple concept of the church was set forth by its founder, the Lord Jesus Christ, in a memorable conversation with his disciples one day in the unlikely area of pagan Caesarea Philippi. During the next four Sunday evenings we will examine "The Church Jesus Built."

There is no part of the Holy Land more beautiful, serene, or majestic than the area in which the ancient city of Caesarea Philippi was located. Twenty-five miles north of the Sea of Galilee, this city was situated near the base of snow-capped Mount Hermon, which formed the northernmost boundary of Palestine in Jesus' day.

The ancient inhabitants of Canaan dedicated many places on the mountains and hills to the Phoenician god Baal. Here also the so-called universal god Pan was worshiped. In fact, the ancient name for Caesarea Philippi was Paneas, in honor of the god Pan.

It was to this area that Jesus had taken his disciples, presumably for a retreat, away from the pressing crowds that seemed to claim every waking moment of Jesus' time. At a lull in their conversation on this particular day. Jesus may have gazed up at the side of Mount Hermon. Following his gaze, the disciples likely were able to see one or more of the cave sanctuaries dedicated to Baal or Pan. Thus it was in this most unorthodox setting that Jesus chose to introduce to his disciples the most revolutionary and electrifying revelation of all time—the truth about the *ekklesia*, the church, which he was to establish. But before he did this, some preliminary matters had to be rectified.

I. The perspective.

A. *First, the perspective of the disciples regarding the true identity of Jesus had to be clearly spelled out and understood (Matt. 16:13–15).* So Jesus asked his disciples a simple question: "Whom do men say that I the Son of man am?" This leading question was designed to make them compare the attitudes of others with their own attitudes about his identity. The answers the disciples gave were interesting. For, according to their report, the people associated Jesus with the three great voices of salvation history in the Bible. First, there was John the Baptist, the forerunner, the herald of the new age of God's grace in which salvation is through identification with the only true sacrifice for sin—the Lamb of God who takes away the sins of the world.

B. *Second, some identified Jesus with Jeremiah, the prophet whose message clearly was reform and hope.* So distressed was that ancient prophet that he was called "the weeping prophet." He saw his people committing spiritual suicide; he watched them rush down a dead-end street destined to end in humiliation and defeat. But shining through Jeremiah's message of judgment there was always present the call to reform, to surrender, and then to cherish the hope that comes when one's faith is placed in God.

C. *Third, still others were sure that Jesus was Elijah, the prophet of power and miracles, who had come back to earth.* For they had witnessed the miracles Jesus had performed, and their hearts had been gripped by the power with which he spoke. But the sad thing about these associations the people made with Jesus is that not one of them saw him as the Messiah of God, the Light of the World, the Savior of sinners! John the Baptist, Jeremiah, and Elijah were all preparers of the coming of Christ, but they were not the Messiah.

D. *How do people view Jesus Christ today?* Relatively few people in our century have not heard his name. In our Western culture where

Christianity is the dominant religion, most believe in the *historical* Jesus—that he lived two thousand years ago in Palestine and died a martyr's death. But many do not recognize him as the risen, ascended Christ, seated at the right hand of the Father in heaven, ever living to make intercession for his people. But to believe that Jesus lived on earth and was a good man and a supreme teacher is not enough! To be saved you have to believe in him as the living God and allow him to be Lord of your life.

II. The profession.

A. *This brings us to the second stage in the discussion Jesus was having with his disciples that day near Caesarea Philippi (Matt. 16:15–17).* Jesus asked, "But whom say ye that I am?" (v. 15). Peter's answer was calm and calculated, born out of the experiences he had had with Jesus throughout the months he and the other disciples had been with him. It came after he and the others had answered Jesus' first question, "Whom do men say that I . . . am?" He had had time to weigh this question thoroughly and fully. His answer did not come on the crest of some high emotional experience. It was a deliberate response.

B. *What did Peter's profession contain?* He said, "Thou art the Christ" (Matt. 16:16). *Christ* is the Greek equivalent of the Hebrew *Messiah,* which means "the Anointed One." Peter said that Jesus was the Christ, the only Messiah.

C. *Peter also said that Jesus was "the Son of the living God" (Matt. 16:16).* God indeed has many "sons and daughters" through spiritual birth into his kingdom, but Jesus was the "only begotten" Son of God. Jesus complimented Peter for his answer, telling him that what he believed about the Messiah had not come from his head, but from his heart. It was not born of his intellect, but it was a revelation to him from the heavenly Father.

III. The product.

A. *Now the stage was set.* Jesus had laid the foundation for the amazing revelation he was about to make. What he said next amounted to the "product" of the profession of faith Peter had just made (Matt. 16:18), for Peter's confession amounted to the foundation upon which Jesus would build his church. It would be built on *confessing people*—those who had professed him as Lord and Christ, just as Peter had done. Peter's name meant "rock." The foundation of the church will also be consistent and unmovable as a shelf of rock. Upon that foundation, Jesus' church would rise, be strengthened, and stand until he returned.

B. *Then, in one piercing statement, Jesus destroyed any possibility that the church would ever be conceived as a citadel or fortress.* He declared instead that his church would be a marching army, designed to storm the battlements of Satan's kingdom of darkness with the good news of salvation.

C. *Most important, Jesus said, "I will build my church" (Matt. 16:18).* Because the church belongs to Christ, he is its head. He determines its structure; it is his gospel that comprises its message. Most important, it is his love that gives the church its magnetism, its drawing power.

Conclusion

The church does not save—not by baptism, membership, or doctrine. It is Christ who saves. Those he saves he adds to his church, this incomparable and inimitable fellowship of believers who recognize him as the head of the church and who confess him as Lord and Master. These, then, become the "living stones" that make up this remarkable spiritual organism.

WEDNESDAY EVENING, AUGUST 4

Title: Worthy Is the Lamb!

Text: "Worthy is the Lamb that was slain to receive power, and riches, and wisdom, and strength, and honour, and glory, and blessing" ***(Rev. 5:12).***

Scripture Reading: Revelation 5:12–13

Introduction

Somewhere along the way the church has lost one of the books of the Bible: once we had sixty-six books, but now in practice we have only sixty-five. The last book of the Bible has been essentially lost. Of course, as you turn to the last part of the Bible, you will find it is still printed. But what I am saying is that we have lost it in the sense that we fail to use it.

There are several reasons why Revelation has become a lost book: some fear it; others do not understand it; and many cannot agree on how to interpret it. Some people are so opinionated that to even discuss Revelation is to become caustic toward and intolerant of those who do not agree. Another extreme position is that everything in Revelation has been fulfilled, and it is simply a dead, dry, dull book of history—so why read it? Opposite all these negative views there is a sound biblical basis on which one may draw a wealth of spiritual help from this invaluable book.

The ultimate message of the book of Revelation is that Christ is worthy. He is worthy because he established the church, he controls history, he is victor over all, and he reigns forever in heaven.

I. Christ is worthy because he established the church (Rev. 1–3).

A. *The first three chapters of Revelation give us our first reason for stating that Christ is worthy: he is worthy because he alone established the church.*

In Matthew 16:18 Christ says that he will build his church. In Ephesians 5:25 we are told that Christ loved the church and gave himself for it.

B. *In Revelation 1:5–6 we are told that Christ is worthy because the church was cleansed through his blood.* Christ addresses the church that he has purchased (2–3:22); in fact, he addresses churches in seven different locations.

1. He admonishes the church at Ephesus to return to its first love.
2. He assures the church at Smyrna that regardless of poverty and persecution and tribulation, he never forgets them.
3. In his letter to the church at Pergamos, he reminds the people that they must never condone heresy by allowing those who teach it to belong to the church.
4. His message to the church at Thyatira is that doing good does not excuse impure doctrine.
5. He says to the church at Sardis that a good reputation is not enough. Rather, they are to have a life that backs up their name.
6. From our Lord's correspondence to the church at Philadelphia, we learn that every church that stays true to his Word and refuses to compromise his truth or deny his name has opportunities to serve him.
7. The message to the church at Laodicea is that mediocrity, self-dependence, compromise, and uncertainty prevent any church from being of value in God's kingdom.

Each of these letters has a message for every church today. At any given time in the history of the church, there have been churches that could be described by one or more of these seven churches.

II. Christ is worthy because he determines history (Rev. 4–19:10).

A. *This passage of Revelation proclaims that Christ is worthy because he alone—not Domitian, not Hitler, and not any contemporary terrorist—determines history.* In these chapters John uses symbols and language that are foreign to us but very clear to the recipients of the letters. Why does John use such language? During the time he was in prison, he had received wonderful reports of how the churches were prospering. Also, he had received the sad message of how they were being persecuted. He now faced the difficulty of getting a message to them that they needed badly while facing the opposition of the Roman government and hostile religious groups. The Holy Spirit inspired him to use a "code language" that the non-Christian world would not understand but the Christian world would understand very well.

B. *John used three basic codes.* He used numbers, colors, and animals to express truth the Jewish recipients would readily understand. The message read, "Worthy is the lamb."

III. Christ is worthy because he triumphs over all (Rev. 19:11–20:15).

The battle between Satan and Christ has raged as long as humankind has been in existence. Here is a description of that battle in this passage.

A. *The claim (10:11–18).* This passage presents the two universal powers at work in our world—the power of God and the power of Satan. Only God is sovereign, but Satan has challenged that claim. This is seen in Christ's temptation experience as recorded in Luke 4:1–13. Here Satan challenges Christ's right to rule over history, over humankind, and over nature. This inevitably leads to conflict.

B. *The conflict (19:19).* This conflict lies basically in that God repudiates Satan's false claim. In his death on the cross, Christ broke Satan's power over people. In Christ's resurrection, God gave him complete victory over sin and death. Christ affirmed this fact in Matthew 28:18 when he appeared to his disciples. He said, "All power is given unto me in heaven and in earth." At that point the conflict had been won. Satan continues to resist our Lord, but the issue has been decided and the outcome is certain.

C. *The conquest (20:10).* In the broad sweep of the divine revelation, John views Christ in heaven riding the white horse of victory (19:11–16). Throughout the battle against the evil forces, not one blow is struck with a material sword. Rather, the sharp sword proceeding from the mouth of our Lord (the gospel) is the lethal weapon.

IV. Christ is worthy because he reigns in heaven (Rev. 21–22).

A. *John gives far more attention to the destiny of the saved in contrast to the destiny of the lost.* He expresses the destiny of the redeemed in the symbolism of the tabernacle (21:1–8), the city (21:9–26), and the garden (22:1–5).

B. *Our unbroken and perfect fellowship with God the Father, Son, and Holy Spirit is dramatized in the portion of Scripture dealing with the tabernacle.* In this fellowship our Lord will wipe away all tears from our eyes; all that is negative and hurtful will cease.

C. *The protection of God is dramatized by the analogy of the city described in 21:9–26.* The high walls of the city speak of our absolute protection. The twelve gates of the city proclaim the abundant entrance that is open to all who come through the suffering of Jesus Christ. The twelve foundation stones grant assurance that the city will never be shaken.

D. *Revelation 22:1–5 speaks of the abundant provisions that will be made by our Lord.* In order for humans to live forever, they must have water, food, and health. In the garden symbolism, all three are provided—the water of life, the perpetual fruit of the tree, and the leaves that provide for healing.

Conclusion

Jesus Christ, the Lamb, is forever worthy. We must never allow our inability to understand every detail of Revelation to cause us to set it aside. We must remember that Revelation proclaims that we are the victors. Our Lord is King of Kings and Lord of Lords.

SUNDAY MORNING, AUGUST 8

Title: Is There a Tomorrow?

Text: "Seeing then that all these things shall be dissolved, what manner of persons ought ye to be in all holy conversation and godliness, looking for and hasting unto the coming of the day of God, wherein the heavens being on fire shall be dissolved, and the elements shall melt with fervent heat?" ***(2 Peter 3:11–12).***

Scripture Reading: 2 Peter 3:1–13

Hymns: "I Know That My Redeemer Liveth," Pounds
"What If It Were Today?" Morris
"Morning Has Broken," Farjeon

Offertory Prayer: Dear Lord, on this summer day we are grateful for life. Help us to use our lives in their best, most fulfilling, and most God-honoring manners. We thank you for the other gifts from your hands. And now as we give gifts from our hands, we pray that you would bless them, use them, and multiply them through the power of your Holy Spirit. In Jesus' name and for his sake we pray. Amen.

Introduction

The *Bulletin of the Atomic Scientists* has for many years pictured a doomsday clock on its cover. The position of its hands shows the minutes before midnight. According to this symbolism, when the hands reach midnight, humankind will have brought about its own end. Will there be a tomorrow?

A young couple looks with pride at their new baby who has just been born. But with their pride in her life there is also a haunting question about her future. What kind of world will this lovely child grow up to inherit? Will there even be a tomorrow? This is another question often asked of ministers, which we will address in today's message.

Christian faith knows that the time will come when the world as we know it will be brought to an end. This will occur at the return of Christ.

Second Peter 3 sounds very contemporary. In the day of the Lord's return, Peter said, the heavens will pass away with a great noise. The earth and everything in it will be burned as the elements melt in fervent heat. As the ancient world perished by means of the flood, this present world will be destroyed by fire. In place of that which is destroyed, there will be new heavens and a new earth in which righteousness will dwell. The word translated "new" means "new in kind." Thus, there will be a new kind of heaven and earth, one marked by righteousness.

Knowing that the present world order would not last forever, Peter asked a significant question: "Seeing then that all these things shall be dissolved, what manner of persons ought we to be . . . ?"

I. When we ask, "Will there be a tomorrow?" there is an anticipation.

A. *We anticipate the second coming of Christ.*

1. Some people may scoff at Christians' belief in the Lord's imminent return. In Peter's day scoffers looked at the world around them and could detect no outward change. They were sure the belief that Christ would return and the world would end had no substance.
2. A historical reminder. To scoff at belief in the second coming of Christ is to ignore at least one historical fact: God destroyed the world once before.

B. *We live as citizens of two worlds.* Christians have never centered their lives in this world alone. We have always known that we are citizens of two worlds. Our belief in God is that even when this world is brought to an end, we still have a greater world in which to live eternally. This world is not our home; heaven is our eternal home.

II. Will there be a tomorrow? The return of Christ is an actuality.

A. *Sometimes the return of Christ seems distant.* Even so, it will happen. We are reminded that God does not reckon time as we do. For the Lord a day is as a thousand years, and a thousand years are as a day. Removed from the time and space limitations of the earth, time is reckoned differently.

B. *The delay in Christ's return is an act of mercy.* While we may wonder at the apparent postponement of Christ's return, Scripture says that this is an indication of God's mercy rather than an oversight. The longer he delays his return, the greater the opportunity for people to turn to him in repentance and faith.

C. *The Lord will return suddenly and unexpectedly.* Therefore, we must not ignore and cannot escape his return. While life goes on as usual, suddenly, as a thief in the night, Christ will return and our world will end.

III. Will there be a tomorrow? Consider our attitudes.

A. *Holiness.* We are to live wholesome Christian lives in anticipation of Christ's coming. This is not the time for one last fling or for sowing wild oats while we can. If anything is an incentive for Christian living, it ought to be Christ's imminent return.

B. *Hope.* We are to have an attitude of hope. While the end of the world carries a threat, it also carries a hope. We know that God will institute his eternal kingdom.

C. *Witness.* We are to use Christ's imminent return as an opportunity for Christian witness. We are told that the delay of Christ's return is for our good (2 Peter 3:9, 15). It gives us an opportunity to witness of his grace and others an opportunity to accept his grace.

Conclusion

Jesus repeated the warning many times that we should be prepared for his return. One day he will return. At that time we will meet him either with joy or with sadness, depending on the preparation we have made. What will it be for you? Will there be a tomorrow? There can be an eternity of tomorrows in Christ's presence.

SUNDAY EVENING, AUGUST 8

Title: Remembering the Lord
Text: "But let a man examine himself, and so let him eat of that bread, and drink of that cup" ***(1 Cor. 11:28).***
Scripture Reading: 1 Corinthians 11:23–28

Introduction

To perpetuate the purpose and function of the church, our Lord established two ordinances—the Lord's Supper and baptism. In this second sermon of our series, we will consider the memorable ordinance of the Lord's Supper.

Memory is a unique phenomenon God built into people's ability to think and reason. There are all kinds of memories. Some bring a smile and a warm feeling; others are agonizing and torturous to us. In close connection with memory is the tendency to forget. Many times there is a conscious reason for our forgetfulness. We don't want to remember certain things. Some things we should forget—like those times we have been wronged by others.

Jesus knew that we would be prone to forget some things, so when he instituted the Lord's Supper, he told his disciples, "Every time you eat this bread and drink this wine, remember me" (1 Cor. 11:24–25, author's paraphrase). He intended that the sacrament of the Lord's Supper become a significant part of the worship of those who constituted his church.

I. Remembering the setting (1 Cor. 11:23).

A. *"The Lord Jesus on the night when he was betrayed took bread" (RSV).* Satan had already entered the heart of Judas. Judas, the materialist, the money-grabber, the lover of the things of this world, had already crept out of that upper room and into the darkness of the night to carry out his deed. The trap was set. The Savior was about to become a victim in the hands of evil men. So what did Jesus do, knowing all this?

B. *He went on with his work, carefully attending to every detail of the task at hand.* He laid out before the disciples the meaningfulness and symbolism of the Lord's Supper that he was instituting for them and for all believers in the ages to come. Here is an incomparable example for all believers. Should one slacken his or her pace because there are only a few more hours to work? On the contrary, because of the brevity of time, one's diligence to carry out the task should be all the greater!

An old farmer, a man of faith and strong Christian character, was asked, "What would you do if you knew today would bring the end of the world?" Without hesitating a moment, he replied, "Plow!" And why not? Before Jesus ascended back to the Father, he told his followers to "occupy till I come" (cf. Luke 19:13). In other words, "Be busy about the tasks at hand, and let me find you doing that when I come!"

II. Remembering the symbolism (I Cor. 11:24–25).

A. *When we come to the Lord's Table, not only should we be remembering the setting in which Jesus instituted this memorial supper, but we also should be remembering the symbolism of what our Lord did that night.* Some Christian groups refer to the Lord's Supper as the Eucharist. *Eucharist* comes from a Greek word meaning "to give thanks." As Jesus began the acting out of this symbolic drama, he took a piece of bread, thanked God for it, and then broke it before the disciples. There, in his open hands, lay the broken piece of bread.

B. *"This is my body, which is broken for you," Jesus said.* The picture was obvious: just as the bread was broken in Jesus' hands, so would his body be broken. And for whom? "For you," he said as he no doubt looked around the table at the disciples. His point was that until the bread was broken, it was not effective. As he passed the bread among the disciples, he symbolized the sharing of his broken body.

C. *Jesus continued this symbolic representation of his sacrificial death when, next, he took one of the cups of wine on the table before him.* Holding it up as he had held up the bread, he said, "This cup is the new covenant in my blood. Do this, as often as you drink it, in remembrance of me" (v. 25 RSV). God had made an offer to sinful humankind. Those who would repent of their sins and believe that Jesus Christ is God's Son would be saved. That was God's covenant of salvation. To attest to the divine and eternal truth of it, he sealed it with the blood of his Son.

III. Remembering the significance (I Cor. 11:26).

A. *It is unfortunate that we think of "preaching" only in terms of a sermon delivered from a pulpit.* Rather, it comes also at other moments: in the conduct, the attitudes, and the spontaneous expressions of those in whose hearts the Lord Jesus lives. There are two ways all of God's people preach a powerful yet wordless message to the world—through the sacred ordinances of baptism and the Lord's Supper.

B. *When people are baptized, Christ bears witness to their conversion experience.* They are acting out the miracle of the new birth—the death and burial of the old life of sin and the resurrection to "walk in newness of life" (Rom. 6:4). Can you imagine the impact left on the people of Jerusalem when, in one day, three thousand people were baptized to affirm their faith in Jesus Christ?

C. *Likewise, when fellow believers in the Lord Jesus come together to partake of these elements representing the broken body and spilled blood of their Lord, they are preaching another sermon.* Baptism is a sermon for the unsaved; the Lord's Supper is a declaration to the powers of darkness that the Lord's death has vanquished them! Furthermore, the preaching contained in the Lord's Supper sets forth the hope of the church: we proclaim the Lord's death "till he comes."

IV. Remembering the sacredness (1 Cor. 11:27–28).

A. *What are we to do to prepare for the Lord's Supper?* First, we must remember the Lord Jesus Christ and what he has done for us through his death on the cross.

B. *Second, we must examine our own hearts and lives—not our neighbor's—to see if we harbor unconfessed sins or sins against others that need to be forgiven and rectified.* Self-examination and heart searching must always be a part of the Lord's Supper.

Conclusion

There are four things we must remember when we come to the Lord's Supper if the experience is to have the impact God intends for it to have in our lives: the setting in which it was instituted, the symbolism of its elements, the significance of its purpose, and the respect with which we are to approach it.

Wednesday Evening, August 11

Title: The Resurrection Body

Text: "So will it be with the resurrection of the dead. The body that is sown is perishable, it is raised imperishable; it is sown in weakness, it is raised in power; it is sown a natural body, it is raised a spiritual body" ***(1 Cor. 15:42–44 NIV).***

Scripture Reading: 1 Corinthians 15:35–58

Introduction

Life after death was a dim concept in the Old Testament. Passages such as Job 14:14; 19:25–27; and Psalm 16:10 give us our fullest revelation of future life in the Old Testament. In the four hundred years between the testaments (Malachi to Matthew—the intertestamental period), the concept of future life was more fully developed. In the New Testament, the concept is complete.

I. The resurrection body of Jesus.

A. *It was tangible.* It could be seen and touched.
   1. The Eleven saw him (Mark 16:14).
   2. The women worshiped him (Matt. 28:9).
   3. Mary Magdalene held him (John 20:16–17).
   4. Thomas was invited to touch him (John 20:27–29).
   5. He ate in the presence of his disciples (Luke 24:42–43).
   6. He appeared to Paul (1 Cor. 9:1).

B. *Although it was the same body, it was somehow different.*
   1. Mary did not recognize him until he spoke (John 20:14–15).
   2. The Emmaus disciples did not recognize him at first (Luke 24:13–35).
   3. Thomas recognized him instantly (John 20:24–28).

C. *It was not subject to time or space.*
   1. He appeared in a room where the doors were closed (John 20:19–26).
   2. He disappeared from the disciples at Emmaus (Luke 24:31).
   3. He ascended into heaven (Acts 1:9).

D. *It could not be held by death.* The widow of Nain's son, Jairus's daughter, and Lazarus were merely brought back to life to die again. Jesus was the first to be resurrected (1 Cor. 15:20).

II. The resurrection body of believers (1 Cor. 15:35–50).

A. *It will be like Jesus' resurrected body (1 Cor. 15:49; Phil. 3:21; 1 John 3:2).*

B. *It will be perfectly suited for heaven (1 Cor. 15:44).*

C. *It will be a real body, not just spirit (Luke 24:39; 1 Cor. 15:44–49).*

D. *It will be incorruptible, not subject to decay (1 Cor. 15:42).*

E. *It will be glorious, not dishonored by sin (1 Cor. 15:42).*

F. *It will be powerful, not handicapped by sin (1 Cor. 15:43).*

G. *It will be prepared for heaven in one of two ways:*
   1. By the transformation (1 Cor. 15:50–52; 1 Thess. 4:15–18).
   2. By the resurrection (1 Cor. 15:53–58; 1 Thess. 4:14, 16).

H. *It will not be the same body that is laid in the grave (1 Cor. 15:35–38).*

I. *It will be luminous, dazzling (Matt. 13:43; 17:2; Luke 9:29).*

Conclusion

Benjamin Franklin wrote his own epitaph. This verse conveys the hope we have that Christ has a glorious life for us after we shed the life we are living now.

Like the cover of an old book,
Its contents torn out,
And stripped of its lettering and gilding,
Lies here food for worms;
But the work shall not be lost,
For it will appear once more
In a new and more elegant edition,
Revised and corrected by the Author.

SUNDAY MORNING, AUGUST 15

Title: Why Me, Lord?
Text: "But the word of God grew and multiplied" ***(Acts 12:24).***
Scripture Reading: Acts 12:1–19, 24
Hymns: "Why Do I Sing about Jesus?" Ketchum
"Count Your Blessings," Oatman
"Surely Goodness and Mercy," Peterson and Smith
Offertory Prayer: Dear Lord, we do not presume to understand all of life. And we do not presume to understand your mercy and grace to us. But we are so very grateful to you for those expressions of grace and mercy. As we give gifts back to you, we also pledge to serve you, to carry out your commission, and to give witness to your marvelous works in our lives. This we pray in Jesus' name and for his sake. Amen.

Introduction

"What have I done to deserve this?" a teacher asked his pastor. He went on to explain that he and his wife had tried to do everything they knew in rearing their children. Their oldest son had been in church all of his life. He had been actively engaged in all of the church's youth activities. He had been a good student in school. And now at age seventeen he was hooked on drugs. "Why me, Lord?" was the educator's question.

Perhaps you expressed that question at the death of someone you loved. Death had come unexpectedly, tragically, and you were totally unprepared for it. You may have asked God, "Why did she have to die? What did she do to deserve this?" It is a variation of "Why me, Lord? What have I done to deserve the troubles I am having?"

The simplest and most complete answer to that question is "Nothing." Probably you have done nothing to deserve the troubles you are having.

In the Old Testament people believed that goodness was rewarded and evil was punished in this life. This belief is seen in the approach of the "comforters" who came to visit Job in his time of great trouble. Each of them let him know that he must have sinned in some way to deserve all that was happening to him. Yet Job maintained his innocence to the end. Job's counselors have not all died off. That same approach is often taken today.

To help us deal with the "Why me, Lord?" question, let us look at a unique verse tucked away in Acts 12: "But the word of God grew and multiplied" (v. 24). At first glance, this does not seem to be such a significant verse. But look at the context. In Acts 12 we are told that the persecution of the early church shifted from religious persecution to political persecution; King Herod became involved. Peter had been imprisoned, and the church had prayed for his release. In the midst of this persecution, the church grew. With this in mind, we can begin to formulate some answers to the question, "Why me, Lord?"

I. A theological answer: God owes us nothing.

A. *An assumption.* We act as though we deserve goodness, blessing, and a carefree life. We act as though God is obligated to us. We never question why all of the good that we experience happens to us. It is only when the reverse occurs, when something bad happens, that we question God. We just seem to assume that we will experience the good things of life.

All good things that we experience come from the grace of God. We cannot buy grace, and we do not deserve grace. God has given us grace because he loves us.

B. *An assertion.* All of our good works cannot be used to manipulate God. We cannot put God in our debt.

A very disappointed man went to talk to his former pastor regarding his family. The man had dropped out of school at the sixth grade. His great ambition in life was that his six children would have a good education. By that time, three of the six children were old enough to have graduated from high school, but none had. One had married early and joined the armed services. Another had married and divorced already. The third was awaiting the birth of an illegitimate child. The man said, "Preacher, I just don't understand it. Ever since I have been a Christian, I have tried to serve God. I have been a deacon; I have taught Sunday school; I have tithed. I don't understand why God is doing this to me." Implicit in his statement was the belief that God was obligated to bless him because he had served God. That is blatantly untrue. We can never buy the blessings of God.

II. A psychological answer: count your blessings.

A. *A simple exercise.* At those times when you are beginning to feel that you are the victim of some kind of celestial conspiracy, try a simple exercise. Count your blessings. Literally, write down anything for which you can be thankful.

B. *A profound result.* A profound result can come from the simple exercise of counting your blessings. You may discover that more good things have happened to you than bad things. Whatever the balance between joy and suffering, you can know that God has graced you. This helps you to get life in focus. Too often we develop tunnel vision, thinking that only the bad happens to us.

III. An emotional answer: develop a new attitude.

A. *An attitude of gratitude.* We can develop a positive attitude of gratitude for all the good gifts we have received from God.

B. *An attitude of faith.* We can determine that we will live in faith. Notice the early church in Acts 12. They did not go into hiding or cease witnessing or eliminate their outreach when confronted with the persecution of King Herod. Instead, during that time they grew and were strengthened. They lived by faith.

C. *An attitude of strength.* In 2 Corinthians 4:7 Paul indicated that the treasure of the gospel was found in clay pots, a metaphor for Christians. This shows that the power in our lives comes from God and not from ourselves.

Conclusion

In our times of trouble, we tend to look inward and feel that we are the only ones experiencing difficulty. Then we want to know what we have done to deserve those troubles. But we can look outward toward God and live in faith, knowing that he always goes with us. Job never did find the answer to why he suffered. But he found God (Job 42:5), and that was enough.

Sunday Evening, August 15

Title: Providing the Power Structure

Text: "Fear came upon every soul: and many wonders and signs were done by the apostles. And all that believed were together, and had all things common" ***(Acts 2:43–44)***.

Scripture Reading: Acts 2:1–13, 41–47

Introduction

At Caesarea Philippi Jesus dropped a veritable bombshell on his disciples. He told them in that weird pagan setting that he was going to establish something called "the church" (Gk. *ekklesia,* "called out ones"). The forces of evil would do all in their power to impede the progress and growth of the church, if not to destroy it altogether.

So the Lord designed a "power structure" for the church, which as long as the church relied on it, would make it impregnable to the attack of the evil one and his emissaries. He determined to infuse the church with his supernatural power, an extension of his own being, the Holy Spirit. Pentecost is one of the towering mountain peaks of the New Testament. It was the time and place God chose to provide the power structure for the church.

I. The receptacles of this power.

A. *God's power was dispensed to the church on the day of Pentecost.* Pentecost was the second of the three great annual feasts of the Israelites. Jews living great distances from Palestine usually preferred to attend the Feast of Pentecost, since sailing weather on the Mediterranean was much better than at Passover, which came early in the sailing season. Thus, in many ways, Pentecost had become the most popular and best-attended feast of the Jewish year.

B. *When the day of Pentecost arrived, the Christians "were all with one accord in one place" (Acts 2:1).* For ten days these 120 believers had been meeting, waiting, and praying as Jesus instructed before he ascended back to his Father in heaven. Because we are curious human beings, we wish that God would have allowed Luke to record for us what happened during that ten-day prayer meeting. There may have been several reasons for his silence. The most significant reason may have been that there were some personal matters that had to be rectified between them and God, and perhaps between each other! Whatever the case, when the prayer meeting was over, the believers experienced a oneness and a spiritual togetherness they had never known.

C. *Then, when God knew they were ready for this event, the Holy Spirit came.* So climactic was his arrival that it was accompanied by some rather dramatic manifestations. First, there was a sound "as of a rushing mighty wind." Why did God use the sound of wind? Perhaps because, throughout the Old Testament, wind was used as a symbol of the Spirit of God. God told Ezekiel to "prophesy unto the wind" (37:9), and when he did, something began to happen among the dried, bleached bones in the valley he beheld. Jesus, in his conversation with Nicodemus, referred to the wind as an expression of the Holy Spirit. He said, "The wind blows wherever it pleases. You hear its sound, but you cannot tell where it comes from or where it is going. So it is with everyone born of the Spirit" (John 3:8 NIV).

D. *Then there was a visible manifestation of God's Spirit among the 120.* They saw "what seemed to be tongues of fire that separated and came to rest on each of them" (Acts 2:3 NIV). At the burning bush on the backside of the Midian desert, God spoke to Moses. In that experience, the fire represented the presence of God, for out of that fire, God gave Moses his instructions. John the Baptist foretold the arrival of one who would baptize "with the Holy Spirit and with fire" (Matt. 3:11 NIV).

E. *The climax came when all of the people in the upper room were filled with the Holy Spirit.* The sound of the wind and the appearance of the tongues of fire were merely accompaniment. The focal point of the event was the filling of every believer with the Holy Spirit. When the people streamed down from the upstairs room into the streets of the city, they began to speak the languages of the people around them, telling of Jesus Christ.

II. The recipients of this strange, new message.

A. *Who heard this joyous message proclaimed by miracle demonstrations (Acts 2:5–13)?* There were in Jerusalem God-fearing Jews from every nation under heaven. When some of those who heard these Galilean believers in Christ speaking in their own language of the glory and grace of God, they were not only amazed, but "in bewilderment" (v. 6 NIV). There is evidence that this group of recipients of the message was smitten with conviction. They could not dismiss this lightly. "Tell us more!" they may have said. "We recognize the power of God among you. We cannot discount the evidence of divine approval upon what you are doing, but we cannot understand it. Tell us more!"

B. *But there was also a negative reaction.* "Others mocking said, 'These men are full of new wine'" (Acts 2:13). Here is evidence of what always happens when the gospel is presented: some respond to the Spirit's influence; others mock, scoff, and reject it. God, in his sovereign creative plan, chose to allow people to make that decision.

III. The results of the preaching of these first-century evangels (Acts 2:41–47).

The results that came because of the preaching and sharing of these first-century Christians on the day of Pentecost has remained a model for Christians in all ages since.

A. *The converts of this ministry joyfully received the gospel, were baptized, and thus identified themselves with the church.*

B. *The communion of these believers consisted in steadfastness of purpose, doctrinal teaching, Christian fellowship, observance of the Lord's Supper, and prayer.*

C. *The moral and spiritual influence of these new converts profoundly affected their community.*

D. *The liberality of these believers abounded toward the needs of the entire body of Christ.*

E. *The service of these people toward God reflected constancy, unity, fellowship, joy, and sincerity.* The spiritual prosperity of this first Christian congregation is reflected in its victorious praises, its favor with the community, and the success of its evangelistic fervor and witness. What an inspired guideline we have for the church!

Conclusion

Thus we have the power structure God has so marvelously provided for the church. He chose as receptacles for this power men, women, and young people who have committed themselves to him through repentance and faith. Some recipients of our message will receive Christ, while others will mock and turn away. As a result, the church will grow numerically and spiritually. This is the church against which "the gates of hell shall not prevail" (Matt. 16:18).

WEDNESDAY EVENING, AUGUST 18

Title: Rewards in Heaven
Text: "Now he who plants and he who waters are one; but each will receive his own reward according to his own labor" ***(1 Cor. 3:8 NASB).***
Scripture Reading: 1 Corinthians 3:8–15

Introduction

We are saved by grace (Eph. 2:8–9) because salvation is the gift of God (Rom. 6:23), but we will be rewarded in heaven according to our works on earth. And not all believers will receive the same reward.

I. Our heavenly rewards are conditional.

A. *They are contingent on our work for Jesus (Matt. 16:27; 1 Cor. 3:8; 2 Cor. 5:10).*
B. *They are contingent on our faithfulness to our assigned task (Matt. 5:11–12; Luke 19:12–27).*
C. *They are conditional according to how we use our abilities (Matt. 25:14–30).*
D. *They are conditional according to our faithfulness to our opportunities (Matt. 20:1–16).*

II. These rewards often are called crowns.

"Crown" is simply a symbolic word that speaks of a heavenly reward (see Rev. 3:11). Different crowns or rewards are spoken of in the New Testament.

A. *The "crown of life" (James 1:12; Rev. 2:10).*
B. *The "crown of righteousness" (2 Tim. 4:8).*
C. *The "crown of glory" (1 Peter 5:4).*
D. *The "incorruptible crown" (1 Cor. 9:25; 1 Peter 1:4).*
E. *The "crown of rejoicing" (1 Thess. 2:19).*

III. These rewards are described by other symbols in the New Testament.

A. *One reward is "to eat of the tree of life" (Rev. 2:7), or to have eternal life with Christ.*
B. *One reward is protection from the "second death" (Rev. 2:11).*

C. *One reward is to eat the "hidden manna" (Rev. 2:17).*
D. *One reward is to receive the "white stone" (Rev. 2:17).*
E. *One reward is to be given a "new name" (Rev. 2:17; 3:12).*
F. *One reward is to have "power over the nations" (Rev. 2:26).*
G. *One reward is the gift of the "morning star" (Rev. 2:28).*
H. *One reward is to be arrayed in white garments (Rev. 3:5; 7:13–14).*
I. *One reward is to be made a "pillar in the temple of . . . God" (Rev. 3:12).*
J. *One reward is to sit with Christ on his throne (Rev. 3:21).*

Conclusion

We need to understand that most of these terms are symbolic. However, what they do say is that heaven is a place of rewards for believers and that these rewards will be different for different believers. Let us serve our Lord with joy and give him blessings fitting his honor.

Sunday Morning, August 22

Title: What Can I Do to Make This World a Better Place?

Text: "Jotham was twenty and five years old when he began to reign, and he reigned sixteen years in Jerusalem. His mother's name also was Jerushah, the daughter of Zadok. And he did that which was right in the sight of the Lord, according to all that his father Uzziah did: howbeit he entered not into the temple of the Lord. And the people did yet corruptly" ***(2 Chron. 27:1–2).***

Scripture Reading: 2 Chronicles 27:1–2

Hymns: "Stand Up, Stand Up for Jesus," Duffield
"Am I a Soldier of the Cross?" Watts
"How Firm a Foundation," Rippon

Offertory Prayer: Dear Lord, we are thankful for the reminder of the seasons of life as reflected in the seasons of the year. Help us, dear Lord, to take time for the restoration and renewal of our spiritual lives. Make us good givers we pray, and accept our gifts today. We pray in Jesus' name and for his sake. Amen.

Introduction

For the last several Sunday mornings we have been addressing questions that are frequently asked of pastors. Our question for today is, "What can I do to make this world a better place?" When we ask that question, we are usually thinking of some grandiose scheme, some way to single-handedly influence the world, such as a way to eradicate world hunger or bring about world peace.

Mother Teresa of Calcutta, India, had a different view. When asked what individuals might do to help make this world a better place in which to live, she answered quietly, "Go home and love your families." Too simple? Hardly. Persistence in loving is something only God can effect. By loving our families, by loving those around us, we can influence those around us. This then radiates out, like circles radiating outward when a rock is thrown into water.

We have a good example of this in King Jotham of Judah. Jotham became king when he was only twenty-five years old. He was born to be king. Both his father and his grandfather had been kings of Judah. He was a good and energetic king, a builder. It was said of him, "He did that which was right in the sight of the LORD" (2 Chron. 27:2).

But notice one negative statement: ". . . howbeit he entered not into the temple of the LORD." That might not strike us as being so awful, since a lot of people do not go to church. But that statement has to be tied into two other statements to give us a true perspective on this issue. The first of those is the concluding statement of verse 2: "And the people did yet corruptly." The king was a good man, but he did not worship God. His influence caused the people to live corrupt lives. The second significant statement is found in 2 Chronicles 28:1, describing King Ahaz, the son of King Jotham: "But he did not that which was right in the sight of the LORD." This is a divergence in the description of the lives of the kings. Jotham's son Ahaz did not follow in the footsteps of the previous kings as far as their personal lives were concerned. We cannot help believing that Ahaz's disobedience was at least in part because of the influence of his father, who did not worship God. Faith must be lived out daily. Let us flesh out this idea in our own lives.

I. You can make the world a better place because you have influence.

A. *Each of us influences someone.* Although you may think yourself rather insignificant and unimportant on the scale of the world's influential people, you do have influence. Each of us influences someone.

Do you remember the verse you learned as a child?

I have a little shadow
That goes in and out with me,
And what can be the use of him
Is more than I can see.

—*Robert Louis Stevenson*

We learned as children that the shadow was ourselves. Each of us influences someone as the shadow of our life falls on that person.

Take Simon Peter, for instance. In John 21, after the resurrection of Jesus, Peter announced that he was going fishing. There is some indication that he had in mind returning to the business of fishing, not just a friendly little fishing trip. When you read the list of those who went with him, it is evident that he was influencing others. Then Jesus met with them on the seashore and gave Peter a ministry of feeding his sheep. Peter's life was transformed; so were others' lives as a result. In Acts 5:15 people were laying their sick on the streets so that Peter's shadow could fall on them.

B. *That influence may be unconscious.* You may not be aware that you are influencing someone else. More things are caught than taught. This has been illustrated by the father who sped down the highway with his child on the lookout for police officers. That father should not be surprised later if his child has a disregard for the law. He will have caught that attitude from his father. Ahaz may have a disregard for God from Jotham, his father.

II. As you influence your world, your influence is active.

A. *Influence may be actively bad.* We all are aware of the possibility of a bad influence: a bad influence can be exerted in a good place. A parent was very upset when he learned that his teenage son was dependent on drugs. "But he only goes to church and to school," he said. Then the parent discovered that someone from the youth group at church had introduced his son to drugs.

B. *Influence may be actively good.* We have all known ways in which someone has influenced others for good. Loving sacrificially is a way to witness for God.

III. Your influence is ending.

A. *Influence is not self-directed.* It is not a matter of your directing to whom you want your influence to go nor how far you want it to spread. Since influence is often unconscious, you may not be aware of how far it spreads. A man once told a former university science professor how he had helped him to retain his faith. The professor was not aware of it and asked how it had happened. The man replied that once when he was a student, he had sat behind the professor in church. When he saw him bow his head in worship and prayer, he realized that he could keep his faith and explore scientific knowledge at the same time. His teacher had influenced him without realizing it.

B. *Influence has a ripple effect.* Consider the influence of Jotham the king: because he did not worship God, disregard of God rippled throughout the kingdom and the people acted corruptly. Now consider how Jesus made his presence known in the world: in one place with one dozen followers. Jesus set influences in motion that continue to this day.

Conclusion

You *can* influence your world. It happens in ways you may not understand. It begins right where you are.

Sunday Evening, August 22

Title: Issuing the Marching Orders
Text: "Go ye therefore, and teach all nations, baptizing them in the name of the Father, and of the son, and of the Holy Ghost: teaching them to observe all things whatsoever I have commanded you: and, lo, I am with you always, even unto the end of the world" ***(Matt. 28:19–20).***
Scripture Reading: Matthew 28:16–20

Introduction

In our last message on the church, we looked at the church as the *ekklesia*, the "called out ones," a universal, living organism composed of all believers in Jesus Christ of all time and infused with the power of the Holy Spirit. In tonight's message we will see another description of the church—an army of Christian soldiers under marching orders. This definition of the church sets it apart from any other earthly organization. It makes the church more than a club, social gathering, or fraternal organization.

Such a concept of the church immediately suggests that there is a "commanding officer" who not only has designed the strategy for the church's existence, but who has issued specific orders for the day-by-day functioning of its members. This commanding officer is not a pastor or bishop. He is none other than the Lord Jesus Christ, whom the apostle Paul called the "head" of the body, the church. The orders Jesus has issued are clear.

I. The validation of the orders.

A. *First, there is the validation of these orders: "Jesus came and spake unto them, saying, All power is given unto me in heaven and in earth" (Matt. 28:18).* Note how the word "all" dominates this entire conversation Jesus had with the disciples. He used "all" power, "all" nations, "all" things, and he promised he would be with them "always" (literally, "all the days" of their lives). In other words, all the limitations and boundaries were about to be removed. Now, because of his resurrection, the spheres in which he exercises absolute authority include not only Palestine but all heaven and earth. He presented himself as the one through whom all of God's authority is channeled. He had been rejected, despised, and humiliated. Now came his vindication. God had "highly exalted him, and given him a name which is above every name" (Phil. 2:9).

B. *But the thrilling emphasis is that this authority would be transmitted to his followers.* He was about to give them an overwhelming task; but before he described it, he gave them the assurance there would be available a limitless resource of power, extending even over the powers of darkness. This truth is behind the promise John gave in his epistle: "Greater is he that is within you, than he that is within the world" (1 John 4:4).

C. *The word "power" translates a word that means "divine authorization."* It is the power of Christ's presence within us that makes it possible to resist the evil one. We have, in the indwelling Holy Spirit, all the authority and power necessary to put evil to flight. Thus, before Jesus issued the marching orders to the church, he promised the power and authority to carry them out. He gave his followers the validation for what he was about to command them to do.

II. The vision.

A. *There is one main verb, or action word, in Jesus' commission (Matt. 28:19–20).* It is the word translated "teach," which is literally "make disciples." All of the other verbs in these verses are subordinate to, or dependent on, "make disciples." They are participles; they radiate like spokes from a hub, and the hub is "make disciples."

B. *First, Jesus said, "Therefore, while you are going into the world," or "as you are going into your world," wherever that sphere of activity may be.* Your world may be the world of business, education, medicine, engineering—anywhere you go regularly to make your living. Ideally there should be within all Christians a consciousness of our primary mission as soldiers in the army of the King of kings. We are to be sensitive to every opportunity to share our testimony for Christ.

C. *Subsequent to making disciples, we are to be "baptizing them."* Jesus was not making one's salvation experience contingent on water baptism. But the fact that he included it in his commission indicates that he considered it important in a believer's developing spiritual life. What is baptism? It is an ordinance, carrying no saving power. It has historical significance in that it looks back on what has happened to believers: spiritual death, burial, and resurrection. It is symbolic of the old life of sin and of the resurrection "to walk in newness of life." It constitutes a powerful witness for the believer, both in its symbolism and its significance. It has been compared to a soldier's uniform. The uniform does not make the soldier; the uniform is worn to declare a soldier is present. In that sense, baptism is the Christian's uniform; it is the badge declaring what has happened in his or her life.

D. *How are believers to be baptized?* Literally "into the name of the Father, and of the Son, and of the Holy Spirit." The preposition "into" suggests a coming into relationship with, or a coming under the lordship of God, as he is expressed here in his triune being. It is symbolic of a believer's pledged submission to the lordship of Christ. It is more than a mere formality of church membership. It is a sacred and holy experience because of its serious and far-reaching implications both for those who observe it and for the candidate.

E. *Then Jesus becomes specific in regard to the subject matter we are to teach these new disciples: "Teaching them to observe all things whatsoever I have commanded you" (Matt. 28:20).* Salvation is not just a once-for-all, climactic experience; it is a continuing relationship with Christ. When we fail to teach new believers faithfully and consistently, we leave the impression that conversion is both the beginning and the ending of their experience. They must be nurtured continually and consistently in the faith.

III. The victory.

A. *The last phrase of Jesus' command contains the ringing note of victory with which Matthew concludes his gospel.* It is the victory promised those who accept and implement these marching orders of the church: "Lo, I am with you always, even unto the end of the world" (Matt. 28:20). "Lo" means "surely." Jesus erased all doubt that we would be called upon to carry out this task apart from his continuing presence with us.

B. *How long is the interval of time between the commission and the consummation of the age?* We do not know. The disciples wanted desperately to know. Jesus would only say, "Watch . . . for ye know not what hour your Lord doth come" (Matt. 24:42). But in the interim, during that period of grace, we are to be diligent in making disciples and preparing them for life.

Conclusion

We have no idea how much time we have left to carry out our Lord's marching orders. It only stands to reason that some of us will have less time than others. There is not now, nor has there ever been, time for "playing church" or considering it a club or a social gathering. The church is an army continually engaged in spiritual warfare. God help us to be at our posts of duty when opportunities come each day to represent our Lord.

Wednesday Evening, August 25

Title: Will We Know Our Loved Ones in Heaven?
Text: "For now we see in a mirror dimly, but then face to face; now I know in part, but then I shall know fully" ***(1 Cor. 13:12).***
Scripture Reading: 1 Corinthians 13:12

Introduction

George MacDonald (1824–1905), a Scottish novelist and poet, was once asked, "Shall we know one another in heaven?" MacDonald's terse reply was, "Shall we be greater fools in Paradise than we are here?" Dr. George Truett, pastor of First Baptist Church, Dallas, Texas, for forty-seven years, was often asked the same question. His answer was, "We shall certainly know more in heaven than we have ever known on earth."

What does the Bible say in answer to our question?

I. The Old Testament people believed they would.

A. *Abraham was reunited with his loved ones (Gen. 25:8).*

B. *David said he would go to his infant son (2 Sam. 12:23).*

C. *King Saul knew Samuel when he appeared from the other world (1 Sam. 28:12–20).*

II. The New Testament people believed they would.

A. *Jesus talked to Moses and Elijah (Matt. 17:1–8).*

B. *Peter, James, and John recognized Moses and Elijah (Matt. 17:4).* Moses had died about 1350 BC, and Elijah, about 870 BC. But they reappeared on earth during the early decades of the first century.

C. *The rich man in hell knew Lazarus in heaven (Luke 16:19–31).* Memory is immortal (v. 25).

D. *Jesus was recognized in his resurrection body (Luke 24:13–33; John 20:15–18, 26–29; et al.).* Since our resurrection body will be like that of Jesus (1 Cor. 15:49; 1 John 3:2), we too will be recognizable.

E. *Jesus still retains his resurrection body, and when he returns we will recognize him (Acts 1:9–11).*

F. *Long after his ascension, Jesus appeared to John on Patmos (Rev. 1:10–18).*

G. *Jesus told us we would know each other (Matt. 8:11–12; Luke 13:28–29).*

III. The concept of heaven demands it.

A. *Heaven's occupants will be God's family.* God is our Father, Jesus is our Elder Brother, and believers are brothers and sisters in Christ. Family members know each other (Eph. 3:14–15).

B. *Heaven is described in the Bible as a home (John 14:1–3).*

C. *Heaven is a place of complete knowledge (1 Cor. 13:12).* We will know more there than we have known here. Our knowledge will be perfect.

D. *Heaven is a place of perfect love.* Since love never dies (1 Cor. 13:13), our love for our family members will exist in heaven.

Conclusion

English minister and novelist Charles Kingsley (1819–75) had written on his wife's headstone: "*Amavimus, Amamus, Amabimus*": "We have loved, we love, we shall love."

Sunday Morning, August 29

Title: Does It Pay to Be Good?

Text: "Fret not thyself because of evildoers, neither be thou envious against the workers of iniquity. For they shall soon be cut down like the grass, and wither as the green herb. Trust in the LORD, and do good; so shalt thou dwell in the land, and verily thou shalt be fed" ***(Ps. 37:1–3).***

Scripture Reading: Psalm 37

Hymns: "Leaning on the Everlasting Arms," Hoffman
"Make Me a Channel of Blessing," Smyth
"God of Grace and God of Glory," Fosdick

Offertory Prayer: Dear Lord, accept our gratitude for this day. And accept our gratitude for the life you have so graciously given us and the blessings you have so lavishly bestowed upon us. Accept, also, these gifts that we leave at your altar. They are gifts that represent life itself for us, and they are gifts that reflect but a measure of your gifts to us. With these gifts, we give ourselves. Please use these gifts to carry the message of Jesus Christ to our community and to the world. We ask this in Jesus' name and for his sake. Amen.

Introduction

Does it pay to be good? You face that question when you leave home for the first time. You face it when you are confronted with a temptation that seems too strong to handle. You face it when business seems to be going badly and you see an opportunity to make some quick but legally questionable money. You face it when the problems at home get sticky and you meet someone who is attentive and appealing. You face it when you have to make a decision of honesty that probably no one but you will ever know.

Some look at life and say, "Life bears it out. It does not pay to be good." I read of a woman who is embittered because her husband does not make very much money and she cannot keep up with their more affluent friends. What galls her is that at one time she could keep up with the best of them. Her husband used to be the sales manager in a large private corporation. He drew a big salary, and they lived in a big house. One day the president of the company asked him to endorse certain household appliances that were defective products being rebuilt and sold as new products. The sales manager protested that it was dishonest, and he would not do it. The employer warned him that he had better do it if he wanted to keep his job. He refused. So now he is drawing a small salary and living in a small house. His wife is bitter. She does not think it pays to be good.

We have come to the end of our study of the questions most frequently asked ministers. The question we ask today is a far-reaching one. Does it really pay to be good? What does it profit a person to follow God?

This is not a new problem. It bothered the ancient Hebrews too. They had always felt that there was a perfect equation between conduct and reward—when you did good you were rewarded, and when you did bad you were punished. But some people were evidently beginning to question this.

They had seen some people who had not done good who were apparently rewarded with success and comfort, and others who had served God and had not fared so well.

Psalm 37, a wisdom psalm, addresses our question. The form of the psalm is an alphabetic acrostic, with each succeeding line beginning with the next letter of the alphabet in the original language.

I. It pays to do good when you see the results.

A. *A word of advice (Ps. 37:1–2).* The psalmist begins by advising his readers not to get jealous of unjust persons who seem to prosper. He warns against using their prosperity as an excuse to imitate them and to do something unwise.

A young actress once asked, "Why shouldn't I let the producers make love to me? The other actresses do, and they are happier and more successful than I am. Sure, I have my ideals, but they don't get me anywhere." This young actress and many other people need to take the advice of the psalmist.

B. *Consider the contrasts.* The contrasts begin in verse 2 and run through verse 35. Verse 2 says that the wicked will wither in the sun. Verse 35 indicates that once the wicked seemed to prosper as a spreading tree, but later they could not even be found. Notice particularly verse 13: God laughs at them.

II. It pays to be good when you examine the alternatives.

A. *Evil is still evil (Ps. 37:13–16).* Although evil persons seem to prosper, evil is still evil regardless of how successful it appears in wealth and power.

B. *You can bankrupt your resources in times of tragedy (Ps. 37:18–19, 24).* Where will you turn when trouble strikes you? The psalmist assures us that the righteous in their poverty are better off than the unrighteous with their wealth. The reason is that the righteous person possesses inward resources that the unrighteous person does not possess. There is no guarantee in Christianity against trouble, but there is a guarantee against defeat.

C. *You may lose the respect of those you respect (Ps. 37:25).* The word "seed" in this verse refers to children. People are most interested in having the love and respect of their family. That is worth more than money.

D. *You may lose your place with God (Ps. 37:11).* One's standing with God is very important. Jesus quoted this verse as part of the Beatitudes (Matt. 5:5).

III. It pays to be good when you consider some principles.

A. *Trust in God (Ps. 37:3).* Five successive verses outline principles that will guide a person in trying to be good. These principles begin with trust in God. Only by faith can we place our trust in him alone for salvation and guidance.

B. *Delight in the Lord (Ps. 37:4).* When we delight in the Lord, in doing his will and in following him, our deep desires for acceptance, mercy, security, and peace are found.

C. *Commitment to God (Ps. 37:5).* Unreserved commitment of the life to God is necessary. This verse was often on the lips of David Livingstone, the missionary pioneer in Africa.

D. *Rest in the Lord (Ps. 37:7).* This verse counsels us to be patient, to wait on the Lord, and to be still in his presence. We too often try to run before God. We must wait for him and for his action. To wait on the Lord is to be dependent on him. This kind of dependence will allow us to live successfully for him.

Conclusion

Does it pay to be good? We ask this question each day in many different forms. The psalmist points us toward an answer. When we measure life in more than commercial terms, we can understand it. Following Christ does pay great dividends.

SUNDAY EVENING, AUGUST 29

Title: Whose Church Is It?
Text: "On this rock I will build my church" ***(Matt. 16:18).***
Scripture Reading: Matthew 16:13–18

Introduction

Church signs tell you a lot about the heritage and pride of the church members. They range from small painted plywood rectangles to elaborate, eye-catching signs that cost as much as a new car. The point of signs is obvious: they tell whose church meets there. But more than a sign by the road is needed to tell adequately whose church it is. In fact, it becomes serious business when we try to reflect on whose church it really is. This is today's topic.

I. Our Lord's church.

A. *What does that mean?* It means he planned the church and set its purposes and boundaries; he is the church's architect. The apostle Paul wrote that "he hath chosen us in him before the foundation of the world" (Eph. 1:4).

He called the church into being. "I will build my church," he said (Matt. 16:18). He didn't have a denomination in mind. Nor was there a hierarchy, an organization, or an architectural structure set in his plan. What he had in mind was a mission: the church he called into being was a group of people who would confess him as Savior and represent him in the world.

Today we proudly proclaim Jesus as the Lord of the church. "Christ died and lived again, that he might be Lord both of the dead and of the living" (Rom. 14:9 RSV). It is his church. He has a right to rule it.

B. *What should it mean to us that Jesus is the Lord of the church?* It should remind us that belonging to the Lord's church is the most distinctive honor we will ever have. Imperfect as we are, the Lord has claimed us for his own and called us to serve him in the world. We can never thank him enough for reaching out and laying hold of us.

Our gratitude motivates us to persevere in the church. We are on the winning side. One of the church's severest critics has said that the church is like a sinking ship. On that ship, he said, festivities are still being held and glorious music is being heard, but below the water line a leak has sprung. The vessel is setting lower with each passing hour though the pumps are being manned day and night. That is the opinion of one critic looking at the church from the outside. We had better take Jesus' estimate. He insisted that the gates of Hades would not prevail against it. Instead of giving up on the church, let us see what is wrong with our part of the ship and correct the problem.

Christ gave his all for us, and he expects us to do the same for him. He wants us to accept his mission, use his gifts, trust him completely, go where he leads, and complete his work with all the energy he gives us.

II. Your church.

A. *The apostle Paul wrote, "Now you are the body of Christ and individually members of it" (1 Cor. 12:27 RSV).* Each Christian in a church should be able to say, "It is my church. I am thankful for it. I am proud of it. It is real to me. I am glad to serve Christ in it."

B. *Have you found satisfaction in the church?* Do you feel good knowing that the church stands for God and his way of life? It stands for the Bible, for people, for the home, and for life after death. It is a place of discovery. In the church you can discover Christ, your best friends, yourself, joy, and God's help. What you need most you can find in the church. It is your church.

III. Our church.

A. *No individual owns the church; many members make up the body of Christ.* "To each is given the manifestation of the Spirit for the common good," stressed Paul (1 Cor. 12:7 RSV). Each part of the body has its proper function, and the body grows as the various parts do what they were made to do (see Eph. 4:16). All people in the church have to live in their own skin. They have unique backgrounds. They have their own set of problems. They have special gifts from God.

B. *With all its differences, however, the church is made up of people who share many important things.* Most important, we share life in Christ. As Christians, we all share the servant status Christ gave us. We share the goal of trying to become like Christ. We share a common need for each other and a common concern for each other.

IV. Their church.

A. *The church is also for those now outside of Christ.* This idea picks up the true spirit of missions. Christ loves the whole world and died for every person in the world. He wants the church to reach out to the outsiders. Jesus constantly was reaching out to the dirty, the sinful, the foreign, the irreligious, and the snubbed. The early church decided to walk in Jesus' footsteps. The book of Acts describes how the Holy Spirit led the church to cross man-made boundaries and to preach the gospel to all nationalities, all classes, and all colors.

B. *Every person you meet is a potential follower of Christ.* You should desire to learn to share Christ with persons who are different and should be willing to accept every Christian as your brother or sister in Christ.

Conclusion

Whose church is it? Christ's. Yours. Ours. Theirs. Those four answers give us four valid ways of understanding what the church is. Let us thank God for all that the church represents for us and for the world.

SUGGESTED PREACHING PROGRAM FOR THE MONTH OF SEPTEMBER

■ Sunday Mornings

To be effective members of the body of Christ, we need to examine what Christ desired. A series on the nature and function of Christ's church titled "Let the Church Be the Church in Your Life" is suggested.

■ Sunday Evenings

"Responding Positively to the Call of God," a series that shows the response to God of specific people in the Bible, is this month's suggested theme. The responses of each of these characters urges listeners to let Jesus Christ be Lord and Savior.

■ Wednesday Evenings

Finish the "Looking Heavenward" series on the first week of September. Then begin a new series, "The Personal Concern of Jesus for Individuals," which is intended to awaken listeners to God's care for us. At times the love of Jesus seems far removed from our lives. But Jesus continually showed interest in particular individuals during his life on earth. That intimacy extends to us today.

WEDNESDAY EVENING, SEPTEMBER 1

Title: What About Our Christian Dead?
Text: "And he said to him, 'Truly I say to you, today you shall be with me in Paradise'" ***(Luke 23:43 NASB).***
Scripture Reading: Luke 23:39–43

Introduction

It is only natural for us to want to know where our dead Christian loved ones are; our love for them does not die when they do. Are they with Jesus? Are they asleep until the resurrection? What does the Bible say about our Christian dead?

I. They are with God.

A. *At death the spirit returns to God (Eccl. 12:7; Matt. 17:1–3; Luke 16:20–22, 25; 23:42–43).*

B. *At death the spirit is immediately with Christ (Luke 23:43; John 14:1–3; Rom. 8:35–39; 2 Cor. 5:6–9; Phil. 1:23).*

C. *Jesus will bring the believer's spirit with him when he returns (1 Thess. 4:14).*

II. They are in paradise.

Paradise is a Persian word meaning "garden." It appears three times in the New Testament.

A. *Jesus' spirit entered Paradise the day he died (Luke 23:43).*
B. *The converted thief's spirit entered Paradise the same day he died (Luke 23:43).*
C. *Those who overcome will live in Paradise (Rev. 2:7).*
D. *Though the word is not used, Paradise is described in Revelation 22:1–2.* The Bible opens with humankind being expelled from a garden (Eden), and it closes with redeemed humankind back in the garden of God (Paradise).

III. They are alive and conscious.

The New Testament does not teach a disembodied state between death and the resurrection.

A. *Jesus told the Sadducees that God is the God of the living, not the dead (Matt. 22:32).*
B. *Jesus said believers would never die spiritually (John 11:26).*
C. *Jesus said Lazarus was alive and conscious in "Abraham's bosom" (Luke 16:22, 25).*
D. *Moses and Elijah appeared alive on the Mount of Transfiguration though they had been absent from their earthly bodies for centuries (Matt. 17:3).*
E. *Paul said that to die is to be with the Lord (2 Cor. 5:1, 8).*
F. *Paul also said that to die and be with Christ is far better than life here (Phil. 1:23).*

IV. They are at rest.

A. *Heaven offers rest to the weary (Rev. 6:9–11; 14:13).* Note the word "rest" in each passage. It means "to be refreshed after toil."
B. *Believers with Jesus are at rest and conscious of happiness.* Note the word "blessed" in Revelation 14:13; it means "happy." Also, see the contrast in Luke 16.

Conclusion

Although believers who have died in the Lord are with Jesus, their state is incomplete. It shall be complete only when their bodies are raised and glorified and their bodies and spirits are reunited at the resurrection (1 Cor. 15).

SUNDAY MORNING, SEPTEMBER 5

Title: When a Church Worships

Text: "Then said Jesus to them again, Peace be unto you: as my Father hath sent me, even so send I you" ***(John 20:21).***

Scripture Reading: John 20:19–25
Hymns: "Brethren, We Have Met to Worship," Atkins
"So Send I You," Clarkson
"Holy, Holy, Holy," Heber
Offertory Prayer: Dear Lord, we thank you today for the revelation of yourself through Jesus Christ. We thank you for the salvation that has been obtained for us by his death on the cross. We thank you for the continuing presence and convicting power of your Holy Spirit. We are grateful for the work you have done in our lives and for blessings and strength. So we give these gifts to you. Please accept them and bless them for your use. We pray in Jesus' name. Amen.

Introduction

Peter Marshall, in a sermon called "The Risk of the Reach," told of a young German soldier in a dirty, blood-stained uniform standing on the firing step of a trench in World War I. It was an early summer afternoon, and the battlefield was quiet. The young soldier had a wistful, faraway expression on his face.

Suddenly a butterfly fluttered into view and alighted on the ground almost at the end of his rifle. It was a strange visitor to a battleground, so out of place. But it was there, a gorgeous creature with wings like gold splashed with carmine swaying in the warm breath of spring.

As the war-weary youngster watched the butterfly, he was no longer a private in a field-gray uniform. He was a boy once more, fresh and clean, swinging through a field in sunny Saxony, knee-deep in clover, buttercups, and daisies. That strange visitor to the front-line trench recalled to him the joys of his boyhood, when he had collected butterflies. It spoke to him of days of peace. It was a symbol of the lovelier things of life. It was the emblem of the eternal, a reminder that there was still beauty and peace in the world.

He forgot the enemy a few hundred yards across no man's land. He forgot the danger and deprivation and suffering. He forgot everything as he watched that butterfly. He reached out toward the butterfly; his fingers moving slowly, cautiously, lest he frighten away this visitor to the battlefield. But showing one kind of caution, he forgot another. The butterfly was just beyond his reach—so he stretched, forgetting that watchful eyes were waiting for a target.

He brought himself out slowly, with infinite care and patience, until now he had just a little distance to go. He could almost touch the wings that were so lovely. And then a sniper's bullet found its mark. The stretching fingers relaxed, then dropped flat on the ground. For the private soldier in field-gray, the war was over.

Risk is always involved when one reaches for the lovelier, finer, more fragile things of life. And that is what worship is: reaching for the beautiful. This can be seen in a gathering of the earliest followers of Jesus just after his crucifixion and resurrection. From the experience of these disciples met by the resurrected Christ, we can see what happens when a church worships.

I. There is a designated period for worship (John 20:19).

A. *A special time for worship.* Notice that these people met on the first day of the week for worship. It was not on the seventh day—the Sabbath—but on the first day—the Lord's Day—that they met.

Christians generally worship God on Sunday, the first day of the week. The seventh day was a memorial to the Creation. The first day of the week is a memorial of the resurrection, the new creation.

B. *The significance of a special time for worship.*
1. Things we do not schedule do not get done.
2. A time dedicated to God. Every day has meaning to God, and for a Christian, every day is sacred. Even so, there is something special about this one day each week that we dedicate to God. The dedication of this one day to God is symbolic of time being in God's hand. We owe God a part of life, a portion of time, in worship.
3. A call to respond to God. Something deep within us needs a day to worship God. A group of explorers in Africa found that the natives traveling with them would not work on the seventh day. When asked for an explanation, they answered, "We no go today. We rest today to let our souls catch up with our bodies."

II. There is a purpose for worship (John 20:19–20).

A. *We worship to see God.* The disciples were glad when they saw Jesus. We, too, want to see Jesus when we worship. There is a time when we have to move aside all of the other things in life that crowd out God. We need to see his face.

B. *Why do we need to see God?*
1. Our fears drive us to God.
2. Our uncertainties push us to God.
3. Our guilt moves us to God.
4. Our fellowship leads us to God.

III. Christ is the center of worship.

A. *We can claim the promise that Christ is in our midst (Matt. 18:20).* Christ's presence as our focus is what sets worship apart from any other gathering.

B. *We can claim Christ's promise that he is with us to the end (Matt. 28:20).*

IV. There is a product of worship (John 20:21–23).

A. *We receive comfort from Christ.*

B. *We receive peace from Christ.*

C. *We receive a commission for service from Christ.*

D. *We receive the Spirit of power from Christ.*
The Holy Spirit gives us the power to receive the forgiveness of sins and to witness to that forgiveness.

Conclusion

Worship is the starting point of a church's ministry. When a church worships God, wonderful things happen.

SUNDAY EVENING, SEPTEMBER 5

Title: Understanding the Providence of God
Text: "As for you, you meant evil against me; but God meant it for good, to bring it about that many people should be kept alive, as they are today" ***(Gen. 50:20 RSV).***
Scripture Reading: Genesis 45:1–15; 50:19–20

Introduction

The theme of the life of Joseph in the book of Genesis is the providence of God. The word *providence* comes from the Latin *pro* and *vid,* as in *video,* which together mean "to see before." The story of God's providence is the story of God's "seeing before" us. Joseph's experience illuminates our understanding of God's providence.

I. Time and providence.

A. *To see providence at work requires time.* We rarely realize something to be of God at the very moment that it occurs. We can best recognize providence from retrospect. Joseph no doubt found it impossible to see God using anything that happened to him for good until he emerged on the other side. Then he saw that God was using the series of misfortunes to bring about good. Viewing them in isolation, all of his misfortunes seemed to comprise a series of senseless tragedies. We can understand how Joseph may not have seen providence at work when his brothers sold him into slavery, when Potiphar's wife framed him, and when the butler forgot to recommend his release to the pharaoh. But *after* Joseph had interpreted Pharaoh's dreams and warned him of coming famine, and *after* Joseph had risen to the second highest office in the land, and *after* Joseph saw how God was going to use the entire experience to reunite his family, he could *then* see God's providence at work.

B. *The corollary to this point is this: often it takes time for God's providence to bring something good from that which is evil and perverse.* It took thirteen years of Joseph's life for him to enter the service of Pharaoh after being sold as a slave (Gen. 37:1–2; cf. 41:46). It took another seven years for him even to see his brothers again (41:53) and to realize more clearly than ever that God had been at work in his misfortunes. Joseph was not sold into slavery one day only to praise God for working so providentially the next. God did not snap his fingers, as it were, to rectify immediately the wrongs inflicted upon Joseph. God did enter Joseph's human situation in a gentle but powerful way to begin the process that would result in good for Joseph. But this process took time.

II. The extent of providence.

Joseph's experience assures us that we are never out of the reach of God's providence. We cannot sink to a depth lower than where God can work.

A. *God's providence extends to a foreign land.* Surely Joseph experienced providence in his loneliness, cut off from his family and friends. Many today may live in a far country emotionally or relationally, if not geographically. God's providence is there.

B. *God's providence extends to any age.* Joseph found God's providence in the years of his youth and middle age. No age or marital status—single, divorced, or widowed—is beyond the working of providence.

III. Our assistance of providence.

A. *God's providence works best as we seek his will.* Joseph, when approached by Potiphar's wife, asked her, "How then can I do this great wickedness, and sin against God?" (Gen. 39:9). The great men of the Bible were the "cannot men," who in whatever situation "could not" do other than the will of God. We will aid the working of God's providence as we pray that his will be done and as we seek to put that part of his will that we do know into practice.

B. *God's providence works best when we ourselves strive to grow.* The Pharaoh told Joseph, "None are so wise and discreet as you are" (Gen. 41:39). This had not always been the case. Joseph's indiscretion in bragging to his brothers about his dreams of authority over them had in part incited them to sell him into slavery in the first place. Our personal growth gives providence more opportunities in which to work.

C. *God's providence works best with the person who tries to make the most of his or her situation.* Joseph recognized that he had committed no crime worthy of imprisonment (Gen. 40:15) but resolved to do his best while serving in the house of Potiphar. Joseph is an example of "blooming where you are planted." Paul was much the same in the New Testament.

D. *God's providence works best when we persist.* If it sometimes takes years for God's providence to bring his purpose to pass, then our perseverance until then is a necessity. "Hanging in there" is imperative. What if Joseph had quit at some point along the way before the final chapter of his life's story was written? Prayer, seeking God's will, and service advance the ways in which providence can work.

E. *God's providence works best as we recognize God's presence with us in our lives.* Joseph's story stresses this over and over. When Joseph first arrived in Egypt and became a slave of Potiphar, the Bible says, "The Lord was with Joseph, and he became a successful man" (Gen. 39:2 RSV). Again, in Genesis 39:21–23, after Potiphar's wife had Joseph imprisoned, we read, "But the Lord was with Joseph and showed him steadfast love, and gave him favor in the sight of the keeper of the prison. . . . The Lord was with him; and whatever he did, the Lord made it prosper."

We can experience God's providence in the form of his presence. God is involved in your life and mine. God does not leave us when we have no more money, or when we break the law, or when heartache attacks a marriage, or when somebody dies. God is here, and he is here in loving, gentle power.

Conclusion

Joseph expressed his affirmations about God's providence in the names of his children. He named his first son Manasseh (which sounds like the Hebrew for *forget*) and said, "It is because God has made me forget all my trouble and all my father's household" (Gen. 41:51 NIV). The second son he named Ephraim (which sounds like the Hebrew for *twice fruitful*), and said, "It is because God has made me fruitful in the land of my suffering" (v. 52 NIV). We can be assured that we worship and commit ourselves to a sovereign God who watches over us and causes all things to work together for our good (Rom. 8:28).

Wednesday Evening, September 8

Title: The Sinful Woman of Galilee

Text: "Wherefore I say unto thee, Her sins, which are many, are forgiven; for she loved much: but to whom little is forgiven, the same loveth little" ***(Luke 7:47).***

Scripture Reading: Luke 7:36–50

Introduction

There are times when being religious would prevent us from being Christian. Christ spoke vividly of this concept while he was in the home of a very religious man. The encounter with the woman of Galilee illustrates that Christ would not allow a narrow faith to reduce the efficacy of salvation to the lost.

I. The situation.

A. *Place.* This incident took place in an unknown city in Galilee. Some contend that it was in Nain, Capernaum, Magdala, or even Jerusalem.

B. *Time.* This occurred during Christ's more public ministry in the second part of his Galilean mission. It occurred during a meal, but it is not certain whether it was a noon or an evening meal.

C. *Circumstance.* Jesus was a guest in the house of Simon the Pharisee (Luke 7:40), who apparently considered his invitation to Christ to be an honor bestowed on him. Simon the Pharisee was a hospitable but curious Jew desiring a close relationship with the Lord. Since Christ was a popular teacher, it was fitting that Simon should entertain Christ in his home. Yet he neglected the courtesies usually afforded an honored guest, such as washing the traveler's feet.

D. *Description of the person.* The woman who invaded this dinner was an outcast, apparently because of immorality. It is obvious from the conversation and her deeds that she was brokenhearted over her sin and felt a strange attraction to Christ. Her deep sense of conviction led her to ignore all the obstacles in the way. Simon the Pharisee's response connotes that she must have been a known prostitute and entered his house contrary to proper decorum.

E. *The action.* Christ sympathetically watched the woman and allowed her the attention she desired. He defended her against her accusers and acknowledged that she was a great sinner. In so doing he revealed himself to be friend of the worst of sinners. Christ received her immediately, not asking her to prove herself or her sincerity. He ministered not only to her but to Simon the Pharisee, for he read the Pharisee's thoughts and then used a vivid illustration so that Simon might apply to himself the lesson Christ felt he needed.

II. The result.

A. *The fallen woman received peace and the promise that her sins were forgiven (Luke 7:47).* She was assured that her faith had saved her (v. 50).

B. *The rift widened between Christ and the Pharisees after this experience.* The Pharisees would not understand the full implications of God's grace for themselves or for others.

Conclusion

Times may come when "religious people" may question the wisdom of our efforts to reach certain kinds of people. But we, like our Savior, realize that God loves everyone and that his Son died that all may come to know him. We must reach out without respect of persons with the gospel of our Savior.

Sunday Morning, September 12

Title: When a Church Prays

Text: "Now, Lord, consider their threats and enable your servants to speak your word with great boldness. Stretch out your hand to heal and perform miraculous signs and wonders through the name of your holy servant Jesus" *(Acts 4:29–30 NIV).*

Scripture Reading: Acts 4:23–31

Hymns: "Sweet Hour of Prayer," Walford
"Teach Me to Pray," Reitz
"Tell It to Jesus," Lorenz

Offertory Prayer: Dear Lord, we thank you for this day in which we can come into your presence in the midst of your people. Among the many blessings for which we give you thanks is the privilege of prayer. Help us to be people of prayer. As the earliest of the followers of Jesus asked him to teach them to pray, we ask you to teach us. Accept our gifts this day, we pray, and bless them. We ask this in Jesus' name and for his sake. Amen.

Introduction

Harry Emerson Fosdick once posed this possibility: suppose that we could pray, that we could enter the throne room of God's grace, only once every twenty-five years. And suppose that it had been ten years since you had prayed and fifteen years before you would be permitted to pray again. Would you not look forward to that day?

But how we have neglected our opportunity to pray every day. Probably one of our greatest weaknesses as a church is our weakness in prayer, our reluctance to pray. It was not so in the early church; prayer was very much a part of the church's life, as evidenced by the accounts we read in Acts.

Prayer is one of the significant ministries of a church. What happens when a church prays?

I. Prayer is a response (Acts 4:23–24).

A. *Prayer is a response to God's grace.* When Peter and John were released from prison, they joined the other Christians in Jerusalem. While Acts does not say it, the church there may have been praying for Peter and John's freedom at the very moment they were released.

What did they do when they were set free? Did they hold a conference? Did they try to find a way to keep from getting arrested again? Did they plan retaliation? No. They prayed. Prayer is the natural response of the Christian to God's grace.

B. *God is described in these verses as having a number of attributes.*

1. The sovereign Lord (vv. 24, 28).

2. The self-revealing Lord (vv. 25–27).
3. The seeing Lord (v. 29).

II. There is a request (Acts 4:29).

Knowing of and relying on these attributes of God will make us a more prayerful people.

A. *Request—petition—is only one element of prayer, but it is that part of prayer that we practice most often.* Prayer should involve praise, thanksgiving, confession, and intercession as well as petition.
B. *The nature of the requests that we make of God centers on obedience to God and concerns our tasks for God.* Notice that the early church's request centers on obedience to God and to the task of witnessing for God. They did not pray, "Grant that we may be kept safe," or "Grant that Peter and John may be protected," or "Lord, don't let it happen again." Instead, they prayed, "Lord, help us get on with the job of proclaiming the gospel." We should pray for boldness in proclaiming the gospel.

III. There is a resource (Acts 4:30).

A. *Expectancy.* The early church prayed with expectancy. They expected God to do something for them. They knew that there was an adequate and powerful resource in the hand of God, and they claimed it.
B. *Availability.* The greatest resource of all time—the power of God in Jesus Christ—is available to all Christians. In *The Power of Positive Praying,* John Bisagno tells of an elderly Russian woman who was being moved into low-income housing provided by the state. When a friend inquired about why she had not heard from her son who had emigrated to the United States, she replied that he had written her, but all he ever sent to her were little pictures of people whom she thought must be his friends. The friend asked if she had kept the pictures. She had. She led him into a room that was covered with five-, ten-, and twenty-dollar bills pinned to the walls. The poor woman had been saving them so her son could tell her who his friends were when he came back to visit. She was a rich woman with many resources available, but she had not called on them. God's resources are available to us through prayer.

IV. There are results (Acts 4:31).

A. *We can know the presence of God.* The presence of God was with the early church. When we are in the presence of God, something will happen. It may not always be just like you expected it to happen. There are times when God may deny the form of the prayer to grant the substance of the prayer. Augustine's mother, Monica, prayed that God would keep him from going from North Africa to Italy. But it was in

Italy that he came under the influence of Ambrose, found salvation in Christ, and began his ministry as a Christian thinker. The form of Monica's prayer was denied, but the substance was granted.

B. *We can know the power of God.* The place was shaken with the power of God. In many ways we can know the power of God in our lives when we pray.

C. *We can have boldness for mission and ministry, Christ's work.* The early church had prayed in verse 29 for boldness in speaking the Word of God. In verse 31 we are told that they spoke the Word of God with boldness. When a church prays, that church can have boldness in its ministry.

Conclusion

A major ministry of a church is prayer. When a church prays, it has power.

Sunday Evening, September 12

Title: The Burden of a Great Potential

Text: "The woman bore a son, and called his name Samson; and the boy grew, and the Lord blessed him" ***(Judg. 13:24 RSV).***

Scripture Reading: Judges 16:18–31

Introduction

Someone said that the heaviest of all burdens to bear is that of a great potential. This was Samson's problem. Born sometime after 1200 BC to aged Hebrew parents living fifteen miles west of Jerusalem, Samson showed potential from his earliest days. Even his birth itself was an answer to prayer. His devout parents had every concern to nurture Samson in a way that would honor God. They even asked God for direction in parenting. Samson grew and was blessed by God.

Samson was born to be a Nazirite, which meant he was to let no razor cut his hair, to abstain from strong drink, and to have no contact with a corpse (cf. Judg. 13:8, 24–25). Before Samson had even reached adulthood, the Spirit of the Lord began to stir in him. In every way Samson's life spoke of a great potential: he had charisma, leadership, strength, and good spiritual upbringing. God's people, oppressed by the Philistines as they were, had dire need of such a person.

But the promise of Samson was never fulfilled. He never realized his potential. Instead, his life was one of the great tragedies of the Bible. Where did things go wrong? When we understand the reasons for his downfall, we can see pitfalls to avoid as we become the disciples of Christ that God intends us to be.

I. Bearing the burden of a great potential requires choosing the right companions.

A. *Samson had no problem making friends.* He was no ninety-seven-pound weakling who was always getting sand kicked in his face at the beach! His name meant "Sunny man." Evidently he was the Brad Pitt of his day, a man over whom the young women swooned.

B. *Samson had no problem making friends, but he had a problem choosing the right friends.* The Bible shows us that Samson's fate directly resulted from his refusal to break off all contact with the Philistines. In particular Samson had a weakness for Philistine women. His adult life is largely the story of the three women in his life and the difficult time he had due to their influence on him.

C. *We remember the story of Samson's marriage.* He saw a Philistine girl and announced to his parents that he wanted her for his wife. In fact, he told them to get her for him. The custom of the time was for parents to choose a spouse for their child. Here Samson made the highly irregular choice himself and demanded that his parents support it. The in-law trouble began before the marriage ceremony was over. His wife and her father, caught in the crossfire between Samson and the Philistines, were killed.

D. *The second woman in Samson's life was a Philistine prostitute (Judg. 16:1).* Samson now showed that he was not interested in marriage or love. This time he just wanted a woman, and any woman would do.

E. *In Judges 16:4–21 we read the story of Samson's romance with Delilah.* Delilah accepted a bribe of approximately twenty-five thousand dollars, according to today's currency, to deliver Samson to the Philistines. Samson never learned to guard his heart. It cost him. Because he refused to break off these contacts with the Philistines, he came to his premature and tragic death.

F. *We have our own Philistines.* For example, while many factors go into the process by which we choose our spouses, one consideration should be that person's Christian commitment. The life of Samson reminds us that the persons we choose to be close to can dictate the kind of persons we will become. First we make our relationships, and then our relationships have a way of making us.

II. Bearing the burden of a great potential requires dealing seriously with sin.

A. *Had Samson heard Jesus teach us to pray, "Lead us not into temptation, but deliver us from evil," he most probably would have snickered.* For in truth, temptation bothered Samson the most when he could not find any. His life is one long story of episodes in which he tried to get as close as he could to sin without yielding. His death is a natural consequence.

Samson was a sport, a tease, a prankster: he liked to play with sin and temptation. He was playing with sin when he decided whom he would marry. On another occasion, he played a prank by setting some Philistine wheat fields on fire. Three times he teased Delilah about the secret of his strength. The fourth time, in a moment of indiscretion, he revealed the secret, and while he slept, Delilah betrayed him.

B. *The writings of Paul in the New Testament remind us that the Christian life is warfare against sin.* We might prefer to think that a truce has been declared in this war and that peace negotiations are going on with the forces of evil at this very moment. The Bible reminds us, however, that we can declare no truce in this spiritual battle; it is a fight that must be fought to the finish. While we are accustomed to those who say such things out of a smug, moralistic attitude, one lesson from Samson's life remains true: if you play with sin long enough, it will get to you. Samson thought sin was something he could manipulate, but he discovered that sin had its final manipulation on him.

C. *Samson presents a graphic portrayal of the result of sin: he was blinded, harnessed, and set to a grinding wheel like a beast of burden.* Someone noted, "Sin blinds, binds, and grinds." Sin that seems so much fun leaves us brute beasts.

D. *Judges 16:20 says, "He did not know that the Lord had left him."* Samson was to regain his strength but not his sight or his freedom. Sin has its consequences. When sin becomes our lord, we are our own victims. When we live in sin, we may not regain the wasted years, a wasted family, or a wasted body.

III. Bearing the burden of a great potential requires seeking God's will, not our own.

A. *Part of Samson's problem was that God's will mattered too little to him.* He was a man of the first person: "I" and "me." His words to his parents upon spotting the Philistine beauty who was to become his bride, "Get her for me; for she pleases me well" (14:3 RSV), were indicative of the way he faced life. Samson was a man accustomed to getting what he wanted, and he was willing to use force to get it. Samson's strength was a frightening sort of undisciplined power.

B. *Samson spent his life fighting the wrong battles.* As a Nazirite, Samson's sole purpose in life was to demonstrate the spiritual and physical power that would free God's people from their Philistine oppressors. This was God's will for his life. But Samson chose his own way. Perhaps the greatest tragedy of Samson's life was that he used the power that God entrusted to him for unworthy goals. The power and gifts of personality that he might have used for good, Samson used instead for sabotage, lust, and personal vendettas. Instead of leading a campaign for the freedom of God's people or becoming a spiritual warrior in the service of a noble cause, Samson engaged in his own private war of revenge. When we seek God's will above our own, we will fight the right battles. Attaining our potential requires that we say to God, "Thy will be done!"

Conclusion

Realizing our God-given potential begins with a decision to make Jesus Christ the Lord of life and to take an active role in his church. We can say to God in this hour what Samson failed to say: "Thy will be done!"

WEDNESDAY EVENING, SEPTEMBER 15

Title: The Jerusalem Pharisees
Text: "The scribes which came down from Jerusalem said, He hath Beelzebub, and by the prince of the devils casteth he out devils" ***(Mark 3:22).***
Scripture Reading: Mark 3:29–30

Introduction

Our Scripture reading for today depicts our Lord reaching out to people. They, however, refused his offer of mercy. In the eyes of men, it appears that he failed. We need to take heart in the fact that though we reach out to all people equally, there are some who refuse our testimony. This experience is also recorded in Matthew 12:22–40; Luke 11:14–23; and John 10:19–21.

I. The situation.

A. *Place.* These accusations were made against Jesus in Capernaum in Galilee, in a house where Jesus apparently was staying. Perhaps it was the house of Simon Peter. The people were gathered in the house and were crowded around the door.

B. *Time.* The incident takes place on the day called "the busy day," which continues through Luke 8:39 and Mark 5:20. It occurred at a time when there was widespread demonic activity.

C. *Circumstance.* Jesus was wearied from his strenuous preaching tour and was searching for quietness and rest. He was now on his second tour of Galilee and had just healed a blind and mute man (Matt. 12:22–23). Walter Lowrie describes this experience as "the culmination of trouble." Rumors had reached Capernaum that Christ was losing his mind (Mark 3:21). The crowd was so pressing that Christ did not even have time to eat (v. 20).

D. *Description of persons.* The people who had gathered around Christ, with the exception of his immediate followers, were very antagonistic toward him. They were arrogant and prideful religious leaders seeking to find fault with Christ. They were actually attempting to change the attitude of the crowd toward Christ. In doing this they were insinuating that Christ was a magician, that he was mad, and that he was in league with the devil.

E. *The method.* Christ allowed their own words to condemn them (Mark 3:23–24). He also used simple illustrations, such as a house divided against itself (v. 25), a thief entering a strong man's house (v. 27), a tree bearing fruit of its own kind (Matt. 12:33), and Jonah's experience. Christ used very descriptive terms to make clear their spiritual condition. He refuted their argument and looked deeply into their souls.

II. The result.

A. *The Pharisees demanded that Christ show additional signs.* In Matthew 12:38–45 we discover that they gained no new faith whatsoever, but rather remained bitter and antagonistic.

B. *It is in this passage (Mark 3:29) that Christ introduces what has come to be known as the unpardonable sin.* When we study this passage in its context, this sin is knowingly and willingly attributing to the devil what we know to be the work of God. It is to take an obvious evidence of the Holy Spirit and to believe that this is the work of Satan. According to Christ's own words, a Christian is incapable of committing this sin. For Christ said that Satan could not cast out Satan in verse 23. It is equally true that the Holy Spirit will not refute the Holy Spirit.

C. *This sin is one that would be committed at the end of a long, long road of many, many years of deliberately resisting the work of the Holy Spirit.*

Conclusion

The fact that there are those who will not accept our testimony does not free us from the responsibility of sharing it. Our duty is to proclaim Christ. The responsibility of others is to accept it. Let us be faithful in proclaiming the message of Christ whenever and with whomever we have the opportunity.

SUNDAY MORNING, SEPTEMBER 19

Title: When a Church Witnesses

Text: "They continued stedfastly in the apostles' doctrine and fellowship, and in breaking of bread, and in prayers. . . . And they, continuing daily with one accord in the temple, and breaking bread from house to house, did eat their meat with gladness and singleness of heart, praising God, and having favour with all the people. And the Lord added to the church daily such as should be saved" ***(Acts 2:42, 46–47).***

Scripture Reading: Acts 2:35–47

Hymns: "Tell It Out with Gladness," Harkness

"We Have Heard the Joyful Sound," Owens
"Stir Thy Church, O God, Our Father," Price

Offertory Prayer: Dear God, you have given us the ability to provide for our needs, to make money, and to enjoy the blessings of life. Your blessings to us have been rich and unlimited. Now help us to give of our material means to spread the gospel of Jesus Christ in the world. Give us the motivation to be witnesses of your grace, and give us the power for that witness. Please accept and use these gifts in your service, we pray. In Jesus' name and for his sake. Amen.

Introduction

Suppose that you saw a car wreck, and a lawsuit resulted from that wreck. Since you had seen the wreck, the court summoned you as a witness. On the witness stand you were sworn to tell the truth, the whole truth, and nothing but the truth. What would you report?

As a witness in a court of law, you would not tell what you thought had happened, what you wished had happened, or what someone else said had happened. To be a faithful witness, you would have to tell exactly what you knew had happened from your own experience.

That is also what a Christian witness does. D. T. Niles gave one of the best definitions of evangelism when he said that it was one beggar telling another beggar where to find bread.

How are we to go about witnessing? Jesus himself set the pattern for us. Leighton Ford pointed out in *The Christian Persuader* that evangelism in the New Testament combined three strands: the witness of fellowship, the witness of service, and the witness of proclamation. Jesus evangelized by loving (Mark 2:16), serving (1:34), and telling (1:14).

The early church followed this pattern. Their witness was through loving fellowship, compassionate service, and faithful proclamation. This is seen in the verses following the record of the Pentecostal experience (Acts 2).

A major ministry of a church, which is itself a mark of a church, is witness to the grace of God in Jesus Christ. From the early church's experience, we can see what happens when a church witnesses.

I. There is a loving fellowship.

A. *The development of community is Christian fellowship.* Notice that those who believed "were together" (Acts 2:44). They were so much together that they did not consider their belongings even their own. They held things in common to meet each others' needs.

People today need a sense of community. With one in five Americans moving to a new residence each year, there is little sense of community. Christian fellowship helps to meet that need.

B. *Fellowship attracts people to Christ.* Loving others sacrificially is unique to those who follow Christ. This selfless outpouring of love is a neon sign advertising the power of Christ. It draws people to Christ; they want to know what enables anyone to love that way.

C. *Fellowship ties people to Christ and the church.* The first person Paul saw after he was converted on the Damascus Road was Ananias. The first words he heard as a Christian was "Brother Saul" (Acts 9:17). Too often churches freeze out visitors rather than bringing them into the warmth of Christian fellowship.

II. There is compassionate service.

A. *Service meets the material needs of people.* Service is a part of the Christian witness. One of the reasons the early Christians owned things in common was so that they could meet the material needs of people.

B. *Material needs are real needs.* Many people may not be able to hear the verbal witness because of their material needs. God takes our material needs seriously.

C. *In meeting the needs of others, Christian service provides the way for Christian witness.* We are bombarded with countless pitches to sell us something to convince us that a particular product is the best. Because of that, many will not hear the message until they see its demonstration in meeting the practical, material needs of others.

Jesus set the example: he put a towel around his waist and washed dirty feet. He told us to give a cup of cold water in his name.

Compassionate service issues in effective witness. In his book *The Reluctant Witness*, Kenneth Chafin tells of a prebaptismal interview with an elderly lady who was a citizen of Mexico and spoke very little English. The interview had to be done with the aid of an interpreter. She was a well-traveled woman of culture and refinement. Chafin asked her what caused her to believe. She said that she had come to Houston, Texas, as a stranger and was very lonely. One of the women in the church came to visit her. At Christmas the woman gave her a book wrapped in pretty paper. The present was fine; the best gift was that the woman invited her to her home for a meal. It was in that experience, she said, that she knew that the story in the book about God's love was true.

III. There is faithful proclamation.

A. *The proclamation of Jesus Christ is essential.* In the Acts account the proclamation of Jesus Christ was central to all the early church did. Peter's sermon at Pentecost was a faithful proclamation. Acts 2:42 tells what they taught the new believers.

B. *Proclamation takes a verbal witness.* To be a witnessing church, we must tell others about Jesus Christ. The late Sam Shoemaker once said that a verbal witness is necessary because one cannot tell others of Jesus' atoning death and resurrection just by being good. The emphasis is then too much on the person and too little on Christ.

Conclusion

A witnessing church carries out Christ's commission. Witness is a threefold task: loving fellowship, compassionate service, and bold proclamation.

SUNDAY EVENING, SEPTEMBER 19

Title: On Dealing with the Call of God

Text: "The LORD came and stood forth, calling as at other times, 'Samuel! Samuel.' And Samuel said, 'Speak, for thy servant hears'" ***(1 Sam. 3:10 RSV).***

Scripture Reading: 1 Samuel 3:1–21

Introduction

Few questions in life are more serious than "What will I do with my life?" The alternatives are endless. Business? Science? Education? All are vocations into which a person may be called. There is also a call to the ministry. Let us examine this by looking at Samuel's life.

I. Hearing God's call.

A. *We will hear God's call in many ways.* We wish we knew if God called Samuel with an audible voice. It either was audible or so real to Samuel that he felt it was spoken. The narrative certainly presents it as being direct and personal, rather different from God's general guidance today (through circumstances, thoughts, inclinations, abilities, and the Bible).

B. *We will hear God's call as one call among many.* Other good and even noble voices call to us: occupation, financial solvency, family. In other moments we may hear the voices of self-doubt or group pressure. So many voices can drown out the sound of God's voice. Or we can confuse God's call with that of another. So many voices calling to us require us to decide which one we will heed.

C. *We will hear God's call even when the day is dark.* God called the boy Samuel in what many term "the Dark Ages of Hebrew history." "The word of the Lord was precious in those days: there was no open vision" (1 Sam. 3:1). God still speaks in dark days of peril, even in our day of "gloom and doom and threats of boom."

II. Understanding God's call.

A. *God calls us to a variety of ministries.* Sometimes we limit our view of God's call to think that God only calls persons to serve as missionaries, evangelists, or pastors. God also calls people to be deacons, Sunday school teachers, farmers, school teachers, computer programmers, homemakers, nurses, and scores of other types of workers.

B. *God calls us in alignment with our gifts, talents, and potentials.* Too often we mistakenly assume that God delights in forcing square pegs into round holes! As a rule, God does not call mission doctors into agricultural missions or skilled musicians as accountants for mission boards.

The call of God comes to us in light of our potential. You may not have the skill or training in hand at the time you feel God calling you. Skills can be acquired later. Samuel surely did not have every skill that he would need as a prophet at the time he heard the Lord's voice, but he had the potential to acquire all that he would need.

C. *God calls and gives us assistance to understand.*

1. A devout home. Samuel came from a devout home and was blessed with a godly mother. To know the Scriptures and the mind of God from the earliest days in the home is an asset in interpreting God's voice.
2. Worship. Samuel grew up in the tabernacle, even sleeping there. We are more likely to hear and understand the call of God if we put ourselves in places that allow us to hear God's voice. Unfortunately, at times we may give God the same kind of attention that a teenager does to a parent talking over the full blast of the music in their earbuds. Worship can assist us in interpreting the call of God!
3. Wise counsel and advice. Samuel had a trusted friend who could help him interpret the call of God. God may have placed an "Eli" near you—perhaps a pastor, a spouse, or a parent.

Our understanding of God's call to us can grow through the years. Samuel misunderstood God at first and thought Eli was calling him. As youth, many feel the conviction that God is calling them to serve as missionaries, only to decide ten years later that God's call was to serve in Christian education or counseling. Our understanding of God's mission for our lives can take time to develop and mature.

III. Obeying God's call.

A. *Hearing and understanding God's call are of no value until you obey it.* Obedience is not always easy. God can call you to what promises to be a difficult task. God charged Samuel with breaking some grim news to the aged Eli. Sometimes we draw back and think God's call demands too much from us and that we are not capable of meeting the demands. We may sell God short! Our faith in his promises needs to increase.

Obeying the call of God can be a stretching experience. God calls disciples of Christ to tough challenges. His work is not easy work, but with his help, it can be done.

B. *Samuel's response in verse 10 is a model: "Speak, for your servant is listening" (NIV).* Other great prophets, when called, made excuses. Samuel obeyed. When we respond to God's call, his Spirit certifies our response (1 Sam. 3:19–21). That Samuel was God's spokesman was clear to all. People might not have obeyed what God said to them through Samuel, but they did not doubt that it was God who was speaking. Samuel had something special: "The Lord was with [him]" (v. 19 NIV). He had God's stamp of approval. God gives the power to fulfill his call. Those he calls find his grace sufficient for every task.

Conclusion

Samuel's obedient response brought a new prophetic era to Israel. With the calling of this boy, the entire nation reached a turning point. With Samuel's ministry, the Dark Ages of Hebrew history came to a close.

Your obedience to the call of God can also be a turning point. It may not affect an entire nation, but it will affect your family, your church, and your community. God can work with you and through you to encourage people, to heal pain, and to share the love of Christ.

Wednesday Evening, September 22

Title: The Wild Man of Gadara

Text: "They came over unto the other side of the sea, into the country of the Gadarenes. And when he was come out of the ship, immediately there met him out of the tombs a man with an unclean spirit" ***(Mark 5:1–2).***

Scripture Reading: Mark 5:1–20

Introduction

Within the dramatic change realized in the life of the wild man of Gadara we see the change that can be realized in the life of any individual once he or she comes to know Christ as Lord and Savior.

I. The situation.

A. *Place.* This experience took place between the two cities of Gerasa and Gadara. The former is a city in Arabia; the latter is a city in Judea. This must have occurred on the east side of the Jordan, for Mark 5:1 tells us that Jesus and his disciples came over to the other side of the city.

B. *Time.* The closing verses of the previous chapter in Mark reveal that this occurred on the same day that he stilled the tempest at sea. The storm probably was at night, and this experience was on the following morning.

C. *Circumstance.* Christ had just passed through the storm at sea and now was on land. The story begins as he steps onto the east shore of the Sea of Galilee.

The people of this area were selfish and mercenary, unconcerned and fearful. Mark and Luke say there was one man, whereas Matthew says there were two. This apparent contradiction can be reconciled by the conclusion that there were two men, one being more prominent.

D. *Description of the person.* A study of the accounts recorded by Matthew, Mark, and Luke reveals that this man was demon possessed and naked. He was living in abandoned tombs in a wasteland between Gerasa and Gadara. Because of his demon possession, he had strength beyond that of a normal man (Mark 5:4). Furthermore, he was self-destructive, inflicting wounds on his own body. He would well be described as a dangerous man, violent and alienated from society.

II. The method.

Christ used his strong personality to attract the man. We see in Mark 5:7 that even demons recognize Jesus to be the Son of God. Christ then authoritatively called the demon out of the man (v. 8). In verse 9 he asked this man his name, and speaking for the demons, he replied that his name was Legion, "for we are many." It is obvious that, although others feared this man, Christ had no fear whatsoever. Along with his boldness, Christ expressed his love.

The manner in which Christ dealt with this man reveals that he made a distinction between the man and the demons possessing him. He first dealt with the demons and then with the man. Christ encouraged him to do what every person should do after conversion—carry the good news back to his own people.

III. The result.

A. *Some surprising results came from this experience.*
   1. The anger of businessmen was aroused (Mark 5:17).
   2. The wild man was made whole emotionally, physically, and spiritually.
   3. Instead of the people rejoicing, many of them feared Christ (Mark 5:18). Following the instruction of our Lord, the man then turned and personally bore testimony of his experience with Christ throughout the cities of the Decapolis (v. 20).

B. *Although we never seek confrontation for its own sake, there will be times when it will come because of the message we bring.* We need to find comfort in the thought that we are not alone if we are rejected or reviled because we are doing the work of God (Mark 5:17).

C. *The wild man of Gadara became a new creature.* He was gentle and obedient; he became an effective witness of the grace of God.

Conclusion

Even though a person may be unloved, unwanted, and perhaps even feared by others, we are to take the gospel to him or her with love and compassion. We need the same determination with which we would reach out to the most moral of persons. We are able to do this because of the power of God released through the saving presence of Jesus Christ.

Sunday Morning, September 26

Title: When a Church Cares
Text: "It was good of you to share in my troubles" ***(Phil. 4:14 NIV).***
Scripture Reading: Philippians 4:10–20
Hymns: "Do You Really Care?" Cates
"Where Cross the Crowded Ways of Life," North
"Send the Light," McCabe
Offertory Prayer: Dear Lord, the season is crowded with the rush of work, the pressure of school, the demands of life. In this time of great activity, help us to slow down enough to hear your voice, to heed your Spirit, to respond to your call. Enable us to remember the essential things of life as we are caught up in the busy things. Our Christian stewardship is essential. Remind us always that we are stewards in your house, not the master of the house. Help us, then, to be good stewards. From a heart of love, we give these gifts to you. Bless them and use them, we pray. In Jesus' name and for his sake. Amen.

Introduction

In an article in the *Baptist New Mexican* some years ago, Charles Myers told of visiting a family that had some financial losses, personal problems, and a general run of misfortune. The family had been brought to his attention, and he went to see them. He represented a church that could help them financially and people who could provide employment. Since he had some experience in counseling, he could help the family with some of their family problems. But since they were not members of the church he served as pastor, he was not obligated to visit them. He visited them because he wanted to help.

When Myers arrived at the home, the mother came to the door. When he introduced himself, he was not invited in. Standing on the porch, he explained his interest in the family and his desire to help in whatever way he could. The woman listened to his offer. When he had finished, she looked at him for a moment with a cold piercing stare; then she said with deep feeling, "You don't really care."

He was stunned. His first reaction was one of anger. Then he thought he would try to explain. His third reaction was to walk away without saying anything. He was not really sure what he did, but he never broke the barrier and finally left. Her response caused him to question whether he did care.

This is the question that returns to haunt us again and again: Do you really care? Or do you just go through the motions of caring because of what is expected of you?

One of the characteristics of a true church of the Lord Jesus Christ is that it really does care. The church at Philippi cared. They cared about Paul. They cared so much about him that they sent him money while he was in prison at Rome. Probably he had already thanked them for the gift, but he ended this personal letter to the church with a reference to their care for him and what it had meant.

What happens when a church cares?

I. It gives expression to its concern.

A. *Concern must be expressed.* In verse 10 Paul indicated that the church at Philippi had shown that they cared for him. They were concerned enough about Paul that they had sent him money.

It is easy to say that we are concerned. We can make the proper facial expression, adopt the right tone of voice, and even say the right words. But what the world is looking for is an expression of that concern.

B. *Concern must be expressed tangibly.* How did Paul know these people were concerned about him? They expressed it tangibly by sending him money. How can you express your concern? When a mother is sick, care for the children, do the wash. When a person suffers loss, provide groceries, buy a coat. When a person is not a Christian, share Christ.

A cart had overturned on a road in old England. A number of people were standing around expressing their concern. One man spoke up to say, "I'm sorry five pounds for our neighbor. How sorry are you?"

II. It seizes the opportunity to act.

A. *Opportunities to act cannot be scheduled.* The indication is that the people of Philippi had always been concerned about Paul. They just had not had an opportunity to act previously. When you really care, you will seize the opportunity when it comes. You cannot always schedule when another person might need you or your help. It is not a matter of doing what is expected of you; anyone can do the expected. It is doing the unexpected because that is what is needed at that time.

B. *Opportunity comes through a sensitivity to needs.*

1. This means that timing is important. We become sensitive to the needs of others and act when the time is ripe. The best actors and athletes are known for their good sense of timing. Likewise, the Christians who serve best are those with the best sense of timing. They are ready to act at the time it is needed.
2. This means responsiveness, even when it is inconvenient.

III. It shares in the lives of others.

A. *That church is involved in the work of others.* In Philippians 4:14–16, Paul praised the Philippians for sharing in all that he had done. They became a part of the life and ministry of Paul by helping him financially. We become a part of the lives and ministries of those we help.

B. *That church multiplies its life and witness.* Consider what supporting another does to multiply the life and witness of the church. The life of the church at Philippi was multiplied through Paul's ministry.

IV. It receives a blessing itself.

A. *Caring blesses the one who gives as well as the one who receives.* Paul's real joy in the gift was not what it did for *him*, but what it did for *them*. He expressed that blessing in material terms (Phil. 4:17) and in sacrificial terms, the terms of worship (v. 18).

B. *Caring causes us to shift attention from ourselves to others.* This frees the Holy Spirit to work more mightily in our lives.

C. *Caring meets two needs: yours and theirs.* A young journalist and his wife attended a reception at the home of a well-known religious figure who lived in the same city. On the way home, they discussed how much they would enjoy knowing the man and his wife more. But they also knew that they must be so popular and their schedule so crowded that they would never have time for them. They dismissed the idea of inviting them to their home for dinner. A few years later that religious leader expressed in an address how lonely he and his wife were during that particular time and how much they would have welcomed the opportunity to meet and visit with other Christians. The journalist realized that if he and his wife had acted on their initial impulse, they would have met the needs of two couples. Caring meets both the needs of the one cared for and the one caring.

Conclusion

When a church cares, that care is expressed in actions. Those actions result in a ministering stance that marks a church of the Lord Jesus Christ who cared for us.

SUNDAY EVENING, SEPTEMBER 26

Title: The Sins of a Self-Made Man

Text: "Saul answered, 'Am I not a Benjaminite, from the least of the tribes of Israel? And is not my family the humblest of all the families of the tribe of Benjamin?'" ***(1 Sam. 9:21 RSV).***

Scripture Reading: 1 Samuel 9:1–3, 15–21

Introduction

King Saul epitomizes many of the values that Americans hold dear. He represents a person who arose from a background of personal obscurity to become not just a figure of prominence, power, and prestige, but the political head of an entire nation. Saul was an effective leader and warrior. During his reign, Israel reclaimed much land lost to the Philistines. The Bible speaks of his great height. Apparently Saul was a person of athletic bent, charismatic personality, and handsome appearance. With all his success, Saul remained a person of conscience. On more than one occasion he admitted his guilt. It takes a "big" person to do that. "Small" people do not admit their errors. Someone has called Saul a "self-made man."

Yet Saul's life ended in failure. His biography is one of the great tragedies of the Bible. Saul appears in the Bible as a man in the prime of life who had already realized much of his potential. Saul had it all, but he let it slip away. We cannot read of Saul's life without thinking of the little boy giving his dad the sports news of the neighborhood softball game: "We had 'em 18–0 but blew it in the bottom of the first!" That was Saul.

Saul was beset by some sins of a self-made man.

I. Thinking too little of yourself. Result: Playing to others' approval.

A. *In 1 Samuel 9:1–21, we read of the incident that led to Saul's anointing as king of Israel.* Evidently a fairly wealthy man, Saul's father had sent him to look for some missing livestock. While gone, Saul encountered the prophet Samuel. As Samuel communicated the news of God's favor to Saul, Saul replied that he was from the humblest family in the least prestigious of the twelve tribes of Israel.

Saul thought little of himself—too little. Somebody needed to tell Saul that it is as much a sin to think too little of yourself as it is to think too much. We need to appropriate the truth that each of us is special, made in the image of God. Giving ourselves unjustified insults is as black a sin as conceit. Often we mistake ego strength for egocentricity.

B. *We see the bitter fruit of this sin in 1 Samuel 15:12–21.* In this passage, Saul disobeyed by not slaying Agag, king of the Amalekites, and consecrating the battle's booty to the Lord. Saul blamed the people (cf. vv. 15, 21). Samuel's comment is revealing: "Though you are little in your own eyes . . ." (v. 17 RSV). Saul is moved to confess the truth: "I have sinned; for I have transgressed the commandment of the LORD and your words, because I feared the people and obeyed their voice [instead of God's]" (v. 24 RSV). We wish that we could have reminded Saul of Joshua's resolution: "But as for me and my house, we will serve the LORD!" (Josh. 24:15 RSV). Because Saul thought too little of himself, he became vulnerable to the desires of the crowd. He showed a sinful craving for peer approval. The motivation of many self-made persons is to secure the approval of others and show themselves they are valuable through their achievements. Saul should have felt affirmed by Samuel's words (v. 17) that he was God's man anointed to do God's work.

A healthy respect for who God made us to be can liberate us from craving the approval of others.

II. Thinking only of yourself. Result: Leaving God out of your life.

A. *Self-made people are prone to think that all of the credit is theirs.* Thinking only of yourself and your world leads to the failure to see yourself and your world with the eyes of faith. Saul thought only of himself. He did not see that God was a part of the picture of reality too.

B. *In 1 Samuel 13:8–14 Saul was camped at Gilgal as the Philistines threatened.* He had been instructed not to begin the military campaign until Samuel had made the proper sacrifice. After waiting seven days for Samuel to come, Saul took matters into his own hands and made the sacrifice himself. He evidently thought, "Sacrifice is a mere formality anyway. Who needs God when you have a sharp sword? I can pray as well as any chaplain. Let's make the sacrifice and get on with it!" By Saul's action we can see that he left God out of his worldview and took an attitude of "I can handle this one by myself."

C. *The danger of telling yourself that you really are self-made is that sooner or later you are likely to believe it.* Your pride is your strength; you are your god. Whoever you are, then, you think is to your own credit. At that point you forget that life is a partnership with God and begin to attribute success solely to human genius and work.

III. Thinking too long by yourself (away from God). Result: Failing to view life with God as an ongoing relationship to nurture.

A. *Self-made people may think that they do not normally need God.* Saul stayed too long away from God. He did not see his life with the Lord as anything more than a panic measure to which he could resort in an emergency. We wish we could have shared Jesus' words, "If any man will come after me, let him deny himself, and take up his cross and follow me" (Matt. 16:24), with Saul.

B. *We read of the last days of Saul's life in 1 Samuel 28:3–14.* Samuel the prophet had died, and a new Philistine invasion threatened Israel. Without Samuel to advise him, Saul was afraid. He had banished all mediums and spiritists from the land, but when he inquired of the Lord and found no answer by dreams or by Urim and Thummim, Saul in desperation sought the witch of Endor to conjure up Samuel from the dead. Saul had stayed too long away from God. Now God was through with Saul. An emergency arose, and Saul had no relationship with God to see him through it. Saul literally self-destructed. His death is the only suicide recorded in the Old Testament.

Our relationship with Christ is something to nurture daily. We cannot stop giving time to this relationship at age fourteen and come back to it at age forty-four and expect much to be there. Several years ago a friend in her seventies broke her hip. Spry and active all of her life, she asked the doctor, "Isn't there anything that I can eat to make it heal faster?" The doctor replied, "Lady, it's what you put into your body day by day that makes for healing." An add-water-and-stir-instant-potatoes spirituality will not suffice for the lack of ongoing spiritual nurture.

Conclusion

Spiritually speaking, a self-made person is a terrible tragedy. We do have an option: the Christ-made person. When we finally confess our own inability to find fulfillment, purpose, and true life in and of ourselves, Christ beckons us to try life his way. You can find God's help today.

Wednesday Evening, September 29

Title: The Adulteress
Text: "The scribes and Pharisees brought unto him a woman taken in adultery; and when they had set her in the midst, they say unto him, 'Master, this woman was taken in adultery, in the very act'" ***(John 8:3–4).***
Scripture Reading: John 8:1–11

Introduction

The condemnation of Christ on the self-righteous and the compassion of Christ for the penitent are both demonstrated in this poignant experience. From this encounter of our Lord, we learn how not to be swayed by the opinion of others and how to reach out in loving concern to the morally derelict.

I. The situation (John 8:1–10).

A. *Place.* This is one of those experiences in the life of our Lord that is easy to locate. Verse 2 tells us that it occurred in the temple just after Christ had come from the Mount of Olives.

B. *Time.* Again verse 2 makes the time easy to identify, for it says, "And early in the morning." This event also occurred during the latter part of Jesus' ministry, possibly during his same visit to Jerusalem when he healed the blind man.

C. *Circumstance.* As Christ was teaching in the temple court, the people were coming to him in a constant procession. The scribes and Pharisees rudely interrupted the worship experience of Christ and those gathered around him (v. 3). To bring as much embarrassment as possible to the accused, they placed her in the midst of the people (v. 3).

Having accused the woman of being caught in the very act of adultery, the scribes and Pharisees then began to inform Christ what the law had to say about this matter, as though Christ needed such tutoring (vv. 4–5).

Verse 6 indicates that their main desire was not really to gain a verdict from Christ but rather to discover a means of trapping him.

The entire situation was doubtlessly planned far in advance; these same scribes and Pharisees had recently had a controversy with Christ about the Sabbath.

One of the goals of the confrontation was to undermine Christ by proving he was friendly with sinners. They wanted to make it appear that Christ was inclined to relax all laws of morality. At the same time, these scribes and Pharisees were attempting to get Christ to conflict with civil authorities.

D. *Description of persons.* From John's account it is easy to conclude that the woman was an immoral individual, perhaps disheveled and sullen. On the other hand, she was respectful of Christ and calm in his presence. It is interesting that the holiness of Christ brought to her soul a sense of peace and acceptance, whereas the alleged spirituality of the scribes and Pharisees brought fear and rejection. This prompts us to ask ourselves whether our presence causes sinners to feel accepted and loved or rejected and disdained.

E. *Method.* According to verse 6, Jesus wrote on the ground, literally the pavement in the temple. We do not know what he wrote, but it is obvious in verse 7 that he placed those who would hinder the salvation of the woman in the jaws of dilemma.

Having exposed the scribes and Pharisees to be the sinners and hypocrites they were, he then turned and spoke privately to the accused woman (v. 10). Though she indeed was a fallen person, he respected her as a human being and thought in terms of the future. Though he expressed a vicarious shame and obvious compassion, he was not lax in his attitude toward immorality. Both the accused woman and her accusers were convicted by the Holy Spirit of their sins.

II. Results (John 8:11).

A. *Jesus offered no excuse for the woman's conduct, but he did accept her repentance and grant her forgiveness.* Christ is not a cruel Lord, and he never asks us to do what he does not also empower us to do.

B. *Christ told the woman, "Go and sin no more" (v. 11).* He had at this point infused her with the power that comes to every Christian to live above such sin.

Conclusion

Three important truths emerge from the account of the woman caught in adultery. First, we should reserve our condemnation of others until we have exhausted every effort to reach them with the grace and salvation of Jesus Christ. Second, we should always realize that we cannot change anyone; only the Lord is strong enough for that. Third, like our Lord, we should not be intimidated by the self-righteous, but rather should reach out to the downtrodden, regardless of the price we may have to pay.

SUGGESTED PREACHING PROGRAM FOR THE MONTH OF

OCTOBER

■ Sunday Mornings

A series of evangelistic sermons titled "Make Sure You Are Right with God" is suggested for this month. These messages make an appeal for a decisive commitment to Jesus Christ as Savior.

■ Sunday Evenings

God has given us the responsibility over much. We need lessons on how to best use all that he has given us. "Where Does Stewardship Begin and End?" is the theme for these messages.

■ Wednesday Evenings

Continue and complete the series of messages based on Christ's encounters with individuals. The theme is "The Personal Concern of Jesus for Individuals."

SUNDAY MORNING, OCTOBER 3

Title: How Sin Entered the World

Text: "Now the serpent was more subtle than any other wild creature that the LORD God had made. He said to the woman, "Did God say, 'You shall not eat of any tree of the garden'?" ***(Gen. 3:1 RSV).***

Scripture Reading: Genesis 3:1–24

Hymns: "O Worship the King," Grant

"Christ Receiveth Sinful Men," Neumeister

"He Included Me," Oatman

Offertory Prayer: Gracious Father in heaven, thank you for the bounty of your provision for us. Help us, Father God, to be generous in spirit as we think of helping others in need of your great salvation. Bless these tithes and offerings that others may come to know Christ as Savior. In his name we pray. Amen.

Introduction

Genesis 1 tells us of the creation of the universe. Genesis 2 tells us in a fuller way of the creation of humanity—God's risk. Genesis 3 tells us about the fall of man and how evil entered the world, a dramatic and tragic event.

In chapters 1 and 2 we see that a good God created a good world. By his mighty word he spoke the world into being, and by the dust of the earth he made man. But something has happened to our world. How is it that a good world made by a good God is so full of evil? Why is there violence and war, bitterness and hatred, resentment and prejudice? This evil exists in our world because it lives within us. You see, every person is like Adam. This is our story in Genesis 3.

I. The drama of temptation (Gen. 3:1–7).

A. *In beautiful literary form, the author of Genesis 3 depicts the drama of temptation and the entry of sin (vv. 1–7).* He begins with the serpent, the instrument of the temptation. Revelation 12:9 speaks of "that old serpent, called the Devil, and Satan." The external source of temptation comes to a person and invokes an answering response and desire within that person. According to James, the anatomy of temptation includes both. Evil comes from without. But lest we say, "The devil made me do it," James plainly teaches that the external power of evil meets a responding chord of desire within us. That is what occurred with Eve in Eden.

B. *The serpent asked the woman an almost rhetorical question: "Hath God said, Ye shall not eat of every tree of the garden?"* Obviously, he knew that Adam and Eve were permitted to eat of every tree in the garden except one. His intent was to plant a seed of doubt concerning the goodness of God.

Here was a woman with everything a human could desire. But Satan knew her weak point and fed her the big lie. He said, "You shall not die. The reason God told you not to eat of that tree is that he knows that if you eat it you will know good and evil. You will be like God. You will have moral perception and understanding. You won't die." The woman began to look at that tree again.

C. *Eve discovered three things about the tree.* First, she noted that the fruit on the tree was good for food. Then she saw that it was delightful to look at. It not only appealed to her hunger; it appealed to her aesthetic sense. But it was the third appeal that was tempting. Satan told Eve that the fruit was "desired to make one wise" (v. 6). Who could resist that kind of temptation? Eve couldn't. She ate the fruit.

D. *Eve not only ate the fruit, she shared it.* We seldom sin alone. When we sin, it usually involves other people.

E. *What was the fruit Eve ate?* Tradition says that she ate an apple, but the Bible doesn't affirm that. That tradition came about due to the similarity of two words in Latin. The word for apple is *malum,* and the word for evil is *malus.* They sound much alike.

The woman was deceived and tempted. She ate the fruit and offered some to her husband. He immediately rebelled against God's command not to eat of the fruit. Then they were called to account.

II. Called to account (Gen. 3:8–13).

A. *In verses 8–13 we have a vivid illustration of the text "Be sure your sin will find you out" (Num. 32:23).* There is no such thing as secret sin. We know, and God knows. Soon someone else will know. Adam and Eve violated the known will of God, his express prohibition. Then Adam and Eve heard the sound of the Lord walking in the garden in the cool of the day.

B. *What did they do?* They heard the sound of God walking in the garden in the cool of the day, and they hid from God. They had been made in his likeness and image. They had lived in a garden paradise in close fellowship with the very presence of God. After they sinned, when God came around, they hid in the bushes.

C. *Sin separates.* It separates us from our best selves. It separates us from other people. It ruptures relationships and cuts us off from God. Sin makes us uncomfortable in church, at prayer, and in worship. We feel strange in God's presence.

Adam and Even tried to hide from God but weren't successful. The first recorded emotion in the Bible is Adam's elation at the creation of the woman. The second recorded emotion is fear due to sin.

D. *When they were confronted by God, they began to make excuses.* Adam blamed the woman. "She gave me fruit of the tree" (v. 12 RSV). Then sort of parenthetically, he said, "And I ate" (v. 12). He did not blame only the woman for his temptation and sin; he blamed God as well. He said, "The woman *you gave me*, she gave it to me, and I ate" (v. 12, author's paraphrase).

God cross-examined the woman, and she blamed the serpent. "The serpent beguiled [seduced] me" (v. 13). God didn't bother to ask the serpent. He knew the serpent was the deceiver. Neither Adam nor Eve took responsibility for their sins. They tried to blame someone else. They ultimately blamed God. People still play that game.

III. Judgment pronounced (Gen. 3:14–19).

A. *The result of the fall came upon Adam, the woman, and the race.* God set forth a series of curses. First, the serpent was cursed. Enmity was put between the serpent and humanity. We are in conflict with an enemy in this world, and his name is Satan, the power of evil. You may personify evil or define it in some kind of philosophical terms, but you cannot deny that it is real. We have to fight it and struggle with it. We not only have the external influence of evil, but we also have the inward answering response of our own desire.

B. *The curse on the woman was that per pain would be multiplied both in childbirth and in domination by her husband.* If any curse has ever come to pass, the painful domination of women has. That all resulted from the fall. In Galatians we read that in Christ "there is neither male nor female" (3:28). Christianity has a oneness that is not found anywhere else. Christ is the great liberator of women, men, and children. Faith in Christ lifts the eternal curse of sin.

C. *God cursed the man, striking the very nerve of man's existence—his work.* Remember, work is not a curse. God was depicted as a gardener, and he placed Adam in the garden of Eden to cultivate and care for it. That is work. Work was given to man before the fall. The curse is not work. A curse was placed on the ground. The result of the curse is toil, thorns, and thistles.

D. *But the ultimate curse for all is found in verse 19: "For dust thou art, and unto dust shalt thou return."* Prior to Genesis 3:19 there was no mention of death. Indeed, there was a clear promise of eternal life. For one of the trees in the garden was the Tree of Life. The clear implication spelled as late as Revelation 21 is that the Tree of Life is a symbol of immortality. The curse of sin is death. Mortality is the result of the fall. Only faith in Christ brings immortality. Scripture says that only God is immortal (1 Tim. 6:16). He gives eternal life to those who believe. Here we find that the judgment of God fell on the first couple as a result of their sin against the known will of the Father. The ultimate curse is the curse of death—"the last enemy" (1 Cor. 15:26).

IV. The promise of mercy (Gen. 3:22–24).

A. *Let us quickly recap the highlights.* Genesis 1 tells about the beauty and brightness of God's creation. Genesis 2 shows the crown of God's creation—man and woman. Genesis 3 describes the origin of evil—that which is amiss in the world and within our own lies. In verses 22–24 we are told that God drove Adam and Even out of the garden of Eden. That was an act of mercy. He drove them out of the garden lest they eat of the Tree of Life and live forever in this dying world.

Once Adam and Eve had sinned, God in his mercy set a cherubim, a divine security guard, at the gate of the garden. He drove them out and would not let them return to eat of the Tree of Life and live forever in the world. It would be hell to live forever in our dying, degenerating bodies.

B. *There is also a bright note of hope there.* In verses 20–21 we are told that Adam gave the woman a name—Eve, which means "the mother of all living." Every time a child is born, it is one more bit of evidence that God has not given up on the race! It was through Eve that salvation ultimately came.

V. The note of hope (Gen. 3:15, 20–21).

A. *The other note of hope is in verse 15.* This is what the church fathers called the *protoevangelium* in Latin. It means the gospel in embryo or the gospel before the Gospels. The promise was that the woman would bruise the heel of the serpent. What does that mean? It promises that through a woman the defeat of evil would eventually come. And so it did: her name was Mary.

B. *Through the seed of Eve, through another woman, the bruising of the serpent's head came to pass.* In Christ we have hope for the defeat of evil and triumph of good.

Conclusion

We cannot return to Eden. We can no sooner go back to the utopian garden than Adam and Eve could. We cannot return, but we can enter the kingdom of God. The new Eden is described in Revelation 21 as paradise regained. Just as surely as Adam and Eve once lived in the presence of God and in daily communion with him, one day you and I, by faith in the Lord Jesus Christ, will enter the presence of God to enjoy his fellowship forever.

If you have not yet turned from your sin and entered the kingdom of God by faith in the work of Jesus Christ on Calvary, do so today.

SUNDAY EVENING, OCTOBER 3

Title: Ownership Versus Stewardship

Text: "But when he had heard these things, he became very sad; for he was extremely rich. And Jesus looked at him and said, 'How hard it is for those who are wealthy to enter the kingdom of God! For it is easier for a camel to go through the eye of a needle, than for a rich man to enter the kingdom of God'" ***(Luke 18:23–25 NASB).***

Scripture Reading: Luke 18:18–30

Introduction

The most important factor in a person's relationship to material things is not whether he or she has much or little. One may have few worldly goods and still be greedy, treating the goods as his or her god.

A story has circulated for years about a man who had neglected service to God and the ministry of the church until his only son lay in the intensive care unit of a hospital in a coma as the result of a motorcycle accident. He was distraught, desperate, and anxious as he hurried to the hospital chapel to pray. He said, "God, I don't bother you much and haven't asked for much; and I think I have this request coming to me. That's my only boy between life and death now. I want you to save him." Then he said God brought very clearly to his mind the words, "Whose boy is that? If he is only yours, you take care of the problem. Give him to me, and we'll see what can be done!" The concept of ownership is sometimes at war with the concept of stewardship.

I. When we see ourselves as owners, our possessions own us.

A. *Our text says that the ruler who wanted eternal life was "very sad" when Jesus instructed him to give away his possessions (Luke 18:23 NASB).* He likely thought he had no choice in the matter. An exchange of his possessions for eternal life seemed a poor bargain to one who thought his possessions were his life.

B. *That the man owned enough goods to be described as "extremely rich" (Luke 18:23 NASB) was deemed by him to be his most important characteristic.* His control of things (his ownership) was the greatest factor he saw in his identity. Obsessed with the ownership of things, he became slave to them.

II. When we see ourselves as owners, our possessions become barriers to eternal life.

A. *Jesus revealed the heart of the issue when he emphasized the difficulty of the rich receiving eternal life.* The analogy that it is easier for a camel to go through the eye of a needle than for a rich man to enter God's kingdom (Luke 18:25) underlines the truth that riches can be barriers to a right relationship with God. He indicated that only by God's power can the rich come to grace (v. 27). An act of God is necessary for a rich man to be willing to trade in his possessions.

B. *The clause "for he was extremely rich" (Luke 18:24 NASB) is given as the total explanation for the man's going away sorrowfully.* This matter-of-fact statement indicates that is what you would expect of the very rich when confronted with the gospel. To the rich, the control of much now seems preferable to something that appears to be only a future possibility. It is too much to give up if one is obsessed with the ownership of things.

III. When we give our possessions to God, our lives become his.

A. *For those who struggle through ownership to stewardship, life takes on new meaning.* If we do not worry about possessions because we see them as being on loan from God, we are not obsessed with keeping them (Luke 18:29–30). Jesus pointed out that the one who gives things into God's hands has his or her gift multiplied. God also then is able to relate to that person in a fuller way than ever before.

B. *The bottom line, however, is that eternal life comes as a gift to those who acknowledge that God is owner and Christ is Lord.* When our quest is for God instead of for treasure, God gives the treasure the world cannot give.

Conclusion

For believers, God is the owner and giver and we are stewards. One great decision in life revolves around our view of the things to which we hold title. They belong to God, and he has given us trusteeship over them for a while. This means we will tithe and be good stewards of all of God's blessings.

Wednesday Evening, October 6

Title: A Man Born Blind
Text: "One thing I know, that, whereas I was blind, now I see" ***(John 9:25).***
Scripture Reading: John 9:1–41

Introduction

The fact that John gives an entire chapter to the account of the healing of the man born blind shows the importance he attaches to it. From it we learn lessons on the healing power of Christ, the spontaneous testimony of the saved, and the resistance with which the work of God is met.

I. The situation.

A. *Place.* The concluding verse of the previous chapter depicts Christ leaving the temple and walking through the midst of the people. The opening verse of John 9 tells us that as he went along, he encountered a man born blind. Therefore, we know this healing occurred at the temple.

B. *Time.* This experience occurred during Jesus' visit to Jerusalem when he attended the Feast of Tabernacles. This was the final day of the feast, the Sabbath.

C. *Circumstance.* John 9:2 informs us that the disciples asked the reason for this man's affliction. Apparently it was of such severity that this was a rather natural question. It is a question we often ask as well, and as was the case with the disciples, an improper question.

The disciples made the blind man the subject of theological discussion rather than the object of healing and compassion. Such a person as the blind man was considered vile and sinful. Thus, the question came as to who was responsible for this man's plight.

D. *Description of persons.* This blind man was full of emotion, ignorant but truthful. Although he had had this handicap from birth, when he encountered Christ, he was immediately obedient to him. After he was healed, the man was enthusiastic about his blessing but remained stern in the face of the Pharisees.

E. *Method.* Christ took the initiative in this situation and was spontaneous (John 9:6). By using clay he veiled his power under a material means. Despite the "prop," Christ selected a means of healing that, in and of itself, would be incapable of producing sight.

Christ altered his method of dealing with people according to the type he encountered. For example, he spoke kindly to the blind man and spoke with judgment to the Pharisees.

Christ first healed the man's physical sight and then his spiritual sight. Christ seized the opportunity of using this man's affliction as an instrument for his own glory. He encouraged him to exercise faith in the Son of God (John 9:37). Christ also used the man's blindness as a symbol of the Pharisees' spiritual blindness in the concluding three verses of this chapter.

II. The result.

Immediately the man's sight was restored, and with it came a firm faith in Christ as a man of God. Later that faith turned into belief in Jesus as the Son of God.

A. *This man's neighbors were amazed, and they desired to see Jesus.* They took this matter to their spiritual leaders. These leaders proved to be enemies of our Lord by insisting that the law did not allow even healing to be done on the Sabbath. In the episode described in John 9:13–38, it is obvious that the scribes and Pharisees attempted to intimidate the people so they would no longer believe in or identify themselves with Christ.

B. *Like many a new convert on our mission fields, this man was thrown out of his "church" after he had gained a personal knowledge of Jesus Christ as Savior.* Nevertheless, it should be pointed out that vast numbers of people were bound to be persuaded of Christ's messiahship because of his healing of this man and because of this man's willingness to be bold in the proclamation of his faith.

Conclusion

The things that are impossible with humans are always possible with God, and this we must never forget. At the same time, we must not attempt to limit what God can do or how God can do it. When we feel as though we have total knowledge of the work of our Lord, we run the risk of being numbered among the scribes and Pharisees of our Lord's day.

SUNDAY MORNING, OCTOBER 10

Title: Have You Been Converted?
Text: "I tell you, Nay: but, except ye repent, ye shall all likewise perish" ***(Luke 13:3).***
Scripture Reading: Luke 13:1–8
Hymns: "This Is My Father's World," Babcock
"I Know That My Redeemer Liveth," Pounds
"The Way of the Cross Leads Home," Pounds
Offertory Prayer: O God, our eternal Father, you have blessed us beyond measure. You have provided us with food, shelter, and clothing. You have dressed us in the righteousness of your dear Son. You have caused

our names to be written in heaven. Out of gratitude for your generosity toward us, we bring these gifts. They seem so small when we consider the blessings you have bestowed upon us. We ask you to receive them. In the glorious name of your Son we pray. Amen.

Introduction

Have you been converted? The question sounds old-fashioned. Your immediate reaction is probably to dismiss it as obsolete. But before you dismiss the question, you need to consider what Jesus says to us. If we take his Word seriously, no question can be more relevant.

When Jesus says, "Repent," he calls for radical conversion of our lives. "Except ye repent, ye shall all likewise perish," is a call to make a decision about God and to set the direction for life. It is a call to turn from sin and turn to God to live a life of obedience under his rule.

I. The universality of sin makes conversion necessary.

A. *The historical incident.* These words were spoken "at that season" (Luke 13:1). Jesus had just spoken to the crowd about the urgency of getting right with God. The people then countered with the observation about the Galileans being killed by Pilate. Evidently Jesus interpreted this as an attempt to justify themselves and to indicate that they did not need to get right with God. They did not need conversion, they thought, since they were the sons of Abraham and lived in Jerusalem.

We know nothing about the tragic death of the Galileans except what is found in the text. Such a slaughter would not have been unusual for Pilate. The Galileans were a volatile group, so it may be that they were involved in some kind of political insurrection. What we do know is that they were in the process of offering a sacrifice in the temple when Pilate found them. His soldiers cut them down and caused their blood to become mingled with the blood of their sacrifices.

Jesus' response to the crowd shows that he thought they felt the Galileans deserved their fate. They reflected an idea that has been around for a long time: tragedy falls in direct proportion to sin. The Judeans always suspected that the Galileans deserved judgment. But Jesus responded in a very direct way: "Suppose ye that these Galileans were sinners above all the Galileans, because they suffered such things? I tell you, Nay: but, except ye repent, ye shall all likewise perish" (Luke 13:2–3). Jesus denied that the tragic death was evidence of greater transgression before God on the part of the Galileans.

Instead of accepting their interpretations of the event, Jesus reminded them of an event that had involved Judeans. "Or those eighteen upon whom the tower in Siloam fell, and slew them, think ye that they were sinners above all men that dwelt in Jerusalem? I tell you, Nay: but, except ye repent, ye shall all likewise perish" (Luke 13:4–5). Again we do not know the details of this incident. Efforts were made to build defense installations around some of the key water projects of the city. Probably these eighteen were working on a defense project near the pool of Siloam. The collapse of the tower was evidently an accident. The wall under construction fell on these men and crushed them to death.

Was this a sign that they had been guilty of some great transgression? Jesus denies it. In fact, a little observation will reveal that such accidents happen to the good and the bad about equally. Rather, what Jesus affirms is that "all," including the Judeans, will perish unless a radical turning from sin and turning to God takes place. The great underlying assumption of our Lord in this passage is that all of us are sinners against God and are thereby deserving of the judgment of God. All will perish unless they repent.

B. *The present application.* People today have a hard time accepting this view of humanity, especially of ourselves individually. We have come up with other explanations for our moral shortcomings. We do not want to think of ourselves as deserving of the judgment of God. We do not want to think of ourselves as sinners. But Jesus says that "all" are in need of conversion because "all" are sinners. Would you admit that he might know more about human nature and human need than you?

II. Conversion is needed now.

A. *The certainty of the judgment makes it urgent.* "Except ye repent, ye shall all likewise perish" (13:3). Repentance is an imperative urged upon us by the certainty of perishing without it. "Likewise" does not mean that we will perish in the same way as the Galileans or the Judeans on whom the wall fell; rather, it means "also." It is an indication of the certainty of judgment.

The great truth underlying this word from Jesus is that everything that is not rightly related to God will perish. The only thing that will survive the fire of judgment is that which has been brought under the saving protection of God.

B. *The justice of judgment makes it urgent.* Jesus emphasizes the justice of the judgment with the parable of the fig tree. The details of the parable are familiar: the owner of the vineyard had come to inspect his fig trees again. One tree in particular he had been watching carefully for some time. For three years he had been expecting fruit from the tree, but he had received only disappointment. At last he called for the keeper of the vineyard to cut down that tree. If the tree was removed from the vineyard, something that would bear fruit could be planted in its place. Otherwise it was just using up the resources of the vineyard without giving anything in return.

This little parable is disturbing. When you begin to think about God's claim on your life, you may become uncomfortable. Surely God would be just in cutting you out.

III. The goodness of God makes conversion possible.

The parable of the fig tree does more than warn of the impending judgment of God. It calls our attention to the goodness of God, who makes repentance possible.

A. *We see the goodness of God in his provisions.* The tree in question was a fortunate one: it was not left to tend to itself in the wild. Rather, it was planted in a vineyard where it received the best of care. Its needs were provided day by day. It was ever under the careful eye of the keeper of the vineyard. Some have seen this as a picture of the care that God had bestowed upon the people of Israel, and so it is; but it is also a picture of the goodness of God toward us all.

B. *We see the goodness of God in his patience.* This is the thrust of the parable. The owner had been patient for three years. He could have justly condemned the tree after the first fruitless year, but he waited and watched. Oh, the patience of God! The intercession of the keeper of the vineyard is probably meant to remind us of the intercession of the Lord Jesus on our behalf. The only reason that we have not already perished is that God is patient and long-suffering. It is the goodness of God that makes it possible for you to have the opportunity to repent. You must not presume upon this goodness. There will be a day when it will run out.

Conclusion

Have you been converted? This is the question for you to face this morning. Unless there has been a radical decision in which you turned from sin and turned to God, you are on a collision course with the judgment of God. Surely you mean to repent sometime. An aged rabbi routinely told people that they needed to repent on the day before they died. They would reply to him, "But we do not know the day of our death." He would wisely answer, "Then you had better do it now." This is the word that Jesus is giving to us. You need to be converted to God now!

SUNDAY EVENING, OCTOBER 10

Title: Concerning the Collection

Text: "Now about the collection for God's people: Do what I told the Galatian churches to do. On the first day of every week, each one of you should set aside a sum of money in keeping with his income, saving it up, so that when I come no collections will have to be made" ***(1 Cor. 16:1–2 NIV).***
Scripture Reading: 1 Corinthians 15:51–16:4

Introduction

The remarkable abruptness with which Paul moves from the climax of his victorious declaration of the believers' resurrection from the dead to his discussion of the collection for the saints has amazed many Bible readers. A seminary professor told the story of his experience on a Sunday afternoon in a large city where he was serving as an interim pastor. He had seen an advertisement in the local paper for a seminar on the prophecies of the Bible, and he decided to go hear for himself the teachings of this expert. To his amazement and amusement, at the appointed time the speaker said something like this: "I'm not going to preach on prophecy, but I am going to preach on tithing and Christian stewardship. You wouldn't have come to hear my sermon on tithing, which means you desperately need it." The professor said one of the most uneasy groups of people in the world is a "prophecy crowd" having to hear a stewardship sermon. Paul did not employ this tactic, but the connection seems to say that people who acknowledge the resurrection by meeting on the first day of the week will be moved to good stewardship.

I. Paul tells the time of the collection.

A. *Paul's readers were expected to make a weekly expression of their stewardship, and it was to be done first.* The first day of the week would coincide with their celebration of the resurrection of our Lord from the dead, the Lord's Day.

B. *Periodic and spontaneous gifts that are special expressions of love and thanksgiving are always appropriate.* The injunction here, however, is for systematic stewardship expressed on a regular basis.

II. Paul tells of the participants in the collection.

A. *"Each one of you" (1 Cor. 16:2) is a phrase that indicates no believer is excluded from the responsibility or the privilege of stewardship of material things.*

B. *The church at Corinth may have included some members who were at the bottom of the economic scale, but these too were exhorted to join in giving.*

III. Paul tells the responsibility of each in the collection.

A. *"In keeping with his income" (1 Cor. 16:2) indicates that our giving should be proportionate to what we have.* The injunctions elsewhere in the Bible that speak of tithing follow a consistent pattern for stewardship. Proportionate giving is enjoined.

B. *Recognizing that we have been prospered as opposed to the concept that we have earned our blessings is a key to proper stewardship.*

IV. Paul tells the reasons for this collection.

Paul may not have enumerated all of the reasons for this collection, but he did make some of them clear.

A. *The witness of the church in its own community would be enhanced by good stewardship.* "So that when I come no collections will have to be made" (1 Cor. 16:2) suggests that Paul wanted to forgo the troublesome experience of taking up special offerings and possibly having to upbraid the Corinthians for poor stewardship.

B. *The witness of the Corinthian church to Jerusalem saints and others would be enhanced by good stewardship.* Paul was eager for the saints in Jerusalem to be impacted by the Corinthians' generosity. The fellowship between Jewish and Gentile Christians could be strengthened and the cause of Christ advanced.

Conclusion

Are you moved by the wonderful victory Christ has purchased for you? Do you look forward to his glorious return? Then you should be moved to proper Christian stewardship. Paul gave us the instructions. Now we must do it.

WEDNESDAY EVENING, OCTOBER 13

Title: An Inquiring Lawyer

Text: "Behold, a certain lawyer stood up, and tempted him, saying, Master, what shall I do to inherit eternal life?" ***(Luke 10:25)***.

Scripture Reading: Luke 10:25–37

Introduction

We should never ask Christ a question unless we really want an answer. And that answer may prove to be most disturbing, as it was in the case of this inquiring lawyer. To answer him, our Lord pointedly related the story of the good Samaritan.

I. The situation.

A. *Place.* Somewhere in or near Jerusalem Christ encountered this inquisitive lawyer. Certainly Christ's illustration indicates that he was in the vicinity of Jerusalem.

B. *Time.* Soon after the return of the Seventy-two in AD 28, Christ had this conversation with an expert in the law. Thomas M. Lindsay, in his book *The Gospel According to St. Luke,* contends that this occurred in the six-month period between the Feast of Tabernacles and the beginning of Passion Week.

C. *Circumstance.* Christ had recently sent out the Seventy-two and then had gone to the Feast of Tabernacles. During the feast, he had forgiven the adulteress brought to him in the temple. Only recently the Seventy-two had joyfully returned from their mission, and the Pharisees were pressing their efforts to trick Christ into making a false statement.

D. *Description of person.* The inquiring lawyer apparently worked on civil and ecclesiastical matters as an expounder of the Jewish law. Luke lets us know very clearly in 10:25 that the lawyer had an ulterior motive: he wanted to make Christ look bad. Verse 27 informs us that the lawyer apparently had a thorough knowledge of the Old Testament. He asked the right question but in the wrong spirit (Luke 10:25). He was flippant and irreverent, self-righteous and conceited, expressing a false sense of superiority and struggling to maintain his reputation.

E. *Method.* Christ reversed the direction of the lawyer's question when he asked, "What is written in the law? how readest thou?" (Luke 10:26). In verse 28 Christ complimented the lawyer on his interpretation. Then Christ further clarified the lawyer's answer by telling the parable of the good Samaritan.

Christ was attempting to lead the lawyer to see that it is humanly impossible to live the perfect life demanded by the law. In verse 37 Christ led the lawyer to condemn himself and acknowledge his own lack of mercy for others.

II. The result.

A. *In Luke 10:30–35, Christ revealed three attitudes that people have toward possessions.* The thieves said, "What is yours is mine, and I will take it." The priest and the Levite said, "What is mine is mine, and I will keep it." But the good Samaritan said, "What is mine is yours, and I will share it."

B. *Christ revealed the lawyer's true nature.* He got nothing out of Christ that he did not already know. It appears that the lawyer went away unjustified, although Christ challenged him to do as the good Samaritan had done.

Conclusion

Christ's answer does not imply that if you give to others in compassion as the Samaritan you will inherit eternal life. Christ does say, however, that one who knows the saving power of God through Christ will be characterized by such compassion.

The inquiring lawyer's question, "Master, what shall I do to inherit eternal life?" could also well be answered by Paul and Silas when they replied to the very same question of their jailer by saying, "Believe on the Lord Jesus Christ, and thou shalt be saved" (Acts 16:31).

Sunday Morning, October 17

Title: The Sinner's Prayer

Text: "And the publican, standing afar off, would not lift up so much as his eyes unto heaven, but smote upon his breast, saying, 'God be merciful to me a sinner'" ***(Luke 18:13).***

Scripture Reading: Luke 18:9–14

Hymns: "Jesus Paid It All," Hall
"Love Lifted Me," Rowe
"I Saw the Cross of Jesus," Whitfield

Offertory Prayer: O God, our heavenly Father, we bring our gifts to you. We follow in the path that your Son walked before us. He gave himself for our sins. We come to bring gifts that express our gratitude for your gift. While our gifts are not as costly as yours, they do express our love. May you be pleased to bless these gifts to further the good news of your Son. In the name of your Gift, Jesus Christ, we pray. Amen.

Introduction

Not everyone who goes to church experiences God. Nor does everyone who goes to church go to heaven at death. Nor do all "good" people go to heaven when they die. Indeed, only sinners go to heaven. Do these statements seem startling? They are all based on the parable of the Pharisee and the publican.

We do not have to wonder about the message of this parable, for Jesus made it clear. "He also told this parable to some who trusted in themselves that they were righteous and despised others" (18:9 RSV). Such would surely apply to the Pharisees who were constantly resisting the ministry of Jesus. But such could also be applied to some who had become followers of Jesus. This parable would not have found its way into our Bible if it did not speak to a need in the hearts of humanity in general.

The primary message is that if you want to be right with God, if you want to have a part in the eternal kingdom of God, you must pray the sinner's prayer. The prayer of the publican is the prayer for all.

I. The sinner's prayer is prayed with great humility.

A. *The contrast between the two characters in the parable is clear.* The Pharisee was a religious man, outwardly proper in his religious practices and in his conduct. He was known for the "good" life that he lived. The publican was a tax collector, an irreligious man notorious for his neglect of religious practices and for wayward living. He was the last man you would expect to be commended by Jesus.

B. *But that contrast was all external; the real contrast between the two men became obvious when they went into the temple to pray*. The Pharisee used the occasion to commend himself on how well he was doing and to express some of his contempt for the publican. But the publican came into the temple with a profound sense of unworthiness that expressed itself in humility.

C. *The place.* The publican's humility was seen in the place he stood. Unlike the Pharisee who stood as close to the Holy of Holies as possible, the publican stood "afar off" (v. 13) He was just barely inside the courtyard. He felt himself at a guilty distance from God, unworthy to make any approach to God. People who pray the sinner's prayer always feel this way.

D. *The posture.* The publican's humility was seen in the posture he assumed. While men ordinarily stood as they prayed and lifted their eyes up toward heaven, the publican did not wish to lift his eyes toward heaven. All that he knew of himself made him feel unworthy of looking upon God. Surely God was too holy for him. He was approaching God with a genuine sense of unworthiness.

E. *The power.* Jesus closed this parable with a saying that he used on other occasions. "For every one who exalts himself will be humbled, but he who humbles himself will be exalted" (18:14 RSV). A person cannot pray the sinner's prayer unless he has recognized his unworthiness and is prepared to acknowledge it before God. As long as he is impressed with who he is and what he has done, he cannot pray this prayer. His prayers will be empty, like that of the Pharisee.

II. The sinner's prayer is an expression of great need.

The Pharisee evidently felt no need as he entered the temple. If he felt any need of God, he gave no expression of it. He felt that what he was doing was sufficient, so he had no need to ask God for anything. He stands in sharp contrast to the publican.

A. *The gesture.* The publican expressed his need through his gesture. Jesus says that the man "beat his breast" (18:13 RSV). There is obviously no merit in the gesture itself, but there is in the sense of need that the gesture expressed. The repeated beating of the breast was an expression of sorrow. It was as though he acknowledged that the heart within his breast was the source of all the wrong. It was an expression of the burden of guilt and sin he felt. It was an expression of the despair and hopelessness he felt. By the gesture, he was declaring that he was guilty before God, and there was nothing he could do to remove the guilt. Only God could be of any help.

B. *The prayer.* But it was the prayer that supremely expressed the sense of need: "God, be merciful to me a sinner!" (18:13 RSV). The petition is very personal. The publican was not there to confess the sins of anyone else. He could not speak for others. He spoke only for himself. "It is me, O Lord, standing in the need of prayer." He seems to have been oblivious to others, including the proud Pharisee. The Pharisee was very conscious of others, but the man with the sinner's prayer was aware only of God and himself.

The petition is specific: "Be merciful." It is not the usual word for mercy. The usual word appeals for pity and compassion. This word means "be propitious toward me." Literally, the prayer is that God will deal with the sin of the person in such a way that his anger will be removed. It is a prayer for reconciliation to God, for the removal of the alienation that sin has brought. All those who properly pray this prayer acknowledge that sin has severed them from God and that they can no longer live without him.

The petition is urgent. The English text misses something of the force of the petition. The man literally prayed, "God be merciful to me *the* sinner." By the use of the definite article, he puts himself in a class of his own. He feels like he must be the chief among sinners.

Are you able to identify with the petition? Unless you feel honest with those words on your lips, you are not even close to the kingdom of God. The sinner's prayer comes out of a great conviction of need.

III. The sinner's prayer is heard by God.

No one heard the Pharisee's prayer except the Pharisee—God makes no response to such expressions of pride and arrogance. Actually, there was no response to make since the man made no petitions of God.

A. *The assurance.* But what good news for sinners! "I tell you, this man went down to his house justified rather than the other" (18:14 RSV). Our Lord knew that many sinners would read these words as they searched for hope, so he emphatically said, "I tell you." The sinner went home right with God while the "good" man went home without meeting God.

B. *The answer.* "Justified" is the key word. The word is passive, which shows God is the agent. The man did not justify himself before God, but rather God justified the sinner. All the man did was acknowledge his need and make a plea for mercy. God did the rest.

"Justified" means "to declare righteous, to acquit." God sovereignly acted to cancel the publican's debt of sin and to accept him as a righteous man. God established a relationship with the man as if the man had fulfilled the law and had been righteous in all his conduct.

Conclusion

Do you remember the observations with which we began? Not everyone who goes to church experiences God. Nor does everyone who goes to church go to heaven at death. Nor do all "good" people go to heaven when they die. Indeed, only sinners go to heaven. But not all sinners go to heaven—only those sinners who have prayed a sinner's prayer as did the publican in the parable. Have you prayed this prayer?

Sunday Evening, October 17

Title: You Cannot Afford Poor Stewardship
Text: "But God said unto him, Thou fool, this night thy soul shall be required of thee: then whose shall those things be, which thou hast provided? So is he that layeth up treasure for himself, and is not rich toward God" ***(Luke 12:20–21)***.
Scripture Reading: Luke 12:13–21

Introduction

An adage about unwise frugality declared that some decisions are "penny wise and pound foolish." This archaic language speaks of an individual's efforts to save pennies that will actually cause him to spend a much greater sum of money later. An example would be the "thrifty" act of refusing to spend money for routine auto maintenance. Such an effort of thrift will eventually lead to costly and otherwise needless repairs. In the Scripture passage for tonight, Jesus tells about the foolishness of valuing things more than life. Poor stewardship is overpriced.

I. Bondage to things is a probable price of poor stewardship.

A. *Pursuing the acquisition of things often leads to that pursuit becoming the most powerful influence on your decisions.* When this occurs, you have become the servant of your possessions; they actually possess you.

B. *Other factors may influence your decision-making process, but as your covetousness demonstrates itself in poor stewardship, your life will be marked by a growing bondage to your goods.* Commitment to the acquisition and preservation of possessions will eventually cause you to heel like a trained puppy, and then you will be enslaved.

II. A distorted sense of value is a price of poor stewardship.

A. *God called the man in Jesus' parable a fool because he valued material things more than his relationship with God.* The blessings he saw as important were things people could give. He overlooked the gifts of life and health and many other blessings only God can provide. His focus was certainly on secondary things, and in his quest to acquire and preserve that which was secondary, he missed that which was primary. He valued livelihood more than life and paid a terrible price for the error.

B. *Distortion of values is the most painful problem of spiritual blindness.* The parasite that carries the disease is covetousness. The proper treatment for the malady is right stewardship.

III. A false sense of well-being is a probable price of poor stewardship.

A. *In Jesus' parable, the man's prognosis of his immediate future differed radically from God's declaration about his fate.* He had addressed his total attention to acquiring things of no eternal significance. Now he would stand before God bankrupt. He had depended on wealth to meet any need that might come, but material wealth had no impact on his greatest need, a right standing with God.

B. *Jesus' terse commentary is that one who spends the resources of God on material goods without attention to a relationship with God deserves to be named a fool.* He thinks his goods make him invincible.

Conclusion

Nobody wants to be a slave, but a failure to be a good steward dooms one to a servitude to things. The antidote to this kind of slavery is proper stewardship. After one receives Christ's salvation, stewardship is an important step on the road that leads to richness in God. Tithing and a right sense of stewardship will not buy you wealth in this world, but it will give you a life in the wealth of God's blessings.

WEDNESDAY EVENING, OCTOBER 20

Title: The Rich Young Ruler

Text: "As Jesus started on his way, a man ran up to him and fell on his knees before him. 'Good teacher,' he asked, 'what must I do to inherit eternal life?'" ***(Mark 10:17 NIV).***

Scripture Reading: Mark 10:17–31

Introduction

Unlike many of the other encounters Christ had with individuals, here he does not deal with physical healing, but rather with money and a man's relationship to it. Underlying this whole conversation is the man's need for total commitment to Jesus Christ.

I. The situation.

A. *Place.* Bible scholar A. T. Robertson suggests that Jesus' encounter with the rich young ruler occurred in Perea. David Smith, in his *Commentary on the Four Gospels,* contends that it occurred as Christ was coming out of his home.

B. *Time.* This encounter occurred during the last months of A.D. 28. Most likely, it occurred in the afternoon.

C. *Circumstance.* Jesus had recently come from Galilee to Perea and had of late presented his teachings on divorce. The preceding four verses in Mark 9 record how Christ expressed his feelings toward children.

D. *Description of person.* Youthful, wealthy, earnest, honorable, worshipful, pure, honest, influential, virtuous, and uninformed about spiritual matters—all these adjectives accurately depict the ruler. Apparently he had some knowledge of eternal life, as evidenced by his question. Although he had a touch of self-satisfaction, he was anxious about the life to come. Beneath his concern about his spiritual welfare was an underlying infatuation for riches.

E. *Method.* Our Lord began with the known (Mark 10:19) and moved to the unknown. Apparently the rich young ruler was familiar with the basic commandments of the Lord. From this point Christ led him progressively toward the truth.

Although Christ said that the man knew the commandments of the Lord, he made no acknowledgment of the man's goodness. In verse 21 Christ shattered the man's self-complacency as he revealed that, though he claimed to have kept the law, he had violated the most important requirement—to love God unreservedly. He asked the man for an entire revolution of his life and an absolute surrender of his will to the will of God. Christ dared to put the man's desire to inherit eternal life to the test.

It is vitally important that John stresses (Mark 10:21) that Jesus loved the lawyer throughout the encounter. It is doubtful that the man questioned that Christ loved him, even though his demands were strenuous.

II. The result.

A. *It is significant in this experience that Christ did not always "succeed" in his efforts to win people to faith in him.* What consolation we find in this experience when we also fail in our efforts.

B. *This encounter resulted in sorrow in the life of the young ruler, amazement on the part of the disciples, and a lesson to the disciples on the relation of riches and eternal life.* The man left thoroughly unsettled about his future and likely went back to his old ways.

Conclusion

Often we feel that because a person is good and respectable, that person will find it easy to commit his or her life to Jesus Christ. Our Lord refutes this: until a person is willing to place Christ absolutely first—above family, riches, and other goals in life—he or she cannot truly become a follower of our Lord.

SUNDAY MORNING, OCTOBER 24

Title: The Word of Forgiveness
Text: "When he saw their faith, he said unto him, Man, thy sins are forgiven thee" ***(Luke 5:20).***
Scripture Reading: Luke 5:17–26
Hymns: "Christ Receiveth Sinful Men," Neumeister
"My Faith Looks Up to Thee," Palmer
"Great Redeemer, We Adore Thee," Harris
Offertory Prayer: O God, our eternal Father, we bless you for your goodness. You have enriched our lives with abundance. As an expression of our gratitude, we bring these gifts from among the things that you have placed in our hands. We petition you to receive them and to use them for the glory of your name. Keep us mindful that you are the source of all good things. In the name of your Son, we pray. Amen.

Introduction

Jesus spoke the word of forgiveness to the man in our Scripture text. As a result, the man was healed and the critics were shocked. It was the boldest word Jesus ever spoke.

How the man got to Jesus is a story in itself. He had been paralyzed for an unknown period of time. Concern for his condition prompted his friends to carry him to Jesus on a pallet. When they arrived at the home in which Jesus was meeting with a company of religious leaders, they could not enter the house with their friend. The crowd was so absorbed in Jesus' confrontation with the teachers and scribes that they gave no attention to the apparent need of the man.

The man's friends were men of faith. They carried him up to the roof of the house, tore up some of the tiles, and let him down into the presence of Jesus. While this was a bold act on their part, it would not have been a very difficult feat. A stairway would have been available on the side of the house, and the tiled roof would have been flat, so the task would have been fairly easy to accomplish. Their persistence in the project was a sure sign of their faith. This was the thing that Jesus noticed about them.

Jesus said to the man, "Friend, your sins are forgiven" (5:20 NIV). This is the word of forgiveness!

I. The word of forgiveness needed.

If you had asked the man's friends, "What is the greatest need of your friend?" doubtlessly they would have said, "Our friend is in desperate need of physical healing. The paralysis is keeping him from being able to function as an ordinary human being." But Jesus knew that the man had a need that went deeper than the physical. He knew the spiritual disease of guilt.

A. *Forgiveness is needed because of what guilt does to a person's relationship to God.* It was surely a serious matter that this man could no longer walk physically with his friends, but it is more serious that he could no longer walk with his God. Above everything else, humans were created to know God, to walk in communion with him day by day, to enjoy his fellowship forever. We are not told the nature of this man's transgression, but we can know that it had shut him out from the presence of God. It was imperative that this barrier be removed.

B. *Forgiveness is also needed because of what guilt does to a person.* Perhaps Jesus knew that in this particular case the main physical condition was directly related to his transgression against God. We can say this without teaching that all physical maladies are the result of a particular transgression. Guilt is a terrible destroyer of human happiness and well-being!

Forgiveness is needed by all: not one of us is without sin. Our relationship with God, ourselves, and others has been seriously affected. Will you admit the need?

II. The word of forgiveness spoken.

A. *We need to look carefully at what Jesus said to the man.* "Friend, your sins are forgiven" (5:20 NIV). Jesus' using the plural "sins" lets us know that particular acts of sin were forgiven, not just the condition into which the man was born. "Are forgiven" is a Greek perfect. This means that the sins had been forgiven and stood forgiven. To forgive means "to remove, to cancel, to send away." The man's sins had been removed!

B. *The religious leaders who heard this word from Jesus had an immediate reaction; they rightly understood the implications of this word.* They did not express their thoughts aloud, but Jesus read them. They were thinking, "Who is this fellow who speaks blasphemy? Who can forgive sins but God alone?" They were right! Several Old Testament leaders had performed most of the same deeds as Jesus and had acted as he did, but not one of them ever claimed authority to forgive sins. This was new and startling. Unfortunately, Jesus' critics came to the wrong conclusion. They reasoned, "Only God can forgive sin. This man claims the authority to forgive sin, so this man is guilty of blasphemy." They did not consider the possibility that Jesus might be God.

C. *Jesus accepted the challenge by relating the forgiveness of sin and the healing of the man.* He asked, "Why are you thinking these things in your hearts? Which is easier to say, 'Your sins are forgiven,' or to say, 'Get up and walk'? But that you may know that the Son of Man has authority on earth to forgive sins . . ." He said to the paralyzed man, "I tell you, get up, take your mat and go home" (5:22–24 NIV).

The conclusion is clear. Jesus Christ has the authority to forgive sin, and this is to be seen as a sign of who he is. He is the earthly manifestation of the eternal God. He can and does forgive sin.

III. The word of forgiveness received.

The religious leaders might have had a problem with the word of forgiveness, but the paralyzed man did not. It was very good news to him.

A. *Received by faith.* Luke indicates that Jesus spoke this word when he saw "their faith." Whose faith did he see? Surely he must have seen the faith of the man's friends, for they had just demonstrated remarkable faith in their deed. But he must have been including the faith of the paralyzed man too. It required some faith for the man to consent to the actions of his friends. So we can expect that the word of forgiveness was received by faith by the crippled man.

   We do not have to wonder about this: the man demonstrated faith. When Jesus said to him, "I tell you, get up, take your mat and go home" (5:24 NIV), that is what he did. The authoritative way in which Jesus gave the command prompted him to attempt the impossible.

   The word of forgiveness must always be received by faith. Even this poor man could have refused to believe, and the word would have been to no avail. He could have refused to receive the offer of forgiveness. Do you believe that Jesus has the power and the willingness to forgive you? Are you ready to receive forgiveness? Then use your faith to ask him for it! To ask is an act of faith. He responds to such faith with full pardon.

B. *Received with joy.* The word of forgiveness was also received with joy: "Immediately he stood up in front of them, took what he had been lying on and went home praising God" (5:25 NIV). Forgiveness brought a renewed sense of the favor and peace of God. It filled the man's heart with peace, joy, and praise to God.

Conclusion

What would have to happen for you to experience God's wonderful forgiveness this morning? First, you must admit your need. Second, you must place your trust in the authority and willingness of Jesus Christ to forgive sin. Third, you must claim your forgiveness by faith. There is no better way to do this than by simply asking for it in a prayer addressed to God through our Lord Jesus Christ.

God will do the rest. He will cleanse the record of heaven and your own defiled conscience. Won't you do it right now?

SUNDAY EVENING, OCTOBER 24

Title: That's Gratitude for You

Text: "And Jesus answering said, Were there not ten cleansed? but where are the nine? There are not found that returned to give glory to God, save this stranger. And he said unto him, Arise, go thy way: thy faith hath made thee whole" ***(Luke 17:17–19).***

Scripture Reading: Luke 17:11–19

Introduction

"I forgot to tell Grandma thank you, Mommy!" is often the confession of a child who is growing in responsible gratitude. Parents are normally very concerned that their children learn to be grateful, for gratitude is a key to a life with meaning. In tonight's text Jesus teaches a great lesson about gratitude.

I. An ingredient of gratitude is the cultivation of memory.

A. *Somebody has suggested that most people are quite selective with their memories.* They tend to forget their own debts and instead remember that which is owed them. The reason for this may be a concern for self rather than for others. Surely all ten lepers had anticipated how grateful they would be if a cure came, but when they discovered that they were cured, nine did not remember to show gratitude.

B. *Jesus' simple yet penetrating question, "Where are the nine?" (v. 17), probed at the dynamics of ingratitude.* "This stranger" refers to the fact that this one who returned was not considered a true Israelite. However, he faced the vivid memory of his former plight as a leper, his cry to Jesus for help, and the ensuing cure; and he had faith to believe what Jesus had done. His faith was born of gratitude, and his gratitude was the child of a willing memory that made him return to give thanks.

II. A result of gratitude is the opening of the channel of blessings.

A. *Many interpreters have suggested that the nine missed the greater blessing.* The nine went on with life, remembering Jesus as a miracle worker only. They never learned the lesson about faith that made the grateful one truly whole.

B. *Perhaps the nine hurried on, driven by fear that the cure might not last, or maybe they were reluctant to accept the responsibility that true gratitude carries.* A story, probably apocryphal, has circulated that says the nine appeared before the priests to be declared ceremonially clean and free to go back into society only to find that their leprosy had returned. The text does not tell us that they got their leprosy back, but their lack of gratitude suggests that they needed it. They could not be trusted with wholeness, for they forgot the Giver of all gifts. With their attitude, they would never be good stewards of life.

C. *The Samaritan who returned to Jesus had the same urgent duties that kept the others from returning; but having received the great gift, his focus was turned to the Giver.* With a grateful heart, he worshiped Jesus, and in so doing he opened the channel of greater blessings.

Conclusion

Your blessings are abundant. God's physical blessings are incomprehensible, and his spiritual blessings cause the finite mind to marvel. The key question is, can you be trusted with God's gifts? You can if your response to them is a gratitude that impacts the way you live. Thanksgiving is an outgrowth of gratitude. True gratitude toward God will be expressed in part by proper stewardship.

WEDNESDAY EVENING, OCTOBER 27

Title: Bartimaeus

Text: "And they came to Jericho: and as he went out of Jericho with his disciples and a great number of people, blind Bartimaeus, the son of Timaeus, sat by the highway side begging" ***(Mark 10:46)***.

Scripture Reading: Mark 10:46–52

Introduction

Christ's encounter with Bartimaeus is recorded also in Matthew 20:29–34 and Luke 18:35–43. In these accounts you may find your own heart's yearning for the mercy of the Lord and his willingness to grant that mercy to all who acknowledge that need.

I. The situation.

A. *Place.* Some concern exists that there appears to be a conflict as to exactly where the healing of Bartimaeus took place. For example, Mark says that Christ was going out of Jericho; Luke says that Christ was entering Jericho (Luke 18:35). A logical reconciliation is found in that there was an old and new Jericho, and apparently Christ was departing one of the Jerichos and entering the other.

Jericho was on the border of Ephraim, about two hours' journey from the Jordan. This was a blooming oasis in the midst of a sandy plain. The city had been built by the Canaanites and destroyed by Joshua and later rebuilt. It was the most luxurious resort area in Palestine. In fact, from the time of Herod the Great, Jericho had been the winter residence of the court.

B. *Time.* Christ's encounter with this blind man occurred sometime in AD 29, probably after the conversation in which Jesus foretold his death to his disciples. Commentator Philip Schaff says that the event occurred around noon on Friday, the eighth of Nisan, a week before Jesus' crucifixion.

C. *Circumstance.* Christ had reached the end of his last journey and was about to consummate his life in Jerusalem. A great multitude was gathered when this healing took place.

D. *Description of person.* Obviously Bartimaeus was blind. His name itself tells us that he was the son of Timaeus, since the prefix *bar* means "son of." That he continued to cry out to Christ—even when others told him to be quiet—reveals the persistency of his faith (Mark 10:48). His prayer was believing in origin (v. 47), urgent in character (v. 48), and specific in aim (v. 51). It is interesting that his faith came by hearing (v. 57). Bartimaeus was a man of humility, poverty, and importunity.

E. *Method.* Christ moved in a compassionate manner, which was noticed by the man even though he could not see. Christ turned from the multitude and gave personal attention to one needy person. In doing so, he disregarded the desire of the crowd for the blind man to be silenced. In fact, Christ encouraged the man to speak when he asked him, "What wilt thou that I should do for thee?" (Mark 10:51). Revealing his genuine concern, Christ inquired further into the man's need. In extending his offer to help, Christ satisfied the man's deepest desire and used the practical act of healing to reach him.

II. The result.

A. *Bartimaeus was healed of blindness.*

B. *Our Lord was moved with compassion, and Bartimaeus was saved by faith.* The natural result was that he followed Christ. When teaching this passage, it should be pointed out that Christ told the man, "Thy faith hath made thee whole" (Mark 10:52), which is also what Paul teaches in Galatians. Also it should be noted that when one is genuinely saved, he will want to follow Christ "in the way" (v. 52), wherever that way may lead.

Conclusion

The last stage of our Lord's earthly life was brought to a close with this compassionate deed of healing one for whom others had neither time nor cure. From this experience we should learn that one needy soul requires that we turn from the multitudes of those around us to extend the grace and mercy of God in love. Also, we should put into practice the example set by our Lord and not be influenced by others who feel that some solitary soul is not worthy of our efforts.

SUNDAY MORNING, OCTOBER 31

Title: Life's Most Important Question
Text: "Jesus and his disciples went on to the villages around Caesarea Philippi. On the way he asked them, 'Who do people say I am? . . . But what about you?' he asked. 'Who do you say I am?'" ***(Mark 8:27, 29 NIV).***
Scripture Reading: Mark 8:27–30

Hymns: "All Hail the Power of Jesus' Name," Perronet
"Fairest Lord Jesus," from the German
"Blessed Assurance, Jesus Is Mine," Stites

Offertory Prayer: O God, our eternal Father, we bring our gifts to you. They are a part of the bounty with which you have blessed us. We ask you to receive our gifts and to use them in the service of your kingdom. Grant that we will always be mindful of the source of every good and perfect gift. In the name of Jesus we pray. Amen.

Introduction

Jesus knew how to ask a question; it was one of his favorite teaching tools. He used a question to drive a truth into the heart. He also used a question to call for a decision. Of all the questions that Jesus ever asked, this one in Mark 8:29 is the most important. There is something about this question that still probes the depth of our beings.

This question marked a critical turning point in Jesus' ministry. He had invested months of ministry in the lives of his disciples. Now he took them away from the busy scene of ministry to a place near Caesarea Philippi. There he first made a rather innocent inquiry about what the crowds were saying about him, but then he asked what his disciples had come to understand about him.

Jesus asked the question only after he had spent some time alone in prayer. He knew this question to be of ultimate importance to his disciples, to the outcome of his ministry in their lives, and to his mission in the world. For them and for us it is the most important question Jesus asked. Let us consider why.

I. It concerns life's most important person.

A. *"Whom say ye that I am?"* The question concerns our understanding of the most important person who ever lived. It is obvious that the crowds had not yet begun to realize his importance. They were identifying him with some of the great names of the past. His boldness and message made them think of John the Baptist. Some who did not know him very well were saying that he must be a resurrected John the Baptist. Others who knew of his mighty works and miracles thought of Elijah. Many expected Elijah to make another appearance before the coming of the Messiah. Still others identified him with the old prophets. They knew that he was uniquely from God, but they were not certain who he might be.

B. *Jesus' unique nature makes him life's most important person.* The disciples had only begun to realize the uniqueness of his nature. When Peter boldly answered the question with "You are the Christ" (Mark 8:29 NIV), he indicated something of their understanding of his uniqueness. In Matthew's account of the same incident, he adds that Peter confesses, "You are the Christ, the son of the living God" (16:16 NIV). It was an affirmation of the uniqueness of Jesus' relationship to God.

Jesus was fully God and fully man—that is, he was God and became a man. If Jesus had been just another great religious leader, the question would have been of limited importance. But since he is who he is, this question is of the utmost importance.

C. *Jesus' unique mission makes him life's most important person.* Peter confessed, "You are the Christ" (Mark 8:29 NIV). *Christ* is the transliteration of the Greek word into English, but Peter actually used the Hebrew word for Messiah, the "Anointed One." Peter was confessing him to be the Messiah that God had promised to send to the nation of Israel.

The mission of the Messiah was to be threefold, as understood by the Old Testament prophets. He was to be the Prophet who would reveal the will of God fully to the people. He was to be the Priest who would offer the complete sacrifice for the sins of the world. He was to be the King who would rule the world in righteousness and judgment. His mission was to bring the kingdom of God to the affairs of a broken and lost world. Never before or since has another ever been sent on such a mission: a mission to serve as revealer, redeemer, and ruler.

II. It concerns life's most important issue.

As Luke presents the question and answer, it might seem to be just an innocent question that our Lord presented to his disciples. It might seem to be just a matter of curiosity on his part. But when you study this question in its greater context, it is obvious that the issue goes much deeper. Indeed, no greater issue has ever been raised.

A. *The issue is personal.* The key word in the question is "you." Jesus is interested in the ideas being formed by the crowd, but he knows all that really matters is what you think.

How would you respond to this question? Would you be inclined to answer, "Well, my church teaches that you are the Son of God"? Jesus will not accept that. The question is personal.

You might even want to answer, "Well, the Bible says that you are the Christ, the Son of the living God." While what the Bible says about Jesus is of supreme importance, that is not the question. He wants to know your personal view of him. Who do you understand him to be?

B. *The issue is eternal.* If my eternal destiny depends on my relationship to Jesus Christ, then this is life's most important question. If you ask me about my understanding of the current president of the United States, that is not an eternal issue. I have lived long enough to learn that presidents come and presidents go. Most of the problems of human existence, however, stay with us. Our understanding of any mortal is a temporal issue, but our understanding of Jesus Christ is an eternal issue.

III. It concerns life's most important commitment.

Peter's answer was, "You are the Christ" (Mark 8:29 NIV). This understanding changed everything about Peter's life—his vocation, his relationship to his family, the way he conducted his daily affairs. When Jesus raised this question with his disciples, he touched on the most critical matter of life. Your understanding of who Jesus is will affect the kind of commitment you make to him. The kind of commitment you make to him will affect everything else in your life.

A. *This is a commitment of the control of life.* If Jesus is who we say he is, then he must have lordship over our lives. We must either change what we say about him or change our commitment to him.
B. *This is a commitment for eternity.* Jesus discussed the implications of committing one's life to him with Peter and the others. It involves a death to self and a cross-bearing lifestyle. It involves a commitment from which there is no retreat.

Conclusion

Simon Peter did not wait until he understood everything about Jesus to make his commitment and his confession. If he had waited, he never would have made it. Rather, based on the best evidence that was available to him, he took a step of faith. By faith he declared that to him Jesus was the Christ, the Son of the living God. Based on this confession, he made a commitment to the extent of his ability. He became a disciple of Jesus Christ.

Jesus is asking you life's most important question. Can you make a confession of faith based on the best evidence that is available to you?

SUNDAY EVENING, OCTOBER 31

Title: Where Stewardship Begins and Ends
Text: "So each of us shall give account of himself to God" ***(Rom. 14:12 RSV).***
Scripture Reading: Genesis 1:27–31

Introduction

It is possible to do the right thing for the wrong reason or from a poor motive. The most impressive church building in the world is St. Peter's Basilica in Rome. It is impressive for more than just the splendor of its architecture. Raising money to build St. Peter's contributed to the Protestant Reformation, the breakup of the Roman Catholic Church in Europe, and decades of war. The massive fund-raising effort drained so much gold from England that Henry VIII was able to break away and establish himself as head of the Church of England.

You may recall that scene in the film *Martin Luther* where John Wetzel was selling indulgences to build St. Peter's. He even had a jingle: "Soon as the coin in the basket rings, a troubled soul from purgatory springs!" We, too, can employ a low motive in the service of a high cause. Therefore, we need to consider the following.

I. Where stewardship begins.

A. *Stewardship has its roots in Genesis 1 and the account of creation.* God made the world, including the wonder of every minute cell. He created the universe in its vast expansiveness—100 billions suns in each of the one billion galaxies. God also created humankind, male and female. We are to "have dominion" over the world. This means we are his trustees, his stewards who are intended to care for creation. "We are laborers together with God" (1 Cor. 3:9).

That is where stewardship begins. "The earth is the Lord's, and the fullness thereof; the world, and they that dwell therein" (Ps. 24:1). Theologian George Buttrick said that many people think "the earth is the devil's." The Bible takes evil seriously, but it teaches that God made the earth, and it is good. This gives divine warrant to our daily work, to science and farming, medicine and art, marriage and human sexuality. "The earth is the Lord's."

B. *Some believe the world belongs to man and is his to do with as he pleases.* Such ownership is thought to be "in perpetuity." But people have often mismanaged stewardship of the earth. We have denuded the forests and allowed topsoil to erode. We misuse atomic power for destruction instead of using it for peaceful purposes, such as the generation of electricity.

Do we own the earth? We came here with nothing, and we cannot hold title to anything a minute after our death. We are not owners of anything; we are only trustees. God expects us to act as responsible stewards of his creation. Stewardship begins with our recognition that the earth is the Lord's and so are we.

II. Stewardship ends with our accountability.

A. *"Every one of us shall give account of himself to God" (Rom. 14:12).* We are not to exploit creation but to use it, develop it, and improve it. Once Daniel Webster attended a dinner in his honor at the Astor House in New York City. During the evening someone asked, "Mr. Webster, what is the most important thought you ever had?" The famous American replied, "My responsibility to God."

B. *God has a prior claim on our time, abilities, opportunities, and resources.* All we have is his. God is concerned that we earn our livelihood honestly, spend it wisely, and give it generously.

We must not play games with God when it comes to stewardship. A friend told me about a boy who sent his grandfather a birthday card. Inside he wrote, "I love you very much. I would have enclosed money, but I'd already sealed the envelope."

Conclusion

Let us not be like that grandson. Our call to mission and stewardship of life is expressed in Ed Seabough's hymn:

Lord, you placed me in this world
of time and place and missiles hurled.
With eyes I've seen the ghetto gloom.
With ears I've heard the sonic boom
And man cry out for breathing room.

Lord, I give my life to you,
my time, my talents, each day new
With faith to witness to your plan,
With hope to gladly take my stand,
And love to minister to man.

I cannot wait, I cannot wait!
Here is my life, I want to live it.
Here is my life, I want to give it.
Serving my fellowman,
Doing the will of God,
Here is my life, here is my life,
Here is my life!

SUGGESTED PREACHING PROGRAM FOR THE MONTH OF

NOVEMBER

■ Sunday Mornings

We live in a selfish, competitive, materialistic world that emphasizes acquiring and keeping. In stark contrast to this trend, the children of God are encouraged to be generous like the Father. How can we do this? "God, the Gracious Giver, Loves the Hilarious Giver" is the suggested theme for the first three morning messages this month, designed to help us be more extravagant in our practical love for others.

On the last Sunday of the month, begin a series that leads up to Christmas titled "Jesus Introduces Himself." Jesus' identity can be found by looking at what he did but also by examining what he called himself. A close look at these names records much about the glory of Christ.

■ Sunday Evenings

"The Proclamation of the Coming of the King" is the theme for the Sunday evening messages this month.

■ Wednesday Evenings

Begin the series "The Spiritual Disciplines That Make Prayer Meaningful." Prayer is a vital part of the Christian life that is often discussed and frequently misunderstood. Many people complain that their prayers seem to "bounce off the ceiling." This is most unfortunate, as prayer is such a significant means by which Christ is real in our lives. This series will run through the end of the year.

WEDNESDAY EVENING, NOVEMBER 3

Title: Call to Him; He Will Answer
Text: "Call to me and I will answer you, and will tell you great and hidden things which you have not known" ***(Jer. 33:3 RSV).***
Scripture Reading: Jeremiah 33:1–3; Luke 18:1–8

Introduction

When the prophet Jeremiah was in prison for his preaching, God revealed to him the coming destruction of Jerusalem and the captivity of the people. While others panicked, Jeremiah prayed. The Lord came to him again and assured him of blessings yet to come: the captives would return and the city would be rebuilt. Jeremiah experienced the truth of the promise he was given: "Call to me and I will answer you." The prophet's assurance is ours. This prayer promise belongs to every believer.

I. God requests us to pray.

A. *"Thus says the LORD who made the earth . . . the LORD is his name: Call to me" (v. 2).* The eternal Creator requests that we enter into his presence. Even with that encouragement, prayer has been called "the most neglected ministry in the church today."

B. *Our God's request is ignored for many reasons.* Some say prayer does not work; prayers go unanswered. Others view prayer as a flight from reality. Some have stopped praying because they feel that, since God knows all, prayer is superfluous. God who desires his will to be done, says, "Call to me." Praying is seen as inferior to action; many people prefer to *do* something rather than *pray* for something. All the excuses for lack of prayer fail to quiet the request of our God: "Call to me" (Jer. 33:2 RSV).

C. *This bidding of God affirms the dynamic of prayer as our link with the God of the universe.* What audacity we believers have: we appeal to the power at the top! Finite man is requested to share with the infinite God. We are encouraged to "come boldly unto the throne of grace" (Heb. 4:16). This is a miracle in and of itself. Consider this: it is virtually impossible for the average citizen to obtain a personal visit with the president, yet in prayer we converse with the Lord of all creation.

D. *Prayer is intensely personal.* In *Prayer: Conversing with God,* Rosalind Rinker defines prayer as "a dialogue between two persons who love each other." Could the reason for prayer becoming a struggle be the loss of the reality that God our Father is personally involved in our lives? Jesus taught us to pray by focusing on "Our Father" (Matt. 6:9). He used the term *Abba* (Mark 14:36), a tender term meaning "Daddy." This marks a radical way to address God. Jesus encourages us to approach God in personal conversation between Father and child. Our loving Father asks his children, "Call to me." Prayer is speaking with the one who loves us more powerfully and hears us more clearly than anyone else.

II. God assures us of results.

A. *"I will answer you" (Jer. 33:3 RSV).* God does answer prayer. The Word says it; why should we doubt it? Why should we be content to live and work within the confines of our own limitations when the power of the Almighty waits to be released?

B. *Prayer must not be an excuse for us to do nothing.* We are to do all we can and pray for God to do what only he can. When you pray as he calls you to pray, be certain of the promise—"I will answer you" (Jer. 33:3 RSV). Jesus assures us of the results when we pray (Matt. 7:7–8).

C. *Skeptics say prayer is the universe's greatest knock-knock joke.*

"Knock, knock."
"Who's there?"
"Nobody."

Jesus said that when we knock, the answer shall be opened to us (Matt. 7:7). Some prayers will be answered even before we pray, and other answers will be delayed, but God always answers prayer. Andrew Murray said, "Prayer consists of two parts, a human and a divine. The human side is the asking, the divine is the giving."

Conclusion

A man visited a hydroelectric plant and walked with the guide out on the long dam. Noticing the water going over the dam, the visitor asked, "What percent of the power from this river do you actually transform into electricity?" The guide replied, "We don't even use 1 percent of it!" Similarly, we Christians lose vast amounts of spiritual power because of our prayerlessness. The Lord of all creation implores us, "Call to me and I will answer."

SUNDAY MORNING, NOVEMBER 7

Title: Why Does God Love the Cheerful Giver?

Text: "Each one must do as he has made up his mind, not reluctantly or under compulsion, for God loves a cheerful giver" ***(2 Cor. 9:7 RSV).***

Scripture Reading: 2 Corinthians 9:6–15

Hymns: "Take Time to Be Holy," Longstaff
"I Gave My Life for Thee," Havergal
"Trust, Try and Prove Me," Leech

Offertory Prayer: Loving Father, we thank you for the gifts of forgiveness and life. We thank you for the gifts of love, hope, and peace. We thank you for the gifts of wisdom and understanding. Today we pray that you will give to us a sense of security in your grace that will enable us to become cheerful, hilarious givers of ourselves for the welfare of others. Bless these gifts as aids to that end, we pray. In Jesus' name. Amen.

Introduction

Pastor Jack Taylor has declared that "cheerful givers do not travel in large herds." Many people look upon giving as a painful procedure, but it should be a spontaneous, joyous experience. Giving should not be considered a begrudged obligation, but rather an opportunity to participate with God in ministering to people.

The Greek word *hilarion,* translated "cheerful" in our English Bibles, is the word from which *hilarious* comes. The apostle Paul declares that God loves the hilarious giver. Paul discovered that the Father God is that kind of giver. He affirmed in his epistle to the Romans concerning the Father that "he that spared not his own Son, but delivered him up for us all, how shall he not with him also freely give us all things?" (8:32).

Why is it that people do not look upon the act of giving as a joyous privilege? Is it possible that this is because people, away from God, seek to find their security in material possessions? When we find our security in material possessions, it is impossible for us to see giving as anything but a threat to our security. This takes the joy out of giving and causes us to assume a protective attitude toward our resources.

When believers come to find their security in the grace and goodness and faithfulness of God, it then becomes possible for them to be cheerful in their giving. Let us raise the question, why does God love the cheerful giver?

I. In the cheerful giver, God sees the reflection of his own nature and character.

As a father delights to see traits of himself in a child, so does the heavenly Father rejoice as he sees his own nature and character duplicated in the lives of his children.

A. *God is an extremely generous giver.* God gives freely, liberally, perfectly, wisely, appropriately, purposefully, practically, graciously.
B. *We need to recognize that God is not covetous, greedy, selfish, stingy, insecure, or poor.* He also is not a miser, a collector, an accumulator, a speculator, a beggar, or a robber.
C. *God never gives grudgingly.*
D. *God always gives freely, extravagantly, and joyfully.*
E. *God does not want to impoverish us.*
F. *God gave to humans an Eden at the beginning, and he is preparing a paradise at the end for those who trust and love him.*
G. *God loves the cheerful giver because God himself is that kind of giver.*

II. In the cheerful giver, God sees imitation of the lifestyle of Jesus (Mark 10:45).

A. *Jesus did not come into this world to be a receiver. Instead, he came to be a giver.*
B. *Jesus gave in many ways:*
   1. Healing the sick.
   2. Loving the unlovely.
   3. Providing light to those in darkness.
   4. Being truth to those troubled by conscience.
   5. Providing peace to those in turmoil.
   6. Granting forgiveness to the sinful.
C. *Jesus came to give heaven to those who were headed for hell.* On one occasion, Jesus said to his disciples, "Freely ye have received, freely give" (Matt. 10:8). Here he made clear our proper response to God's gifts.

D. *Paul quotes Jesus as saying, "It is more blessed to give than to receive" (Acts 20:35).* It is more Christlike to be a giver than to be a receiver. We will experience the abundant life in the here and now when we imitate our Lord's lifestyle with unselfish giving.

III. In the cheerful giver, God sees the Holy Spirit allowed to work.

A. *The Holy Spirit is God's gift to every believer.*

B. *The Holy Spirit is given to us to reproduce within us the nature and character of Jesus Christ (Gal. 5:22–23).*

C. *The Holy Spirit is seeking to give to believers all of those inward traits and characteristics they need to be the true sons and daughters of God.*

D. *The Holy Spirit came to equip the church with the gifts needed for the work of the living Christ in this world. Without the gifts of the Spirit to the believer, the church would be helpless.*

IV. In the cheerful giver, God sees hope for the salvation of souls.

A. *God loves this unsaved world, and he gave his Son, Jesus Christ, that this world might be saved.*

B. *Christ loved this world to the extent that he gave himself in obedience to his Father, and he gave his life for us on the cross.*

C. *The Holy Spirit is seeking to give the gospel to all of the world today through those who constitute the body of Christ.*

D. *If we see ourselves as reservoirs into which the blessings of God are to come for our own delight, then we are receiving the grace of God in vain. Paul encourages us "not to accept the grace of God in vain" (2 Cor. 6:1 RSV). We must not be a mere container or consumer of the blessings of God.*

E. *God wants us to be a worker, a giver, a helper, a channel through which he can pour out his blessings upon the world.*

Conclusion

Are you a cheerful giver? Do you want to become a cheerful, hilarious giver? If so, remember your security is in the grace of God rather than in the gadgets that money can buy. Put your faith in the Father who feeds the birds of the air and clothes the lilies of the field with their beauty.

When you become a cheerful giver, the Father will take special delight in you. He will increase your capacity and your ability to be a giver. He will increase your joy in giving. The Father will also increase your inward security in the grace of God as you give.

SUNDAY EVENING, NOVEMBER 7

Title: The Heavenly Inauguration

Text: "Yet have I set my king upon my holy hill of Zion. I will declare the decree: the LORD hath said unto me, Thou art my Son; this day have I begotten thee" ***(Ps. 2:6–7).***

Scripture Reading: Psalm 2:1–12

Introduction

John Quincy Adams (1767–1848) became president of the United States by a strange turn of events. In 1824, since none of the candidates—Adams, Henry Clay, Andrew Jackson, or William Crawford—had received an electoral majority, the presidential contest was taken to the House of Representatives. When the House voted on February 9, 1825, the deciding vote was cast by New York. But the New York delegation was divided equally. General Stephen van Rensselaer held the tie-breaking vote. Some of his colleagues urged him to support Crawford, and others, Adams. When it came time to vote, Van Rensselaer was thoroughly perplexed. Being a pious man, he dropped his head on the desk just before the ballot box reached him and prayed for guidance. When he lifted his head and opened his eyes, he saw a ballot on the floor by his seat with Adams's name on it. He interpreted this as an expression of God's will and cast his vote for Adams, and as a result, Adams won New York—and with it, the presidency of the United States (Paul Boller Jr., *Presidential Anecdotes,* Oxford Press, 1981).

Though the inauguration of John Quincy Adams may have resulted from an odd election or a political accident, such has never been the case with the heavenly inauguration of our Lord.

Some commentators have associated Psalm 2 with the crowning of King David. Others have compared it to the enthronement ceremonies of ancient Egypt. But it is more than an ancient royal psalm; it is a messianic psalm. God has set apart his King.

I. The King will be opposed (Ps. 2:1–3).

A. *Scripture teaches there will be those who oppose God.* They plot against him and his ways. The term "imagine" in v. 1 is the same word translated "meditate" in Psalm 1. One may exercise his or her thought life in a positive or negative direction toward God. A famous Bible teacher once said that our thoughts not only reveal what we are, but predict what we will become. Are you meditating on the world or on the Word?

B. *The passage also suggests that there are those who "take counsel together against the LORD."* Remember Acts 4:25? Peter and John held the first group prayer meeting after Pentecost. They reminded the disciples that Herod and Pilate had conspired against Jesus but that Jesus' power had overcome. They asked that the threats against them be considered, and they prayed that God would give them the power to speak the word of Jesus with boldness. They knew they would be opposed. They quoted Psalm 2:1–2.

C. *The psalmist predicted further opposition.* "Let us break their bands asunder and cast away their cords." What does this mean? The bands were a horse's bridle and reins. Picture a chariot racer circling an arena. Someone has cut into the bands. When just a little stress comes, the tear in the leather begins to pull. Suddenly, in an almost dramatic Hollywood *Ben Hur* fashion, the chariot breaks loose, and the racer is dragged behind the horse until he dies. It is a vivid picture of what a lost man tries to do to a Christian.

II. The King reigns (Ps. 2:4–6).

A. *In v. 4 we encounter some unique biblical imagery describing the power of the reigning King of the universe: he laughs!* This glimpse at God's humor reminds us of a little boy play-wrestling with his father. The father holds the boy back while the boy swings as hard and fast as he can, crying, "I'm wrestling, Daddy. I'm winning." The father laughs with amusement, knowing the child is actually helpless. Compare humankind's strength to the power of God, the mortal to the omnipotent. I am not suggesting that God winks at people's sin, but rather that he finds it laughable that people think they are getting away with it.

B. *In addition to God's laughing, we also see here his wrath and displeasure over evil.* The Hebrew language pictures the moist nostrils of a snorting bull. How interesting that Paul used similar imagery in portraying Christ's victory over Satan in 2 Thessalonians 2:8: "The Lord Jesus will overthrow with the breath of his mouth" (NIV).

III. The King is the King's Son (Ps 2:7–9).

A. *Foreshadowed in the words "Thou art my Son" is a beautiful portrayal of the sonship of Christ.* The New Testament writers understood Psalm 2 to refer to Jesus. Luke recorded in Acts 13:32–33: "What God promised our fathers he has fulfilled for us, their children, by raising up Jesus. As it is written in the second Psalm: 'You are my Son; today I have become your Father.'"

B. *Notice what else the psalmist reported: the inheritance of the people.* "I shall give thee the heathen for thine inheritance, and the uttermost parts of the earth for thy possession" (Ps. v. 8). It was common in the ancient world for the firstborn son to receive by right property as part of a permanent possession. God gave his Son all the rights of being a king and a high priest as a gift. Hebrews 5:5 quotes from Psalm 2, "Christ also did not take upon himself the glory of becoming a high priest. But God said to him, 'you are my Son'" (NIV). The right of possession of this inheritance came with Christ's desire to receive the lost into God's family that they might be saved from separation from him.

IV. The King demands loyalty (Ps. 2:10–12).

In rapid-fire succession, the psalmist lists conditions to be met for one to be counted loyal to the king. Look at them for a moment.

A. *First, he says, "Be wise" (v. 10).* Imagine an employee working for his boss: the worker must use wisdom and discretion in his job. Christians should be wise in serving God.

B. *Second, "Be instructed" (v. 10).* Visualize being teachable and open to God's Word. Our teachability allows God to disciple and instruct us. Have you memorized any Scripture this month? Have you had any time alone with God recently? Have you led someone to Christ this year? If not, then you need to be listening to the Lord. Be instructed.

C. *Third, "Serve the Lord" (v. 11).* The word *serve* literally means "to work." Remember Paul's ideal of Romans 12:11: be "fervent in spirit; serving the Lord." Look for opportunities to serve. What new ministries has God given you? Are you fulfilling them? If not, why not?

D. *Fourth, "Rejoice" (v. 11).* A good spirit and attitude enhance your service to God. A negative, critical spirit infects all your other work. Doubtful, critical attitudes cancel out positive possibilities for your ministry as a Christian.

E. *Fifth, "Kiss the Son" (v. 12).* In the ancient world, when a king was inaugurated, oil was poured on the head of the king, and the foot of the king was kissed. These symbolized commitment and loyalty. Symbolically, we must be willing to commit ourselves to Christ completely. Are you willing?

F. *A promise of blessing is contingent upon the five above conditions being met.* "Blessed are they that put their trust in him" (v. 12). What a special promise God has given us in Jesus Christ.

Conclusion

Over one hundred years ago, Abraham Lincoln came out to the platform over the steps of the eastern portico of the Capitol to be sworn in as president of the United States. He was carrying three things: a manuscript of his speech, a cane, and a tall silk hat. He placed the cane under the table and held on to his manuscript, but he did not know what to do with his hat. Senator Stephen Douglas stepped forward, took the hat, and returned to his seat. He leaned over to one of Mrs. Lincoln's cousins and commented, "If I can't be president, I can at least hold his hat" (Boller, *Presidential Anecdotes*).

Probably neither you nor I will be president, but Jesus is Lord of Lords and King of Kings. We can sit in the heavenly inauguration and hold his hat. We can support him, love him, and praise him. I hope you will be there.

Wednesday Evening, November 10

Title: Unhindered Prayer
Text: ". . . that your prayers be not hindered" ***(1 Peter 3:7).***
Scripture Reading: 1 Peter 3:7–12

Introduction

The promises of prayer are conditional. Prayer is not like an automatic dispensing machine into which we deposit our requests and receive what we desire. Prayer can be hindered. Peter warned husbands and wives to maintain good relationships "in order that your prayers be not hindered" (1 Peter 3:7). The apostle gave the basis for unhindered prayer: "For the eyes of the Lord are over the righteous, and his ears are open unto their prayers" (v. 12). Unhindered prayer is the result of a sound relationship between us and the Lord. How may we be sure of unhindered prayer?

I. Abide in Christ and let no sin hinder prayer.

A. *The righteous are assured of access to the Lord in prayer.* "The prayer of a righteous man has great power in its effects" (James 5:16 RSV). "The desire of the righteous will be granted" (Prov. 10:24 RSV). If righteousness supports prayer, sin hinders it. "If I had cherished iniquity in my heart, the Lord would not have listened" (Ps. 66:18 RSV).

B. *Jesus put this in a positive way.* "If you abide in me, and my words abide in you, ask whatever you will, and it shall be done for you" (John 15:7 RSV). The secret to unhindered prayer is to abide in Christ. To abide in Christ is to forsake sin and live a righteous life. To abide in Christ is to follow his example rather than the prevailing community standards.

C. *Since prayer is in Jesus' name, we cannot expect to prevail in prayer if our lives are out of harmony with Christ.* Abiding in Christ is not some unseen spiritual experience reserved for the Christian elite. It is obedience to Christ, obedience to his Word—being Christlike. Because sin keeps us from abiding in Christ and sin hinders prayer, we must examine ourselves and lay aside every sin.

II. Some sins that hinder prayer.

Peter noted some sins that hinder prayer. These are representative of the wide range of relationships and attitudes that affect prayer.

A. *Family dissension (1 Peter 3:7).* A lack of compassion and respect between spouses will hinder prayer. When family relationships are fulfilled with Christ's love, the prayer life of each family member will be vital.

B. *Church fellowship (1 Peter 3:8 RSV).* "Have unity of spirit, . . . love of the brethren." It is inconceivable to expect much of prayer if one's attitude toward the church is harsh, critical, or indifferent. Love for one another is one test of discipleship. Prayer is a primary trait of the discipled life. Lack of love is a failure of discipleship and a hindrance to prayer.

C. *Cold selfishness (1 Peter 3:8).* This sin must be overcome by "sympathy . . . and a tender heart [compassion]." A woman was attacked, beaten, and molested by three people while a crowd stood by ignoring her pleas for help. That happened in our "Christian America" where more and more people keep their distance and refuse to involve themselves. Our prayers can, indeed, be hindered by cold selfishness.

D. *Arrogance and pride (1 Peter 3:8).* These attitudes must be replaced by a "humble mind." Luke 18:11 gives a glimpse of two men in prayer. One thanked God that he was "not like all other men" (RSV), but Jesus said his attitude of arrogant pride made him unacceptable to God. Certainly his prayers were not heard.

E. *Refusal to forgive (1 Peter 3:9).* Jesus taught us to pray, "Forgive us our debts, as we forgive our debtors" (Matt. 6:10). A little boy, smarting after punishment, finished his prayers with the usual blessings for all the family but one. Then, turning to his father, he said, "I suppose you noticed you weren't in it." Refusal to forgive makes meaningful relationships impossible and blocks effective prayer.

Conclusion

An older pastor would often ask, "Are you on praying ground?" He did not have a physical location in mind, but rather the spiritual position, the relationship that encourages prayer. Are your prayers hindered by fractured family and church relationships, cold selfishness, arrogant pride, or lack of forgiveness? We must "turn away from evil and do right" (1 Peter 3:11 RSV), lest our prayers be hindered.

SUNDAY MORNING, NOVEMBER 14

Title: Five Steps Toward Good Stewardship

Text: "Moreover it is required of stewards that they be found trustworthy" ***(1 Cor. 4:2 RSV).***

Scripture Reading: 1 Corinthians 4:1–5

Hymns: "We Have Heard the Joyful Sound," Owens
"I Gave My Life for Thee," Havergal
"Our Best," Kirk

Offertory Prayer: Heavenly Father, we thank you for the greatness of your grace toward us. We recognize you as the giver of every perfect gift. We give ourselves to you for service in our world. Accept our gifts and bless them to your glory and to the salvation of those who need Jesus Christ as Savior. In his name we pray. Amen.

Introduction

In our text the apostle is describing the indispensable ingredient for good stewardship. The minister or layperson must be dependable and trustworthy if he or she wants to please God and be helpful to others.

The position of steward in biblical days was an honored position. It is a term used for house manager, a position of trust and responsibility. Stewardship is something much more than giving an offering to the Lord's work on Sunday. It is recognizing God's ownership and our trusteeship. Being a good steward means bringing the totality of life into an attitude and activity of cooperation with the purposes of God to be pleasing to God. We do not have the option of deciding to be a steward or not. Our choice is whether we will be a good steward or a poor one.

We find the abundant life and experience spiritual success when we give rather than when we seek to receive. Jesus was describing the fulfillment that comes to a good steward who sees life as an opportunity to give when he said, "It is more blessed to give than to receive" (Acts 20:35).

There are at least five things we can do that will help us to be good stewards.

I. We can give God the first hour of every day.

A. *We can begin the day with a prayer of gratitude and a prayer for guidance and help.* This suggestion should not be taken legalistically or literally. I am not talking about sixty minutes so much as I am talking about letting God come into the very beginning of the day.

We are wise to spend some time reading and thinking about the great truths of God's Word at the beginning of the day.

B. *Many find the use of a daily devotional helpful.* This can help us lift our thoughts toward God and determine to live all of the day in his will.

When we give the first hour of the day to God, we can rejoice in his goodness and report for duty (Ps. 118:24).

II. We can give God the first day of the week.

A. *In our modern day, we are rather confused about the weekend.* Some people think of the weekend as beginning Friday afternoon and closing as they go to work on Monday. We need to reexamine our calendar. The weekend comes to a conclusion on Saturday. Sunday is the beginning of the week. Modern society has secularized the sacred. We may attempt to live by bread alone, but our souls will starve if we secularize Sunday.

B. *The Sabbath was made for people, not people for the Sabbath.* We were created as upward-looking creatures, and God intended that we worship and rest.

C. *We must rest.* We miss our destiny if we neglect or refuse to worship the true and living God. Jesus encouraged people to rescue the ox that had fallen into the ditch on the Sabbath as Moses had permitted. Modern people sometimes push the ox into the ditch and then rescue it on the day of worship.

III. We can give God the first portion of our paycheck.

A. *God is no pauper.* He is no beggar. Likewise, he is not seeking to impoverish us or to deprive us of any of the necessities of life.

B. *We shouldn't be shocked to discover that our tithes and offerings do not enrich the God who is the Creator of all things.*

C. *When we faithfully bring our tithes and offerings to the Lord, we are accepting him as the owner of all.* Even we are his. Because people are insecure in the face of physical needs, they hoard to provide for days of insecurity. We need to find a balance between working for and trusting God for our needs.

D. *When we become givers, we become like our God, the great Giver.* For God, loving meant giving his Son to die on a cross for us. For Jesus Christ, loving us and loving God meant giving his life on the cross.

E. *We never discover the highest joy of living until we, like our God and like our Savior, give ourselves for the well-being of others.* Paul declares that God loves the cheerful giver. Why is that? It is because as we give, we demonstrate a similarity of character to our God.

IV. We can give God first consideration in every decision we make.

A. *We all face decisions every day.* These decisions affect our family, our friends, and the people with whom we work. The Bible teaches us that the natural man does not think the thoughts of God. We put self at the center. We make many of our decisions on the basis of the profit that we hope to reap as a result of our decisions.

B. *Decisions are often made on the basis of pain that has been experienced in the past.* We try to avoid in the present or future that which has been painful in the past.

C. *Some of us make decisions on the basis of tradition and custom.* We seek to do that which has been done in the past, and sometimes this is anything but good.

D. *As we face the various decisions of life each day, we need to ask, "What would Jesus do in this set of circumstances?"* We can trust the Holy Spirit to help us with the complex issues we face.

V. We can give God first place in our hearts.

A. *The great commandment calls us to love God foremost and supremely.* The next commandment calls us to love our neighbor as ourselves. We must love ourselves properly to know how to love our neighbor.

B. *First among persons should be our mates.*
C. *Only God deserves first place in our hearts.* Every other person or thing that might claim first place will ultimately disappoint us.

Conclusion

The abundant life is within the reach of each of us if we will truly be good stewards of all that God has placed in our care. To do this we need to take these five steps:

1. Give God the first hour of each day.
2. Give God the first day of each week.
3. Give God the first portion of our paychecks.
4. Give God the first consideration in every decision.
5. Give God first place in our hearts.

If we will earnestly seek to do these, we will live a life of joy.

SUNDAY EVENING, NOVEMBER 14

Title: The Solid Rock
Text: "I called upon the LORD in my distress: the LORD answered me, and set me in a large place. The LORD is on my side; I will not fear: what can man do unto me?" ***(Psalm 118:5–6).***
Scripture Reading: Psalm 118:5–7, 19–22, 25–29

Introduction

The historical setting of Psalm 118 has puzzled scholars for years. It may have been written during the time of the rebuilding of the temple, during the time of Ezra, or before the exile. Some have suggested that it might be about a feast held in celebration of the Jews' return home from Babylon. Others have described it as being about an autumn festival. Though mystery surrounds its history, the opposite may be said of its prophecy. One commentator has labeled it the "Battle Hymn of the Old Testament."

As a processional song for a multitude of voices, the psalm symbolizes the restoration of a king. Jesus may have had this psalm on his lips when he arose to go to Gethsemane. Some scholars suggest that this is the actual hymn sung after the Lord's Supper (Matt. 26:30). Psalm 118 often found its way into the New Testament. Its basic message centers around the Messiah. Let us examine the image of Christ in this psalm.

I. Jesus is the Christ of care (Ps. 118:5–7).

A. *Regardless of what you face today, God cares for you.* Notice in verse 5, "I called upon the LORD in distress: the LORD answered me, and set me in a large place." The term "distress" comes from a word that means to be squeezed in a narrow, tight place and then to be set free from it. Have you ever gone camping and tried to get into a small sleeping bag? When you try to turn over, you feel like a mummy!

B. *The word "distress" is also used to describe a predicament where you are surrounded.* It was often used in Texas "Alamo" fashion in the Old Testament when the enemy surrounded. But God is with his people! "The LORD is on my side; I will not fear: what can man do unto me?" (v. 6). God on your side does not mean you can get what you want all the time. Nor does it mean that we trick God. The psalmist was not referring to God lining up with our ideals; rather, he was suggesting that we conform to God's standard. We must align ourselves with God's way to receive his protection.

II. Jesus is the Christ of salvation (Ps. 118:19–22).

A. *Verses 19–22 have tremendous christological significance because Jesus applied them to himself.* Look carefully at verse 19. We read, "Open to me the gates of righteousness." The gates of righteousness symbolize our obedience and faithfulness to God. In the ancient world, the gate to a city was the entrance and exit point. But more important, it was the security of the city and the "civic center." Every person entering the city had to pass through the gate. It became the center of legal transactions. Sometimes religious discourses were shared there. The gate, however, was the point of vulnerability for the city wall. Be reminded that we gain strength at our weakest point. We are strengthened by allowing God's righteousness and power over our lives.

B. *The psalmist celebrated God's presence.* "I will praise thee: for thou hast heard me, and art become my salvation" (v. 21). Here the Hebrew language presents a strong grammatical construction for the concept "to be." Often, to express simple existence, the Hebrew verb is left out. Here the verb is included, not only suggesting existence, but also presence. Many people believe in the existence of God. The problem is that they are not sensitive to his presence. True salvation comes by receiving the gift of eternal life by entering into a relationship with God through Christ.

Look at the powerful symbolism of verse 22: "The stone which the builders refused is become the head stone of the corner." In Matthew 21:42 when Jesus completed the parable of the tenants, he said, "Have you never read in the Scriptures: 'The stone the builders rejected has become the capstone'? The Lord has done this, and it is marvelous in our eyes" (NIV). Jesus is either our foundation or the stone we stumble over.

III. Jesus is the Christ of loyalty (Ps. 118:26).

A. *The psalmist cried, "Blessed be he that cometh in the name of the Lord" (v. 26).* Here the triumphal entry of Jesus is idealized. In Matthew 21, Mark 11, Luke 19, and John 12, the crowds spread their cloaks and palm branches on the road and shout, "Hosanna," the Hebrew expression meaning "Save."

B. *Psalm 118:26 connects neatly with the accounts of the triumphal entry of Jesus to Jerusalem.* Of interest is the Hebrew translated "cometh" in the King James Version. The idea was of a person having given his word and the promise actually coming to pass. Jesus has given us his word. His word does come to pass!

Conclusion

Perhaps the best doxology to this psalm can be found in the words of the famous hymn "The Solid Rock" by Edward Mote:

My hope is built on nothing less
Than Jesus' blood and righteousness;
I dare not trust the sweetest frame,
But wholly lean on Jesus' name.

When darkness seems to hide his face,
I rest on his unchanging grace;
In every high and stormy gale,
My anchor holds within the vale.

His oath, his covenant, his blood
Support me in the whelming flood;
When all around my soul gives way,
He then is all my hope and stay.

When He shall come with trumpet sound,
Oh, may I then in Him be found;
Dressed in His righteousness alone,
Faultless to stand before the throne.

On Christ, the solid Rock, I stand;
All other ground is sinking sand,
All other ground is sinking sand.

Wednesday Evening, November 17

Title: Ask in Faith and in God's Will

Text: "And this is the confidence that we have in him, that, if we ask any thing according to his will, he heareth us" ***(1 John 5:14).***
Scripture Reading: Mark 11:22–24; 1 John 5:14–15

Introduction

Sam Levenson said of prayer, "Even those who wouldn't step out of the house for a prayer service still expect room service and 'Make it fast!'" Prayer is not that easy. Two essential elements must be present for effective prayer: We must ask in God's will and in faith. If these two elements are present, we can be confident in coming before God with our requests.

I. Praying in God's will.

A. *Discovering God's will is the beginning of praying in his will.* The condition of praying in God's will hinders—instead of encourages—many in their praying. Can anyone know God's will? Andrew Murray wrote, "First [we must] find out if our prayers are according to the will of God. We can determine this through the word of God received and kept in our hearts and through the Holy Spirit indwelling and leading us." The Bible contains the principles of God's will. We need to apply these principles to the situations that underlie our prayer concerns. If our request does not fall within the limits of God's revealed will, we ought not to present it. Romans 8:26 promises the Holy Spirit will intercede "according to the will of God." Prayer is in God's will when the Spirit and the Word unite to affirm the petition we make.

B. *Commitment to do God's will must be present.* To pray according to God's will involves a commitment to do his will as he reveals it to us. Jesus said, "Thy will be done in earth, as it is in heaven" (Matt. 6:10). God will not bless us if we are not now doing the part of his will we already know.

C. *Place no personal limits on God's will.* It is his will we seek. We are not praying in his will when we place personal limits or guidelines on our requests. We present the needs; he provides the solutions.

D. *Follow Jesus' example.* Jesus in Gethsemane set the best example of praying in God's will when he prayed, "Not my will, but thine, be done" (Luke 22:42). The horror of the cross was before him. His human emotions recoiled at the thought; his mind and body gave evidence of the struggle as he sweat drops of blood. The victory came when his will pulled alongside the will of the Father. Effective prayer is praying in God's will. It is also something more.

II. Asking in faith.

Jesus said, "I tell you whatever you ask in prayer, believe that you receive it, and you will" (Mark 11:24 RSV). In Mark 11:22–24, Jesus defines the faith required in prayer.

A. *Faith in God.* Faith focuses on the resources of an all-powerful God. With God all things are possible. Augustine said, "He loves us everyone as though there were but one of us to love." "Have faith in God" (v. 22 RSV).

B. *Have faith without doubt.* Our faith must be without doubt—"and does not doubt in his heart" (v. 23 RSV). James 1:6–7 (RSV) reminds us to "ask in faith, with no doubting." Rosalind Rinker suggests that we "ask only for that which you confidently believe He could do." She illustrates this by her daughter's concern for an unsaved friend. Her prayers for him began with a request for courage to talk with him. Then she prayed for his willing acceptance of a New Testament. Step by step she prayed in faith without doubt until two weeks after her first request, the friend openly trusted Christ. Believing God *can* is not the same as believing God *will.*

C. *Direct faith to a specific need.* "*Whatever* you ask in prayer" (v. 24 RSV). Focus faith on a specific need, a definite request. Specificity in prayer shows we are earnest.

Conclusion

Mark 9:22–23 records a father seeking help for his ill son. He approached Jesus and said, "But if you can do anything, take pity on us and help us." Jesus bluntly replied, "If you can! All things are possible to him who believes" (RSV). Jesus was willing, the man believed, and the boy was healed! To be effective, prayer must be in faith and in God's will.

Sunday Morning, November 21

Title: The Sacrifice of Thanksgiving

Text: "I will offer to thee the sacrifice of thanksgiving and call on the name of the LORD" ***(Ps. 116:17 RSV).***

Scripture Reading: Psalm 116:16–19

Hymns: "Rejoice, Ye Pure in Heart," Plumptre
"I Will Sing the Wondrous Story," Rowley
"Praise Him!" Crosby

Offertory Prayer: Father in heaven, today we offer you the thanksgiving of our lips and the love of our heart. Help us, Father God, to become the instruments of your love to others. Help us to let your blessings flow through us that others might come to know you. In Jesus' name we pray. Amen.

Introduction

The founding fathers of the United States were following many biblical words of encouragement when they established the observance of an annual day of national thanksgiving.

Psalms 103–18 contain many expressions of praise and thanksgiving. In these psalms, each of us is encouraged to be thankful to God. Our text speaks of thanksgiving as an offering to the Father God. The writer of the epistle to the Hebrews has a similar thought in mind when he encourages believers to offer up through Jesus Christ a sacrifice of praise to God. "Through him then let us continually offer up a sacrifice of praise to God, that is, the fruit of lips that acknowledge his name. Do not neglect to do good and to share what you have, for such sacrifices are pleasing to God" (Heb. 13:15–16 RSV). People often think of bringing tithes and offerings as a sacrifice to God, but how many think of a sincere expression of thanks as being a sacrifice that is well-pleasing to the Father? Again we hear the psalmist speak: "Offer to God a sacrifice of thanksgiving, and pay your vows to the Most High; and call upon me in the day of trouble; I will deliver you, and you shall glorify me" (Ps. 50:14–15 RSV). God delights in our sacrifice of thanksgiving. We hear the psalmist speaking for our Lord again when he says, "He who brings thanksgiving as his sacrifice honors me; to him who orders his way aright I will show the salvation of God!" (v. 23 RSV).

Today let us all offer up to our God the sacrifice of thanksgiving.

I. Let us thank God for his many gifts to us through people.

A. *Most of us have parents for whom we can be thankful to our God.* We should express this gratitude to God and to our parents also.

B. *Those of us who are married can be thankful to God for our companions.* An attitude of gratitude that expresses itself in words of affection and thanksgiving will do much to enrich a marriage and to help solve the problems that every couple faces.

C. *Have you thought of friends as being the blessings of God to you?* Have you thanked God for your friends? Have you thanked your friends for being your friends?

D. *We can thank God for our helpers.* Most of us have people who help us in our time of need. Some of these are family members. Many of us have helpers without being aware of them. How long has it been since you expressed thanks for law enforcement officers who help your community be a safe place in which to live? Are you grateful for the doctors and nurses who are available around the clock to minister to you and your family in medical emergencies? How long has it been since you thanked God for the fire department that is available to come in case your home should catch fire?

E. *As we offer up a prayer of thanksgiving to God, let us give expressions of thanks to persons who are a blessing to us.* Make a phone call. Write a letter. Speak up. Offer the gift of thanksgiving.

II. Let us thank God for the gift of spiritual life.

A. *The psalmist expressed gratitude to God for this gift when he said, "For thou hast delivered my soul from death" (Ps. 116:8 RSV).*

B. *Spiritual death is a present reality for those who have not yet experienced the miracle of the new birth.*
C. *Spiritual birth and life come to us through faith in Jesus Christ (John 1:12).* Through faith in Jesus Christ we move out of the realm of spiritual death and receive the gift of eternal life (1 John 5:11–12). Physicians can cooperate with God in the healing process and add years to our physical lives, but only Jesus Christ can give us the gift of eternal life.
D. *Let us offer up to God the sacrifice of thanksgiving for this gift of new life (cf. 1 John 3 RSV).*

III. Let us thank God for leading us in triumph.

Paul encouraged the Corinthians to offer the sacrifice of thanksgiving for spiritual victory in life. He wrote, "But thanks be to God, who in Christ always leads us in triumph" (2 Cor. 2:14 RSV).

A. *Let us offer thanks to God for victory over evil within.* All of us struggle with an inclination that makes it easy for us to surrender to attitudes that lead us to activities for which we are ashamed. We discover a weakness within that brings embarrassment to us. Romans 7 describes Paul's inward struggle with his own personal weaknesses, and he brings this chapter to a close with a question and then an answer. The question is, "Wretched man that I am! Who will deliver me from this body of death?" He has the answer for himself and for us when he says, "Thanks be to God through Jesus Christ our Lord!" (Rom. 7:24–25 RSV). Our living Lord uses many spiritual forces to help us overcome evil.
   1. God gives us a new nature that causes us to hunger and thirst after righteousness.
   2. God gives us the Holy Spirit, who seeks to bring about purity within.
   3. God gives us the Bible to help us day by day.
   4. God gives us the church as a family, where we can associate with those whose influence can be elevating.
   5. God uses chastisement when it is needed (Heb. 12:3–11).

B. *Let us offer thanks to God for victory over our enemy Satan.* Each of us has a spiritual foe in Satan, who wants to bring about our spiritual defeat and prevent us from being the servants our Father would have us to be (1 Peter 5:8). Our enemy seeks to camouflage his presence (2 Cor. 11:13–15). If you have become so sophisticated that you do not believe there is an evil enemy of God and people, then you need to recognize that Satan has already won a great victory over you.

   James, a prominent leader in the Jerusalem church following the resurrection of our Lord, gives practical advice on how we can achieve victory over the evil one (James 4:7–8). Paul gives us equally good advice (Eph. 6:1–20).

Conclusion

Let us offer up to God the sacrifice of thanksgiving. Let us verbalize this, not only to him, but to those around us.

Jesus Christ has died for our sins. Only Christ has conquered death for us. Only through Christ are we offered forgiveness. Only through Christ are we offered eternal life. Only through Christ do we find a doorway into heaven.

Let Jesus come into your heart today as King, Lord, Friend, and Helper.

SUNDAY EVENING, NOVEMBER 21

Title: The Real Jesus
Text: "Thou wilt shew me the path of life: in thy presence is fullness of joy; at thy right hand there are pleasures for evermore" ***(Ps. 16:11).***
Scripture Reading: Psalm 16:9–11

Introduction

Some theologians have called Psalm 16:9–11 the Romans 8:38–39 of the Old Testament. One might suggest that Psalm 16 is a resurrection prophecy. David probably was not thinking of a christological resurrection theology when he penned this passage. He did, however, have a glimpse of the future hope, even though he did not understand fully the meaning of the resurrection in a Christian sense.

C. S. Lewis, in *Reflections on the Psalms,* suggested one should let Jesus come out of this passage through the eyes of the New Testament and not attempt to press Christ legalistically into the mold of this psalm. As David wrote the psalm, he probably was concerned about preservation *from* death. Now that we can see through the New Testament clearly, we know that Christ taught preservation *through* death.

As Peter interpreted this psalm in his Pentecost sermon, he preached with assurance that indeed David did see something of the resurrection and recorded it in Psalm 16. Note the profound practical wisdom he gives for resurrection living here and now.

I. Have you experienced fellowship with God (Ps. 16:9)?

David wrote, "Therefore my heart is glad and my tongue rejoices; my body also will rest secure" (v. 9 NIV). Examine these three phrases.

A. *First, "My heart is glad."* The term used for "glad" means to be of good cheer. Picture the inner life being at peace with God. Take time to meet God in a quiet time of fellowship.
B. *Second, "My tongue rejoices."* "Rejoice" comes from a word that means to circle around. The idea is that of deep inner joy. The outward expression of the self comes from what has taken place in the heart.

C. *Finally, "my body also will rest secure."* For believers there is pleasant peace and tranquility in Christ. Note the facets of Christian fellowship with God: the inner self, the outer self, and the body resting securely. Recess to a place alone with God. Confess him to others. As a result, you will be secure in your fellowship with him.

D. *If you have come to church and have not experienced time alone with God during the week, or if you have gathered here without inviting someone to church with you, then you are missing full fellowship with God.* I am not suggesting that you should not come to church if you have not witnessed or spent time alone with him. I am saying, however, that you will receive a greater blessing if you do these things. You will better understand true Christian fellowship.

II. Are you aware that you encounter God at death (Ps. 16:10)?

A. *A man's wife was killed in an automobile accident several years ago.* A friend of the deceased came across some Bible study notes that the woman had taught her before the tragedy. The friend gathered up the written material and sent it to the victim's widower with a letter of explanation. For the first time, the husband saw the notes taken under his deceased wife's teaching. Through the notes, the late wife showed her assurance that if something ever happened to her physically, life would still go on spiritually. As the widower read the notes, he wept for his spouse with the reassurance of her eternal destiny.

B. *According to verse 10, God will not abandon us or leave us.* We may be assured that God will be with us through Christ now and for all eternity.

III. Your fellowship experience will determine the destiny of your encounter (Ps. 16:11).

A. *Some commentators have made strong cases for the confident expectation of the resurrection foreshadowed in this particular passage.* They are correct. But remember other glimmering lights of the resurrection in the Old Testament too. Enoch walked with God and then was not. Elijah was taken away. Their destiny was determined by their relationship with God.

B. *The psalmist wrote about knowing the path of life.* What is the path of life? It is a familiarity with God's will and God's way for your life. Invest your life for God!

Suppose you were given $86,400 with the stipulation that you had to spend it all tomorrow. The only thing you would get out of the $86,400 would be what you bought. That would be the only dividend of the investment. What would you do? Would you buy a boat? A car? (After a tithe, of course!) God has given you 86,400 seconds tomorrow. He wants you to show him how you are going to invest that time to make eternal dividends.

Conclusion

A grandfather walked in the woods with his grandson. The man tied white rags to trees as they walked through the forest. He and his grandson hunted for rocks and looked at animals. They always got home safely. How? They followed the path of the white cloths. Jesus has gone before us to show us the way to God. His resurrection has provided the trail to the Tree of Life. Fellowship with God today!

WEDNESDAY EVENING, NOVEMBER 24

Title: Enter in with Praise and Thanksgiving
Text: "Enter into his gates with thanksgiving, and into his courts with praise: be thankful unto him, and bless his name" ***(Ps. 100:4).***
Scripture Reading: Psalm 100

Introduction

Prayer is first of all an approach to God and not the presentation of a celestial shopping list. We come first to give rather than to take; offer rather than request. The psalmist describes the priority of prayer: "Enter into his gates with thanksgiving, and into his courts with praise." In prayer we should approach the loving Father with our praise and thanksgiving. This is the picture of true worship found in Revelation. The four living creatures praise the Lord and give "glory and honor and thanks to him." The twenty-four elders "fall down before him . . . and worship him . . . singing, 'Worthy art thou, our Lord and God, to receive glory and honor and power'" (4:9–11).

I. Praise and thanksgiving acknowledge the nature of God.

A. *To pray with praise and thanksgiving is to acknowledge God's holiness and majesty.* Remember he is the Lord. "It is he that hath made us, and not we ourselves; we are his people, and the sheep of his pasture (Ps. 100:3). In prayer we affirm our dependence on the Lord. We adore him and express our reverent praise for his steadfast love and faithfulness.

B. *Jesus taught us to approach the Father with praise and adoration.* "Our Father which art in heaven, hallowed be thy name" (Matt. 6:9). To hallow the Lord's name means to regard him as holy and separate and to respond with awe and reverence. Praise him in prayer. Enter in with praise and thanksgiving.

II. Praise is an action of the will.

A. *A problem in our prayer life is the vacillation of our emotions.* Sometimes we do not feel like praying. Each person has the capacity to know, feel, and decide. If we let our emotions determine our prayer life, we will certainly fail. With the will we must decide to pray. Emotion frequently limits the meaning of prayer, but we can still will to praise and thank him. Paul acknowledged this reality: "Rejoice always, pray constantly, give thanks in all circumstances; for this is the will of God in Christ Jesus for you. Do not quench the Spirit" (1 Thess. 5:16–18 RSV).

B. *God does not tell us to feel grateful always.* He does, however, command us to give thanks always. Even when we do not feel emotionally grateful, we can still choose to give thanks and praise to God: "I *will* bless the LORD at all times: his praise *shall* continually be in my mouth" (Ps. 34:1 RSV, emphasis added). Psalm 43 reflects the depressed emotions of one caught in difficult circumstances. With a decision of the will the psalmist determines to praise God. Our feelings do not alter the Lord's loving presence and powerful nature.

III. Some encouragements for praise and thanksgiving.

A. *The will is prompted to praise by various encouragements.* Recollection of God's nature—his creative power, his personal presence, his steadfast love, and his abundant mercy—will bring much praise to our lips.

B. *The memory of blessings encourages praise.* "Count your many blessings, name them one by one" is good advice for praise. Ten lepers met Jesus and sought healing of their dreaded disease. They all were cleansed, but only one came back to offer thanks (Luke 17:11–19). This one leper then received full communion with the Lord through faith. Failure to offer thanks can clog the channel of blessings. Count your blessings and praise the Lord.

C. *Praise is encouraged through the use of God's Word.* Meditate on Scripture. The words will become your own expression of praise and thanks. Put yourself in the place of the writer; feel his experiences of deliverance, joy, and spiritual blessings. Praise and thanksgiving will erupt.

D. *The psalmist utilized "joyful songs" (v. 2) to praise and thank the Lord.* Christ placed a new song in the heart of the redeemed. With music we can also "praise God from whom all blessings flow."

Conclusion

When prayer enters in with praise and thanksgiving the result is what Whittier had in mind when he prayed:

> Drop thy still dews of quietness,
> Till all our strivings cease;
> Take from our souls the strain and stress
> And let our ordered lives confess
> The beauty of Thy peace.

SUNDAY MORNING, NOVEMBER 28

Title: Jesus, the Bread of Life
Text: "Jesus said to them, 'I am the bread of life; he who comes to me shall not hunger, and he who believes in me shall never thirst'" ***(John 6:35 RSV).***
Scripture Reading: Exodus 16:4–16; John 6:35–51
Hymns: "Great Is Thy Faithfulness," Chisholm
"Come, Thou Long-Expected Jesus," Wesley
"O Come, All Ye Faithful," Wade
Offertory Prayer: Father, may the pattern of our loving be like the pattern of your loving. May it lead us to the grace of giving. In the name of the Christ child. Amen.

Introduction

We rejoice at Christmas because God sent his Son, his ultimate gift, into the world as a baby. We celebrate Christmas in honor of the birth of the one who gives us life. We sing on Christmas morning because Christ's coming to earth to dwell in human flesh is the most significant event in human history. In short, Christmas is important because of whose birthday it is.

Who is Jesus? I suggest we allow Jesus to answer that question. Our Advent sermons will come from Jesus' own statements concerning who he is.

In the New Testament text we read earlier in our service, Jesus declared, "I am the bread of life." Bread is a basic substance of life. We all realize that if we refuse to eat we will surely waste away and die. Bread is something on which we all depend. Jesus is much more than physical bread: he is the bread that nourishes a relationship between God and humans. We depend on Jesus, the Bread of Life, for eternal life. By calling himself the Bread of Life, Jesus speaks of two movements: his coming to us through the incarnation and our coming to him for salvation.

I. Jesus came to us.

A. *Jesus' coming brings a divine revelation and begins a divine-human reconciliation.*

We all are fond of the nativity scene. We picture a stable with straw; a few sheep, cows, donkeys, goats, and camels; a mother and father; humble shepherds; and a baby in a manger. But that scene is more than a sentimental picture of a sweet baby. It is in fact a revealing picture into the very heart of the Father.

B. *The birth of the Christ child says that God can identify with us.* A medical drama with a scene in which a white doctor attempted to be sympathetic to the plight of a black doctor may help us understand how Christ's coming as a human helped him identify with humans.

The black physician rebuked the white physician, saying, "As well as you try and as sincere and well meaning as you are, you will never know what it means to be me simply because you are white and I am black—just like you will never know how your wife feels because she is a woman and you are a man."

That Baby in a manger almost two thousand years ago reminds us that God does know how we feel. As a baby he whimpered when hungry, soiled his diapers, stumbled and fell learning to walk, and learned to say words and then sentences. He grew up experiencing all the daily joys and trials of life, then suffered when he was betrayed and deserted. God can identify with us. That is good news!

C. *The Babe lying in a manger shows us the way to God.* You have probably asked a group of persons for directions to a particular place, and suddenly two, three, or four began to speak at once—each giving you "definitive" directions. Which voice did you listen to?

In this world many voices compete for our ear about ultimate matters. Christian faith reminds us to listen to Jesus. John begins his gospel with that magnificent prologue: "In the beginning was the Word, and the Word was with God, and the Word was God" (John 1:1). Jesus is the ultimate expression of God, the incarnation of God. He can tell us what God is like because he has come down from God; he can show us the way to God because he is from God. "The Word was made flesh, and dwelt among us (and we have beheld his glory)" (v. 14). The babe of Bethlehem shows us the way to God. That is good news!

D. *The baby in swaddling clothes announces joy to the world.* We do not live in a happy age. Perhaps the best illustration of this tragic truth is a study of contemporary humor. It is a humor without joy: comedians depend on—and people laugh at—cynicism, sarcasm, and ridicule. Life for many is grim, meaningless, and hopeless.

It is the message of Christmas that Christ gives hope and joy in times like these and makes life meaningful, purposeful, and enjoyable. The babe of Bethlehem brings joy to the world. That is good news!

E. *Mary's baby unites us with God.* In the sixteenth century the emperor of Germany received a very expensive piece of pie. He owed an international banker one million dollars, and one Christmas the banker put a canceled debt note in a Christmas pie. When the emperor ate the pie, a million-dollar liability was canceled.

The birth of God's Son that first Christmas is God's Christmas pie to us. He is saying as loudly and as clearly as he possibly can that our sins are forgivable. He is saying that he desires friendship and reconciliation with human beings. The babe of Bethlehem unites believers with God. That is good news!

II. Jesus calls us to come to him.

Jesus as the Bread of Life calls us to come to him for salvation. The gift of life requires the believing reception of the gospel. Jesus calls us to put our faith in him, to believe in him as the Bread of Life (John 1:12). It is accurately said that you can lead a horse to water, but you cannot make him drink. Any parent knows that you can set food down in front of a child, but you cannot make the child eat. (Some bribes work some of the time, but no bribe works all of the time.) You may want to be someone's friend, but you cannot be that person's friend until he or she wants you as a friend too. It is that way with Jesus. Jesus was born as a babe in Bethlehem because he wants to be our Friend, but he will not force us to like him against our will. Christian relationship means that we accept Jesus as our Friend.

III. Jesus invites us to eat his flesh and drink his blood (John 6:47–58).

Eating the Lord's Supper is not cannibalism, but rather symbolism. The image of eating Christ's flesh and drinking his blood grows out of a world in which animals were sacrificed to false gods but not all of the animal was burned on the altar. Part was kept by the priest and part was returned to the worshiper, who then ate it, believing that he had literally eaten of his god, that he was god-filled. Though we do not practice this type of thing, against the backdrop we are invited symbolically to eat of Jesus' flesh and to drink his blood to picture an experience of an authentic union.

Maybe an illustration can help you understand what Jesus meant when he invited us to eat his flesh. Imagine you have just received a new book. You know you will like it, because its author is a favorite of yours. Yet instead of devouring it right away, you place it on your shelf. You know the effects of this. Until you read it, the enjoyment, information, inspiration, and assistance of that book will always remain external. Someday, however, you will read it, and only then will it really be your book. You will know its contents and be helped by its insight. You will be able to draw upon it to enrich your life.

That is the way it is with Jesus. As long as Jesus remains on pages—even holy ones—in a book, he cannot give your life nourishment and sustenance. You must digest the Bread of Life for salvation.

Conclusion

Who is that babe in the manger? He is the Bread of Life. He comes to give us real, meaningful, abundant, full, eternal life. Will you come to him today? Will you accept his love? Will you eat his body and drink his blood and have abundant and eternal life?

SUNDAY EVENING, NOVEMBER 28

Title: "Where Is God?"

Text: "My God, my God, why hast thou forsaken me? why art thou so far from helping me, and from the words of my roaring?" ***(Ps. 22:1).***
Scripture Reading: Psalm 22:1–31

Introduction

At Jesus' baptism, he heard the voice of his Father. When he was tempted, he quoted Scripture. Throughout his ministry, he called on God, and the Father answered. At Jesus' transfiguration, God was present. As Jesus taught by parables, wisdom from God confounded those around him. Even when he was betrayed by Judas, there was a sense of divine destiny.

But all changed on the cross. For the first time, Jesus asked the question that confronts all of us: "Where is God?" Jesus identified with our humanity on the cross in order to assume our sin. He experienced that which he had never known before: the void, the absence of God. He knew fully what it was to be human.

The psalmist's prayer had brought him no relief from difficulty. His persistent petitions seemingly accomplished nothing. Hence, the language and the mood of Psalm 22 have led many to believe it could be titled "The Psalm of the Cross." Consider the questions the psalmist raised about our existence.

I. Where is God when we ache?

A. *There were many forms of rejection on the cross.* The Romans cast lots for Christ's clothes. The crowd passing by the crosses mocked him. The sinners for whom he was dying scorned him. Religious leaders rebuked him. Facing rejection, Jesus cried out in agony, "My God, my God, why hast thou forsaken me?" (Matt. 27:46; Mark 15:34). He was really asking, "Where is God?"

   A similar question was asked recently by a little boy whose father was mysteriously murdered. In another instance, a teenager's home was destroyed by a tornado. He cried, "Why our home? We are good." On the cross, Jesus Christ identified with the human experience. He encountered the absence of God.

B. *Look carefully at the New Testament counterparts to Psalm 22.* In Matthew 27:46 Jesus cried out, *"Eli, Eli, lama sabachthani?"* The first phrase in this cry is Hebrew, meaning "my God." Hebrew was not the common vernacular of the people, but rather the religious language. Jesus spoke privately to God. Consequently, many of those around the cross thought he was speaking to Elijah. In Aramaic the people's language, he then cried, *"Lama sabachthani,"* meaning "Why have you forsaken me?" So Christ's public cry of abandonment was understood easily by the crowd. He felt abandoned and cried out publicly. But he still had talked privately with the one who had abandoned him.

   Do you feel abandoned by God? Does he seem silent to you? Talk to him. Ask Him, "Lord, where are you?" Jesus did so on the cross.

II. Where is God when the unjust are unfair?

The vigilante-style killing of four youths in a New York City subway several years ago was at first applauded by New York City residents. Why? People were tired of injustice. Criminals seemed to have more rights than the innocent. Where is God when injustice seems to rule? What hope do we have?

A. *Consider the familiar messianic symbols of the cross.* In Psalm 22:14 examine the quote, "All of my bones are out of joint." In verse 16 recognize the symbolism of Christ's pierced hands and feet. In verse 18 read about the gambling away of Christ's clothes at the cross. But look at the odd clause in verse 6: "I am a worm."

Here the Hebrew word for "worm" is a unique one. Do not associate this with an ordinary earthworm. Rather, consider the special worm used in industry in the ancient world. These tiny creatures were crushed to produce a crimson-colored juice. The resulting liquid was used to dye royal robes and clothing. It was an expensive procedure only kings could afford.

B. *As the worms were crushed, robes for royalty were made.* What symbolism! Jesus Christ was "crushed," so that by his precious crimson blood, the robes of royalty might be dyed for Christians to assume kingship and share in his glory!

C. *Where is God when the unjust are unfair?* We can answer this by seeing where he has been. The cross shows he understands; he has identified with the human drama of injustice.

III. Where is God when we are in dire necessity?

Note three Hebrew verbs in verse 19–21: "Help me, deliver me, and save me." Each carries an important meaning.

A. *The term "to help" is a military term.* God could have sent a legion of angels to help Jesus.

B. *Look at the second phrase: "Deliver me."* God could have delivered Christ from the cross. The term meant to escape. Yet he did not escape; he bore the brunt of the penalty of humankind's sin.

C. *The term "to save" used in this particular verse means "to widen or make sufficient" rather than "to narrow or restrict."* He asked for salvation, and now it is offered to us.

D. *Where is God when we are in dire necessity?* Being a Christian does not exempt us from problems. In 1983 Aleksandr Solzhenitsyn, speaking in Britain, called us back to God as a civilization. He told of his experiences as a fifteen-year-old Marxist atheist. As he grew he began challenging the Russian system in his writings. As a result, he was sentenced to eight years in Siberia. There he physically became sick unto death and found God. When you find yourself in the most difficult of circumstances, God is near. The breakthrough may come when you realize you are so deprived that total adherence to God is your only refuge.

Conclusion

God has come! We find the fulfillment of Psalm 22:27–30 in Hebrews 2:10–14: "Since the children have flesh and blood, he too shared in their humanity so that by his death he might destroy him who holds the power of death" (v. 14 NIV). God has come. From Bethlehem to Calvary's cross, God has come. "Where is God?" Let the Bible answer the question for you. He has come!

SUGGESTED PREACHING PROGRAM FOR THE MONTH OF

DECEMBER

■ Sunday Mornings

Continue with the theme "Jesus Introduces Himself" throughout the Christmas season. Then close out the year with a message for the new year.

■ Sunday Evenings

Use the theme "Responding to the God of Encouragement" for the Sunday evening messages this month. Paul spoke of "the God of steadfastness and encouragement" (Rom. 15:5 RSV). We will study the Scriptures from the standpoint of seeing how God seeks to encourage his people.

■ Wednesday Evenings

Complete the series "The Spiritual Disciplines That Make Prayer Meaningful."

WEDNESDAY EVENING, DECEMBER 1

Title: Pray for One Another

Text: "Moreover as for me, God forbid that I should sin against the LORD in ceasing to pray for you" ***(1 Sam. 12:23).***

Scripture Reading: 1 Samuel 12:23; James 5:13–18

Introduction

Have you ever said, "All I can do is pray," when faced with another's problem? We often underestimate the efficacy of prayer. But what a gift to another! Alfred, Lord Tennyson wrote, "More things are wrought by prayer than this world dreams of. Therefore, let thy voice rise like a fountain for me night and day." Intercessory prayer is the Christian's highest privilege. Samuel said, "God forbid that I should sin against the LORD in ceasing to pray for you" (1 Sam. 12:23). The Word commands us to "pray one for another" (James 5:16).

I. Intercessory prayer is our work as priests of the Lord.

A. *Christians are a "holy priesthood, to offer up spiritual sacrifices acceptable to God by Jesus Christ" (1 Peter 2:5).* A priest brought people to God. He went into the Holy of Holies and interceded for them. Isaiah prophesied, "You shall be named the priests of the Lord" (6:16).

B. *Each Christian has the responsibility to pray for others.* Samuel recognized it was sin to fail in that work.

II. Intercessory prayer follows the pattern of Jesus.

A. *When we pray for one another, we walk in Jesus' steps and follow his example.* In the Sermon on the Mount, Jesus taught us to pray for our persecutors (Matt. 5:44). During the Last Supper, Jesus turned and said, "Simon, Simon . . . I have prayed for thee" (Luke 22:31–32). In Gethsemane Jesus prayed for us (John 17:9). At the cross he prayed for others—"Father, forgive them" (Luke 23:34).

B. *Jesus' continuing ministry in glory involves intercessory prayer—"He always lives to make intercession" (Heb. 7:25 RSV).* If we would be like Christ, then we must pray for one another.

III. Opportunities for intercessory prayer (James 5:13–18).

James gives several life situations that are opportunities to pray for one another.

A. *Suffering (v. 13).* When you suffer affliction brought by the injustices of others, you should pray. Praying for the person who wrongs us will change our attitude toward that person. If you cannot pray, "Father, forgive," at least begin by asking God to work with the individual. Praying for one who has brought suffering to you will enable the passion of sinful anger to melt into forgiveness.

Suffering may come upon us in the grief of death. A friend said to a grieving woman whose husband had recently died, "I want you to know that our family has been praying for you."

"Thank you," replied the widow. "The prayers of many people have been like a blanket of love to me."

B. *Happiness (v. 13 NIV).* "Is anyone happy? Let him sing songs of praise." Intercessory prayer includes praise and thanksgiving for others. When others experience happiness and blessings, there is a special need to pray for them to be free from pride and selfishness and to give God the glory. Pray they will retain proper priorities.

C. *Illness (v. 14).* Illness is a result of the fall. It is not part of God's eternal will, but he permits it in our lives. Nevertheless, no illness can frustrate God's ultimate will. All healing is of God in Christ, our Great Physician. Many times he chooses to heal in what appears to us as a miracle. These miracles are always for his glory.

D. *Sins (vv. 15–16).* The worst malignancy is sin. Pray for the salvation of your family and friends. Our sovereign Lord desires all to have life and none to perish. James encourages prayer for spiritual healing of the sin problem. "Confess your sins to each other and pray for each other" (v. 16 NIV). Unless we are willing to repent of our sin, we have no right to pray for another's sin. "The prayer of a *righteous* man is powerful and effective" (v. 16 NIV, emphasis added).

Conclusion

We need never apologize to someone by saying, "All I can do is pray." Praying for another is doing the best we can. May Samuel's commitment be ours: "God forbid that I should sin against the Lord in ceasing to pray for you" (1 Sam. 12:23).

Sunday Morning, December 5

Title: Jesus, the Light of the World

Text: "Again Jesus spoke to them, saying, 'I am the light of the world; he who follows me will not walk in darkness, but will have the light of life'" ***(John 8:12 RSV).***

Scripture Reading: Isaiah 9:2–7; John 8:12–30

Hymns: "We Have Heard the Joyful Sound," Owens
"O Little Town of Bethlehem," Brooks
"The Light of the World Is Jesus," Bliss

Offertory Prayer: Father, you loved and therefore you gave; help us to see that as our pattern for loving. In the name of the Christ child. Amen.

Introduction

On the evening of the first night of the Feast of Tabernacles, there was a ceremony called the Illumination of the Temple, which involved the ritual lighting of four golden candelabras in the Court of Women. For additional reflection, each person lit four candlesticks and set them in a floating bowl, producing such a spectacle of illumination that it is said that all Jerusalem reflected the light. All night long the light glowed. In celebration and anticipation, the greatest, wisest, and holiest of Israel's men danced before the Lord and sang psalms of joy and praise while the people watched and waited.

They watched and waited, hoped and prayed, because this festival reminded the citizens of Israel that God had promised long ago that a child would be born who would be the Anointed One, sent by the great Yahweh to redeem his people. The great prophet of the golden age of prophecy, Isaiah, had proclaimed that the coming of God's new age would be as the coming of a great light (9:2–7).

For Israel it was a time of darkness and despair. The nation was occupied by a foreign power, and thus the Jews' aspirations, dreams, and hopes were blunted by reality and blighted by circumstance. So they longed for the birth of the one who would restore their rejoicing and revive their joy, the prophet who would renew their glory, release them from bondage, and reestablish their independence.

Against this backdrop Jesus defined who he is: "I am the light of the world!" What a magnificent setting—the darkness of the countryside surrounding the brilliance of the light coming from the temple area—for a declaration that God's new age had dawned in the birth, person, and work of the humble Nazarene!

Light enables one to see. It illuminates. "To shed light on the matter" means to reveal, to disclose truth. Jesus is the Light of the World in that he enables us to see the truth about ourselves and the truth about God. He illuminates our understanding both of ourselves and of God. In Jesus, the Light of the World, we see ourselves as God sees us, and we see God as he desires that we see him.

I. The child born in Bethlehem illuminates the way we feel about ourselves.

A. *We live in an age of despair and gloom.* It is an age that tells us that we are not worth much unless we brush with the right toothpaste, wash our hair with the right shampoo, wear the appropriate designer labels, and use the latest jargon. A great sense of worthlessness, of "nobodiness," permeates our day.

B. *But Jesus as the Light of the World can illuminate our feelings at precisely this point.* We have worth because of who our Creator is. "The Word was made flesh" (John 1:14); this reminds us that we are the good product of the creative, loving activity of God as he moved to bring order out of chaos, light out of darkness, and humans out of the dust of the ground. The biblical picture is one of excitement, ecstasy, anticipation, and fondness as God forms a man into his own image and breathes the breath of life into his nostrils. He looks upon creation with delight, calls it good, and declares that he likes it.

C. *Not only have we been created by the Word because he loved us, but also the Word became flesh because he loved us.* Sure, humans ate the forbidden fruit, but the message of Christmas is that we are nevertheless loved and deemed more valuable than precious jewels. That toddler in Nazareth assures us that we are still the apple of the Father's eye—even in our sin. Jesus is the incarnating—the in-the-fleshing—of God's love for us. We are of ultimate worth because we have a redeemer.

II. The child born in Bethlehem illuminates the way we feel about God.

A. *Where do you think John, the great apostle of love, got the idea to write such a stunning verse as "For God so loved the world that he gave his one and only son that whoever believes in him shall not perish but have eternal life" (John 3:16 NIV)?* The Holy Spirit inspired him. During his three years with Jesus, John learned that, indeed, the boy born of Mary was the Light of the World who could illuminate our understanding of how God feels about us.

B. *Where do you think Paul, the great apostle of grace, got such a preposterous idea as to reduce the gospel to "God demonstrates his own love for us in this:*

While we were still sinners, Christ died for us" (Rom. 5:8 NIV)? He got it from interpreting the life and ministry of Jesus through the Holy Spirit. To Paul, Jesus was the Light of the World. In Jesus, Paul learned ultimately how God felt about him and that faith in the child born of the virgin was the way to be right with God.

Conclusion

When a tour group gets to the bottom of the magnificent Carlsbad Caverns in New Mexico, the lights are turned off to show utter darkness. After the lights are turned off, it does not take long before you can even feel the darkness; you start getting anxious for the lights to come back on. The tension is relieved only when the lights return.

In our world of darkness—a world of sin and guilt, desperation and despair, estrangement and alienation—Jesus is the Light!

SUNDAY EVENING, DECEMBER 5

Title: The Need for Encouragement
Text: "Jonathan, Saul's son, arose, and went to David at Horesh, and strengthened his hand in God" ***(1 Sam. 23:16 RSV).***
Scripture Reading: 1 Samuel 23:15–18

Introduction

Jonathan's experience with David illustrates the reality of the ministry of encouragement. Romans 15:5 says, "May the God of steadfastness and encouragement grant you to live in such harmony with one another, in accord with Christ Jesus" (RSV). So, God the Father gives encouragement. Romans 15:4 says that he encourages us with the Scriptures. Philippians 2:1 says, "So if there is any encouragement in Christ . . ." (RSV). John 14 speaks of the encouragement of the Holy Spirit. He is our ever-present encourager, the Paraclete, who dwells within us.

All of us need to be encouragers, and all of us will need encouragement sooner or later. At times we will need extra encouragement. When do you need encouragement? Let us look to the Bible for the answers to this question.

I. If you are busy in your work or ministry.

A. *Leaders need to help workers with words of encouragement.* Second Chronicles 35:2 says, "He set the priests in their charges and encouraged them to the service of the house of the Lord." King Josiah encouraged the priests in their service. Hezekiah did the same in 2 Chronicles 29:11. There is a principle here: those in authority need to encourage those under them. Employers may do this for their employees. Fathers need to encourage their children. Husbands need to encourage their wives by a word, touch, smile, or hug. And pastors need to encourage their staff members and congregations.

B. *Those under authority yearn to be encouraged.* They need to know they are benefiting the one they serve. When they get encouragement, their hands are strengthened for work.

II. If you are facing a new challenge.

A. *The Lord wants his leaders to be encouraged.* The Lord told Moses to commend and encourage Joshua for his good report concerning the land of Canaan: "Joshua the son of Nun, who stands before you, he shall enter there; encourage him, for he shall cause Israel to inherit it" (Deut. 1:38 RSV). This illustrates an important principle: encourage your boss, your teacher, your parents, your husband, your pastor, or whoever your leader may be.

B. *In Joshua 1:6–9 the Lord himself speaks strong encouragement to Joshua.* In fact, he commands Joshua to be encouraged. Anything less would be sin!

III. If you are about to complete a task.

A. *People need to be spurred on to complete a project.* Ezra 6:22 (NASB) says, "They observed the Feast of Unleavened Bread seven days with joy, for the Lord had caused them to rejoice, and had turned the heart of the king of Assyria toward them to encourage them in the work of the house of God, the God of Israel."

The temple at Jerusalem was being rebuilt. Ezra had been confronted with adversaries who were hindering the work. Finally, the temple was completed (Ezra 6:15); Ezra had not given up. Now there came a special encouragement from an unexpected source—the king of Assyria! Who prompted the king to encourage the Israelites? The Bible says it was the Lord!

B. *Do you know someone who is about to finish a task?* Does this person need encouragement? Is the Lord prompting you to encourage that person? Purpose in your heart to do it! It may be an older person completing life or someone sick struggling for restoration of health, or possibly a student about to complete high school or college.

IV. If the Holy Spirit is prompting you.

A. *Daily encouragement is needed, and the Holy Spirit brings it.* We are to hear his voice and encourage others to respond, being sensitive to their needs. It is important for two reasons: first, the heart can become hardened to the Holy Spirit; and second, the heart can be deceived by sin. We may never know just when the Holy Spirit is prompting someone, so we need to be alert to encourage one another.

Hebrews 3:12–13 says, "Take care, brethren, that there not be in any one of you an evil, unbelieving heart that falls away from the living God. But encourage one another day after day, as long as it is still called 'Today,' so that none of you will be hardened by the deceitfulness of sin" (NASB).

B. *How do we do that?* Hebrews 10:24–25 says encouragement is effected by stimulating one another to love and to do good deeds, as well as by worshiping with one another. First Thessalonians 5:11 says we are to build up one another. Ephesians 4:29 says we are to speak encouraging words to others, not discouraging ones, by making positive statements rather than negative ones.

V. If life begins to overwhelm.

A. *When David was overwhelmed by a bitter and angry people, he needed encouragement.* So "David encouraged himself in the LORD his God" (1 Sam. 30:6).

B. *Things may be difficult for you.* All of us face adversity or difficult circumstances at some time. What can we do? We can encourage ourselves in God by reading his Word and praying.

Conclusion

God's Word is full of encouragement. Whatever we need, he gives to us. Be encouraged in the Lord today!

WEDNESDAY EVENING, DECEMBER 8

Title: A Praying Church

Text: "When they had prayed, the place was shaken where they were assembled together; and they were all filled with the Holy Ghost, and they spake the word of God with boldness" ***(Acts 4:31).***

Scripture Reading: Acts 4:23–33

Introduction

Complimentary descriptions of a church often include these words—*evangelistic, spiritual, servant.* All of these are accurate, yet it is impossible to be that kind of church unless the people pray. Prayer is basic for evangelism, growth, spirituality, and service. The first chapters of Acts describe a growing, vibrant, witnessing body of Christians. This vitality came from their prayer life. Acts 4 is an inside look at a praying church.

Peter and John were used of the Lord to heal a man "lame from birth" (Acts 3:2 RSV). The healing created interest, and a large crowd gathered to hear Peter preach. This annoyed the religious leaders, and in jealousy they arrested the apostles, kept them in custody overnight, threatened them, and then released them. Peter and John went to church and reported their experience. A time of prayer followed.

I. A church united in prayer.

A. *"They lifted their voices together to God" (Acts 4:24 RSV).* Jesus said there is power in public united prayer (Matt. 18:19–20). Prayer includes learning to say, "*Our* Father." Prayer is an experience of the family of faith. Strong and growing churches are united in prayer. Paul believed in the power of united prayer (Rom. 15:30; 2 Cor. 1:11).

B. *People need to understand clearly the unique role prayer has in their lives.* Andrew Murray wrote in *With Christ in the School of Prayer,* "Most churches think their members are gathered into one simply to take care of and build up each other. They know not that God rules the world by the prayers of his saints; that prayer is the power by which Satan is conquered; that by prayer the church on earth has disposal of the powers of the heavenly world."

II. The content of the church's prayer.

The Jerusalem church gathered in prayer illustrates the content of vibrant prayer.

A. *It first focused on God (Acts 4:24).* Turning one's face toward the Lord has a way of restoring proper perspective on the problems of everyday life.

B. *The Word gave assurance and guidance (Acts 4:25–26).* This prayer includes a quotation from Psalm 2:1–2. The Word of God offers content for our prayer life.

C. *Past blessings and victories are recalled (Acts 4:27–28).* The Jerusalem church remembered the dark days surrounding Jesus' crucifixion and how the cross became God's exclamation mark at the resurrection. God's faithfulness in the past is assurance of his faithful work now.

D. *Petitions were made for specific needs (Acts 4:29).* The church prayed for boldness in the witness of their leaders. They sought a display of God's power in the hope of turning many to the Lord Jesus.

III. A praying church gets answers.

Luke records the exciting conclusion to the church prayer meeting.

A. *They were all filled with the Holy Spirit (Acts 4:31).* The church is a spiritual body and needs the power of the Spirit to do the work of God. Jesus promised to give the Holy Spirit if we ask (Luke 11:13).

B. *They spoke the word of God with boldness (Acts 4:31).* The immediate blessing of the Spirit's filling is bold witnessing. Christians need the power of the Spirit to tell people about Christ.

C. *The signs of a spiritual body abounded (Acts 4:32–35).* The result of a praying church is a united body—"one in heart and mind" (v. 32 NIV). A spirit of benevolent sharing prevailed, and needs were met (vv. 32–35).

Conclusion

A preacher recited several of the acts of God recorded in the Bible. After each event he exclaimed, "Do it again! Do it again!" That should be the desire of every church member—that the experiences of this praying church would occur again and again.

SUNDAY MORNING, DECEMBER 12

Title: Jesus, the Good Shepherd

Text: "I am the good shepherd. The good shepherd lays down his life for the sheep" ***(John 10:11 RSV)***.

Scripture Reading: Psalm 23; John 10:11–18

Hymns: "There's a Song in the Air," Holland
"The First Noel," Traditional English Carol
"Angels We Have Heard on High," French Carol

Offertory Prayer: Father, as we think about the gift you gave us in Bethlehem, we are motivated to give you the gift of our hearts and lives. Please accept these offerings as an expression of the gift of our love for you. In the name of the Christ child. Amen.

Introduction

The Israelites, long before they became a settled agrarian people, were nomads in a pastoral setting. It was natural that they would see their relationship with God in a pastoral image. Against this backdrop of a people who pictured themselves as God's sheep, Jesus announced that he was the Good Shepherd. The implication is clear: he is the shepherd who leads us to God. The child of Bethlehem is the true revelation of God and the true way to God and salvation. But how does the Good Shepherd lead us to God?

I. Jesus the Good Shepherd leads us to God by translating God's message for humans.

A. *In the East shepherds lead their sheep by chanting to them in nonhuman sounding utterances that the sheep learn to discern, trust, and obey.* As a shepherd watches his sheep graze, he periodically calls to them in a loud sing-song voice to reassure them. He also calls the sheep to follow him, and they recognize his voice and move to the sound.

B. *Louis Cassels writes of a man who had a humbug attitude toward Christmas.* He was a decent and kind man who loved his family, but he simply could not understand the Christian proclamation of an incarnation. God becoming flesh seemed absurd and silly. One Christmas eve, while his family was at church, a flock of birds was stranded in the snow outside his house. He desired to lead them to the barn where the children's pony was kept, but he was unable to communicate this to the birds. He tried to lead them into the barn by waving his arms, leaving a trail of bread crumbs, and carrying out a variety of other schemes. He finally realized that in order to communicate to the birds, he himself would have to become one. It was at that moment that the church bells rang, announcing the glad tidings of Christmas. As he heard the bells, he finally understood the reason for the incarnation: God could now communicate with us in a way we could understand so he could lead us to safety!

C. *Jesus has come to lead us into the barn, to show us that God loves us and wants to save us.* When you look at a nativity scene, remember that Jesus was born so that God could communicate with you, that he could call you to himself. Jesus relays God's message in a way we can understand.

II. Jesus the Good Shepherd leads us to God by personally giving us God's message.

A. *Jesus knows us and calls us by name, and we know him.* The Good Shepherd knows each of us intimately. In the East sheep are raised not to eat, but for their wool. Thus, a shepherd grows to know each one and even gives them nicknames—often based on their physical characteristics, such as Brown Leg or Black Ear.

B. *Before the incarnation of God at Bethlehem, we humans could only speak of God at best in the abstract, as a stranger.* He was "out there," not a native. We could not say for sure if he liked us, if he was an ally or an adversary. We could only guess. That baby born on the first Christmas fleshes out for us our understandings of God and his feelings for us. Recall that beloved verse, John 3:16, and personalize it by inserting your name.

III. Jesus the Good Shepherd leads us to God by a loving sacrifice.

A. *The Good Shepherd lays down his life for his sheep (John 10:11, 15).* It was not an uncommon occurrence for a shepherd to risk his life to protect the flock. Sometimes the threat would be from wild and dangerous animals—wolves, bears, or lions; but sometimes the threat was from another sort of animal—humans bent on theft. Shepherds would sometimes have to engage in desperate fights with savage beasts or thieves, and the faithful shepherd would lay down his life to defend his flock.

B. *Jesus is the Good Shepherd who gladly and voluntarily sacrifices his own life.* God gave at Bethlehem and Jerusalem, in a manger and on a cross, in life and in death. Jesus did not have to die; he could have followed the advice of friends such as Peter, or he could have called a legion of angels to his assistance. But the Good Shepherd died because that is what would bring life to the sheep—you and me. He laid down his life so that we, his sheep, might have life—abundant and eternal.

Conclusion

One day Jesus told a story to reveal what the Father is like. A shepherd had one hundred sheep in his care, and during the course of the day's labors, he lost one. Tired, hungry, thirsty, and desiring to be with family, he nevertheless began to retrace the many and difficult steps of the day's journey. He finally found the kid, which had strayed off and become frightened. Then he tenderly and joyfully put it on his own shoulders, returned home, and gave a party to celebrate finding the lost sheep. Then Jesus made the point: God is like that shepherd. He wants us all safely in the fold. He has gone on a long search—the incarnation. He rejoices when one person is found—salvation.

That, my friends, is the meaning of Christmas. That baby in the manger is God looking for you.

SUNDAY EVENING, DECEMBER 12

Title: The Who of Encouragement
Text: "I will ask the Father, and He will give you another Helper, that He may be with you forever" ***(John 14:16 NASB)***.
Scripture Reading: John 14:16–18, 26; 15:26

Introduction

Paul emphatically says in Romans 15:5, "God gives . . . encouragement." First Peter 5:7 says, "He cares for you" (NASB). God cares in all types of situations. He is the God of encouragement. His nature is fully revealed in his Son, Jesus Christ, who also had a ministry of encouragement. And when Christ left the earth, he left his ministry of encouragement in the care of the Holy Spirit. Now, for believers, the Holy Spirit is the "who" of the ministry of encouragement. How does the Holy Spirit encourage us?

I. The Holy Spirit encourages us through his person (John 14:16–17, 26).

A. *The Holy Spirit is a person, though some prefer to use the pronoun* it *as though he were a thing.* The word translated "spirit" is the Greek word *pneuma.* It is neither male nor female, but the personal pronoun *he* is always used to refer to the Spirit.

B. *The Holy Spirit acts as a person.* He does things a person does. He dwells, guides, speaks, and teaches. He witnesses, hears, and knows. He works, loves, glorifies, and gives. All of these are personal acts.

The Holy Spirit reacts as a person. He can be grieved, blasphemed, and sinned against. People react to him as a person. He may be received, resisted, insulted, glorified, and quenched.

C. *Although the King James Version translates* pneuma *by the word "ghost," that word today is not appropriate for an accurate translation of the Greek word.* The word *ghost* refers to the returning spirit of a dead person.

The Holy Spirit is not a ghost; he is a person, the third person of the Trinity.

II. The Holy Spirit encourages us in his presence (John 14:16).

A. *He is to us all that Jesus was to his disciples in fellowship and service.* The presence of Jesus was powerful, stabilizing, and encouraging. In Mark 4:35–41, Jesus stilled the storm on the sea and the storm in his disciples' hearts. In John 6:16–21, the disciples were frightened, and Jesus came walking on the sea, speaking words of encouragement: "Do not be afraid" (NASB). Wherever we see the words "do not fear" or "be not afraid," they are powerful words of encouragement. In John 21 the disciples fished all night and caught nothing. When Jesus came they made a great catch; his presence encouraged them greatly! Now we experience the presence and encouragement of Christ through the Holy Spirit.

B. *John 14 is important for understanding the Holy Spirit.* In the New American Standard Bible the Holy Spirit is called "the Helper" (v. 16). In the King James Version he is called "the Comforter" (v. 16). He is also called "the Spirit of truth" (16:13).

Each word in these verses is important in understanding the Holy Spirit. The personal pronoun "I" (John 14:16) is emphatic. "I [myself] will ask the Father." He prayed, and the Father answered his prayer. He sent the Holy Spirit on the day of Pentecost.

In verse 17 "world" refers to those who disregard God. They cannot receive the Holy Spirit, they do not know him by experience, nor do they see him. But the disciples knew him—from the moment they first believed in Jesus Christ. We, as believers today, know him. He dwells with us and in us. We do not have to pray for him to come. He has already come. We already have the Spirit. We just need to surrender control of our lives to him.

The Greek word for "another" in verse 16 means "another of the same kind." So the Holy Spirit is another just like Jesus.

The word "comforter" is the Greek word *paraclete,* which means "one being called to one's side, to one's aid." It describes a lawyer who is called to stand with a client in court, especially a defense lawyer. It is a word used in a court of justice to denote a counsel for the defense, an advocate.

C. *We have two advocates—the Holy Spirit (Rom. 8:26–27) and Jesus Christ (v. 34).* Christ intercedes in heaven before God (v. 34), and the Holy Spirit intercedes for us, sometimes with groanings too deep for words, according to the will of God (vv. 26–27).

D. *Our response to their intercession is vital.* We cannot hinder or help Christ's intercession for us, because his intercession continues without ceasing. We can facilitate or frustrate the Holy Spirit's intercession in us by our cooperation or resistance. We are the object of Christ's praying; we are the subject of the Holy Spirit's praying, so that he can pray through us. He prays for us to enable us to pray.

E. *The Holy Spirit is an incredibly precious gift.* All that Jesus had been to his followers during his earthly ministry, the Holy Spirit has been since and will continue to be in the future. Jesus' walked alongside his disciples; the Holy Spirit dwells in us. Jesus spoke to them through their ears; the Holy Spirit speaks to our hearts. Jesus' followers could not always be with him; but we are never away from the presence of the indwelling Spirit. Are you aware of the Holy Spirit's presence in your life?

III. The Holy Spirit encourages us in our praying (Rom. 8:26–27).

Romans 8 is a chapter about the Holy Spirit and his work. One way he encourages us is that he helps us to pray.

A. *The key word in these verses is "helps."* This is a verb in the Greek language that expresses the idea of facing someone who has a burden too heavy to lift alone, taking hold of it with the person, and lifting it together. The word is used only one other time in the New Testament. In Luke 10:40, Martha, speaking of her sister, said to Jesus, "Tell her to help me" (NASB), or tell her to get under part of the load.

B. *Are you burdened about something?* Is it hard to pray about it? This is how the Holy Spirit "helps" our praying. We are on one side of the burden, and he says, "I will get on the other side. Let us stand facing one another and each take hold of it. Together we can lift your burden—our burden—up to the Father." Have you ever lifted a load and groaned under it? Well, the Holy Spirit does our groaning for us as he helps us!

C. *Notice another thing: "our weakness."* Paul is not just referring to weaker Christians, or to Christians young in the faith, or to the spiritually immature. He is including himself. The point is, all of us are weak, and we always will be. We are weak so that we may be dependent on the Holy Spirit. We are to rest in our weakness instead of striving in it. To rest is faith; to strive is works. One is of the Spirit; the other is of the flesh. This weakness, therefore, leads us to depend on the Holy Spirit. He helps our weakness as we cooperate with him so he can do for us what we could never do for ourselves!

IV. The Holy Spirit encourages us with his peace (John 14:26–27).

A. *Jesus promised the gift of peace, and he gives this peace through the Holy Spirit.* His peace is not the absence of trouble; it is an attitude of a calm heart and mind in the midst of trouble.

Two artists portrayed their concept of peace. One painted a scene of a sunny meadow beside a small lake. A tree, with not a leaf stirring, was located in the center of the meadow. There was not a ripple on the lake. Standing in the shade of the tree was a cow contentedly chewing her cud.

The other painted a rugged mountain scene. Black clouds split with lighting heralded an approaching storm. The trees were bent before the wind. To one side was a high waterfall that hit the rocks far below. At the end of the waterfall, lots of spray suggested the roar of water and the force with which it hit. It was a scene of wild turmoil, but on a ledge behind the waterfall was a little bird, its throat bursting with song.

B. *The Holy Spirit encourages us with that kind of peace!* Whatever your storm is, or whatever the climate of your circumstances, the Holy Spirit is eager to give you peace if you will let him.

Conclusion

We need a fresh awareness of the Holy Spirit in our lives and in the church. The Holy Spirit encourages us in the Christian life, and we can appropriate his encouragement as we acknowledge God's Word and apply it to our lives. Be encouraged!

WEDNESDAY EVENING, DECEMBER 15

Title: The Power of Earnest Prayer
Text: "So Peter was kept in prison, but the church was earnestly praying to God for him" ***(Acts 12:5 NIV).***
Scripture Reading: Acts 12:1–16; Acts 13:1–12

Introduction

Acts 12–13 offers interesting glimpses of two congregations at prayer. The Jerusalem church is described in Acts 12 and the Antioch church in Acts 13. These chapters show the relationship between prayer and some crucial concerns in the life of a church.

Herod's persecution brought James's death and Peter's arrest. While Peter was in jail, "the church was earnestly praying." At Mary's house "many were gathered together praying" (12:12). Peter was delivered and arrived at the house, where he was greeted by an amazed congregation. Why should they be amazed after "earnestly praying" for this very event? Was their faith lacking? Were they surprised God did it without their physical help or personal intervention to the authorities? Earnest prayer has amazing results! Let us wait on the Lord and see in *our* church the amazing power of earnest prayer.

I. Pray earnestly for God to bless the church's outreach.

A. *The close of this chapter gives the long-term results of prayer: "The word of God grew and multiplied" (Acts 12:24).* This is an excellent description of church growth. The prayer meeting at Mary's house showed the Jerusalem church a useful lesson: God uses a people prepared by prayer.

B. *The marvelous movements of people toward God have all been launched with God's people in fervent prayer.* The miracle of Christian multiplication in Korea is the result of prayer. Many trace the growth in recent years to a prayer commitment made by four missionaries of different denominations. Hundreds of Korean Christians even today gather at early hours of the morning. Prayer and church growth travel together.

II. Pray earnestly for the Lord to bless his laborers.

The Antioch church became the center of Christian outreach; the church is an inspiring example of prayer for the laborers in the field.

A. *Prayer is involved in sending out.* The church worshiped, prayed, and fasted, and then the missionary workers were chosen and set apart (Acts 13:2). Jesus instructed us to pray for laborers (Matt. 9:37–38); the needs of the world are great, and the laborers are few.

B. *Prayer is involved in the success of the laborers.* Paul spoke for every believer when he said, "Pray for us also, that God may open to us a door for the word" (Col. 4:3). Our prayers affect the success of the warriors on the front lines (2 Thess. 3:1).

C. *Prayer is involved in the safety of the Lord's laborers.* Paul requested prayer "that we may be delivered from wicked and evil men; for not all have faith. But the Lord is faithful" (2 Thess. 3:1–3).

III. Pray earnestly for the Lord's power over the enemy.

A. *The laborers left Antioch and soon encountered a personal servant of the devil (Acts 13:6–12).* Paul confronted him and had victory in dealing with him. Our battle is against the "spiritual hosts of wickedness in the heavenly places" (Eph. 6:12 RSV). The armor of the Lord to fight these spiritual forces is to be used with prayer (v. 18).

B. *Jesus promised power against the enemy. Christ's death and resurrection have rendered the devil powerless.* Every Christian participates in that victory. We claim the power of that victory as we "pray at all times in the Spirit" (Eph. 6:18 RSV).

Conclusion

A church is commissioned by God to reach the world. People near and far are the responsibility of our church. Satan will do all he can to frustrate our mission, but earnest prayer will allow God to move in power. The church will grow; workers will go and serve successfully. The forces of evil will be confronted and conquered. Such is the power of earnest prayer!

Sunday Morning, December 19

Title: Jesus, the Resurrection and the Life

Text: "Jesus said to her, 'I am the resurrection and the life; he who believes in me, though he die, yet shall he live, and whoever lives and believes in me shall never die. Do you believe this?'" ***(John 11:25–26 RSV).***

Scripture Reading: John 11:1–6, 33–35, 38–44

Hymns: "Joy to the World!" Watts

"There's a Song in the Air," Holland

"Good Christian Men, Rejoice," Medieval Latin Carol

Offertory Prayer: Loving Father, as it was with Lazarus, may it be also with us—breathe new life into us; and may it show in our giving. In the name of the babe born in Bethlehem. Amen.

Introduction

The raising of Lazarus is the climax of John's gospel. The first half of his story has been devoted to "signs" pointing to the identity of Jesus, called the Christ. The reader has seen that Jesus is called by many names: the Word become flesh, the Lamb of God who takes away the sins of the world, the great I AM, the Bread of Life, the Light of the World, the Good Shepherd, and now the Resurrection and the Life. This episode is the crescendo of the evangelist's story, because the final enemy—death—has been overcome.

The story is the finale much as that in *Hamlet.* In that play Hamlet's discovery of his mother's complicity in his father's death is the climax. The central question of who killed the king is answered fairly early in the drama; the rest of the action becomes only a matter of if, when, and how Hamlet will carry out his vengeance.

So it is here in John's gospel. The author himself declares the purpose of the story: "These are written that you may believe that Jesus is the Christ, the Son of God, and that believing you may have life in his name" (20:31 RSV). With the raising of Lazarus and with Jesus' pronouncement that he is the Resurrection and the Life, the revelation is complete. Now the readers and hearers know the identity of this one born in Bethlehem. Now the meaning and message of Christmas has been unveiled. Now the reason that the "Word became flesh" (1:14) is disclosed. After this time it is all decided. The stage has been set. Many confess their faith in him, while others feverishly and fervently plot his death and destruction. It sets the stage for the revelation of Jesus' glory—crucifixion and resurrection.

I. The names tell the tale.

A. *Lazarus means "God helps."* Lazarus and his sisters were good family friends of Jesus. The one who had "no place to lay his head" (Matt. 8:20) made it a point to visit and stay with this family when he was in the area. He enjoyed them and they, him.

But there would be no more visits with Lazarus. While he was sick his sisters sent word to Jesus of the situation. It is a statement of faith and a petition: "Lord, the one you love is sick" (John 11:3). They figured that Jesus would come and help the one he loved, and they begged him to do just that. But Jesus stayed away until Lazarus had been dead four days. Lazarus, "God helps," is dead—beyond the help of man.

B. *The second name that tells the tale is Bethany, which means "house of affliction."* That is exactly what Jesus and the disciples found there that day—persons torn by the awfulness of separation, the pain of finality, the emptiness of loss. Many friends had come from Jerusalem to console the grieving family.

When Martha heard that Jesus had come, she immediately went to see him. Her message for Jesus was two-pronged: "Lord, if you had been here, my brother would not have died. But I know that even now God will give you whatever you ask" (John 11:21–22). First, Martha almost attacked Jesus for not being there. It is as if she said: "You could have done something. Lazarus was supposed to be the one you loved. Why didn't you come when you got our message? Why didn't you do something?" Then she kind of half asked Jesus to do something "even now." There was an implicit faith that all was not hopeless any time Jesus was present. In her grief she displayed both her simmering anger and her lingering faith.

C. *Jesus responded to the despairing petition with the pronouncement of his identity as the Resurrection and the Life and the demonstration of that truth.* The third name that tells the tale is Jesus, the Resurrection and the Life. The raising of Lazarus was a sign of the resurrection, while Jesus was the reality itself. In Jesus the last day becomes present reality. Faith in Jesus appropriates the victory of God in the present and the defeat of the grave in eternity.

II. What is the meaning of Jesus, the Resurrection and the Life?

A. *The child born in Bethlehem is the proclamation of the death of sin.* Jesus said that a man cannot be so dead in sin that God cannot breathe new life into him. Hardened criminals have been changed by the life-granting forgiveness of sin. Self-righteous people have opened themselves up to abundant life through the life of the risen Christ. Millions throughout history have testified to Jesus' resurrection power in changing their sinful lives to lives free from sin.

B. *The child born in Bethlehem is the proclamation of the death of death.* Jesus brings to focus that death is not the end but rather a passageway to life. Edward the Confessor said, "Weep not, I shall not die; and as I leave the land of the dying, I trust to see the blessings of the Lord in the land of the living." From birth we are on a journey into the sunset, and in Jesus Christ we journey not into the sunset but rather into the sunrise.

Conclusion

Two friends served together in a war. One was wounded and was in no man's land where no one could reach him. His friend risked his life and made it to the wounded soldier, who said simply, "I knew you would come." This Christmas, good news! Christ has come! Jesus has come as the Bread of Life who delivers you from your despair of hunger and meaninglessness, as the Light of the World who delivers you from your darkness of sin and death, as the Good Shepherd who delivers you from your dreaded lostness and ignorance, and as the Resurrection and the Life who delivers you from death and destruction.

SUNDAY EVENING, DECEMBER 19

Title: The How of Encouragement

Text: "I thank God, whom I serve with a clear conscience the way my forefathers did, as I constantly remember you in my prayers night and day, longing to see you, even as I recall your tears, so that I may be filled with joy" ***(2 Tim. 1:3–4 NASB).***

Scripture Reading: 2 Timothy 1:3–12

Introduction

The "when" of encouragement is the many times we need it. The "who" of encouragement is the Holy Spirit, who continues the ministry of Jesus Christ among us. Now let us examine the "how" of encouragement.

Timothy had been shedding tears over the difficulties he faced in his ministry, so Paul encouraged him. He did this by referring to Timothy's godly heritage in his mother and grandmother and in the spiritual gift God had given him. He encouraged him by saying that fear is not from God, but that God gives power, love, and a disciplined life (see 2 Tim. 1:7). What encouragement that must have been to Timothy!

Have you encouraged someone lately? Are you waiting for someone to encourage you? Yield up that expectation to the Lord and be encouraged in him. Put your trust in him. There is great power in encouragement.

How does encouragement come? God is the source; the Holy Spirit is the encourager. Let us look at five ways the Holy Spirit gives encouragement.

I. He encourages us through a personal friend (1 Sam. 23:15–16).

A. *David and Jonathan were intimate friends.* They were covenant friends who had exchanged robes and weapons, sealing their covenant with blood. When Saul was pursuing David to kill him, Jonathan came to David and encouraged him in God. He gave David a word of faith: "Do not be afraid" (v. 17).

B. *God always signs his letters of encouragement.* He sends no anonymous letters. He always personalizes his encouragement! He may send someone to us, for he prompts one Christian to help another.

II. He encourages us through God's Word (Rom. 15:4).

A. *God's written Word has power to encourage.* God's Word has hope! If you have a problem or a need for direction, just believe there is a message for you in the Word of God and seek it!

B. *You can look elsewhere for encouragement, but it will be only temporary.* There is powerful literature outside the Bible, but only God's Word is eternal. Isaiah 40:8 (NASB) says, "The grass withers, the flower fades, but the word of our God stands forever."

III. He encourages us through our spiritual position (Phil. 2:1).

A. *Our spiritual position is that we are in Christ.* "If therefore there is any encouragement in Christ . . ." (NASB). "In Christ" is used approximately 150 times in the New Testament. It refers to our union with Christ. We are "in him," in that we have been crucified with Christ, raised up with him, and allowed to sit with him in heavenly places. We are to take advantage of that relationship. Colossians 3:1 says, "If then you have been raised up with Christ, keep seeking the things above, where Christ is, seated at the right hand of God" (NASB).

B. *His power is made available to us.* "Now to Him who is able to do exceeding abundantly beyond all that we ask or think, according to the power that works within us, to him be the glory in the church and in Christ Jesus to all generations forever and ever. Amen" (Eph. 3:20–21 NASB). Philippians 4:13 says we are totally adequate in Christ: "I can do all things through him who strengthens me." As he is, so are we in the world: "By this, love is perfected with us, that we may have confidence in the day of judgment; because as He is, so also are we in this world" (1 John 4:17 NASB). This is encouragement!

IV. He encourages us through divine intervention (Acts 16:22–26).

A. *God can deeply encourage us through his miracles.* Paul and Silas were beaten by prison guards and thrown into the inner prison where they were guarded securely. It is safe to say that they needed encouragement. But they were not feeling sorry for themselves. They were praying and singing hymns of praise to God (v. 25). Their hearts were encouraged. Then suddenly there came a great earthquake and the foundation of the prison was shaken. God intervened!

B. *Divine intervention proves God's encouragement.* Jesus was asleep during a storm on the Sea of Galilee. The disciples cried out to him, "Do you not care?" Yes, he did care! He commanded the storm to cease and their hearts to be stilled (Mark 4:35–41).

Jesus really does care. He is the Good Shepherd, not a hireling merely tending the sheep in a perfunctory way. In fact, he gives the ultimate of encouragement in John 10: "I lay down my life for the sheep."

Conclusion

We all are a part of the ministry of encouragement. We receive encouragement, and we give it. Believe it and share it every day of your life!

Wednesday Evening, December 22

Title: Lord, Teach Us to Pray

Text: "It came to pass, that, as he was praying in a certain place, when he ceased, one of the disciples said unto him, Lord, teach us to pray, as John also taught his disciples" ***(Luke 11:1).***

Scripture Reading: Luke 11:1–13

Introduction

During the past two months we have sought guidance from God's Word on the discipline of prayer. Some lessons are better caught than taught. We learn by example; Jesus is that perfect example on prayer. Watching and listening to Jesus pray, the disciples felt their own shortcomings and requested, "Lord, teach us to pray." They had seen mighty miracles but did not ask for power. They had heard his matchless preaching but did not ask him to teach them how to preach. They longed for his dynamic prayer life.

Prayer is essential for the Christian's well-being. Without prayer the Christian has a spiritual drought and a fruitless life. We can learn much from the glimpses of Jesus' prayer life as recorded in the Gospel of Luke.

I. Prayer as preparation for life.

A. *Jesus was born into a devout, God-fearing family.* Both Joseph and Mary were sensitive to the voice of God and obedient to his leadership. No doubt Jesus' early childhood was immersed in the prayerful spirit of his parents. A child will be better prepared for life when reared by a mother who shares Mary's commitment (Luke 1:38). Mary's prayer song (1:46–55) expresses praise and thanksgiving to God for salvation and fulfillment of his promises.

B. *When the infant Jesus was dedicated to the Lord, the family was encountered by Simeon and Anna—both of whom prayed for the family and praised God (Luke 2:25–39).* Parents need to expose their children to prayer; it is preparation for life.

C. *The twelve-year-old Jesus learned lessons on prayer while in Jerusalem for the Passover.* In the temple he heard the expressive prayer psalms but also the vain repetitions and meaningless ritual. He returned to Nazareth and continued to grow in maturity (Luke 2:52). The so-called "silent years" must have included much prayer to prepare him for his life's work. Prayer is the best preparation for life.

II. Prayer in the decisive days of service.

A. *Jesus' public ministry began with his baptism by John.* Luke preserves the significant observation that "Jesus also had been baptized and was praying" (Luke 3:21 RSV). Life's decisive moments are best bathed in prayer. How many efforts have crashed on the rocks of failure because we did not begin with prayer?

B. *In his humanity Jesus needed the strength of prayer.* He often withdrew to pray (Luke 4:42; 5:16). If Christ needed prayer, how much more do we? Where is our lovely place where we withdraw to fellowship with the Lord? Without prayer our resources will soon burn out, and we will be useless. Jesus spent a night in prayer before choosing the twelve disciples (6:12–16). Crucial decisions should be made with prayer.

III. Prayer to achieve life's purpose.

A. *The months soon passed, and Jesus set his face toward Jerusalem (Luke 9:51) for the concluding purpose of his earthly mission.* Prayer strengthened him for his sacrificial offering. The transfiguration occurred "as he was praying" (v. 29 RSV). The glory of eternity shone through, and in prayerful dialogue, Moses and Elijah spoke with Christ about his "departure" (v. 31 RSV) soon to come at Jerusalem. Later in the Garden of Gethsemane, Christ achieved victory as he prayed "not my will, but thine, be done" (22:42). None of us will face what Jesus did, but still we need prayer to achieve God's purpose in our lives.

B. *During the weeks leading toward the cross, the disciples asked Jesus to teach them how to pray.* He summarized in stark simplicity the basic content of prayer (Luke 11:2–4). He continued to encourage them to ask the Father simply about all their needs and trust him to respond (vv. 5–13).

Conclusion

Shortly before Jesus entered Jerusalem for that eventful week leading up to the resurrection, he reminded the disciples that "they ought always to pray and not lose heart" (Luke 18:1 RSV). He then posed the question, "When the Son of man comes, will he find faith on earth?" (v. 8 RSV). Will he find us praying? Prayer is the primary step of faith we take daily in our walk with the Lord. Most of us know enough about prayer: practice is the problem. The Master has taught us—now, will we pray?

SUNDAY MORNING, DECEMBER 26

Title: Therefore, Be It Resolved

Text: "Therefore, brethren, since we have confidence to enter the sanctuary by the blood of Jesus . . ." ***(Heb. 10:19 RSV).***

Scripture Reading: Hebrews 10:19–25

Hymns: "Love Divine, All Loves Excelling," Wesley
"I Am Resolved," Hartsough
"My Faith Looks Up to Thee," Palmer

Offertory Prayer: Good Father, in your goodness you have given us the gift of life and the gift of another new year. May we give our lives and this year to you, beginning with this offering. In the name of the one who makes all things new. Amen.

Introduction

Resolutions are abused realities. We make jokes about them, such as, "My only New Year's resolution is to make no New Year's resolutions." That is a shame, because something important is at stake. How do we make commitments? Are we faithful to our commitments? How do we keep them?

The author of the epistle to the Hebrews builds a marvelous case for four resolutions that I commend to you.

I. Whereas.

A. *Whereas "we have confidence to enter the sanctuary . . ."* In Jewish theology the presence of God was to be feared. Quite naturally, then, in Jewish piety there was a shrinking back from the presence of God and even from speaking the holy name. The Holy of Holies, which represented the presence of God, was covered so that persons could neither enter nor see into it. Only once a year, after elaborate rites of purification and precautions (such as tying a rope around his body in order to pull him out in case of death in the presence of God), could a priest enter into the Holy of Holies, and then only in fear and trembling.

In contrast, Christians proclaim that God can be not only approached, but approached with confidence. We approach the presence of God not only unafraid, but with eager anticipation and joy. Jesus spoke of God as "Father" with all of the connotations of intimacy and nearness.

B. *Whereas "what blocked our entry into the presence of God has been rent in two . . ."* Outside of the Holy of Holies was a veil. It covered the place that represented the presence of God. Its purpose was to keep people out. The Christian proclamation is that in the death of Jesus Christ, the curtain has been rent in two from top to bottom. This symbolizes, first, that God did it. Christianity is not about what we can do for ourselves; it is not about our search for God. Rather, the emphasis is on what God has done for us and God's search for us. We come to God not through moralism or mysticism, but through the death of the Son of God. The tearing of the veil from top to bottom symbolizes, second, that we can now enter into the presence of God. Because of the redemptive work of Jesus, we can enter into God's presence: the veil separating us and God has been torn apart.

C. *Whereas Jesus is our great High Priest . . .* The word priest means "bridge builder," which adequately describes the work of Christ. The bold proclamation of the gospel is that Jesus builds bridges of trust and love between humans and the Father. He is the Door, the Rent Curtain, the Way into the presence of God.

In Jesus we now know how much God loves us and all that he will do to redeem us. And it is Jesus' great love for us that draws us to him. The memory of his pierced hands pierces our hearts and draws us. If the cross will not make you come, nothing will. If the cross cannot make you feel welcome, nothing can.

II. Therefore, be it resolved.

The first parts of the resolutions are established: whereas "we have confidence to enter the sanctuary . . ."; whereas "what blocked our entry into the presence of God has been rent in two . . ."; whereas "Jesus is our great High Priest . . ." Now let us examine the endings.

A. *"Let us draw near to God" (v. 22 NIV).* Here we are reminded of the "duty" of worship. As Augustine so eloquently and succinctly put it, "The chief end of man is to glorify God and to enjoy him forever." There is also a word about the "opportunity" of worship. It is mind-boggling for a Jew to think that persons can boldly enter into the presence of God confidently and with joy. This is, indeed, a privilege we all too often take for granted.

Let us draw near to God "in full assurance of faith" (v. 22 NIV). Often a boy will not ask a particular girl out for a date because of the fear of rejection. This is a familiar fear for all. We do not have to worry about that with God. We can draw near to God in the full assurance of faith because Christmas is God's invitation. We are his delight, his joy.

We also draw near to God in the full assurance of forgiveness.

In 8:12 (NIV) the author describes God's forgiveness: "I will . . . remember their sins no more." God will not hold our sins against us. He forgives our sins and wipes the slate clean.

B. *"Let us hold unswervingly to the hope we profess" (v. 23 NIV).* God has been faithful to us; he has provided a way of salvation. Therefore we should keep the faith. It is not always an easy task, but it is the one we have been given to do.

C. *"Let us . . . spur one another on toward love and good deeds" (v. 24 NIV).* Through our words and our deeds, we are to help others. We need to be "encouragers," persons who put "courage into" others. Life is full of "discouragers," self-appointed "cold-water committees." We need encouragers. The name Barnabas means encouragement. It was Barnabas who first believed in Paul and led the others to trust him also. It was Barnabas who encouraged Paul to give John Mark another chance and took the young man himself on a missionary journey.

D. *"Let us not give up meeting together" (v. 25 NIV).* There is no such thing as "Lone Ranger Christianity." William Barclay wrote, "There is no man who can live the Christian life and neglect the fellowship of the church." There is no "secret discipleship." Coals in a group will burn brighter and longer and stay hotter. Sticks in a bundle are harder to break. Fellowship provides strength and energy, resolve and commitment. The church is a vitally necessary "hospital for sinners." To be absent is against your best interests.

Conclusion

God has kept his resolutions to us. He has allowed us to enter his presence, has granted us forgiveness, and has united us with him. All of this has been effected by the death of Christ.

Out of gratitude for all God has resolved, let us resolve to know him better by drawing near to him, keeping faithful, encouraging one another, and enjoying fellowship with the saints.

Sunday Evening, December 26

Title: The Secret to Encouragement

Text: "Now faith is the assurance of things hoped for, the conviction of things not seen" ***(Heb. 11:1 NASB).***

Scripture Reading: Hebrews 11:1–6

Introduction

Everyone needs encouragement from time to time; even the people found in Hebrews 11 did. The epistle to the Hebrews was written to persons struggling in their faith. They needed encouragement to face bitter trials and persecution. These believers needed to see the finality of Christ and follow him. They needed to understand the supremacy of Christ in revelation. They needed personal power just to live day by day. And they needed to respond to Christ in the proper spirit.

Hebrews 11 is the record of great faith. It inspires Christians to draw near to the Lord and stay near him. The secret of these saints' accomplishments in the will of God is their faith. Faith is necessary to become a Christian, and it is necessary to live the Christian life. Deepening our spiritual lives calls for a deepening of our faith. This chapter identifies great faith as the secret to encouragement. Five thoughts support this.

I. Great faith has a great God.

A. *Hebrews 11:6 states that the first fundamental fact of life is that "[God] is . . ."* The Bible does not argue the existence of God; it merely announces it and accepts it. Genesis 1:1 says, "In the beginning God . . ." This is what the Bible declares throughout its pages. It is a book of the experiences of people believing in God—God revealing, people responding.

B. *He is a great God, worthy of our faith.* New discoveries open the curtains to a greater revelation of God's greatness. The immensity of the cosmic system is awesome! The star Betelgeuse in the Orion constellation has a diameter of 270 million miles, which is three times the distance of our earth to the sun. Yet it is dwarfed by Alpha Hercules, a star so fantastically huge that if it occupied our sun's position, it would engulf the earth and extend beyond the orbit of Mars. About 3,500 stars are visible to the naked eye: 12,000 can be seen with good field glasses; and 1.5 billion can be seen with a powerful telescope. God is indeed great.

C. *He is a God of power, knowledge, and purpose.* He has a plan for the ages; his purpose is at work. The people in Hebrews 11 answered the call to faith in God's purpose. And this is the call that comes to us today—great faith in a great God!

II. Great faith has great trials.

A. *Abraham was called a "friend" of God (cf. 2 Chron. 20:7) and was commended for his great faith.* His deep trial of faith is recorded in Genesis 22. Isaac was the promised son and heir of God's promise to bless the nations. God told Abraham to offer him as a sacrifice. Abraham obeyed! The key to understanding his spirit is in his deep belief that God would raise Isaac up again (Heb. 11:19).

B. *This same God who lets us be tried will also fully provide for us.* First Corinthians 10:13 (NASB) says, "No temptation has overtaken you but such as is common to man; and God is faithful . . ." It is the picture of an army trapped in a pass, yet a way of escape is found. We are not sheltered from hardships, but God provides for us and never lets us go beyond his love and care.

III. Great faith has a great commitment.

A. *People of faith have intense commitment.* By faith Noah built an ark to save his family (Heb. 11:7). Faith motivated Abraham to be sent away from his home to an undisclosed land (v. 8). Moses' commitment of faith caused him to turn his back on power, prestige, and fame to dedicate himself to the afflicted people of God (vv. 24–27).

B. *Faith costs something!* Hebrews 12:1–2 says we are to lay aside the weights and the besetting sin of our lives to run with patience the race before us.

A young Christian attorney had staged a successful campaign to become a state senator. Having completed the necessary study for the practice of law, he felt that he could cope with any problem that might arise. During his first session in the senate, he was offered a sum of money to vote in favor of a bill.

In his hotel room he remembered his indebtedness. He still owed for part of his education; he had borrowed money to set up his practice; and he and his wife needed money for the expenses of a new baby. The sum offered would cover all his indebtedness and give him a nice bank account. But he was not in favor of the bill and had planned to vote against it.

Each time he felt he had reached a decision, he would remember the money. In desperation he knelt and prayed, "Dear God, help me to make the decision that you would have me to make." Taking his Bible, he found God's answer! He voted his conscience.

IV. Great faith has its rewards.

A. *Look at the results of great faith.* Abel offered a better sacrifice than Cain. Enoch was translated to see God. Noah was saved from the flood. Abraham's family was as innumerable as the stars of heaven and the sand of the seashore. Moses saw a nation liberated. Jesus was exalted and glorified.

B. *Whatever the cost, faith is worth it all.* At age twenty-four, George Beverly Shea auditioned at CBS with the Lynn Murray singers and was offered a job. He had to make a decision. Rhea F. Miller's poem "I'd Rather Have Jesus" kept ringing in his ears, and he told CBS, "I had better stay where I am." Later he came to know why. He was soon led to Chicago where he met Billy Graham and became a key figure in his evangelistic ministry.

V. Great faith has great inspiration.

A. *We can be inspired to greater faith in only one way.* It is by "looking unto Jesus the author and the finisher of our faith" (Heb. 12:1–2). His example of faith, as seen in the cross and its shame, is great encouragement to any believer.

B. *Here is a modern-day example to show why God inspires us in our faith.* When Alexander Maclaren was sixteen, he had a job near Glasgow, six miles from the city. To go to work, he had to walk through a deep ravine that was supposed to be haunted. He was afraid to walk there in the daylight. At night it was out of the question. But his father told him to come home as fast as he could one Saturday night.

He obeyed. He whistled, he cried—he was terrified. Fear was in his heart. He started to run when he heard footsteps up the ravine. Surely his life was over! But out of the darkness into the pale light came the head and shoulders of the grandest man on earth—his father.

God asks us to have faith to accomplish the impossible because he is there with us. This is our inspiration.

Conclusion

Jesus Christ is our encouragement. The secret to experiencing his presence and power is faith. Respond to him in faith and receive the strength of encouragement.

WEDNESDAY EVENING, DECEMBER 29

Title: Prayers for the Coming Year
Text: "Pray without ceasing" ***(1 Thess. 5:17).***
Scripture Reading: Matthew 6:5–13

Introduction

In our text the apostle Paul encourages the believers in Thessalonica to develop the habit of praying and then not to break that habit.

As we approach the beginning of a new year, we can most appropriately and profitably spend some time in earnest prayer. It is suggested that we let some saints who were poets lead us in this time of prayer. Many of the hymns and songs in our hymnal take the form of earnest, fervent prayers. Let us join together on this last Wednesday evening of the year in singing some prayers to our Lord.

I. Let our lives sing a prayer of adoration and consecration.

Fanny J. Crosby would lead us in praying:

> I am Thine, O Lord, I have heard Thy voice,
> And it told Thy love to me;
> But I long to rise in the arms of faith,
> And be closer drawn to Thee.
>
> Consecrate me now to Thy service, Lord,

By the pow'r of grace divine;
Let my soul look up with a steadfast hope,
And my will be lost in Thine.

Draw me nearer, nearer, nearer, blessed Lord,
To the cross where Thou hast died;
Draw me nearer, nearer, nearer, blessed Lord,
To Thy precious, bleeding side.

II. Let our lives sing a prayer regarding Bible study for the coming year.

All of us need to spend some time with God's Word each day to grow spiritually (Josh. 1:8). Mary A. Lathbury voices for us a prayer that is appropriate when we open up God's Word and read.

Break Thou the bread of life, dear Lord, to me,
As Thou didst break the loaves beside the sea;
Beyond the sacred page I seek Thee, Lord;
My spirit pants for Thee, O Living Word.

Bless Thou the truth, dear Lord, to me, to me,
As Thou didst bless the bread by Galilee;
Then shall all bondage cease. All fetters fall;
And I shall find my peace, my all in all.

O send Thy Spirit, Lord, now unto me,
That He may touch my eyes, and make me see;
Show me the truth concealed within Thy Word,
And in Thy book revealed I see the Lord.

III. Let our lives sing a prayer for spiritual illumination.

Only God can open our eyes and help us see spiritual reality. Clara H. Scott wrote a prayer to God for us at this point.

Open my eyes, that I may see,
Glimpses of truth Thou hast for me;
Place in my hands the wonderful key
That shall unclasp, and set me free;
Silently now I wait for Thee,
Ready, my God, Thy will to see;
Open my eyes, illumine me, Spirit divine!

Open my ears, that I may hear
Voices of truth Thou sendest clear;
And while the wave-notes fall on my ear,

Ev'rything false will disappear;
Silently now I wait for Thee,
Ready, my God, Thy will to see;
Open my ears, illumine me, Spirit divine!

IV. Let our lives sing a prayer to the Master Teacher regarding prayer.

Our Lord's disciples requested not that he teach them how to preach or to teach, but to pray. He is the perfect model and Master Teacher at this point. Albert Reitz voices our prayer for help.

Teach me to pray, Lord, teach me to pray;
This is my heart-cry day unto day;
I long to know Thy will and Thy way;
Teach me to pray, Lord, teach me to pray.

Power in prayer, Lord, power in prayer!
Here 'mid earth's sin and sorrow and care,
Men lost and dying, souls in despair;
O give me power, power in prayer!

My weakened will, Lord, Thou canst renew;
My sinful nature Thou canst subdue;
Fill me just now with power anew;
Power to pray and power to do!

V. Let our lives sing a prayer of commitment to personal witnessing.

A man named Leon Tucker prayed the first stanza of the prayer that we will pray, asking our Lord to lay upon us a new and deeper concern for the souls of the lost about us. With all sincerity let us join in this prayer.

Lord, lay some soul upon my heart,
And love that soul through me;
And may I bravely do my part
To win that soul for Thee.

Lord, lead me to some soul in sin,
And grant that I may be
Endued with power and love to win
That soul, dear Lord, for Thee.

To win that soul for Thee alone
Will be my constant prayer;
That when I've reached the great white throne,
I'll meet that dear one there.

Some soul for Thee, some soul for Thee,
This is my earnest plea;
Help me each day, on life's highway,
To win some soul for Thee.

VI. Let our lives sing a prayer of personal commitment to our Savior as we face the coming year.

Take my life, and let it be
consecrated, Lord, to Thee;
Take my hands, and let them move
At the impulse of Thy love,
At the impulse of Thy love.

Take my feet, and let them be
Swift and beautiful for Thee;
Take my voice, and let me sing
Always, only, for my King,
Always, only, for my King.

Take my silver and my gold,
Not a mite would I withhold;
Take my moments and my days,
Let them flow in ceaseless praise,
Let them flow in ceaseless praise.

Take my will, and make it Thine,
It shall be no longer mine;
Take my heart, it is Thine own,
It shall be Thy royal throne,
It shall be Thy royal throne.

—*Frances R. Havergal*

VII. Let our lives sing a song of faith for the new year.

Ours is not a dead Christ. He is alive from the dead to be our Leader and our King as we face the coming year. Let us rejoice as we respond to his living presence. Ernest W. Shurtleff wrote a prayer of triumphant faith.

Lead on, O King Eternal,
The day of march has come;
Henceforth in fields of conquest
Thy tents shall be our home:
Through days of preparation
Thy grace has made us strong.
And now, O King Eternal,

We lift our battle song.

Lead on, O King Eternal,
Till sin's fierce war shall cease,
And holiness shall whisper
The sweet amen of peace;
For not with swords' loud clashing
Nor roll of stirring drums;
With deeds of love and mercy,
The heav'nly kingdom comes.

Lead on, O King Eternal,
We follow, not with fears;
For gladness breaks like morning
Where-e'er Thy face appears;
Thy cross is lifted o'er us;
We journey in its light;
The crown awaits the conquest;
Lead on, O God of might.

Conclusion

When we pray, we let God come into our lives to help us. We also dedicate ourselves to helping him with his work in the world. Let us rejoice because of the year that is ahead of us.

Miscellaneous Helps

Messages on the Lord's Supper

Title: The New Covenant
Text: "This cup is the new covenant in my blood, which is poured out for you" ***(Luke 22:20 NIV).***
Scripture Reading: Luke 22:14–22

Introduction

Several covenants are mentioned in the Old Testament. One that we will examine today was made at Sinai when God gave Moses not only the Ten Commandments, but the extended legislation that we call the "book of the covenant." The other covenant we will look at was promised by Jeremiah and became a reality in the life, death, and resurrection of Jesus.

I. The old covenant.

A. *When God brought the Israelites out from Egypt, he led them across the Red Sea and then to Mount Sinai.* There they stayed for about eighteen months as God, through Moses, outlined his commandments for their way of life. More than four hundred years previously he had promised Abraham that all the world would be blessed through his seed.

The covenant of law, however, was interposed until the promise became a reality through the coming of the Savior.

B. *Part of the covenant was the sacrificial system.* The major sacrifice was the once-a-year occasion when the high priest went into the Holy of Holies and offered a sacrifice for the people.

II. The new covenant.

God revealed to the prophet Jeremiah a truth that he passed on to the people. God would, in the future, make a new covenant with the nation. It would be based on God's inward presence, not on external observances. The fundamental basis of it would be that God would forgive their sins.

III. Jesus fulfilled this prophecy.

A. *When Jesus sat down with the disciples for his last Passover, he instituted a new ordinance—the Memorial Supper.* He knew that he would go to the cross the next day to die for our sins. His heart was heavy as he told his disciples that the fruit of the vine he poured for them represented his blood. They did not understand. But as we look back at Calvary and the resurrection, we see what they were not yet able to comprehend.

B. *The writer of Hebrews presents Jesus as the one who is the "better" High Priest.* Whereas the high priest under the old covenant offered sacrifices every year, Jesus "offered one sacrifice for sins for ever" (Heb. 10:12). The Memorial Supper speaks of that redeeming work.

Of course, people in Old Testament days were not saved by the sacrifice of animals. They were saved by believing in God's provision for them. Thus, people then were saved by faith as we are now. Though they did not understand all the implications of the sacrificial system, they were justified when they accepted God's plan in that day. One poet said it beautifully:

Not all the blood of bulls and beasts
On Jewish altars slain
Could give the guilty sinner peace
Or take away the stain.

But Christ, the Heavenly Lamb
Takes all our guilt away,
A sacrifice of nobler name
And richer blood than they.

—*Isaac Watts*

Under the old covenant, the sheep died for the shepherd, but under the new covenant, the Shepherd died for the sheep.

Conclusion

Those who observe the Memorial Supper should do so with grateful hearts and fresh resolves. We can be saved only once, but we can reaffirm our faith and should do so periodically. Remember, the blood represents the life. Since Christ gave his blood for us, this means he gave his life for us. We, too, should gratefully give our life in service for him.

Title: Seeing the Savior in Symbol

Text: "For as often as ye eat this bread, and drink this cup, ye do shew the Lord's death till he come" ***(1 Cor. 11:26).***

Scripture Reading: 1 Corinthians 11:23–26

Introduction

Some people can see only the facts; they never see the meaning behind the facts. Some can see only the literal; they never see the symbolic, the truth behind the literal. Jesus spoke often in symbols. He called himself the Door, the Light of the World, and the Truth. He told many stories to illustrate spiritual truth. The prodigal son and the good Samaritan are outstanding examples of spiritual truth through stories.

Because Jesus returned to his heavenly Father, he left us a beautiful picture of his atoning work. We call it by several names. Perhaps the best description is "Memorial Supper," for this is exactly what it is, a service in which we call to mind the most important act Jesus did for us. Though we see the Savior symbolically in many places and in many ways, the picture we have of him in this observance tells us the fundamental truths about him and his work. Three important things about our Savior are present in these verses.

I. He died for us.

A. *One outstanding scholar called Isaiah 53 the "heart of the Old Testament."* This was because it foretold the sufferings of Christ for our sins in a vivid way.

B. *Likewise, the accounts of the death of Christ should be called the "heart of the New Testament."* When Jesus died on the cross, he fulfilled all the prophecies about the coming atonement—both those uttered vocally and those foreshadowed in symbols through the sacrificial system.

Of all the attempts to explain the event, I like the words of the one who wrote, "Jesus paid it all; all to him I owe." A little girl came home from Sunday school and asked her daddy, "Is there anything God cannot do?" He replied, "No, I guess not." She said, "Yes, one thing. He cannot see my sins when they are washed in the blood of Jesus Christ."

II. He arose from the grave.

A. *Although the fact that Jesus rose from the grave is not stated directly in the Corinthians passage, it is certainly implied, as Paul spoke of Christ's coming again as part of the symbolism.* The resurrection of the Savior from the grave was the one event that proved his death was a part of God's plan. When God raised Jesus from the dead, he placed his approval on the atoning death. One religion requires its devotees to travel at least once in their lifetime to the grave of their founder and worship at that spot. Christianity makes no such demand—the Savior is not dead.

B. *The Savior is not dead.* He is alive forevermore. The importance of this truth cannot be overemphasized. A minister stood by the garden tomb conducting a religious service, and he made this striking statement: "If Jesus Christ did not rise from the grave, nothing matters. But if he did arise, nothing else matters!"

III. He is coming again.

A. *When Jesus comes the next time, he will receive his children to himself, and he will judge the wicked.* The first time Jesus came he died; the second time he comes he will pronounce a sentence of death against those who have rejected him.

B. *A young man was arrested for a small violation.* He employed an attorney and was acquitted. Years later he committed a serious crime. When the case came to trial, the man saw his former attorney sitting as judge. He said to him, "You remember me, don't you? You helped set me free years ago. You'll help me again, won't you?" The judge replied, "Things are different now. Then, I was your counselor. Today I am your judge." Christ wants to be your Savior now and plead your case before the Father. If you refuse, he will one day stand as your Judge.

Conclusion

What do you see when you eat the bread and drink the wine? Rather than divide ourselves over the nature of the Memorial Supper, Christians should unite around its central meaning. The one who knew no sin was made to be sin for us that we might become righteous in God's sight. The more this truth grips us, the greater will be our motivation for service.

MESSAGES FOR CHILDREN AND YOUNG PEOPLE

Title: What Do You Have?
Text: "What is that in thine hand?" ***(Ex. 4:2).***
Scripture Reading: Exodus 4:1–9

Introduction

One day while Moses was tending sheep in a desolate part of the country, God spoke to him from a burning bush, saying that he had a great task for him: Moses was to lead his nation out of Egypt and slavery. When Moses protested, thinking he was not skilled enough, God asked him to throw the stick in his hands on the ground. It became a snake. God then performed other miracles to convince Moses he would be with him.

We all at times feel unsure about our abilities. We need to remember that God has equipped us with things "in our hand" to help us. They are talents we can use to make our lives happy and successful. We should use them for God.

I. Our personalities are in our hands.

A. *We should use our personalities for God.* Years ago a minister was walking in the business section of a large city one evening. He passed by a night club where people drank alcohol and watched lewd entertainment. He saw a man with a smile and marvelous outgoing personality inviting people inside. The minister said to himself. "That person could render a great service for God if he could become a Christian." Later he led the man to Jesus, and the man joined his church.

In time the man became the chief usher for the church and used his personality to greet the people as they came to worship, especially making visitors feel welcome.

B. *God has gifted us.* Our personalities can be evil or righteous. God can work in us toward greater righteousness.

II. Our time is in our hands.

A. *A number of years ago a man wrote a book titled* How to Live on Twenty-Four Hours a Day. In it, he said that we all have at least one thing in common: We have twenty-four hours each day. In those hours we have time to do the things we really want to do. Did you ever hear someone say, "I don't have time to do that"? What that person really meant was that he wanted to do something else more than he wanted to do that thing.

B. *A wise man once said, "Do not squander time, for it is the stuff life is made of."* If you waste one year as a young person by failing to get your education at the right time, it may cost you three or four years later when you try to get it as an older person. Jesus said, "As long as it is day, we must do the work of him who sent me. Night is coming, when no one can work" (John 9:4 NIV). Years ago a young man worked at translating a book from Latin into English during the three-minute period he waited for his breakfast coffee to boil each day. We need to use every moment of our time wisely.

III. Our example is in our hands.

A. *Even if we cannot do big things, we can do little things well.* Our quiet, good life may help some people we do not even know about as they struggle with decisions.

B. *A preacher delivered a forty-minute sermon one day, and at the close of it a grown man came down the aisle, accepted Jesus, and joined the church.* Later the preacher asked the man, "What did I say that caused you to make your decision for Jesus Christ?" The man replied, "I didn't hear but a few words you said this morning. I was looking most of the time at that little lady about two pews in front of me. She has been a great example for me, helping me several times when I had difficulty. I decided I wanted to be a Christian and try to help others as she has helped me."

Conclusion

You may have other things to give either to God or to the wicked ways of this world. The decision is yours. A great national leader once delivered a message to his countrymen, telling how good God had been to them. He concluded by saying, "Choose . . . this day whom ye will serve . . . as for me and my house, we will serve the Lord" (Josh. 24:15).

Title: Bad Bargains
Text: "For what is a man profited, if he shall gain the whole world, and lose his own soul? or what shall a man give in exchange for his soul?" ***(Matt. 16:26).***
Scripture Reading: Matthew 16:26

Introduction

Many people like to shop at sales. There is something exciting about getting a good deal. But there can be a problem with this quest for saving money. Sometimes what we think is a bargain is not a bargain at all. Sometimes stores mark up the prices, then take off a percentage of the new heightened price. Those bargains may not be nearly as good as we think they are!

Young people have many decisions to make. We must be careful that we do not make bad bargains by making foolish choices. Let me suggest a few.

I. We should never exchange divine truth for the devil's trash.

A. *The Bible is God's Word for us.* We should begin the habit of reading the Bible daily early in life. Some groups have planned reading programs to guide people in choosing the passages they wish to read. Some people, though, may prefer to map out their own program. This is good—if they will do it—but following a program designed by people who are familiar with the Bible may be better at first.

B. *At first we may wish to read merely for inspiration.* Later we can use good commentaries to help us understand deeper truths. When a Bible passage's background is known, we can gain even greater insight. The important thing, however, is to read the Bible. It is wise not to let our secular reading usurp the time spent in the Word.

II. We should never exchange high standards of living for low standards.

A. *Because God loves us, he challenges us to be like him, and he is holy.* God knows that if we will keep our bodies clean and our conduct proper, we will have a much better chance of succeeding in life.

B. *Paul told young Timothy, "Keep thyself pure" (1 Tim. 5:22).* He explained further, "Flee . . . youthful lusts . . . follow righteousness" (2 Tim. 2:22). A store that dealt with used merchandise put a suit on display with a sign that read: "Slightly Soiled, Reduced in Value." What a lesson for us! A life that is stained even a little by sin is crippled for the encounters and struggles of life.

III. We should never exchange faith for fear.

A. *Of course, we ought always to be careful about things that can hurt.* Perhaps we should fear them. We should be afraid of loaded guns, speeding cars, and hateful attitudes. To face the future, however, always expecting the worst to happen, is not a healthy way to live.

B. *How should you face things you fear?* Someone says, "Have courage," but that is not the best way. The best way is to have faith! If you remember nothing else in this message, let me suggest you memorize this sentence: The opposite of fear is not courage; it is faith. God has promised to take care of us if we trust him. We should be careful in every way and try to take care of ourselves, of course; but when we cannot conquer the foes that wait for us, God will either do it for us or give us the strength to do it. Trust him. He will not fail!

IV. We should never substitute our good deeds for the righteousness of Jesus Christ.

A. *God sent his Son to die on the cross to save us from our sins.* We do not become Christians by trying to do more good things than bad things.

B. *Though we should try to live right, we cannot be good enough to save ourselves.* One becomes a Christian by saying to Jesus: "I am sorry for my sins and will do my best to forsake them. However, I will accept you as my Savior and let you deal with the guilt of my sins. You can write my name in the Lamb's Book of Life, for I have accepted you personally as Lord of my life and forgiver of my sins."

Conclusion

Do not ever trade the best for the worst. In fact, do not even swap the best for the mere good. That is a bad bargain. Accept the most expensive gift of Christ's death for you at no cost. His free gift is the best bargain of all.

Funeral Meditations

Title: What Jesus Says to the Troubled
Text: "Let not your hearts be troubled . . . believe" ***(John 14:1).***
Scripture Reading: John 14:1–6

Introduction

The disciples sat with Jesus around a table in the upper room. They had finished the Passover; Jesus had instituted the Memorial Supper. In a few minutes they would leave the house, walk down the mountain, cross the Kidron Valley, and ascend the Mount of Olives to the Garden of Gethsemane. Jesus knew what awaited him, but his heart ached for his disciples. He realized that the Shepherd would be slaughtered and the sheep would be scattered. Though the burden of his own soul was great, he focused on their needs.

Jesus always has a word for those who find it difficult to cope with tragedies. One of the hardest traumas we face, of course, is the death of a loved one. Christ's words to his followers, therefore, reach us with a firm grip at this particular time.

I. Have faith in God.

A. *Every devout Jew believed in God.* Long ago they had been purified from the pagan view of many gods. To them, the one who delivered their fathers from Egyptian bondage was the supreme fact of life. Most of us—perhaps all—believe in God. Probably we have no atheists among us. The familiar saying during World War II, "There are no atheists in foxholes," might be expanded to include funerals also.

B. *A token belief in a higher power, however, is not enough.* Jesus came to reveal God as a warm, compassionate Father, who, though he hates sin, loves sinners. He calls us to accept him as God's only begotten Son, the Bread of Life, Water of Life, Light of the World, and greatest of all, the Resurrection and the Life. A minister stood beside the Garden Tomb, where many believe Jesus was buried, and said, "If Jesus did not arise from the grave, nothing matters, but if he did arise, nothing else matters."

II. Have faith in heaven.

A. *God promises many things to the believer in this life.* His supreme blessing for us, however, is a heavenly home. We must never allow anyone to minimize this hope. Modern skeptics enjoy ridiculing those who believe in heaven by calling it "pie in the sky." They say we have no business thinking about it too much. According to them, we have all we can do to properly manage things on earth and should live only one world at a time. C. S. Lewis dealt with this attitude in a marvelous way. He said, "We are afraid of the jeer about 'pie in the sky' and of being told that we are trying to escape from the duty of making a happy world here and now into dreams of a happy world elsewhere. But either there is 'pie in the sky' or there is not. If there is not, Christianity is false. . . . If there is, then this truth, like any other must be faced."

B. *Though Jesus did not tell us many details about heaven, he affirmed unquestionably its existence.* An aged saint said, "I am not nearly as sure about the details of heaven as I was earlier in life, but I am far more certain about its fact." Jesus wisely refused to satisfy the curious minds about the technical aspects of our eternal home. Our dull spirits and limited minds could not comprehend the greatness of the things God has provided for us. Let us, however, face the death of our loved ones with a firm faith in God's provision for those who have loved and served him.

III. Have faith in his second coming.

A. *Closely connected with our heavenly home is the blessed hope that Jesus will come again personally and make our salvation complete.* Our loved ones have gone to be with the Lord now: the Bible does not teach "soul sleeping." Those who have gone on are now with the Lord.

The lights are all out in the mansion of clay;
The curtains are drawn for the dweller's away.
He silently slipped o'er the threshold by night
To make his abode in the city of light.

—*Anonymous*

B. *God has not revealed to us the nature of the afterlife.* Paul spoke of death as the way "to depart, and to be with Christ" (Phil. 1:23). He encouraged us by saying that, though we are absent from the body, we are "present with the Lord" (2 Cor. 5:8). These expressions assure us we shall have a conscious life. The great event, however, will be when Jesus Christ comes and those who have gone on earlier shall come with him. At that time, they and the living Christians shall all receive their resurrection bodies. What a glorious day! Have faith in that promise and never forsake it, doubt it, or minimize it!

Conclusion

Death is a form of Christ's coming, for he comes to receive us and take us to himself. Our belief in life after death gives meaning to our present life. Faith is the difference between despair and delight, between hopelessness and hilarity, between tears and triumph.

Title: The Close of a Beautiful Life
Text: "I have fought a good fight, I have finished my course, I have kept the faith" ***(2 Tim. 4:7).***
Scripture Reading: 2 Timothy 4:6–8

Introduction

Sunsets thrill us; they represent the end of a day. If the sunset is beautiful, the day was probably also a lovely one. Lew Sarret writes:

God is at the anvil beating out the sun.
Where the molten metal spills,
At His forge among the hills
He has hammered out the glory of a day that's done.

There is another phenomenon, however, that is more beautiful than a sunset: the sunset of a person's life when it has been lived in harmony with God's will.

Paul had come to the end of his life. He knew he was facing death, but he wrote about it with a glowing testimony of faith. He mentioned three things about his pilgrimage that he knew were true. Each of them suggests a quality that God glorifies in a life.

I. "I have fought a good fight" suggests quality.

A. *Paul had a dedicated spirit.* He would not accept any compromise that lowered the standard of Christian morality. We need this characteristic today. The most important aspect about a life is not how great it is in the eyes of the world, but how great it is in the eyes of God.

B. *Quality should be the goal of every person.* In an airplane factory, a large sign was placed that could be seen by all the workers. It said, "We build airplanes here. We build them inexpensively if possible, but we build good airplanes."

II. "I have finished my course" suggests patience.

A. *The origin of the word* patience *is interesting.* It means literally "to bear under." In modern usage *patience* means to stay at a job and persevere until it is completed successfully. This trait is essential to fulfill one's mission at any task. When William Pitt was prime minister of England, someone asked him what was the most important personal requirement for his job. He replied, "Patience." The person then asked what was the second most important requirement. Pitt said, "Patience." The third? "Patience."

B. *A person with patience has an advantage in accomplishing a task.* Elizabeth Barrett Browning said, "I worked with patience which almost means power." Jerrold Douglas said that patience "kills the great giant Despair," and James Russell Lowell said, "Endurance is the crowning quality . . . patience all the passion of great hearts." In the sonnet of his blindness, John Milton first lamented his inability to see. He then turned to speak of the other side, saying, "Patience, to prevent that rumor soon replies. . . . They also serve who only stand and wait." Thomas Edison showed patience when he replied to his assistant who complained of their several hundred experimental failures, "We know many things that do not work. Now let's find one that does work."

III. "I have kept the faith" suggests trustworthiness.

A. *In one of the races of ancient Greece, each contestant was given a lighted torch.* The object was not to get to the finish line first, but to get there with the torch still lit. Life is like that! The goal is not to accrue wealth or to achieve success as the world counts it.

B. *What does it matter though we get these things if we let the light of character go out?* A commencement speaker told a group of graduates, "Be careful that you do not place too much value on material success or worldly fame, because if you do, you may some day meet a man who cares nothing for them. You will then realize how poor you are." The academicians at the university where David Livingstone received an honorary degree had a favorite custom. They booed the recipient to show their disrespect for the school conferring the honor on someone who had not achieved in book learning. When the degree was bestowed on him, however, they saw a life of trustworthiness and dedication with which they could not argue. They stood and cheered.

Conclusion

These characteristics come from a life that is motivated by Jesus Christ. Worldly aims cannot inspire such living. Jesus Christ can. Being a Christian is more than accepting certain historical facts about Jesus; it involves committing ourselves to his lordship. When these things have become a part of us, our life's end will also be a beautiful sunset.

Title: God Supplies Our Need
Text: "My God will supply every need of yours according to his riches in glory in Christ Jesus" ***(Phil. 4:19 RSV).***
Scripture Reading: Psalm 23:1–6; 90:1–2; 91:1

Introduction

We never are ready for the loss of a loved one. Sometimes those we love die quickly; often they linger for a long time. Sometimes, seeing their suffering, we know deep in our hearts that it is far better for them to "depart and be with Christ" (cf. Phil. 1:23). Yet when the moment comes for them to leave the body, we find that we are not ready for it.

Yet death comes to all. It comes to the aged as they walk on faltering feet. Its summons is heard by those who have scarcely traveled half the journey of life; sometimes it even hushes the laughter of little children. The Scripture says that "it is appointed unto men once to die" (Heb. 9:27).

As in all situations, God's Word has a message for us when the family circle is broken or when a friend goes to be with the Lord. In a "love letter" to his Philippian friends, Paul said many helpful things but none more assuring than "My God shall supply all your need according to his riches in glory by Christ Jesus" (4:19). Let me elaborate with three simple thoughts.

I. Your need.

A. *You and I are needy people.* From the womb to the tomb we stand in need of help from each other and from God. Though we hear the word *independent* used often, no one is truly independent. We all need each other.

B. *The greatest need we have, however, is to answer the mystery of life and death.* No one understands death. In fact, no one understands life. I looked at dictionary definitions once and was amazed to find that life is defined as the "absence of death" while death is defined as "the absence of life." That does not help very much, does it? To us, death means a loved one has gone and emptiness has overtaken us.

We need help. We are wise to admit the need rather than to try to imagine it does not exist.

II. God will supply that need.

A. *How marvelous that we have friends to aid us in our time of need.* They help tremendously. Where would we be without our friends? Shakespeare said, "The friends thou hast and their adoption tried, grapple them to thy soul with hoops of steel." Oliver Wendell Holmes wrote:

> Fame is a scentless sunflower
> with a gaudy crown of gold.
> But friendship is a breathing rose
> with sweets in every fold.

Friends are indeed wonderful and helpful. They bring food to the home, send flowers to the funeral parlor, speak kind words, and try in every way to help meet the need.

B. *With all due respect and appreciation for our friends, however, ultimately only one person can supply our need to deal with death.* According to Pascal, a God-shaped vacuum exists in every heart. Only our divine heavenly Father can fill it. We are made for God, and we are restless until we rest in him. We need to remember in our times of grief that God still loves us and does all things well. John Greenleaf Whittier said so beautifully:

> I know not what the future holds
> Of marvel or surprise,
> Assured alone that life and death
> God's mercy underlies.
>
> And if my heart and flesh are weak
> To bear the untried pain,
> The bruised reed He will not break
> But strengthen and sustain.
>
> And so beside the silent sea
> I wait the muffled oar;
> No harm from Him can come to me
> On ocean or on shore.
>
> I know not where His islands lift
> Their fronded palms in air;
> I only know I cannot drift
> Beyond His Love and care.

Oh, brothers, if my faith is vain,
If hopes like these betray,
Pray for me that feet may gain
The sure and safer way.

And Thou, O Lord, by whom are seen
Thy creatures as they be,
Forgive me if too close I lean
My human heart on Thee.

God alone can supply the need that we have at this time in our lives.

III. He does it through Christ.

A. *What method does God use to meet our need?* He is not some vague, abstract, nebulous First Cause or Unmoved Mover. Rather, he comes to us by his warm, personal presence in Jesus Christ. Years ago a philosopher said, "If there is a God, we wish that he would give us some word about himself to take away the darkness from our eyes." John had the reply: "In the beginning was the Word . . . and the Word was made flesh and dwelt among us" (John 1:1, 14).

B. *In this message from God in the form of his Son, we have the answers to problems that haunt our souls.* Only Jesus has conquered death and has the authority to say, "Because I live, ye shall live also" (John 14:19).

Conclusion

Today is a time to reevaluate all of our priorities. God meets our needs, but he also challenges us to take a fresh look at our lives. The way our loved one has gone, we too shall go some day, perhaps sooner than we think. God calls on us to comfort one another and seek to continue the ministry of compassion and intercession that he began when he was on earth.

WEDDINGS

Title: Marriage Ceremony

Holy and happy is the sacred hour when two devoted hearts are bound by the enchanting ties of matrimony. Marriage is an institution of divine appointment and is commended as honorable among all men. Marriage is God's first institution for the welfare of the race. In the quiet of Eden, before the forbidden tree had yielded its fruit or Satan had touched the world, God saw that it was not good for the man to be alone. He made a helpmate suitable for Adam and established the rite of marriage while heavenly hosts witnessed the wonderful scene in reverence.

The contract of marriage was also sanctioned and honored by the presence and power of Jesus at the marriage in Cana of Galilee and marked the beginning of his wondrous works. It is declared by the apostle Paul to be honorable among all people. So it is ordained that a man shall leave his father and mother and cleave unto his wife, and they shall be one flesh, united in hopes and aims and sentiments until death alone shall part them.

If you, then, ______ (Groom) and ______ (Bride), after careful consideration, in the fear of God, have deliberately chosen each other as partners in this holy estate, and know of no just cause why you should not be united, in token thereof you will please join your right hands.

Groom's Vow

______, will you have this woman to be your wedded wife, to live together after God's ordinance in the holy estate of matrimony? Will you love her, comfort her, honor her, and keep her in sickness and in health, and forsaking all others keep yourself only unto her so long as you both shall live?

Groom: I will.

Bride's Vow

______, will you have this man to be your wedded husband, to live together after God's ordinance in the holy estate of matrimony? Will you love him, honor him, and keep him in sickness and in health, and forsaking all others keep yourself only unto him so long as you both shall live?

Bride: I will.

Vows to Each Other

I, ______, take thee, ______, to be my wedded wife, to have and to hold from this day forward, in prosperity or adversity, in sickness or in health, in advances or reverses, to love and to cherish till death do us part, according to God's holy ordinance, and thereto I pledge thee my faith.

I, ______, take thee, ______, to be my wedded husband, to have and to hold from this day forward, in prosperity or adversity, in sickness or in health, in advances or reverses, to love and to cherish till death do us part, according to God's holy ordinance, and thereto I pledge thee my faith.

Then each belongs to the other for richer or poorer, for better or worse, in sickness and in health, till death alone shall part you.

From time immemorial, the ring has been used to seal important covenants. The golden circlet, most prized jewel, has come to its loftiest altar. Its untarnishable material is of the purest gold. Even so may your love for each other be pure and may it grow brighter and brighter as time goes by. The ring is a circle, thus having no end. Even so may there be no end to the happiness and success that come to you as you unite your lives together.

Do you, ______, give this ring to your wedded wife as a token of your love for her?

Will you, ______, take this ring as a token of your wedded husband's love for you, and will you wear it as a token of your love for him?

Do you, ______, give this ring to your wedded husband as a token of your love for him?

Will you, ______, take this ring as a token of your wedded wife's love for you, and will you wear it as a token of your love for her?

Having pledged your faith in love to each other in the sight of God and these assembled witnesses, and having sealed your solemn marital vows by giving and receiving the rings, acting with the authority vested in me as a minister of the gospel by this state, and looking to heaven for divine sanction, I pronounce you husband and wife.

What God hath joined together, let not man put asunder.

Prayer

Title: A Wedding Ceremony

Tonight is a very special night. It is a time that many have looked forward to with great anticipation. We have come to unite in marriage ______ and ______.

The marriage relationship was conceived by God and is thus subject to his purpose, direction, and discipline. The most meaningful and fulfilling of all human encounters, it is more than a civil contract. Rather, it is an intimate, soul-searching experience. Marriage requires the utmost in patience. Kindness and sincerity must pervade every part of the marriage if happiness is to come to this new endeavor.

Marriage is a sacred calling, uniting two members of separate families into the creation of a new and unique family. A oneness is established as man finds his helpmate and woman finds her loving companion who will cherish her as his own self.

Since, as we have said, marriage is God's ordinance, and since this is God's house, I am going to ask that we bow in prayer and ask God's blessing upon the uniting of these two to be husband and wife.

Prayer by the minister, followed by the question: Who gives ______ to be married to ______?

Father (or one giving away the bride): I do. *(If the one giving away the bride wishes, he may say, "Her mother and I.") After this, he will be seated in the audience, probably with the bride's mother unless there are reasons why he should sit elsewhere.*

The time when two devoted hearts come to be bound by the enchanting ties of matrimony is a holy and happy moment. These tokens of joy are made more nearly perfect when the bride and groom come to this time with reverence, humility, and faith. Marriage began when God spoke the marriage words in the garden of Eden. Jesus honored it by attending a wedding early in his ministry. Paul put his full approval on it: he commanded the husband to love his wife as Christ loves the church, and the wife to submit to her husband in all things.

You two have come to me signifying your desire to be united in marriage. If that is now your intention, please join right hands for your vows. *They join right hands.*

______, in taking ______ to be your lawful wife, I require you to promise to love her, care for her, and in every way help her to become her best self until death shall part you. Do you so promise?

Groom: I do.

______, in taking ______ to be your lawful husband, I require you to promise to love him, care for him, and in every way help him to become his best self until death shall part you. Do you so promise?

Bride: I do.

May I have the ring(s).

Through the centuries, the ring has been used to seal important covenants. In the past, the great seal of state was often worn by the king on a ring. Its stamp signified royal authority. Friends have exchanged simple bands of gold to signify goodwill. Today, at the marriage altar, the golden ring has come to its loftiest significance. Two things stand out in symbolism. Untarnishable material—the purest gold—and unique form—the never-ending circle—combine to symbolize the qualities of the ideal marital state.

______, will you give this ring to ______ as a symbol of your love for her?

Groom: I will.

______, will you receive this ring from ______ as a symbol of his love for you, and will you wear it as a symbol of your love for him?

Bride: I will.

This may be repeated in reverse for a double ring ceremony.

You will please rejoin right hands.

Having pledged your faith in and love to each other and having sealed your vows by giving and receiving the ring(s), and looking to heaven for divine approval, you are now husband and wife. Shall we pray?

The wedding party may wish to add a unity candle service or other things to enrich the service for them personally.

Title: A Small Home Wedding

The home, first of all institutions, was established by God. In the beautiful garden of Eden, he gave the first wedding vows. In this home, we have come today to unite ______ and ______ in marriage and thus establish a new home. As the first home was called Paradise because God was there, so he wishes for every man and wife to have a beautiful home where he is present.

Do you ______ take ______ to be your wife and with her seek to establish a home that will bring glory to God? Do you promise to love her as your own self and be faithful to her as long as you both shall live?

Groom: I do.

Do you ______ take ______ to be your husband and with him seek to establish a home that will bring glory to God? Do you promise to love him as your own self and be faithful to him as long as you both shall live?

Bride: I do.

May I have the ring(s)?

The best man (and maid of honor, if it is a double-ring ceremony) will give the ring(s) to the minister.

The ring is used as a symbol to express the covenant between the bride and groom at the time of their wedding. It indicates the mutual love and commitment of each to the other.

Will you give this ring to your bride as an expression of your love for her and your pledge of your faithfulness to her until death part you?

Groom: I will.

Will you receive this ring from your groom, and will you wear it as an expression of your love for him and your pledge that you will be faithful to him until death part you?

Bride: I will.

Minister hands the ring to the groom and says: You will place the ring on your bride's ring finger and repeat after me, "With this ring, I thee wed and promise you that I will love you as long as I live."

The ring service will be repeated in reverse if the bride wishes to give a ring to the groom.

Now that you have pledged your vows to each other and sealed them by giving and receiving the ring(s), and in order that you may establish your own home, I pronounce you husband and wife. Shall we pray?

Minister then leads in a closing prayer. After the prayer, he may say: "Ladies and gentlemen, I introduce to you Mr. and Mrs. ______, who will now establish their own home."

Sentence Sermonettes

Faith is fear that has said its prayers.

Love is the Christian's trademark.

God is not only the great Giver; he is also the great Forgiver.

If you want to be rich, give; if you want to be poor, grasp.

The only real mistake is one from which we learn nothing.

The habits formed in youth can become tyrants in old age.

The longer you put off a job, the harder it becomes.

The more faith we have in God, the greater faith we have in ourselves.

Joy is not the absence of suffering, but the presence of God.

Greed turns my mind toward me.

God says do not wait! The devil says procrastinate!

Love is the heart in bloom.

Pray for a good harvest, but keep on plowing.

Worry is a merry-go-round, but it rides you.

Your soul will live forever somewhere. Where?

Satan fears prayer because God hears prayer.

When you give help, you give hope.

Words either bruise or bless.

Our days on earth are running toward sunset.

Jesus' grace is greater than our needs.

We can only appreciate the miracle of a sunrise when we have waited in the darkness.

Never let yesterday use up today.

Gratitude is a smile in the heart.

A happy marriage is the union of two good forgivers.

The Bible that is falling apart usually belongs to someone who is not.

The church is a hospital for sinners, not a museum for saints.

The wages of sin never go unpaid.

Feed your faith. Starve your doubts.

Choice, not chance, determines destiny.

When a church stops doing, it starts dying.

A day of worry is more exhausting than a week of work.

Love each day so that you will neither be afraid of tomorrow nor ashamed of yesterday.

Laughter is a tranquilizer with no side effects.

Jesus Christ is the Light that knows no power failure.

Every minute you are angry, you lose sixty seconds of happiness.

Footprints in the sands of time are not made sitting down.

You had better make friends on the way up, because you are going to need them on the way down.

It is easier to stare up the steps than it is to step up the stairs.

You are not fully dressed until your face has put on a smile.

Complaining only makes the devil laugh.

Love looks not with the eyes, but with the heart.

Luck comes when hard work and preparation meet opportunity.

It is easier to build a snowman in hell than it is to hide your sins from God.

Persistence is the ability never to give up.

We never know how many tomorrows we have.

Hell hath no jury.

Live so that as people get to know you better, they will know Christ better.

Eternity—a hopeless end or an endless hope.

No God, no peace; know God, know peace.

Love gives presence, not presents.

God does not promise us security from the storm, only security in the storm.

If you do not have Christmas in your heart, you will not find Christmas under the tree.

Subject Index

Index of Scripture Texts